Exploring the Intersection of AI and Human Resources Management

Muhammad Rafiq
UCSI Graduate Business School, UCSI University, Kuala Lumpur, Malaysia

Muhammad Farrukh
Shenzhen Moscow State University-Beijing Institute of Technology (SMBU), Shenzhen, China

Rizwan Mushtaq
EDC Paris Business School, Paris, France

Omkar Dastane
UCSI Graduate Business School, UCSI University, Kuala Lumpur, Malaysia

IGI Global
PUBLISHER of TIMELY KNOWLEDGE

A volume in the Advances in Human Resources Management and Organizational Development (AHRMOD) Book Series

Published in the United States of America by
IGI Global
Business Science Reference (an imprint of IGI Global)
701 E. Chocolate Avenue
Hershey PA, USA 17033
Tel: 717-533-8845
Fax: 717-533-8661
E-mail: cust@igi-global.com
Web site: http://www.igi-global.com

Library of Congress Cataloging-in-Publication Data

Names: Rafiq, Muhammad, 1987- editor. | Iqbal, Muhammad Farrukh, 1988- editor. | Mushtaq, Rizwan, 1985- editor. | Dastane, Omkar, 1983- editor.

Title: Exploring the intersection of AI and human resources management / edited by Muhammad Rafiq, Muhammad Iqbal, Rizwan Mushtaq, Omkar Dastane.

Description: Hershey, PA : Business Science Reference, [2024] | Includes bibliographical references and index. | Summary: "The book publishes the recent methodologies, theories, and perceptive related to AI application within the firms of Asia"-- Provided by publisher.
Identifiers: LCCN 2023041784 (print) | LCCN 2023041785 (ebook) | ISBN 9798369300398 (hardcover) | ISBN 9798369300404 (paperback) | ISBN 9798369300411 (ebook)
Subjects: LCSH: Personnel management--Data processing. | Artifical intelligence--Industrial applications.
Classification: LCC HF5549.5.D37 E97 2024 (print) | LCC HF5549.5.D37 (ebook) | DDC 658.300285/63--dc23/eng/20231220
LC record available at https://lccn.loc.gov/2023041784
LC ebook record available at https://lccn.loc.gov/2023041785

This book is published in the IGI Global book series Advances in Human Resources Management and Organizational Development (AHRMOD) (ISSN: 2327-3372; eISSN: 2327-3380)

British Cataloguing in Publication Data
A Cataloguing in Publication record for this book is available from the British Library.
All work contributed to this book is new, previously-unpublished material.
The views expressed in this book are those of the authors, but not necessarily of the publisher.
For electronic access to this publication, please contact: eresources@igi-global.com.

Advances in Human Resources Management and Organizational Development (AHRMOD) Book Series

ISSN:2327-3372
EISSN:2327-3380

Editor-in-Chief: Patricia Ordóñez de Pablos, Universidad de Oviedo, Spain

MISSION

A solid foundation is essential to the development and success of any organization and can be accomplished through the effective and careful management of an organization's human capital. Research in human resources management and organizational development is necessary in providing business leaders with the tools and methodologies which will assist in the development and maintenance of their organizational structure.

The **Advances in Human Resources Management and Organizational Development (AHRMOD) Book Series** aims to publish the latest research on all aspects of human resources as well as the latest methodologies, tools, and theories regarding organizational development and sustainability. The **AHRMOD Book Series** intends to provide business professionals, managers, researchers, and students with the necessary resources to effectively develop and implement organizational strategies.

COVERAGE

- Employment and Labor Laws
- Work-Life Balance
- E-Human Resources Management
- Executive Compensation
- Employee Relations
- Upward Feedback
- Corporate Governance
- Human Relations Movement
- Personnel Retention
- Succession Planning

IGI Global is currently accepting manuscripts for publication within this series. To submit a proposal for a volume in this series, please contact our Acquisition Editors at Acquisitions@igi-global.com or visit: http://www.igi-global.com/publish/.

The Advances in Human Resources Management and Organizational Development (AHRMOD) Book Series (ISSN 2327-3372) is published by IGI Global, 701 E. Chocolate Avenue, Hershey, PA 17033-1240, USA, www.igi-global.com. This series is composed of titles available for purchase individually; each title is edited to be contextually exclusive from any other title within the series. For pricing and ordering information please visit http://www.igi-global.com/book-series/advances-human-resources-management-organizational/73670. Postmaster: Send all address changes to above address.

AI can enhance recruitment, retention, and employee engagement. The author delve into potential ethical, cultural, and legal issues associated with AI-driven HRM, highlighting the necessity for thoughtful and strategic implementation. Finally, the chapter proposes strategies for successfully incorporating AI in HRM, emphasizing the development of AI competencies, fostering a data-driven culture, and ensuring ethical AI deployment. The discussion provides a foundation for future research, policy development, and practical applications in AI-driven HRM, promoting a future-ready workforce in Asia.

Chapter 11 titled 'Blockchain Technology in the Digital Auditing Paradigm' (Dr. Aziatul Waznah Ghazali, Dr. Nur Aima Shafie, Dr. Yusarina Mat Isa, Zulaikha Amirah Johari, Dr. Hafizah Omar Zaki, Prof. Zuraidah Mohd Sanusi) explores the multifaceted impact of blockchain technology on auditing practices, emphasizing its potential to revolutionize audit methodologies. The fundamental principles of blockchain and its implications in the auditing domain in explored extensively. Moreover, the paper also discusses the role of auditors in navigating the complexities of blockchain. As the digital auditing landscape evolves, blockchain emerges as a powerful tool that promises to improve the credibility of financial reporting, making it imperative for professionals, academics and regulators.

Chapter 12 titled 'AI in Market Research' (authors: Dr. Manisha Paliwal, Nishita Chatradhi) examines the role of artificial intelligence (AI) in market research and its impact on customer insights. While existing research has extensively explored AI's influence on marketing, education, and customer experience, a noticeable gap remains in understanding AI's role in reshaping the market research industry. This study aims to fill that gap by focusing on the unexplored territory of AI-driven market research and customer insights. The review follows a structured methodology, analyzing relevant research articles published between 2000 and 2023 using the TCCM framework. The findings demonstrate AI's significant impact on customer experiences, market segmentation, and personalized services across various industries. By embracing AI's capabilities, businesses can thrive in the data-driven and competitive landscape, forging lasting connections with their target audiences and driving success in the dynamic world of business.

Happy Reading!

Muhammad Rafiq
UCSI Graduate Business School, UCSI University, Kuala Lumpur, Malaysia

Muhammad Farrukh
Shenzhen Moscow State University-Beijing Institute of Technology (SMBU), Shenzhen, China

Titles in this Series

For a list of additional titles in this series, please visit:
http://www.igi-global.com/book-series/advances-human-resources-management-organizational/73670

Leadership Strategies for Effective Diversity Management
Amdy Diene (Liberty University, USA)
Business Science Reference • © 2024 • 300pp • H/C (ISBN: 9798369310502) • US $250.00

Cases on the Interplay Between Family, Society, and Entrepreneurship
Ethel Ndidiamaka Abe (SashBM LLC, USA) and Isaac Idowu Abe (SashBM LLC, USA)
Business Science Reference • © 2024 • 300pp • H/C (ISBN: 9781668487488) • US $240.00

Women of Color and Hair Bias in the Work Environment
Kula A. Francis (University of the Virgin Islands, US Virgin Islands) and Anna M. Clarke (University of the Virgin Islands, US Virgin Islands)
Business Science Reference • © 2024 • 295pp • H/C (ISBN: 9781668487907) • US $245.00

Enhancing Employee Engagement and Productivity in the Post-Pandemic Multigenerational Workforce
Angela M. Even (Purdue University, USA) and Bryan Christiansen (Southern New Hampshire University, USA)
Business Science Reference • © 2023 • 464pp • H/C (ISBN: 9781668491720) • US $235.00

Utilizing Cloud Computing for SME Development
Jonathan G. Sinclair (HighRoads Ltd, UK)
Business Science Reference • © 2024 • 300pp • H/C (ISBN: 9781799896951) • US $250.00

Global Citizenship and Its Impact on Multiculturalism in the Workplace
Randa Diab-Bahman (Kuwait Technical College, Kuwait) and Abrar Al-Enzi (Gulf University for Science and Technology, Kuwait)
Business Science Reference • © 2023 • 351pp • H/C (ISBN: 9781668454367) • US $240.00

For an entire list of titles in this series, please visit:
http://www.igi-global.com/book-series/advances-human-resources-management-organizational/73670

IGI Global
PUBLISHER of TIMELY KNOWLEDGE

701 East Chocolate Avenue, Hershey, PA 17033, USA
Tel: 717-533-8845 x100 • Fax: 717-533-8661
E-Mail: cust@igi-global.com • www.igi-global.com

Table of Contents

Preface xiv

Acknowledgment xxi

Chapter 1
Foundations of AI in Human Resource Management: Transforming Asian Organizations 1
Muhammad Rafiq, UCSI Graduate Business School, UCSI University, Kuala Lumpur, Malaysia
Omkar Dastane, UCSI Graduate Business School, UCSI University, Kuala Lumpur, Malaysia

Chapter 2
AI-Based Performance Appraisal Systems: A Game-Changer in Asia 15
Duan Xiuqing, UCSI Graduate Business School, UCSI University, Kuala Lumpur, Malaysia
Muhammad Rafiq, UCSI Graduate Business School, UCSI University, Kuala Lumpur, Malaysia
Wang Zhumin, Chengdu University of Technology, Chengdu, China

Chapter 3
Implementation of Artificial Intelligence in Human Resource Management in Asia-Pacific 30
Anusha Thakur, University of Petroleum and Energy Studies, India

Chapter 4
Critical Role of HR Professionals in the Adoption and Integration of AI in HRM 47
Atia Aftab, University of Management and Technology, Lahore, Pakistan
Komal Khalid, King Abdulaziz University, Jeddah, Saudi Arabia

Chapter 5
Revolutionizing Work: The Influence of Artificial Intelligence on Employee Experience 66
Pradnya Bhatkulkar, UNA-Brands, Singapore

Chapter 6
A Bibliometric Analysis of Artificial Intelligence and Human Resource Management Studies 85
Azizan Bin Morshidi, Universiti Malaysia Sabah, Malaysia
Nurhizam Safie Mohd Satar, Universiti Kebangsaan Malaysia, Malaysia
Azueryn Annatassia Dania Aqeela Azizan, University of New South Wales, Australia
Rizal Zamani Idris, Universiti Malaysia Sabah, Malaysia
Rafiq Idris, Universiti Malaysia Sabah, Malaysia
Mohammad Shaukhi Md Radzi, Universiti Malaysia Sabah, Malaysia
Sitinurbayu Mohd Yusoff, Universiti Malaysia Sabah, Malaysia
Fauzie Sarjono, Universiti Malaysia Sabah, Malaysia

Chapter 7
Benefits and Challenges Regarding the Adoption of HRM4.0 in Public Universities of Malaysia 118
Saeed Mohammed Qurtas Barzani, Universiti Utara Malaysia, Malaysia
Muhammad Imran, Universiti Utara Malaysia, Malaysia
Irfan Hameed, UCSI University, Malaysia & International University of Rabat, Morocco

Chapter 8
Artificial Intelligence and Green Human Resource Management: Navigating the Challenges 140
Fazeelat Masood, Bahria University, Pakistan
Naveed R. Khan, UCSI University, Malaysia
Erum Masood, Bahria University, Pakistan

Chapter 9
AI-Powered Employee Experience: Strategies and Best Practices 166
Dwijendra Nath Dwivedi, Krakow University of Economics, Poland
Ghanashyama Mahanty, Utkal University, India

Chapter 10
Synergizing AI and HRM: Leveraging Business Analytics for a Future-Ready Workforce....................182
Kamaal Allil, University of Hertfordshire, UK

Chapter 11
Blockchain Technology in the Digital Auditing Paradigm....................202
Aziatul Waznah Ghazali, Faculty of Economics and Management, Universiti Kebangsaan Malaysia, Malaysia
Nur Aima Shafie, Accounting Research Institute, Universiti Teknologi MARA, Malaysia
Yusarina Mat Isa, Faculty of Accountancy, Universiti Teknologi MARA, Malaysia
Zulaikha Amirah Johari, Faculty of Economics and Management, Universiti Kebangsaan Malaysia, Malaysia
Hafizah Omar Zaki, Faculty of Economics and Management, Universiti Kebangsaan Malaysia, Malaysia
Zuraidah Mohd Sanusi, Accounting Research Institute, Universiti Teknologi MARA, Malaysia

Chapter 12
AI in Market Research: Transformative Customer Insights - A Systematic Review....................231
Manisha Paliwal, Sri Balaji University, Pune, India
Nishita Chatradhi, Sri Balaji University, Pune, India

Compilation of References 256

About the Contributors 298

Index 305

Detailed Table of Contents

Preface xiv

Acknowledgment xxi

Chapter 1
Foundations of AI in Human Resource Management: Transforming Asian Organizations 1
Muhammad Rafiq, UCSI Graduate Business School, UCSI University, Kuala Lumpur, Malaysia
Omkar Dastane, UCSI Graduate Business School, UCSI University, Kuala Lumpur, Malaysia

This chapter provides a comprehensive introduction to the role of artificial intelligence in HRM within Asian contexts. It explores the basic concepts, methodologies, and theories of AI, and its transformative impact on HRM practices. The chapter delves into AI applications in recruitment, performance appraisal, workforce planning, and ethical considerations, setting the stage for a deeper understanding of AI integration into HR strategies in Asian organizations.

Chapter 2
AI-Based Performance Appraisal Systems: A Game-Changer in Asia 15
Duan Xiuqing, UCSI Graduate Business School, UCSI University, Kuala Lumpur, Malaysia
Muhammad Rafiq, UCSI Graduate Business School, UCSI University, Kuala Lumpur, Malaysia
Wang Zhumin, Chengdu University of Technology, Chengdu, China

This chapter explores the transformative impact of AI-based performance assessment methods in Asia. It delves into the shift from traditional, often biased, evaluation systems to more objective, data-driven AI techniques. The discussion encompasses the adaptation of these technologies within the unique cultural and organizational contexts of Asian businesses, supported by case studies and empirical data. The chapter concludes with insights into the future potential of AI in enhancing employee development, retention, and organizational growth in the Asian corporate landscape.

Chapter 3
Implementation of Artificial Intelligence in Human Resource Management in Asia-Pacific 30
Anusha Thakur, University of Petroleum and Energy Studies, India

The amalgamation of pioneering technologies such as artificial intelligence in the human resources (HR) department has revolutionized the conduct of businesses nowadays. The inclusion of AI automates the organization's processes, benefiting the administration. Artificial neural networks, fuzzy logic, expert systems, data mining, machine learning, and genetic algorithms are a few of the techniques for the implementation of AI in HR. The chapter contemplates the role and benefits of artificial intelligence in organizations in the Asia-Pacific region to enhance the efficiency and effectiveness of human resource functions. It emphasizes the market players and use cases in the Asia-Pacific, illustrating the decision-making support solutions to deliver high-end value and profitability. This study also focuses on the trends and challenges in the implementation of AI in organizations to discover new potential and strategize for the future.

Chapter 4
Critical Role of HR Professionals in the Adoption and Integration of AI in HRM 47
Atia Aftab, University of Management and Technology, Lahore, Pakistan
Komal Khalid, King Abdulaziz University, Jeddah, Saudi Arabia

In this chapter, HR professionals are spotlighted as pivotal players in integrating artificial intelligence (AI) into human resource management (HRM). Drawing inspiration from literary figures, they champion a culture of continuous learning and adaptation, ensuring that AI adoption complements rather than replaces human capabilities. Ethical leadership, inclusivity, and collaboration underpin their strategies, while a profound emphasis is placed on preserving the essence of human connection. They navigate the complexities of AI-driven decision-making, emphasizing data-driven insights and agile innovation. By fostering a symbiotic relationship between humans and AI, HR professionals elevate HRM, harmonizing technology with the organization's strategic vision. This chapter underscores HR's transformative role in marrying AI's potential with human-centric values.

Chapter 5
Revolutionizing Work: The Influence of Artificial Intelligence on Employee Experience 66
Pradnya Bhatkulkar, UNA-Brands, Singapore

The chapter offers a thorough review of the vital factors to take into account when integrating artificial intelligence (AI) into the employee experience. The urgent need to provide HR teams with a profound awareness of AI's potential and its revolutionary influence on the HR sector is one of the primary issues that are underlined. Recognizing the breadth and depth of AI capabilities and appreciating how these capabilities will influence future HR practices are important components of this understanding. It's crucial for HR professionals to develop their AI skills because this technology will fundamentally alter how HR is conducted, not just as a trendy buzzword. The chapter's conclusion underlines that AI is an essential element of HR that has the potential to greatly influence the field's future. HR workers can open up a world of opportunities by embracing AI and play a crucial role in leading the firm to success in a quickly changing business environment.

Chapter 6
A Bibliometric Analysis of Artificial Intelligence and Human Resource Management Studies 85
Azizan Bin Morshidi, Universiti Malaysia Sabah, Malaysia
Nurhizam Safie Mohd Satar, Universiti Kebangsaan Malaysia, Malaysia
Azueryn Annatassia Dania Aqeela Azizan, University of New South Wales, Australia
Rizal Zamani Idris, Universiti Malaysia Sabah, Malaysia
Rafiq Idris, Universiti Malaysia Sabah, Malaysia
Mohammad Shaukhi Md Radzi, Universiti Malaysia Sabah, Malaysia
Sitinurbayu Mohd Yusoff, Universiti Malaysia Sabah, Malaysia
Fauzie Sarjono, Universiti Malaysia Sabah, Malaysia

The pervasiveness of artificial intelligence (AI) within contemporary organisations is an undeniable phenomenon. The primary objective of this chapter is to undertake a meticulous bibliometric analysis of the scholarly literature that investigates the interconnected exploration of the utilisation and ramifications of artificial intelligence (AI) within the realm of human resource management (HRM). The researchers consulted the valued scientific database Scopus, which proved to be a fount of knowledge. Ninety-one documents were initially retrieved and meticulously chosen for the analysis. The data underwent processing through the esteemed Bibliometrix software and the sophisticated Biblioshiny application tool. The results evince that the application of artificial intelligence (AI) to human resource management (HRM) constitutes an emerging domain of inquiry, characterised by a continuous and unwavering expansion and a promising trajectory for the future. Finally, the discourse examined the comparative themes that emerged before and after the advent of the COVID-19 pandemic.

Chapter 7
Benefits and Challenges Regarding the Adoption of HRM4.0 in Public Universities of Malaysia 118
Saeed Mohammed Qurtas Barzani, Universiti Utara Malaysia, Malaysia
Muhammad Imran, Universiti Utara Malaysia, Malaysia
Irfan Hameed, UCSI University, Malaysia & International University of Rabat, Morocco

The main purpose of this study is to explain the benefits and challenges of adopting HRM4.0 in public universities in Malaysia. Past studies stressed that the public universities of Malaysia are lacking in advanced HRM practices such as use of HRM 4.0. The semi-structured interviews have been conducted in the HR departments of six public sector universities in Malaysia. The findings of the study revealed five factors affecting the use of HRM 4.0 in HR departments of public universities, namely its advantages, system quality and usability, quick decision-making process, user satisfaction, and subjective norms. At the same time, the performance and productivity of the HR departments are positively related to the use of HRM 4.0. This study mainly focuses on the perceived modeling structure of HRM4.0 to assess the contributory factors and challenges that have an impact on the productivity of HRM4.0 in Malaysian public universities.

Chapter 8
Artificial Intelligence and Green Human Resource Management: Navigating the Challenges 140
Fazeelat Masood, Bahria University, Pakistan
Naveed R. Khan, UCSI University, Malaysia
Erum Masood, Bahria University, Pakistan

Artificial intelligence (AI) refers to developing computer systems that can perform tasks that typically require human intelligence, such as learning, problem-solving, and decision-making. Green HRM, on the other hand, is a holistic approach to managing human resources that considers the environmental impact of an organization's operations. The AI-green HRM integration has the potential to create a powerful synergy that can help organizations become more sustainable. For example, AI can be used to analyze data and identify areas of an organization where energy and resources are being wasted. This information can then be used to develop and implement more sustainable practices. First, this chapter generates insights into the significance of AI-Green HRM integration. Second, this chapter illustrates challenges faced by organizations in the adoption of AI in endorsing green HRM practices. Third, this chapter concludes the managerial implications of AI-Green HRM for organizations, in particular the Malaysian context.

Chapter 9
AI-Powered Employee Experience: Strategies and Best Practices 166
Dwijendra Nath Dwivedi, Krakow University of Economics, Poland
Ghanashyama Mahanty, Utkal University, India

AI has become an indispensable tool for businesses seeking to enhance the employee experience. Businesses that implement it can increase employee satisfaction, enhance customer service, and decrease cost per employee served – ultimately adding significant business value. Artificial intelligence instruments can improve employee experiences across several areas: recruitment, onboarding, training, and performance management. Furthermore, this use case will profoundly impact customer experiences overall.

Chapter 10
Synergizing AI and HRM: Leveraging Business Analytics for a Future-Ready Workforce 182
Kamaal Allil, University of Hertfordshire, UK

This chapter explores the integration of artificial intelligence (AI) and human resource management (HRM) practices within the Asian business landscape. It offers a comprehensive examination of the evolution of AI in HRM, emphasizing the benefits and potential challenges associated with implementing AI-driven HRM strategies. The discussion highlights the importance of synergizing AI and HRM through business analytics, offering insights into how AI can enhance recruitment, retention, and employee engagement. The author delves into potential ethical, cultural, and legal issues associated with AI-driven HRM, highlighting the necessity for thoughtful and strategic implementation. Finally, the chapter proposes strategies for successfully incorporating AI in HRM, emphasizing the development of AI competencies, fostering a data-driven culture, and ensuring ethical AI deployment. The discussion provides a foundation for future research, policy development, and practical applications in AI-driven HRM, promoting a future-ready workforce in Asia.

Chapter 11
Blockchain Technology in the Digital Auditing Paradigm 202
Aziatul Waznah Ghazali, Faculty of Economics and Management, Universiti Kebangsaan Malaysia, Malaysia
Nur Aima Shafie, Accounting Research Institute, Universiti Teknologi MARA, Malaysia
Yusarina Mat Isa, Faculty of Accountancy, Universiti Teknologi MARA, Malaysia
Zulaikha Amirah Johari, Faculty of Economics and Management, Universiti Kebangsaan Malaysia, Malaysia
Hafizah Omar Zaki, Faculty of Economics and Management, Universiti Kebangsaan Malaysia, Malaysia
Zuraidah Mohd Sanusi, Accounting Research Institute, Universiti Teknologi MARA, Malaysia

The introduction of blockchain technology has ushered in a new era in the field of auditing. This study explores the multifaceted impact of blockchain technology on auditing practices, emphasizing its potential to revolutionize audit methodologies. The fundamental principles of blockchain and its implications in the auditing domain are explored extensively. Moreover, the chapter also discusses the role of auditors in navigating the complexities of blockchain. As the digital auditing landscape evolves, blockchain emerges as a powerful tool that promises to improve the credibility of financial reporting, making it imperative for professionals, academics, and regulators.

Chapter 12
AI in Market Research: Transformative Customer Insights - A Systematic Review 231
Manisha Paliwal, Sri Balaji University, Pune, India
Nishita Chatradhi, Sri Balaji University, Pune, India

This systematic review examines the role of artificial intelligence (AI) in market research and its impact on customer insights. While existing research has extensively explored AI's influence on marketing, education, and customer experience, a noticeable gap remains in understanding AI's role in reshaping the market research industry. This study aims to fill that gap by focusing on the unexplored territory of AI-driven market research and customer insights. The review follows a structured methodology, analyzing relevant research articles published between 2000 and 2023 using the TCCM framework. The findings demonstrate AI's significant impact on customer experiences, market segmentation, and personalized services across various industries. By embracing AI's capabilities, businesses can thrive in the data-driven and competitive landscape, forging lasting connections with their target audiences and driving success in the dynamic world of business.

Compilation of References 256

About the Contributors 298

Index 305

Preface

INTRODUCTION

The realm of Human Resource Management (HRM) has always been pivotal in shaping the success of organizations. Traditionally focused on harnessing human potential, HRM has evolved with the advent of the digital era. The integration of Artificial Intelligence (AI) in HRM practices marks a significant milestone, presenting both challenges and opportunities, particularly in Asia's diverse business landscapes. This evolution aligns with the growing importance of digital marketing strategies, like those involving virtual reality, in enhancing organizational reach and effectiveness (Zaki et al., 2023).

Exploring the Intersection of AI and Human Resources Management delves into how AI is redefining HRM functions and its integration in Asian contexts. It addresses the need for understanding AI applications in HRM amidst cultural diversity and language nuances typical of Asian organizations. This need mirrors the challenges faced in cross-cultural work engagement and the integration of green practices in businesses, reflecting the complex interplay between organizational strategies and environmental consciousness (Aman et al., 2022; Farrukh et al., 2023).

The chapters in this book, contributed by experts, offer theoretical insights and practical guidance in various HRM domains. They explore applications of AI in recruitment, performance appraisal, and employee engagement, considering the ethical implications of these technological advancements. The book serves as a resource for academics, researchers, policymakers, and practitioners. It reflects the intersection of strategic management, leadership capabilities, and technological innovation in transforming HRM practices in Asia (Haba & Dastane, 2019; Haba et al., 2023b; Rafiq et al., 2023a).

CONTENT OF THE BOOK

The handbook is organised into 12 chapters that uncover fresh theoretical and empirical views on digital natives, digital technology, and digital revolutions in Asian enterprises and society.

Chapter 1 titled 'Foundations of AI in Human Resource Management: Transforming Asian Organizations' (author: Dr. Muhammad Rafiq, Dr. Omkar Dastane) provides a comprehensive introduction to the role of Artificial Intelligence in HRM within Asian contexts. It explores the basic concepts, methodologies, and theories of AI, and its transformative impact on HRM practices. The chapter delves into AI applications in recruitment, performance appraisal, workforce planning, and ethical considerations, setting the stage for a deeper understanding of AI integration into HR strategies in Asian organizations.

Chapter 2 titled 'AI-Based Performance Appraisal Systems: A Game-Changer in Asia' (author: Duan Xiuqing, Dr. Muhammad Rafiq, Dr. Wang Zhumin) explores the transformative impact of AI-based performance assessment methods in Asia. It delves into the shift from traditional, often biased evaluation systems to more objective, data-driven AI techniques. The discussion encompasses the adaptation of these technologies within the unique cultural and organizational contexts of Asian businesses, supported by case studies and empirical data. The chapter concludes with insights into the future potential of AI in enhancing employee development, retention, and organizational growth in the Asian corporate landscape.

Chapter 3 titled 'Implementation of Artificial Intelligence in Human Resource Management in Asia-Pacific' (author: Anusha Thakur) contemplates the role and benefits of artificial intelligence in organizations in the Asia-Pacific region to enhance the efficiency and effectiveness of human resource functions. It emphasizes on the market players and use cases in the Asia-Pacific, illustrating the decision-making support solutions to deliver high-end value and profitability. This study also focuses on the trends and challenges in the implementation of AI in organizations, to discover new potential, and strategize for the future.

Chapter 4 titled 'Critical Role of HR Professionals in the Adoption and Integration of AI in HRM' (authors: Atia Aftab, Dr. Komal Khalid) underscores HR's transformative role in marrying AI's potential with human-centric values. In this chapter, HR professionals are spotlighted as pivotal players in integrating artificial intelligence (AI) into Human Resource Management (HRM). Drawing inspiration from literary figures, they champion a culture of continuous learning and adaptation, ensuring that AI adoption complements rather than replaces human capabilities. Ethical leadership, inclusivity, and collaboration underpin their strategies, while a profound emphasis is placed on preserving the essence of human connection. They navigate the complexities of AI-driven decision-making, emphasizing data-driven insights and agile innovation. By fostering a symbiotic relationship between humans and AI, HR professionals elevate HRM, harmonizing technology with the organization's strategic vision.

Chapter 5 titled 'Revolutionizing Work: The Influence of Artificial Intelligence on Employee Experience' (author: Pradnya Bhatkulkar) offers a thorough review of the vital factors to take into account when integrating artificial intelligence (AI) into the employee experience. The urgent need to provide HR teams with a profound awareness of AI's potential and its revolutionary influence on the HR sector is one of the primary issues that are underlined. Recognizing the breadth and depth of AI capabilities and appreciating how these capabilities will influence future HR practices are important components of this understanding. It's crucial for HR professionals to develop their AI skills because this technology will fundamentally alter how HR is conducted, not just as a trendy buzzword. The chapter's conclusion underlines that AI is an essential element of HR that has the potential to greatly influence the field's future. HR workers can open up a world of opportunities by embracing AI and play a crucial role in leading the firm to success in a quickly changing business environment.

Chapter 6 titled 'A Bibliometric Analysis of Artificial Intelligence and Human Resource Management Studies' (authors: Azizan Bin Morshidi, Dr. Nurhizam Safie Mohd Satar, Dania Aqeela Azizan, Dr. Rizal Zamani Idris, Dr. Rafiq Idris, Dr. Mohammad Shaukhi Md Radzi, Dr. Sitinurbayu Mohd Yusoff, Dr. Fauzie Sarjono, Universiti Malaysia Sabah, Malaysia) offers panoramic view of the field. The pervasiveness of artificial intelligence (AI) within contemporary organisations is an undeniable phenomenon. The primary objective of this article is to undertake a meticulous bibliometric analysis of the scholarly literature that investigates the interconnected exploration of the utilisation and ramifications of artificial intelligence (AI) within the realm of human resource management (HRM). The researchers consulted the valued scientific database Scopus, which proved to be a fount of knowledge. Ninety-one documents were initially retrieved and meticulously chosen for the analysis. The data underwent processing through the esteemed Bibliometrix software and the sophisticated Biblioshiny application tool. The results evince that the application of artificial intelligence (AI) to human resource management (HRM) constitutes an emerging domain of inquiry, characterised by a continuous and unwavering expansion and a promising trajectory for the future. Finally, the discourse examined the comparative themes that emerged before and after the advent of the COVID-19 pandemic.

Chapter 7 titled 'Benefits and Challenges Regarding the Adoption of HRM4.0 in Public Universities of Malaysia' (authors: Saeed Mohammed Qurtas Barzani, Dr. Muhammad Imran, Irfan Hameed) mainly focuses on the perceived modeling structure of HRM4.0 to assess the contributory factors and challenges that have an impact on the productivity of HRM4.0 in Malaysian public universities. The main purpose of this study is to explain the benefits and challenges of adopting HRM4.0 in public universities in Malaysia. Past studies stressed that the public universities of Malaysia are lacking in advanced HRM practices such use of HRM 4.0. The semi-structured interviews have been conducted in the HR departments of Six (6) public sector universities in Malaysia. The findings of the study revealed five factors affecting the use of HRM 4.0 in HR departments of public universities, namely its advantages, system quality and usability, quick decision-making process, user satisfaction, and subjective norms. At the same time, the performance and productivity of the HR departments are positively related to the use of HRM 4.0.

Chapter 8 is titled 'Artificial Intelligence and Green Human Resource Management: Navigating the Challenges' (authors: Dr. Fazeelat Masood, Dr. Naveed R. Khan, Erum Masood). Artificial intelligence (AI) refers to developing computer systems that can perform tasks that typically require human intelligence, such as learning, problem-solving, and decision-making. Green HRM, on the other hand, is a holistic approach to managing human resources that considers the environmental impact of an organization's operations. The AI-green HRM integration has the potential to create a powerful synergy that can help organizations become more sustainable. For example, AI can be used to analyze data and identify areas of an organization where energy and resources are being wasted. This information can then be used to develop and implement more sustainable practices. First, this chapter generates insights into the significance of AI-Green HRM integration. Second, this chapter illustrates challenges faced by organizations in the adoption of AI in endorsing green HRM practices. Third, this chapter concludes the managerial implications of AI-Green HRM for organizations, in particular Malaysian context.

Chapter 9 is 'AI-Powered Employee Experience-Strategies and Best Practices' (source: Dwijendra Nath Dwivedi, Dr. Ghanashyama Mahanty). AI has become an indispensable tool for businesses seeking to enhance the employee experience. Businesses that implement it can increase employee satisfaction, enhance customer service, and decrease cost per employee served - ultimately adding significant business value. Artificial intelligence instruments can improve employee experiences across several areas: recruitment, onboarding, training, and performance management. Furthermore, this use case will profoundly impact customer experiences overall.

Chapter 10 titled 'Synergizing AI and HRM: Leveraging Business Analytics for a Future-Ready Workforce' (authors: Dr. Kamaal Allil) explores the integration of Artificial Intelligence (AI) and Human Resource Management (HRM) practices within the Asian business landscape. It offers a comprehensive examination of the evolution of AI in HRM, emphasizing the benefits and potential challenges associated with implementing AI-driven HRM strategies. The discussion highlights the importance of synergizing AI and HRM through business analytics, offering insights into how

Rizwan Mushtaq
EDC Paris Business School, Paris, France

Omkar Dastane
UCSI Graduate Business School, UCSI University, Kuala Lumpur, Malaysia

REFERENCES

Aman, A., Rafiq, M., Dastane, O., & Sabir, A. A. (2022). Green corridor: A critical perspective and development of research agenda. *Frontiers in Environmental Science*, *10*, 982473. doi:10.3389/fenvs.2022.982473

Bhutta, U., Martins, J. N., Mata, M. N., Raza, A., Dantas, R. M., Correia, A. B., & Rafiq, M. (2021). Intellectual Structure and Evolution of Accounting Conservatism Research: Past Trends and Future Research Suggestions. *International Journal of Financial Studies*, *9*(3), 35. doi:10.3390/ijfs9030035

Dastane, O., & Haba, H. F. (2023). The Landscape of Digital Natives Research: A Bibliometric and Science Mapping Analysis. *FIIB Business Review*.

Farrukh, M., Raza, A., & Rafiq, M. (2023). Environmentally specific authentic leadership and team green creative behavior based on cognitive-affective path systems. *International Journal of Contemporary Hospitality Management*, *35*(10), 3662–3680. doi:10.1108/IJCHM-04-2022-0530

Fernandez, D., Dastane, O., Omar Zaki, H., & Aman, A. (2023). Robotic process automation: bibliometric reflection and future opportunities. *European Journal of Innovation Management*.

Haba, H. F., Bredillet, C., & Dastane, O. (2023a). Green consumer research: Trends and way forward based on bibliometric analysis. *Cleaner and Responsible Consumption*, *8*, 100089. doi:10.1016/j.clrc.2022.100089

Haba, H. F., & Dastane, D. O. (2019). Massive open online courses (MOOCs)–understanding online learners' preferences and experiences. *International Journal of Learning, Teaching and Educational Research*, *18*(8), 227–242.

Mushtaq, R., Dastane, O., Rafiq, M., & Başar, B. D. (2023). Women financial inclusion research: A bibliometric and network analysis. *International Journal of Social Economics*, *50*(8), 1169–1185. doi:10.1108/IJSE-06-2022-0438

Xue, X., Rafiq, M., Meng, F., & Peerzadah, S. A. (2023). 21st anniversary of job embeddedness: A retrospection and future research agenda. *Work (Reading, Mass.)*, *76*(3), 991–1005. doi:10.3233/WOR-220240 PMID:37355920

Acknowledgment

We sincerely thank the chapter contributors for their hard work and support which resulted in the completion of this book - Exploring the Intersection of AI and Human Resources Management. We also like to thank the members of the editorial advisory board for their assistance, suggestions, and review throughout the book preparation. Last but not least, we are grateful to IGI Global's editorial and production team for their assistance throughout the editing process.

Chapter 1
Foundations of AI in Human Resource Management:
Transforming Asian Organizations

Muhammad Rafiq
https://orcid.org/0000-0001-5037-6485
UCSI Graduate Business School, UCSI University, Kuala Lumpur, Malaysia

Omkar Dastane
https://orcid.org/0000-0002-9921-859X
UCSI Graduate Business School, UCSI University, Kuala Lumpur, Malaysia

ABSTRACT

This chapter provides a comprehensive introduction to the role of artificial intelligence in HRM within Asian contexts. It explores the basic concepts, methodologies, and theories of AI, and its transformative impact on HRM practices. The chapter delves into AI applications in recruitment, performance appraisal, workforce planning, and ethical considerations, setting the stage for a deeper understanding of AI integration into HR strategies in Asian organizations.

1. INTRODUCTION TO AI IN HRM

The advent of Artificial Intelligence (AI) in Human Resource Management (HRM) signifies a revolutionary shift in how organizations manage their most valuable asset – their people. AI in HRM represents the convergence of technological innovation with traditional human-centric processes, redefining the landscape of workforce management, talent acquisition, and employee engagement. The integration of AI

DOI: 10.4018/979-8-3693-0039-8.ch001

into HRM practices is more than just an advancement in technology; it is a paradigm shift that challenges conventional HR methodologies and offers new opportunities for organizational growth and efficiency. This integration is particularly transformative in the dynamic and culturally rich Asian business environment, where diversity and technological progress coexist.

AI in HRM encompasses a wide range of applications, from automating mundane tasks to providing strategic insights through advanced data analytics. The impact of AI on HRM is multifaceted, offering organizations the tools to make more informed decisions, enhance employee experiences, and foster a more agile and responsive workforce. In the Asian context, the application of AI in HRM is especially pertinent given the region's rapid economic growth, cultural diversity, and evolving labor market dynamics. The adoption of AI in HRM practices in Asia is not merely a trend but a necessary response to the unique challenges and opportunities presented by the region's distinct business milieu. Today, business rivalry is highly intense, and the business milieu is highly uncertain (Rafiq *et al.*, 2023b), making the role of AI even more crucial. Several studies have highlighted the importance of leadership in navigating this complex environment (Farrukh *et al.*, 2023), where education plays a pivotal role in enhancing an individual's self-efficacy (Farrukh *et al.*, 2021), thereby empowering them to effectively harness AI for strategic advantage.

The integration of AI in HRM in Asia offers a unique perspective on how technology can be leveraged to address specific regional needs. It represents an exciting frontier where traditional practices are being transformed by AI's ability to process vast amounts of data, provide predictive insights, and foster a more inclusive and engaging workplace environment. This evolution is crucial for Asian organizations aiming to stay competitive in a globalized economy, where talent management and organizational agility are key drivers of success. As such, understanding the role of AI in HRM within the Asian context provides valuable insights into the future of work and the ongoing transformation of HR practices globally.

1.1. AI Emergence and Evolution in HRM

The emergence and evolution of AI in HRM is a story of technological progression meeting human-centric management. Initially, AI's role in HRM was limited to automating simple tasks like resume screening and employee scheduling. However, as AI technologies evolved, their applications in HRM expanded, encompassing more complex functions such as talent analytics, predictive modeling for employee turnover, and personalized training programs. This evolution marked a significant transition from traditional HR practices, heavily reliant on manual processes and intuition-based decision-making, to a more data-driven, analytical approach.

In Asia, the adoption of AI in HRM has been accelerated by the region's rapid technological advancements and the growing need to manage diverse and expanding workforces effectively. Countries like China, Japan, and South Korea have been at the forefront of integrating AI into HRM, leveraging technology to navigate the challenges of a dynamic labor market. This evolution has been characterized by a shift from a one-size-fits-all approach to a more personalized, employee-centric model, where AI-driven insights enable HR professionals to cater to individual employee needs and aspirations, thereby enhancing overall organizational effectiveness (Eubanks, 2022). With the rapid development of industrialization, transportation, and urbanization (Aman *et al.*, 2022; Haba et al., 2023), maintaining high calibre employees has become a difficult issue for today's businesses (Rafiq *et al.*, 2022). In response, organizational researchers focused on human resource management (HRM) often grapple with securing a competitive advantage in this fast-paced environment (Aman *et al.*, 2023), increasingly relying on advanced AI tools to manage and retain talent effectively.

1.2. Key AI Technologies Shaping HRM Practices

Several key AI technologies are shaping HRM practices, transforming how organizations manage their human resources. These include machine learning, natural language processing (NLP), and cognitive computing. Machine learning algorithms enable HR systems to learn from data patterns, facilitating predictive analytics in talent management and workforce planning. Natural language processing has revolutionized employee interactions with HR systems, allowing for more natural and intuitive communication through chatbots and virtual assistants.

Cognitive computing, which mimics human thought processes, is being employed to make complex decisions regarding talent acquisition and employee development. These technologies are not only enhancing the efficiency of HR processes but are also enabling a more personalized and engaging employee experience. In the Asian context, these technologies are particularly relevant, as they allow organizations to navigate the region's diverse linguistic and cultural landscape, thereby creating more inclusive and effective HRM practices (Cooke *et al.*, 2020).

2. AI APPLICATIONS IN HRM

The integration of Artificial Intelligence (AI) into Human Resource Management (HRM) has led to a renaissance in workforce management practices, particularly in the Asian context. AI applications in HRM have streamlined numerous processes, from recruitment to employee development, offering unprecedented efficiency and effectiveness. In recruitment, AI algorithms have transformed traditional methods, enabling more precise matching of candidates with job requirements. AI-driven analytics provide deep insights into workforce dynamics, leading to more informed strategic decision-making. AI's impact extends beyond mere automation; it offers predictive insights and personalization that are changing the HR landscape. For Asian businesses, grappling with a competitive and culturally diverse labor market, AI in HRM is not just a technological upgrade but a strategic necessity to remain agile and competitive (Rana and Sharma, 2019).

AI influence on HRM is multifaceted, touching every aspect of employee lifecycle management. AI-driven tools are being used for nuanced employee engagement strategies, identifying potential employee turnover, and tailoring training programs to individual needs. These tools are particularly effective in the Asian market, where diverse cultural backgrounds and workforce needs necessitate adaptable and nuanced HR strategies. AI ability to analyze and learn from large datasets enables organizations to predict future workforce trends, adapt to changing market demands, and create a more responsive and effective HRM system (Lepak and Shaw, 2008). In today's rapidly changing and hectic entrepreneurial environment, positive psychological factors (Ren *et al.*, 2019) are being increasingly recognized, mirroring the growing importance of accounting conservatism research (Bhutta *et al.*, 2021). Additionally, access to finance is evolving as a critical aspect (Mushtaq *et al.*, 2023), influencing both organizational strategies and individual career paths. Concurrently, environmental concerns, such as the rise in solid waste generation due to rapid population growth and urbanization (Rafiq *et al.*, 2023a), are pushing companies and consumers alike to pay greater attention to their impact on nature (Jin *et al.*, 2023), underlining the interconnected nature of modern business ecosystems.

2.1. AI in Recruitment and Talent Acquisition

AI has significantly transformed recruitment and talent acquisition in HRM, introducing a new era of efficiency and precision. In Asia, where the talent pool is vast and diverse, AI helps streamline the recruitment process by automating routine tasks such as resume screening and initial candidate assessments. AI algorithms analyze vast amounts of data, identifying patterns and insights that human recruiters might overlook, thereby enhancing the quality of hire. AI-driven recruitment tools also help reduce unconscious biases, promoting a more inclusive and diverse workforce. By leveraging AI, Asian companies can effectively manage large-scale recruitment drives, ensuring that they attract and retain the best talent suited to their specific business needs and cultural contexts (Stahl *et al.*, 2012).

2.2. AI-Driven Employee Engagement and Retention Strategies

AI-driven employee engagement and retention strategies have become pivotal in HRM, particularly in the competitive Asian business environment. AI tools analyze employee data to identify patterns and predictors of engagement and turnover, offering actionable insights for HR professionals. By understanding the factors that drive employee satisfaction, companies can develop targeted strategies to enhance engagement, increase job satisfaction, and reduce turnover rates. AI's predictive capabilities allow for proactive interventions, addressing potential issues before they escalate into larger problems. In Asia, where employee expectations and cultural nuances vary widely, AI's role in crafting personalized engagement strategies is invaluable, helping businesses retain their best talent and maintain a competitive edge (King, 2019).

2.3. Leveraging AI for Enhanced Employee Training

AI is revolutionizing employee training in HRM, offering personalized learning experiences tailored to individual needs and learning styles. This is especially relevant in Asia, where diverse educational backgrounds and skill levels present unique challenges in workforce development. AI-powered training programs analyze employee performance data to identify skill gaps and recommend customized training modules. This targeted approach ensures that employees receive relevant, effective training that directly contributes to their professional growth and organizational goals. Additionally, AI-driven training programs are scalable and adaptable, allowing companies to efficiently upskill large numbers of employees in response to evolving market demands (Chowdhury *et al.*, 2023).

The use of AI in employee training also extends to the development of soft skills, critical in the Asian business context. AI-driven simulations and interactive modules provide immersive learning experiences, enhancing communication, leadership, and problem-solving skills. This holistic approach to training, underpinned by AI, not only improves individual performance but also fosters a more dynamic, skilled, and adaptable workforce. As Asian businesses navigate a rapidly changing economic landscape, AI's role in employee training becomes increasingly crucial, offering a pathway to continuous learning and organizational resilience (Modgil *et al.*, 2022).

3. AI AND WORKFORCE MANAGEMENT

The integration of AI into workforce management is transforming HR practices in Asia, offering dynamic solutions for complex workforce challenges. AI's ability to analyze extensive datasets provides valuable insights for strategic workforce planning, predicting future talent needs, and understanding workforce dynamics. This technology is particularly beneficial in Asia's diverse and rapidly evolving labor markets, where it helps businesses to stay ahead of talent trends and market shifts. AI-driven workforce analytics enable organizations to make data-driven decisions, optimizing workforce deployment and enhancing overall operational efficiency. These AI applications are reshaping how Asian companies approach workforce management, transitioning from traditional methods to more agile, informed, and strategic practices (Chitturu *et al.*, 2017).

AI's impact extends to workforce dynamics, enabling organizations to identify skills gaps, predict employee turnover, and efficiently manage talent pipelines. In the Asian context, where workforce needs are continually changing, AI's predictive capabilities are invaluable. AI tools provide a nuanced understanding of workforce trends, allowing for proactive talent management strategies that align with organizational goals and market demands. This shift towards AI-driven workforce management represents a significant advancement in HR practices, enabling Asian organizations to be more competitive, adaptive, and future-ready (Chenoy *et al.*, 2019).

3.1. AI in Workforce Planning and Analytics

AI plays a critical role in workforce planning and analytics, offering insights that drive effective talent management strategies. In Asia, where labor markets are characterized by rapid growth and transformation, AI-driven workforce planning is critical. By leveraging AI algorithms and machine learning, organizations can forecast future staffing needs, identify critical skills gaps, and develop strategies for talent acquisition and development. AI analytics help HR professionals in Asian companies to understand complex workforce patterns, enabling them to anticipate and prepare for future changes. This strategic approach to workforce planning, facilitated by AI, supports sustainable growth and competitive advantage in the Asian business landscape.

3.2. AI-Enabled Performance Appraisal Systems

AI-enabled performance appraisal systems represent a significant shift in HR practices, introducing a level of objectivity and precision previously unattainable. In Asian organizations, where performance evaluations often involve cultural sensitivities and hierarchical dynamics, AI offers an unbiased, data-driven approach. AI tools can analyze performance data to provide comprehensive evaluations, highlight areas for improvement, and recommend personalized development plans. These systems reduce the subjectivity and bias often associated with traditional appraisal methods, ensuring fair and accurate assessments. The implementation of AI-enabled performance appraisal systems in Asia signifies a move towards more transparent, equitable, and efficient performance management practices (Stahl et al., 2012).

4. ETHICAL AND LEGAL IMPLICATIONS OF AI IN HRM

The integration of AI in HRM within Asian markets brings with it a host of ethical and legal implications that necessitate careful consideration. As AI systems make increasingly significant decisions about hiring, promotions, and employee monitoring, ethical issues such as bias, transparency, and accountability come to the forefront. Legal challenges also arise, particularly around data privacy, compliance with local and international regulations, and liability in case of AI-driven decisions leading to disputes or discrimination. These complexities demand a nuanced approach to AI implementation in HRM, balancing technological innovation with ethical responsibility and legal compliance.

4.1. Addressing Ethical Concerns in AI Usage

Ethical concerns in AI usage in HRM, especially in Asian contexts, include potential biases in AI algorithms that may perpetuate existing societal and workplace inequalities. For instance, AI-based recruiting tools might inadvertently favor certain demographics, leading to unfair hiring practices. Additionally, transparency in AI decision-making processes is vital to ensure accountability and maintain employee trust. Organizations must adopt frameworks and guidelines that ensure AI systems are auditable, explainable, and free from biases, thus fostering ethical AI usage. It's crucial for Asian companies to engage in continuous ethical audits of AI systems and provide training to HR professionals on ethical AI practices (Liang *et al.*, 2021).

Another ethical aspect is the potential dehumanization of HR processes, where AI-driven decisions might overlook the individual nuances and circumstances of employees. It's essential for Asian organizations to strike a balance between AI efficiency and human empathy, ensuring that AI supports rather than replaces human judgment in HRM. This involves setting clear boundaries for AI usage and maintaining a human-centric approach in HR practices. Ethical AI usage in HRM also demands an inclusive approach, considering diverse cultural, social, and personal contexts within Asian workforces.

4.2. Navigating Data Privacy and Compliance Issues

Data privacy and compliance are critical legal issues for AI in HRM, particularly in Asia, where data protection laws vary significantly across countries. Organizations must navigate a complex legal landscape to ensure compliance with national and international regulations, such as the GDPR in Europe and local data protection laws in Asian countries. This involves implementing robust data security measures, obtaining clear consent for data collection and usage, and ensuring that employee data is handled transparently and responsibly. Failing to comply with these legal requirements can lead to significant penalties and damage to an organization's reputation (Kagan *et al.*, 2011).

Another challenge in navigating data privacy and compliance issues is the cross-border transfer of employee data within multinational companies operating in Asia. Organizations must be aware of the legal constraints and requirements for data transfer between countries and ensure that their practices align with international data protection standards. This may involve establishing data localization policies, conducting regular data protection impact assessments, and engaging with legal experts to stay updated on evolving legal landscapes. Balancing the need for data-driven AI applications with stringent data privacy and compliance requirements is key to the responsible use of AI in HRM in Asia (Teune, 2023).

5. BUILDING AI-ENABLED LEARNING ECOSYSTEMS

In the dynamic business environment of Asia, AI-enabled learning ecosystems are emerging as a transformative force in HRM. These ecosystems leverage AI to provide personalized, scalable, and efficient learning experiences for employees. By integrating AI into learning and development strategies, organizations can not only enhance the skills of their workforce but also adapt to the rapid technological changes and evolving industry requirements. AI-enabled learning ecosystems support continuous learning and upskilling, which are crucial for maintaining a competitive edge in today's fast-paced market.

These ecosystems harness the power of AI to analyze learning patterns, preferences, and outcomes, thereby offering customized learning paths for individual employees (Greller and Drachsler, 2012). AI-driven analytics can identify skill gaps and recommend tailored training programs, making learning more relevant and effective. Additionally, AI can facilitate just-in-time learning, delivering training modules at the point of need, thereby maximizing learning retention and application. By building AI-enabled learning ecosystems, Asian organizations can foster a culture of continuous improvement and innovation, aligning employee development with organizational goals.

5.1. Innovating HRM With AI-Driven Learning Platforms

AI-driven learning platforms are at the core of innovating HRM in Asia. These platforms use sophisticated algorithms to deliver customized learning experiences, adapting content and pace according to the learner's progress and performance. This personalization ensures that employees receive training that is most relevant to their roles and career aspirations (Boxall *et al.*, 2011). AI-driven platforms can incorporate various learning formats, including interactive courses, virtual simulations, and gamified learning, making the learning process engaging and effective.

Furthermore, AI-driven learning platforms can provide real-time feedback and assessments, allowing learners to track their progress and adjust their learning strategies accordingly. These platforms can also facilitate collaborative learning, connecting learners with peers and mentors, thus enriching the learning experience. For HR managers, AI-driven platforms offer valuable insights into workforce competencies, enabling them to align training initiatives with strategic business objectives. Such platforms represent a significant leap in HRM practices in Asia, transforming how organizations approach employee development and performance management.

6. CHALLENGES IN AI IMPLEMENTATION

Implementing AI in HRM within the diverse and multifaceted Asian business landscape presents unique challenges. Organizations often face difficulties in aligning AI applications with existing operational models and employee expectations. These challenges range from managing cultural diversity and resistance to change, to addressing technological hurdles and ensuring seamless integration with existing systems. Addressing these challenges is crucial for the successful adoption of AI in HRM and requires a strategic approach that considers the unique characteristics of the Asian business environment (Budhwar *et al.*, 2022).

One significant challenge is the need to ensure that AI applications are compatible with the varied cultural norms and business practices prevalent across Asia. Organizations must navigate the delicate balance of implementing advanced AI technologies while respecting and adapting to local cultures and traditions. Additionally, the rapid pace of technological advancement can sometimes outstrip the organizational readiness and infrastructure, posing significant challenges in AI adoption and integration.

6.1. Overcoming Cultural Barriers

Overcoming cultural barriers is essential in the successful implementation of AI in HRM, particularly in the culturally diverse Asian region. Cultural barriers can manifest in various forms, including language differences, varying attitudes towards technology, and differing perceptions of AI's role in the workplace (Glikson and Woolley, 2020). To address these barriers, organizations need to adopt culturally sensitive approaches when introducing AI technologies. This includes providing multilingual support, understanding local cultural nuances, and engaging with employees to address any concerns or misconceptions about AI.

6.2. Technological Challenges and Solutions

The implementation of AI in HRM also faces technological challenges, such as data quality issues, integration complexities with existing systems, and the need for robust cybersecurity measures. Organizations must invest in high-quality data collection and processing capabilities to ensure the accuracy and effectiveness of AI applications. Additionally, seamless integration of AI tools with current HR systems is essential for maximizing their utility and minimizing disruption. Addressing cybersecurity concerns is equally important, as AI systems often handle sensitive employee data.

To overcome these challenges, organizations can explore partnerships with technology providers, invest in employee training to enhance technological literacy, and implement stringent data security protocols. Tailoring AI solutions to specific organizational needs and continuously monitoring and updating these systems can also help address technological challenges effectively.

7. THE FUTURE OF AI IN HRM

The future of AI in Human Resources Management (HRM) is poised for transformative growth, with emerging trends and technologies reshaping the landscape of HR practices. In the dynamic Asian market, this evolution is particularly significant, where AI's integration is not only enhancing current HR operations but also paving the way for groundbreaking innovations. The potential for AI to revolutionize HRM lies in its capacity to offer more personalized, efficient, and strategic HR solutions, aligning closely with the ever-evolving business and workforce needs of the region (Singh et al., 2024; Li & Zhang, 2024).

As AI technology continues to evolve, its applications in HRM are expected to become more sophisticated, enabling deeper insights into employee behavior, enhanced predictive capabilities, and more nuanced workforce management. This ongoing evolution promises to unlock new opportunities for HR professionals, offering tools that are more intuitive, intelligent, and integrated with the broader organizational goals (Chen & Sharma, 2022).

7.1. Anticipating Emerging Trends

Anticipating emerging trends in AI and HRM involves staying abreast of the latest developments in AI technologies and understanding their potential impact on HR practices. Key trends include the use of advanced machine learning algorithms for more accurate talent prediction, the adoption of AI-driven analytics for workforce planning, and the integration of AI in enhancing employee experience. These trends signify a shift towards more data-driven, predictive, and employee-centric HR practices, aligning with the dynamic needs of the modern workforce.

7.2. Preparing for the Next Wave of AI Innovations in HRM

Preparing for the next wave of AI innovations in HRM requires organizations to adopt a forward-thinking approach. This includes investing in ongoing training and development for HR professionals to equip them with the skills needed to leverage AI effectively. Organizations should also focus on building robust data infrastructures to support AI applications and foster a culture of innovation that embraces technological advancements. By proactively preparing for future AI innovations, organizations can position themselves at the forefront of HR technology, ensuring they are well-equipped to harness the full potential of AI in HRM.

Embracing the next wave of AI innovations also involves anticipating the changing needs of the workforce and aligning AI strategies accordingly. This may include developing more personalized AI-driven HR tools, exploring the use of AI in enhancing employee well-being, and integrating AI more deeply into strategic HR decision-making. By staying attuned to these emerging trends and preparing for the next wave of innovations, organizations can ensure that their HRM practices remain relevant, effective, and aligned with the future of work.

8. CONCLUSION

This chapter concludes by emphasizing the transformative role of AI in HRM, particularly within the Asian context. It has underscored the potential of AI to revolutionize traditional HR practices, addressing everything from recruitment to workforce analytics. While highlighting the importance of ethical considerations and the challenges in AI implementation, the chapter also looks forward to the emerging trends and innovations in AI that are poised to further shape the future of HRM. This exploration serves as a vital resource for those navigating the evolving landscape of HRM in the age of AI.

REFERENCES

Aman, A., Rafiq, M., & Dastane, O. (2023). A cross-cultural comparison of work engagement in the relationships between trust climate – Job performance and turnover intention: Focusing China and Pakistan. *Heliyon*, *9*(9), e19534. doi:10.1016/j.heliyon.2023.e19534 PMID:37809562

Aman, A., Rafiq, M., Dastane, O., & Sabir, A. A. (2022). Green corridor: A critical perspective and development of research agenda. *Frontiers in Environmental Science*, *10*, 982473. doi:10.3389/fenvs.2022.982473

Bhutta, U., Martins, J. N., Mata, M. N., Raza, A., Dantas, R. M., Correia, A. B., & Rafiq, M. (2021). Intellectual Structure and Evolution of Accounting Conservatism Research: Past Trends and Future Research Suggestions. *International Journal of Financial Studies*, *9*(3), 35. doi:10.3390/ijfs9030035

Boxall, P., Ang, S. H., & Bartram, T. (2011). Analysing the 'black box'of HRM: Uncovering HR goals, mediators, and outcomes in a standardized service environment. *Journal of Management Studies*, *48*(7), 1504–1532. doi:10.1111/j.1467-6486.2010.00973.x

Budhwar, P., Malik, A., De Silva, M. T., & Thevisuthan, P. (2022). Artificial intelligence–challenges and opportunities for international HRM: A review and research agenda. *International Journal of Human Resource Management*, *33*(6), 1065–1097. doi:10.1080/09585192.2022.2035161

Chenoy, D., Ghosh, S. M., & Shukla, S. K. (2019). Skill development for accelerating the manufacturing sector: the role of 'new-age' skills for 'Make in India'. *International Journal of Training Research, 17*(1), 112-130.

Chitturu, S., Lin, D.-Y., Sneader, K., Tonby, O., & Woetzel, J. (2017). Artificial intelligence and Southeast Asia's future. Academic Press.

Chowdhury, S., Dey, P., Joel-Edgar, S., Bhattacharya, S., Rodriguez-Espindola, O., Abadie, A., & Truong, L. (2023). Unlocking the value of artificial intelligence in human resource management through AI capability framework. *Human Resource Management Review*, *33*(1), 100899. doi:10.1016/j.hrmr.2022.100899

Cooke, F. L., Schuler, R., & Varma, A. (2020). Human resource management research and practice in Asia: Past, present and future. *Human Resource Management Review*, *30*(4), 100778. doi:10.1016/j.hrmr.2020.100778

Eubanks, B. (2022). *Artificial intelligence for HR: Use AI to support and develop a successful workforce*. Kogan Page Publishers.

Farrukh, M., Raza, A., & Rafiq, M. (2023). Environmentally specific authentic leadership and team green creative behavior based on cognitive-affective path systems. *International Journal of Contemporary Hospitality Management*, *35*(10), 3662–3680. doi:10.1108/IJCHM-04-2022-0530

Farrukh, M., Raza, A., Sajid, M., Rafiq, M., Hameed, R., & Ali, T. (2021). Entrepreneurial intentions: The relevance of nature and nurture. *Education + Training*, *63*(7/8), 1195–1212. doi:10.1108/ET-01-2021-0028

Glikson, E., & Woolley, A. W. (2020). Human trust in artificial intelligence: Review of empirical research. *The Academy of Management Annals*, *14*(2), 627–660. doi:10.5465/annals.2018.0057

Greller, W., & Drachsler, H. (2012). Translating learning into numbers: A generic framework for learning analytics. *Journal of Educational Technology & Society*, *15*(3), 42–57.

Haba, H. F., Bredillet, C., & Dastane, O. (2022). Green consumer research: Trends and way forward based on bibliometric analysis. Cleaner and Responsible Consumption, 100089.

Jin, J., Rafiq, M., Hayat, N., Yang, Q., & Al Mamun, A. (2023). Discovering the Adoption of Eco-Friendly Furniture Among Chinese Customers. In N. Mansour & L. M. Bujosa Vadell (Eds.), *Finance, Accounting and Law in the Digital Age: The Impact of Technology and Innovation in the Financial Services Sector* (pp. 273–283). Springer International Publishing. doi:10.1007/978-3-031-27296-7_25

Kagan, R. A., Gunningham, N., & Thornton, D. (2011). Fear, duty, and regulatory compliance: lessons from three research projects. Explaining compliance: Business responses to regulation, 37-58.

King, K. (2019). *Using Artificial Intelligence in Marketing: How to harness AI and maintain the competitive edge*. Kogan Page Publishers.

Lepak, D. P., & Shaw, J. D. (2008). Strategic HRM in North America: Looking to the future. *International Journal of Human Resource Management*, *19*(8), 1486–1499. doi:10.1080/09585190802200272

Liang, T.-P., Robert, L., Sarker, S., Cheung, C. M., Matt, C., Trenz, M., & Turel, O. (2021). Artificial intelligence and robots in individuals' lives: How to align technological possibilities and ethical issues. *Internet Research*, *31*(1), 1–10. doi:10.1108/INTR-11-2020-0668

Modgil, S., Singh, R. K., & Hannibal, C. (2022). Artificial intelligence for supply chain resilience: Learning from Covid-19. *International Journal of Logistics Management*, *33*(4), 1246–1268. doi:10.1108/IJLM-02-2021-0094

Mushtaq, R., Dastane, O., Rafiq, M., & Başar, B. D. (2023). Women financial inclusion research: A bibliometric and network analysis. *International Journal of Social Economics*, *50*(8), 1169–1185. doi:10.1108/IJSE-06-2022-0438

Rafiq, M., Dastane, O., & Mushtaq, R. (2023a). Waste reduction as ethical behaviour: A bibliometric analysis and development of future agenda. *Journal of Global Responsibility*, *14*(3), 360–379. doi:10.1108/JGR-09-2022-0098

Rafiq, M., Farrukh, M., Attiq, S., Shahzad, F., & Khan, I. (2023b). Linking job crafting, innovation performance, and career satisfaction: The mediating role of work engagement. *Work (Reading, Mass.)*, *75*(3), 877–886. doi:10.3233/WOR-211363 PMID:36683474

Rafiq, M., Jafar, R. M. S., Ahmad, W., Dastane, O., & Sial, M. A. (2022). Job Embeddedness: Cross-cultural Comparison Between China and Pakistan During COVID-19 Pandemic. *Vision (Basel)*.

Rana, G., & Sharma, R. (2019). Emerging human resource management practices in Industry 4.0. *Strategic HR Review*, *18*(4), 176–181. doi:10.1108/SHR-01-2019-0003

Ren, T., Jin, X., Rafiq, M., & Chin, T. (2019). Moderation of Housing-related Factors on Psychological Capital–Job Embeddedness Association. *Frontiers in Psychology*, *10*, 1618. doi:10.3389/fpsyg.2019.01618 PMID:31649569

Stahl, G., Björkman, I., Farndale, E., Morris, S. S., Paauwe, J., Stiles, P., Trevor, J., & Wright, P. (2012). Six principles of effective global talent management. *Sloan Management Review*, *53*(2), 25–42.

Teune, L. (2023). *Is AI a Diamond in the Rough for HR? Identifying the Attributions Towards AI-enabled HR practices. A Grounded Theory Approach*. University of Twente.

Chapter 2
AI-Based Performance Appraisal Systems:
A Game-Changer in Asia

Duan Xiuqing
UCSI Graduate Business School, UCSI University, Kuala Lumpur, Malaysia

Muhammad Rafiq
https://orcid.org/0000-0001-5037-6485
UCSI Graduate Business School, UCSI University, Kuala Lumpur, Malaysia

Wang Zhumin
Chengdu University of Technology, Chengdu, China

ABSTRACT

This chapter explores the transformative impact of AI-based performance assessment methods in Asia. It delves into the shift from traditional, often biased, evaluation systems to more objective, data-driven AI techniques. The discussion encompasses the adaptation of these technologies within the unique cultural and organizational contexts of Asian businesses, supported by case studies and empirical data. The chapter concludes with insights into the future potential of AI in enhancing employee development, retention, and organizational growth in the Asian corporate landscape.

1. INTRODUCTION TO PERFORMANCE ASSESSMENT IN ASIA

The landscape of performance assessment in Asia has been traditionally dominated by practices influenced by the region's unique cultural and hierarchical dynamics. Historically, in countries like Japan and South Korea, performance evaluations

DOI: 10.4018/979-8-3693-0039-8.ch002

have been shaped by cultural norms that emphasize collective harmony and respect for seniority, often resulting in assessments that might not fully reflect individual performance. This scenario underscores the need for a shift towards more objective and fair methods. Traditional methods, deeply embedded within these cultural contexts, tend to lack the objectivity necessary for the modern, diverse workforce, thus limiting their effectiveness in personal development and organizational growth (De Loo, 2002). We believe that education can enhance an individual's self-efficacy (Farrukh *et al.*, 2021), providing a foundation for more effective performance assessments in such environments.

In response to the evolving business landscape, which is increasingly characterized by technological advancements and a diverse workforce, there's a growing need for performance assessment methods that are both efficient and forward-looking. AI-based systems, utilizing technologies such as natural language processing, machine learning, and predictive analytics, promise a significant transformation in the realm of performance evaluations (Blasch *et al.*, 2021). These AI-driven systems offer advantages such as real-time feedback, personalized development programs, and an objective assessment framework, aligning with the expectations of a contemporary workforce (Chowdhury *et al.*, 2023). Several studies have highlighted the importance of leadership in effectively implementing these advanced systems in organizations (Farrukh *et al.*, 2023). Today, business rivalry is highly intense, and the business milieu is highly uncertain (Rafiq *et al.*, 2023b), making it imperative for leaders to guide their organizations towards embracing these innovative and objective performance assessment methods.

2. TRADITIONAL ASIAN PERFORMANCE ASSESSMENT PRACTICES AND LIMITATIONS

Traditional performance assessment practices in Asia have long been shaped by the region's cultural and hierarchical norms. In many Asian countries, such as China, Japan, and India, performance evaluations often involve a top-down approach, where senior management plays a pivotal role in determining employee evaluations (Varma *et al.*, 2023). As concerns over sustainability are well recognized and encouraged by the United Nations Development Programme (UNDP) (Aman *et al.*, 2022), maintaining high calibre employees has become a difficult issue for today's businesses (Rafiq *et al.*, 2022), especially when the assessment process is influenced by personal biases or favoritism. Additionally, the emphasis on collective harmony over individual achievement, a common cultural trait in Asia, can result in assessments that do not accurately reflect individual contributions and competencies (Earley and Ang, 2003).

Another limitation of traditional performance assessment practices in Asia is their reliance on annual or bi-annual reviews, which can be inadequate in capturing the ongoing performance and development of employees (Baker, 2013). This infrequency can lead to outdated or irrelevant feedback, hindering timely professional development and adaptability to changing job roles or market conditions. Furthermore, these practices often lack a mechanism for incorporating employee self-assessment or peer feedback, which are crucial for a comprehensive understanding of performance dynamics. Organizational researchers focused on human resource management often grapple with securing a competitive advantage in such dynamic environments (Aman *et al.*, 2023).

a. Impact of Hierarchical Structures on Assessment

Hierarchical structures in Asian organizations significantly influence traditional performance assessment practices. In countries like South Korea and Japan, where hierarchical relationships are deeply ingrained in the workplace, performance evaluations are often more reflective of an employee's position within the organization rather than their actual job performance (Horak and Yang, 2019). This can lead to a situation where higher-ranking individuals are evaluated more favorably, irrespective of their actual performance contributions (Goffin and Olson, 2011). Additionally, these hierarchical structures can discourage employees from providing honest feedback or challenging the status quo, further compromising the assessment process.

Moreover, the hierarchical nature of traditional Asian workplaces often results in a lack of transparency in the assessment process. Employees may not receive clear explanations for their ratings or understand how their performance aligns with broader organizational goals. This lack of transparency can lead to demotivation and a sense of unfairness among employees, especially if they perceive the assessment process as arbitrary or biased. In this context, maintaining high calibre employees becomes even more challenging as they may feel undervalued or unappreciated (Clack, 2021).

b. Cultural Norms and Assessment Biases

In many Asian cultures, performance assessment practices are deeply intertwined with prevailing cultural norms, such as respect for authority, collectivism, and indirect communication. These cultural characteristics can introduce biases into the performance assessment process. For instance, in collectivist societies like China and India, there is often a tendency to prioritize group harmony over individual accountability, which can lead to inflated or homogenized evaluations that do not accurately reflect individual performance (Rafiq and Weiwei, 2017). Similarly, the cultural norm of showing deference to authority can result in employees receiving higher evaluations based on their age or tenure rather than their actual job performance (Rafiq and Chin, 2019). These biases present significant challenges to HRM, as organizational researchers strive to develop more equitable and effective performance evaluation methods that cater to the diverse Asian workforce.

3. EVOLUTION OF AI IN PERFORMANCE ASSESSMENT

The evolution of AI in performance assessment, particularly in the last decade, has paralleled the growing importance of accounting conservatism research (Bhutta *et al.*, 2021). As organizations increasingly emphasize prudent financial management and risk assessment, AI's role in evaluating employee contributions to these areas has become more prominent (Bazarbash, 2019). AI systems are now adept at analyzing financial data, aiding in the identification of trends that align with conservative accounting practices, thus integrating financial prudence into performance assessment.

Furthermore, AI's impact on performance assessment extends to understanding and enhancing access to finance (Mushtaq *et al.*, 2023). It refers not just to the availability of financial products but also to their utilization within an organization. AI-driven analytics play a crucial role in identifying employees' competencies in managing financial resources, thereby aiding in strategic decision-making and optimizing financial product usage (Chowdhury et al., 2023). This aspect is particularly relevant in today's business environment, where access to finance is a critical determinant of organizational success.

Amidst these developments, environmental considerations have also become a priority. The increase in consumer awareness about environmental issues worldwide has led organizations to pay greater attention to their nature-related practices (Jin *et al.*, 2023). AI-driven performance assessment tools now include metrics that evaluate employees' contributions to environmental sustainability (Bachmann *et al.*, 2022). This is especially pertinent as solid waste generation continues to rise due to rapid population growth and urbanization (Rafiq *et al.*, 2023a), making sustainable practices an essential component of performance assessment. In today's rapidly changing and hectic entrepreneurial environment (Ren *et al.*, 2019), positive psychological factors such as adaptability and resilience are becoming much more important. AI systems can now analyze performance in these areas, providing insights into how well employees navigate and contribute to sustainability goals (Nishant *et al.*, 2020).

4. AI TECHNOLOGIES IN PERFORMANCE EVALUATION: ADVANCEMENTS AND APPLICATIONS

AI technologies in performance evaluation have seen remarkable advancements, notably in their ability to provide nuanced and comprehensive analyses. One of the key breakthroughs is the development of sophisticated machine learning algorithms capable of assessing performance based on a multitude of variables. These algorithms not only analyze quantitative output but also qualitatively evaluate aspects such as teamwork, creativity, and problem-solving skills. By harnessing vast amounts of data, AI systems offer a more holistic view of an employee's contributions and potential areas for growth (Dwivedi *et al.*, 2021).

Another significant advancement is the application of natural language processing (NLP) in performance evaluation. NLP technologies enable AI systems to interpret and analyze written and verbal communication, providing insights into an employee's communication skills, leadership qualities, and overall engagement. This application is particularly beneficial in assessing soft skills, which are increasingly recognized as crucial in the workplace. Additionally, NLP facilitates the processing of open-ended feedback and peer reviews, extracting valuable insights that traditional methods might overlook (Guetterman *et al.*, 2018).

Predictive analytics also play a pivotal role in AI-driven performance evaluation. These tools can forecast future performance trends and potential challenges, allowing for proactive interventions. Predictive models analyze historical data and current performance metrics to identify patterns and predict outcomes, such as the likelihood of an employee excelling in a particular role or the risk of attrition. This foresight enables organizations to make informed decisions about talent management, succession planning, and employee development strategies (Jackson and Dunn-Jensen, 2021).

5. CULTURAL IMPLICATIONS OF AI IN ASIAN PERFORMANCE ASSESSMENT

The integration of AI in performance assessment within Asian contexts brings forth a set of unique cultural implications. In Asia, where cultural norms and values significantly influence workplace dynamics, the adoption of AI-driven assessment tools must be sensitive to these factors. Asian cultures often place a high value on hierarchical structures, collective harmony, and indirect communication, which can impact how AI systems are perceived and utilized. In countries with high power distance, such as China or South Korea, employees might be less inclined to openly challenge or question AI-generated assessments, especially if these are endorsed by higher management. This deference to authority can lead to underutilization of AI's potential for fostering open dialogue and transparent feedback mechanisms (Da Silva *et al.*, 2022). Furthermore, the collectivist nature of many Asian societies, where group cohesion and conformity are prioritized, might lead to resistance against AI systems perceived as too individualistic or disruptive to team dynamics. Ensuring that AI tools accommodate and respect these cultural nuances is crucial for their successful integration and acceptance (Nguyễn, 2023).

Another cultural consideration is the communication style prevalent in many Asian cultures, which tends to be more indirect and contextual than in Western countries. This has implications for the design and implementation of AI systems in performance assessments. AI tools relying heavily on direct feedback and explicit communication may not capture the subtleties of Asian communication styles, potentially leading to misinterpretations or overlooked nuances in performance evaluations. Thus, customizing AI algorithms to interpret and align with these communication styles is essential. Moreover, the implementation process of AI in performance assessments must be accompanied by sensitization programs that help employees understand and adapt to these new technologies, respecting their cultural background and addressing any apprehensions or misconceptions. This approach will ensure that AI tools are not only technically proficient but also culturally compatible, fostering a more inclusive and effective performance assessment environment.

6. CHALLENGES AND BEST PRACTICES IN AI-BASED PERFORMANCE ASSESSMENT CONCLUSION: TRANSFORMING PERFORMANCE ASSESSMENT IN ASIA WITH AI

Implementing AI-based performance assessment systems in Asia presents a unique set of challenges that need careful navigation. Firstly, the disparity in technological infrastructure across different Asian countries can significantly impact the effectiveness of AI solutions. Advanced economies like Japan and Singapore may readily embrace AI-driven tools, while emerging economies might struggle with the requisite technological adoption due to limited resources and infrastructure (Chin *et al.*, 2021). This disparity necessitates a tailored approach to AI implementation, considering each country's specific technological readiness and resource availability. Another challenge lies in data integrity and privacy concerns. The vast amounts of data required for AI algorithms can raise issues around data security, employee privacy, and the ethical use of information. Organizations must establish robust data governance frameworks to address these concerns, ensuring compliance with local and international data protection laws (Delacroix and Lawrence, 2019). Additionally, there's the risk of algorithmic bias, where AI systems may inadvertently perpetuate existing workplace biases, leading to unfair assessments. To mitigate this, continuous monitoring and adjustment of AI algorithms are crucial, coupled with training programs that sensitize users to potential biases in AI assessments (Lee *et al.*, 2019).

Best practices in implementing AI-based performance assessment systems involve a blend of technological, ethical, and cultural considerations. A key practice is the co-creation of AI systems, involving stakeholders at all levels in the design and development process. This approach ensures that the AI tools are aligned with the organizational culture and employee expectations, enhancing acceptance and effectiveness. Regular training and development programs are essential, equipping HR professionals and employees with the skills to effectively interact with and interpret AI-driven assessments. Moreover, creating a transparent AI environment where employees understand how the AI system works and how decisions are made can foster trust and confidence in the technology. Organizations should also prioritize ethical AI, implementing systems that are fair, unbiased, and respectful of employee privacy and data security. This includes regular audits of AI systems to identify and correct any biases or inaccuracies, ensuring equitable and accurate performance assessments.

In conclusion, AI-based performance assessment systems hold the potential to revolutionize performance evaluation in Asia. By replacing traditional, often subjective methods with AI's objectivity and efficiency, these systems can offer more accurate, fair, and developmental assessments. As organizations navigate the challenges and adopt best practices, AI in performance assessments can lead to enhanced employee development, better talent retention, and overall organizational growth. This transformation, however, hinges on the balanced integration of technology with ethical, cultural, and operational considerations (Zaki et al., 2023). The future of performance assessment in Asia looks promising with AI, with continued research and collaboration between industry and academia crucial for realizing its full potential (Feijóo *et al.*, 2020). These advancements are not just a technological leap but represent a shift towards a more data-driven, objective, and employee-centric approach to talent management in the Asian business landscape.

a. Technological Disparities and Infrastructure

The adoption of AI-based performance assessment in Asia is significantly influenced by the technological disparities across the region. In technologically advanced nations like Japan and South Korea, the integration of AI into HR practices is smoother due to the existing robust digital infrastructure and a workforce familiar with tech-driven environments (Murday *et al.*, 2013). These countries have the bandwidth and technical know-how to incorporate sophisticated AI tools seamlessly into their performance assessment systems. On the other hand, in emerging economies like Vietnam or Indonesia, the scenario is markedly different. The digital infrastructure in these regions might not be as developed, posing significant challenges in terms of bandwidth, data storage, and cybersecurity. Additionally, there is often a lack of skilled professionals who can effectively implement and manage these advanced AI systems. This gap necessitates a phased and more educationally supportive approach to AI integration, focusing on building the necessary infrastructure and workforce capability to leverage AI technologies effectively.

Another aspect of this disparity is the varied levels of AI acceptance and cultural readiness across Asia. While some countries exhibit a high degree of openness to technological innovation, others may exhibit resistance due to cultural norms or apprehensions about data privacy and job security. Tailoring AI solutions to fit the cultural and technological landscape of each country is thus crucial. This involves not just technological adaptation but also educational initiatives to raise awareness and understanding of AI's benefits and applications in performance assessment (Dwivedi et al., 2021). Organizations should collaborate with local governments and educational institutions to develop training programs and workshops aimed at upskilling the workforce for an AI-ready future (Miao *et al.*, 2021).

Furthermore, the technological disparity also impacts the quality and quantity of data available for AI algorithms. In countries with less digital penetration, collecting comprehensive and diverse data sets, which are critical for training unbiased and effective AI models, can be a challenge. This limitation can lead to AI systems that are not fully optimized for the local context, potentially affecting their accuracy and effectiveness. There is a need for a strategic approach to data collection and management, ensuring that AI systems are trained on high-quality, representative data. This could involve collaborations with various stakeholders, including industry partners, government agencies, and international bodies, to create comprehensive databases that can feed into more effective AI performance assessment tools.

b. Algorithmic Bias and Ethical Concerns

Algorithmic bias is a critical concern in the deployment of AI-based performance assessment systems, particularly in a culturally diverse region like Asia. These biases can stem from the data on which AI models are trained, often reflecting historical inequalities or societal biases (Ntoutsi *et al.*, 2020). For instance, if an AI system is trained on data from a predominantly male workforce, it might inadvertently develop biases against female employees. The impact of such biases can be significant, leading to unfair performance evaluations, discrimination, and a lack of diversity in the workplace. To address this, organizations must invest in developing unbiased AI models. This involves using diverse and inclusive training data, regularly auditing

AI systems for bias, and involving a wide range of stakeholders in the development process to ensure different perspectives are considered.

In addition to algorithmic bias, ethical concerns such as data privacy and employee surveillance arise with the use of AI in performance assessment. There is a fine line between using AI to monitor performance and intruding into an employee's privacy. In some Asian cultures, where personal space and respect for individuality are highly valued, this can be particularly sensitive. Organizations must establish clear policies and guidelines around data usage, ensuring transparency in how employee data is collected, used, and stored (Bertot *et al.*, 2014). Employees should be informed about the AI systems in use, their purpose, and the measures taken to protect their data. Ensuring an ethical approach to AI implementation is not just about compliance with regulations but also about building trust and a positive organizational culture. By addressing these ethical concerns proactively, organizations can create an environment where AI-based performance assessment systems are seen as tools for growth and development rather than surveillance and control.

c. Adaptation to Local Cultural Nuances

Adapting AI-driven performance assessment systems to the intricate cultural nuances of Asia is crucial for their effectiveness and acceptance. In a region characterized by diverse cultural, linguistic, and social landscapes, a one-size-fits-all AI solution is impractical and often ineffective (Bibri, 2021). For instance, in countries with high power distance cultures like China and India, employees might accept AI-generated feedback without question, potentially overlooking critical thinking or personal development. In contrast, in more egalitarian societies like Japan, employees might expect more transparency and participation in the AI decision-making process. Tailoring AI tools to these cultural nuances involves not just language localization but also adapting the AI's interaction and feedback mechanisms to align with local communication styles and hierarchical structures.

Moreover, in many Asian cultures, where group harmony and collectivism are valued, performance assessment systems must be designed to promote teamwork and collective achievement rather than just individual performance (Lee & Kim, 2023). AI systems should be sensitive to these cultural values, focusing on collaborative achievements and group dynamics. This approach can enhance the system's relevance and acceptance, ensuring that performance assessments align with employees' cultural and social expectations. Additionally, involving local stakeholders in the development and implementation of AI systems can provide valuable insights into cultural specifics, leading to more effective and culturally competent AI tools.

Lastly, it's essential to consider the impact of these cultural adaptations on the overall objectivity and fairness of AI systems. While customizing AI tools to fit local cultural contexts is important, it should not compromise the system's ability to provide fair and unbiased assessments. Balancing cultural adaptability with the need for standardization and objectivity is a delicate task that requires ongoing evaluation and refinement. Regular feedback loops, involving a diverse group of employees and cultural experts, can help fine-tune AI systems, ensuring they remain effective across different cultural settings while maintaining their core objective of fair and unbiased performance assessment.

d. Implementation Challenges in Diverse Business Environments

Implementing AI-based performance assessment systems in Asia's diverse business environments presents several challenges. First and foremost is the wide variation in organizational structures and business practices across the region. Large multinational corporations might have the resources and infrastructure to integrate sophisticated AI systems seamlessly, while small and medium enterprises (SMEs) may struggle with limited budgets and technical expertise. For SMEs, the cost of AI implementation, including the necessary hardware, software, and training, can be prohibitive. This necessitates the development of scalable and affordable AI solutions that can be customized to fit the needs of different types of organizations.

Another challenge is ensuring that the AI systems are compatible with existing HR processes and technologies. Many Asian companies may still rely on traditional HR systems and practices, making the transition to AI-driven methods a significant change. This requires a careful planning and integration strategy, where AI tools are gradually introduced, ensuring compatibility with existing systems and minimizing disruption. Employee training and change management are also crucial in this process, as employees need to understand and adapt to new technologies and workflows.

Furthermore, the varying levels of digital literacy among the workforce in Asia can affect the adoption and effectiveness of AI systems. In regions with higher digital literacy, employees are more likely to embrace AI tools and use them effectively. However, in areas with lower digital literacy, there may be resistance or difficulty in using these systems. Organizations need to invest in digital education and training programs to ensure that all employees, regardless of their initial digital proficiency, can benefit from AI-driven performance assessment tools (Lee & Wang, 2022).

e. Future Trends and Emerging Innovations in AI and Performance Assessment

The future of AI in performance assessment in Asia is marked by several emerging trends and innovations. One significant trend is the increasing use of advanced machine learning algorithms and data analytics to provide more nuanced and comprehensive performance assessments. These technologies enable the analysis of a wider range of performance indicators, including behavioral patterns, team dynamics, and even emotional intelligence, providing a holistic view of an employee's performance.

Another trend is the integration of AI with other cutting-edge technologies like the Internet of Things (IoT) and wearable devices. This integration can provide real-time data on employee activities and well-being, offering new insights into performance and productivity. For example, wearable devices can track stress levels or physical activity, providing data that can be used to assess work-life balance and overall employee health, which are critical components of performance.

Moreover, AI-driven performance assessment systems are becoming more personalized and adaptive. AI technologies can now learn from individual employee feedback and performance history, adjusting the assessment criteria and feedback mechanisms to better suit each employee's unique strengths and development needs. This personalized approach not only enhances the accuracy and relevance of performance assessments but also contributes to employee development and job satisfaction.

In conclusion, the integration of AI into performance assessment in Asia is an evolving landscape, characterized by rapid technological advancements and innovative applications. As AI technologies continue to advance, they offer the potential to transform traditional performance assessment methods, making them more efficient, fair, and aligned with the unique cultural and business environments of Asia. By staying attuned to these emerging trends and continuing to innovate, organizations can leverage AI to enhance their talent management strategies and drive organizational success.

REFERENCES

Aman, A., Rafiq, M., & Dastane, O. (2023). A cross-cultural comparison of work engagement in the relationships between trust climate – Job performance and turnover intention: Focusing China and Pakistan. *Heliyon*, *9*(9), e19534. doi:10.1016/j.heliyon.2023.e19534 PMID:37809562

Aman, A., Rafiq, M., Dastane, O., & Sabir, A. A. (2022). Green corridor: A critical perspective and development of research agenda. *Frontiers in Environmental Science*, *10*, 982473. doi:10.3389/fenvs.2022.982473

Bachmann, N., Tripathi, S., Brunner, M., & Jodlbauer, H. (2022). The contribution of data-driven technologies in achieving the sustainable development goals. *Sustainability (Basel)*, *14*(5), 2497. doi:10.3390u14052497

Baker, T. (2013). *The end of the performance review: A new approach to appraising employee performance*. Springer. doi:10.1057/9781137347503

Bazarbash, M. (2019). *Fintech in financial inclusion: machine learning applications in assessing credit risk*. International Monetary Fund.

Bertot, J. C., Gorham, U., Jaeger, P. T., Sarin, L. C., & Choi, H. (2014). Big data, open government and e-government: Issues, policies and recommendations. *Information Polity*, *19*(1-2), 5–16. doi:10.3233/IP-140328

Bhutta, U., Martins, J. N., Mata, M. N., Raza, A., Dantas, R. M., Correia, A. B., & Rafiq, M. (2021). Intellectual Structure and Evolution of Accounting Conservatism Research: Past Trends and Future Research Suggestions. *International Journal of Financial Studies*, *9*(3), 35. doi:10.3390/ijfs9030035

Bibri, S. E. (2021). Data-driven smart sustainable cities of the future: An evidence synthesis approach to a comprehensive state-of-the-art literature review. *Sustainable Futures : An Applied Journal of Technology, Environment and Society*, *3*, 100047. doi:10.1016/j.sftr.2021.100047

Blasch, E., Pham, T., Chong, C.-Y., Koch, W., Leung, H., Braines, D., & Abdelzaher, T. (2021). Machine learning/artificial intelligence for sensor data fusion–opportunities and challenges. *IEEE Aerospace and Electronic Systems Magazine*, *36*(7), 80–93. doi:10.1109/MAES.2020.3049030

Chin, T., Hu, Q., Rowley, C., & Wang, S. (2021). *Business models in the Asia-Pacific: dynamic balancing of multiple cultures, innovation and value creation*. Taylor & Francis.

Chowdhury, S., Dey, P., Joel-Edgar, S., Bhattacharya, S., Rodriguez-Espindola, O., Abadie, A., & Truong, L. (2023). Unlocking the value of artificial intelligence in human resource management through AI capability framework. *Human Resource Management Review*, *33*(1), 100899. doi:10.1016/j.hrmr.2022.100899

Clack, L. (2021). Employee engagement: Keys to organizational success. The Palgrave handbook of workplace well-being, 1001-1028.

Da Silva, M., Flood, C. M., & Herder, M. (2022). Regulation of health-related artificial intelligence in medical devices: The Canadian story. *UBCL Rev.*, *55*, 635.

De Loo, I. (2002). The troublesome relationship between action learning and organizational growth. *Journal of Workplace Learning*, *14*(6), 245–255. doi:10.1108/13665620210441207

Delacroix, S., & Lawrence, N. D. (2019). Bottom-up data trusts: Disturbing the 'one size fits all' approach to data governance. *International Data Privacy Law, 9*(4), 236-252.

Dwivedi, Y. K., Hughes, L., Ismagilova, E., Aarts, G., Coombs, C., Crick, T., Duan, Y., Dwivedi, R., Edwards, J., Eirug, A., Galanos, V., Ilavarasan, P. V., Janssen, M., Jones, P., Kar, A. K., Kizgin, H., Kronemann, B., Lal, B., Lucini, B., ... Williams, M. D. (2021). Artificial Intelligence (AI): Multidisciplinary perspectives on emerging challenges, opportunities, and agenda for research, practice and policy. *International Journal of Information Management, 57*, 101994. doi:10.1016/j.ijinfomgt.2019.08.002

Earley, P. C., & Ang, S. (2003). *Cultural intelligence: Individual interactions across cultures*. Academic Press.

Farrukh, M., Raza, A., & Rafiq, M. (2023). Environmentally specific authentic leadership and team green creative behavior based on cognitive-affective path systems. *International Journal of Contemporary Hospitality Management, 35*(10), 3662–3680. doi:10.1108/IJCHM-04-2022-0530

Farrukh, M., Raza, A., Sajid, M., Rafiq, M., Hameed, R., & Ali, T. (2021). Entrepreneurial intentions: The relevance of nature and nurture. *Education + Training, 63*(7/8), 1195–1212. doi:10.1108/ET-01-2021-0028

Feijóo, C., Kwon, Y., Bauer, J. M., Bohlin, E., Howell, B., Jain, R., Potgieter, P., Vu, K., Whalley, J., & Xia, J. (2020). Harnessing artificial intelligence (AI) to increase wellbeing for all: The case for a new technology diplomacy. *Telecommunications Policy, 44*(6), 101988. doi:10.1016/j.telpol.2020.101988 PMID:32377031

Goffin, R. D., & Olson, J. M. (2011). Is it all relative? Comparative judgments and the possible improvement of self-ratings and ratings of others. *Perspectives on Psychological Science, 6*(1), 48–60. doi:10.1177/1745691610393521 PMID:26162115

Guetterman, T. C., Chang, T., DeJonckheere, M., Basu, T., Scruggs, E., & Vydiswaran, V. V. (2018). Augmenting qualitative text analysis with natural language processing: Methodological study. *Journal of Medical Internet Research, 20*(6), e231. doi:10.2196/jmir.9702 PMID:29959110

Horak, S., & Yang, I. (2019). Whither seniority? Career progression and performance orientation in South Korea. *International Journal of Human Resource Management, 30*(9), 1419–1447. doi:10.1080/09585192.2017.1362659

Jackson, N. C., & Dunn-Jensen, L. M. (2021). Leadership succession planning for today's digital transformation economy: Key factors to build for competency and innovation. *Business Horizons*, *64*(2), 273–284. doi:10.1016/j.bushor.2020.11.008

Jin, J., Rafiq, M., Hayat, N., Yang, Q., & Al Mamun, A. (2023). Discovering the Adoption of Eco-Friendly Furniture Among Chinese Customers. In N. Mansour & L. M. Bujosa Vadell (Eds.), *Finance, Accounting and Law in the Digital Age: The Impact of Technology and Innovation in the Financial Services Sector* (pp. 273–283). Springer International Publishing. doi:10.1007/978-3-031-27296-7_25

Lee, N. T., Resnick, P., & Barton, G. (2019). *Algorithmic bias detection and mitigation: Best practices and policies to reduce consumer harms* (Vol. 2). Brookings Institute.

Miao, F., Holmes, W., Huang, R., & Zhang, H. (2021). *AI and education: A guidance for policymakers*. UNESCO Publishing.

Murday, J., Bell, L., Heath, J., Kong, C. H., Chang, R., Fonash, S., & Baba, M. (2013). Implications: People and physical infrastructure. Convergence of knowledge, technology and society: Beyond convergence of nano-bio-info-cognitive technologies, 287-370.

Mushtaq, R., Dastane, O., Rafiq, M., & Başar, B. D. (2023). Women financial inclusion research: A bibliometric and network analysis. *International Journal of Social Economics*, *50*(8), 1169–1185. doi:10.1108/IJSE-06-2022-0438

Nguyễn, T. (2023). *The Influence of ChatGPT and AI Tools on Vietnamese Education*. Academic Press.

Nishant, R., Kennedy, M., & Corbett, J. (2020). Artificial intelligence for sustainability: Challenges, opportunities, and a research agenda. *International Journal of Information Management*, *53*, 102104. doi:10.1016/j.ijinfomgt.2020.102104

Ntoutsi, E., Fafalios, P., Gadiraju, U., Iosifidis, V., Nejdl, W., Vidal, M. E., Ruggieri, S., Turini, F., Papadopoulos, S., Krasanakis, E., Kompatsiaris, I., Kinder-Kurlanda, K., Wagner, C., Karimi, F., Fernandez, M., Alani, H., Berendt, B., Kruegel, T., Heinze, C., ... Staab, S. (2020). Bias in data-driven artificial intelligence systems—An introductory survey. *Wiley Interdisciplinary Reviews. Data Mining and Knowledge Discovery*, *10*(3), e1356. doi:10.1002/widm.1356

Rafiq, M., & Chin, T. (2019). Three-Way Interaction Effect of Job Insecurity, Job Embeddedness and Career Stage on Life Satisfaction in A Digital Era. *International Journal of Environmental Research and Public Health*, *16*(9), 1580. doi:10.3390/ijerph16091580 PMID:31064119

Rafiq, M., Dastane, O., & Mushtaq, R. (2023a). Waste reduction as ethical behaviour: A bibliometric analysis and development of future agenda. *Journal of Global Responsibility*, *14*(3), 360–379. doi:10.1108/JGR-09-2022-0098

Rafiq, M., Farrukh, M., Attiq, S., Shahzad, F., & Khan, I. (2023b). Linking job crafting, innovation performance, and career satisfaction: The mediating role of work engagement. *Work (Reading, Mass.)*, *75*(3), 877–886. doi:10.3233/WOR-211363 PMID:36683474

Rafiq, M., Jafar, R. M. S., Ahmad, W., Dastane, O., & Sial, M. A. (2022). Job Embeddedness: Cross-cultural Comparison Between China and Pakistan During COVID-19 Pandemic. *Vision (Basel)*.

Rafiq, M., & Weiwei, W. (2017). Managerial trust outlook in China and Pakistan. *Human Systems Management*, *36*(4), 363–368. doi:10.3233/HSM-17157

Ren, T., Jin, X., Rafiq, M., & Chin, T. (2019). Moderation of Housing-related Factors on Psychological Capital–Job Embeddedness Association. *Frontiers in Psychology*, *10*, 1618. doi:10.3389/fpsyg.2019.01618 PMID:31649569

Varma, A., Budhwar, P. S., & DeNisi, A. (2023). *Performance management systems: A global perspective*. Taylor & Francis. doi:10.4324/9781003306849

Zaki, H. O., Fernandez, D., Dastane, O., Aman, A., & Sanusi, S. (2023). Virtual reality in digital marketing: Research agenda based on bibliometric reflection. *Marketing Intelligence & Planning*, *41*(4), 505–524.

Chapter 3
Implementation of Artificial Intelligence in Human Resource Management in Asia-Pacific

Anusha Thakur
https://orcid.org/0000-0001-8761-2250
University of Petroleum and Energy Studies, India

ABSTRACT

The amalgamation of pioneering technologies such as artificial intelligence in the human resources (HR) department has revolutionized the conduct of businesses nowadays. The inclusion of AI automates the organization's processes, benefiting the administration. Artificial neural networks, fuzzy logic, expert systems, data mining, machine learning, and genetic algorithms are a few of the techniques for the implementation of AI in HR. The chapter contemplates the role and benefits of artificial intelligence in organizations in the Asia-Pacific region to enhance the efficiency and effectiveness of human resource functions. It emphasizes the market players and use cases in the Asia-Pacific, illustrating the decision-making support solutions to deliver high-end value and profitability. This study also focuses on the trends and challenges in the implementation of AI in organizations to discover new potential and strategize for the future.

DOI: 10.4018/979-8-3693-0039-8.ch003

INTRODUCTION

Organizations are progressively turning to HR analytics and AI to gain valuable acumens in their workforce, in today's data-driven world. Leveraging state-of-the-art technologies and evaluating wide amounts of HR data, enables businesses to seamlessly augment their holistic growth across the world.

Artificial intelligence has matured into a group of influential technologies that offer viable advantages to businesses across industries (Hupfer, 2020). After years of speculation and hype, AI is witnessing an expansion from the realm of science, to become a precedence of any organization. The evolution of artificial intelligence enables HR systems to become unbiased, powerful, productive, and profitable.

The HR systems act as a building block for an organization (Bhardwaj, 2020). A strong and advanced HR team paves the way for wider avenues, unlike a weak system restraining the growth of an organization. Human resources paves opportunities to enable the worldwide digital transformation sweeping organizations.

Workforce skilling and technological advancements, play a significant role in organizations. The technology in human resources refers to the use of self-learning and advanced algorithms for the analysis of the data, predominantly to create recommendations and insights or to automate tasks. HR professionals emphasize on counting on the latest platforms, working ways, and technologies, and becoming strongly positioned in the business (Occean, 2017).

Integration and adoption of intelligent HR-tech solutions are the vital aspects, that enable the systems to develop unprecedented workplace strategies, and substantially design outcome-driven workplace models and processes. The advent of AI-powered solutions in HR automates several repetitive, less value-added, and time-consuming tasks (Ghosh, 2023).

The organizations adopt these automated tools for varied reasons to attain specific goals. For instance, AI-driven plan optimizers relieves the conventional scheduling techniques such as minimizing schedule-related service interruptions, and employee downtime (Amar, 2022). The technology assists human aid managers and stakeholders in making efficacious decisions. Automation in HR, augments work flexibility, creates a balanced workload, and paves the way for several innovative opportunities.

The benefits offered by the technology augment the decision-making and operational activities, enabling the employees to focus on the lesser-mundane tasks. To facilitate the implementation of technology, it thereby becomes essential for the leaders to substantially adapt to the workforce policies.

With the changing business domains, human resource management (HRM) is expected to witness opportunities and challenges, while maintaining growth and development at the same time. The chapter discusses the various benefits offered by the implementation of artificial intelligence in human resources. It discusses the different key market players implementing artificial intelligence in human resources, in terms of country-wise (India, Australia, Singapore, and China). The study further contemplates the restraints and the opportunities hindering and paving way for the businesses in the present and future.

LITERATURE REVIEW

The inception of the pandemic revolutionized the way businesses work. In spite, of the global headwinds, increasing strategies, technologies, and business models help build the thrust for new HR systems. Over the past few years, Asia Pacific has become one of the innovative hubs for human resource technology (Amos, 2022).

Leading organizations are engaged in capitalizing on cutting-edge technologies to source, screen, and manage candidates along with aligning of skill sets, addressing skills gaps, and maintaining compliance, as per the changing industry scenarios. The availability and interest of businesses and individuals in artificial intelligence have witnessed a significant spur over the past few years.

The HR systems emphasize on offering well-informed, better-equipped, and customized learning programs to cater to the changing business scenario (Avila, 2023). AI in amalgamation with strategic insights paves the way for newer business avenues and is expected to transform the function of the HR system holistically. An AI system helps enhance the analysis and performance forecast by gathering and comparing job performance and employee data. The AI-based HR tools in different forms emphasize on segments such as training & development, hiring, employee benefits, and employee engagement, posing to be profitable to the businesses.

ARTIFICIAL INTELLIGENCE AND AUTOMATION IN HR

Automation and AI are vital technologies empowering and accelerating transformation in businesses in the Asia Pacific region. Increasing government policies, innovation, and investments, spur the adoption of technologies. Software automation is gaining significant traction, particularly in this region, with variations existing among the different countries. The companies in the Asia Pacific region account for nearly 60 percent of the workforce of the world, hence, it becomes imperative for these to cope with the changing marketplace (Harshman, 2021).

Increasing computing power of artificial intelligence systems enables prolific applicability of these in businesses. The incorporation of cutting-edge AI technology expedites augmented analytics and enables professionals to autonomously draw insights about the employees, with enhanced operational efficiencies and productivity.

Automation technology in countries such as India, Australia, China, and Singapore are increasingly, witnessing a shift in the way organizations manage human talent while restructuring the different segments. The adoption of robotics and AI platforms helps streamline the processes, with seamless analysis of data, and effective talent strategies.

Hybrid workplace models are expected to be one of the fastest-growing trends in the region. Beyond comprehending the business value of automation technology, it becomes essential for the employees to embrace automation, and ensure that the individuals easily learn to work effectually with the digital assistants and automated processes.

USES OF AI IN HUMAN RESOURCES

With increasing state-of-the-art technologies and digitalization, the need for restructuring different organizational core functions is gaining significant traction. Technological innovations are pushing businesses to make their value-creation processes more customer-friendly and effective. Businesses across different regions are striving towards digital transformation to cope with the dynamic business environment (Mehrotra, 2022).

AI in human resources has revolutionized the way organizations work, resulting in better decision-making and outcomes. The AI-based tools vary in their goals and tasks but share the same method. A few uses of artificial intelligence in human resources (Mackenzie, 2023) are illustrated as:

Recruiting

Artificial Intelligence enables businesses to find the right talent like, the job description. The technology enables HR professionals to locate qualified applicants by identifying and analyzing the suitable features in a CV. The valuation process is significantly AI-driven, from personality assessments to video interview insights. In addition to this, intelligent screening software has the potential to automate the screening of resumes, thereby, allowing the recruiter chatbots to network with the candidates on a real-time basis to determine an individual's appropriateness (Dutta, 2022). Hence, implementing AI technology in human resources saves time and ensures that no potential candidates are missed in the process.

Performance Management

The AI-powered HR system considers factors such as peer feedback, project involvement, and completed tasks, thereby helping to track and analyze the performance of the employee data. At the time of the review process, a report with the inclusion of the areas of improvement, progress, and strengths, is generated. AI in businesses enables professionals to easily track and quantify the performance of the employees and accordingly forecast the employee potential.

AI algorithms enable the evaluation of varied amounts of data, such as feedback, productivity metrics, and engagement levels, thereby, offering the systems with real-time acumens into employee performance. The technology owes the potential to promote incessant performance feedback and create an adaptive and agile system. This data-managed approach thereby allows HR systems to grow customized and targeted employee advancement plans, encouraging organizational success and career growth (Circle, 2023).

Employee Offboarding/Onboarding Processes

With the incorporation of AI in the HR systems, the employees are easily guided and well-versed with the companies' policies, and procedures with proper training sessions. The companies owe the potential to streamline the process a bit extra, to, make quiz questions, craft the onboarding materials and introduction from the beginning, add and recommend the links to the appropriate training content, send mechanized notices to the new individuals, and decode the existing onboarding content to the latest languages, thereby offering customized content (Zavvy, 2023). The AI helps to seamlessly manage the offboarding tasks, and exit surveys, thereby enabling a smoother transition of the individuals.

Talent Development and Training

The AI-based systems help personalize the learning and development processes for the employees. Based on the vision, goals, and role, the technology recommends explicit workshops, webinars, and training courses, thereby motivating the employees to engage in the overall career development processes.

Employee Engagement Initiatives

The inclusion of an Artificial Intelligence survey tool in HR teams automates the process of gauging an employee sentiment precisely. However, businesses often restrict employee communication to performance assessment and annual review activities. Approaches such as limited data analysis, special committees, and employee surveys are not favorable in terms of delivering actionable insights via actual responses. Hence, the advent of employee engagement opens avenues for organizations to work in a better way. A few ways in which AI helps to augment employee engagement (Gautam, 2019) are illustrated as:

- *Behavior Mapping and Predictive Analytics:* One of the major enablers of employee engagement is learning & development. Several organizations value this enabler as a vital aspect in developing and recalling talent by providing career growth and proficient advancement. The incorporation of AI-powered predictive or data analytics, helps organizations to develop customized training programs, position them with various employees' learning needs and forms, and thereby, attain better interaction between the employee and training programs. Offering employee behavior maps and predictive insights, helps HR professionals to generate quitting tendencies of the employees, and address the same. Hence, with the employees feeling valued, and motivated, the businesses can easily sustain and grow in the competitive market.
- *Real-time Feedback and Responsive Tools:* The AI-powered responsive platforms help organizations to gather feedback from the employees on a real-time basis, and address any issues or queries then there itself. Real-time feedback paves the way to understand the perception of the employees. With the help of sentiment analysis, these advanced AI tools offer better insights in the employees' mood at the workplace, thereby easily waning the smallest of issues being faced by the same.
- *Chatbots:* In today's scenario, messenger and social media apps have completely altered the way communication process, with chatbots leveraging the same in a much more informal and interactive way. Implementation of a chatbot in the L&D initiatives leverages natural language processing and Machine Learning (ML) to bolster the learning results in an organization. One of the most common Chatbot use cases is that of the brand "Starbucks", which is engaged in using Facebook messenger bots for seamless demand and distribution processes.
- *Collaboration Tools:* AI-powered tools are engaged in taking care of the menial tasks, giving suggestions on collaborations, and simultaneously safeguarding the leadership positions from decision fatigue. With the delegation of tasks, the team members and managers can emphasize more on work, hence, driving better engagement.

Workforce Planning

Proficient analysis of information such as industry trends, current workforce skills, company growth plans, and future opportunities, with the help of an AI tool, helps predict the forthcoming roles to be looked upon, and accordingly strategize their business models.

ANALYSIS IN THE "ASIA PACIFIC" REGION: INDIA

In India, several organizations are increasingly implementing artificial intelligence to augment the proficiency of human resources. The process focuses on the automated process of recruitment till performance appraisal of employees.

In India, Post-pandemic enterprises are increasingly shifting towards the digital revolution, with HR professionals leaning on the data flowing from digital interaction points to predict the exit and entry of new talents, streamline the coordination and communication processes, plug skill gaps, assess employee performance design compensation packages, and deciding on the work environments in an organization (Goel, 2021).

Instahyre

About the Company: Instahyre, founded in 2014, is headquartered in Delhi. There are nearly 10,000 companies registered with Instahyre, which enables individuals to search for jobs, keeping their privacy intact and valued.

Solutions Offered: The company offers a cutting-edge revolutionary hiring platform, based on artificial intelligence, empowering employers to search and hire talent seamlessly or accurately. With the revamping technology, finding a suitable candidate or a suitable job becomes easy and hassle-free (Instahyre, 2014).

EdGE Networks

About the Company: EdGE Networks, headquartered in Bangalore, offers nextGen technology solutions for the transformation of the workforce, based on artificial intelligence and data science technologies. The company was established in 2012. EdGE Networks offers a talent decision platform to simplify key decisions in talent management and enable organizations to build the team of the future.

Solutions Offered: EdGE Networks is the provider of a combined platform that includes talent acquisition, workforce planning, workforce optimization, and talent transformation, with a layer of useful insights and analytics. The company is engaged in developing efficiency tools, leveraging AI to enable businesses to cater to the challenges in the HR systems. The enterprise solutions offered by the company include HIREalchemy, workforce optimization, and talent acquisition, covering a range of HR requirements (EDGE, 2012).

Mercer LLC

About the Company: Mettl, founded in 2009, is headquartered in Gurugram. The global HR consulting firm *Mercer* announced the acquisition of *Mettl*, an online assessment and data sciences-driven talent assessment company, valued at Rs. 250 crore (BusinessLine, 2018). The company operates in nearly 100 countries, with approximately 1800 clients across the world.

Solutions Offered: The company's proficient in-depth analytics, cloud-based platform, and research-backed assessments help deliver revolutionary outcomes for employees and clients. Mettl offers personalized valuations across employee development, comprising of candidate training, & development, skills assessment, and pre-hiring screening programs for the employees (MercerLLC, 2009). Key segments offered by the company are recruitment, L&D solutions, proctoring, certifications & exams, as well as online talent assessments. Mettl thereby focuses on offering solutions to effectively identify, hire, grow, and engage the best talent, with a restructured value-creation process.

AUSTRALIA

The HR industry has witnessed significant traction, in terms of technological advancements, over the past few years in Australia. The shift towards automation at unparalleled accuracy and speed has led to several diversified benefits for job seekers, employees, and leaders across the industry.

In today's scenario, nearly one in 5 Australian SMEs are engaged in using artificial intelligence in the human resource segments (Burgess, 2023). Usage of this technology in HR segments has significantly automated the manual tasks of scheduling interviews, shortlisting capable candidates, personalizing employee training programs, and matching job descriptions, thereby completely revolutionizing the way of working. In addition to this, Gen AI along with other AI-powered tech, is also increasingly enhancing the way businesses are unleashing growth and productivity in the future in Australia (Nuttall, 2023).

Xref

About the Company: Xref is a Sydney-based, software company founded in 2013. The company operates with offices in the UK, New Zealand, Australia, and North America. Xref is a recruitment technology company that focuses on recruiting, retaining, and remembering the best talent in an organization.

Solutions Offered: Xref is the provider of actionable data-driven insights with exit surveys, employee engagement, and automated reference, enabling businesses to identify, hire, and retain talent across the world. The company is engaged in automating the reference processes that helps make data-driven and fast hiring decisions. Xref works with legitimate companies such as Westpac and Qantas. The AI-driven platform offers features such as automated requests, reporting and insights, people records, security and compliance, integrations, survey builder, additional checks, and template builder. Key solutions offered by the company includes Recruitment Process Outsourcing (RPO), staffing and recruitment firms, talent acquisition, and people and culture (Xref, 2013).

Culture Amp

About the Company: Culture Amp, headquartered in Australia, has operational facilities in nearly 4 locations. The company focuses on enhancing and benchmarking against the best-in-class organizations. Culture Amp founded in 2009, emphasizes on getting employee performance, engagement, and development tools and perceptions to build a category-defining culture.

The company operates with nearly 25 million employees and is now being used by nearly 4,000 organizations (Shu, 2021). The clients range in size from approximately 20 to 30 people to more than nearly 150,000 employees and comprises of BigCommerce, KIND, Unilever, Salesforce, PwC, and SoulCycle.

Solutions Offered: The company is the provider of an HR tech ecosystem that helps to easily collect, interpret, and accordingly take, action, on the feedback received. The AI-based platform offers seamless conduct of activities such as individual employee effectiveness, company-wide engagement, and onboarding surveys (Amp, 2009). The employee experience platform transforms the organization and helps build a competitive advantage in the dynamic business environment. The platform comprises of:

- *Employee Engagement:* Understanding the employees via onboarding, pulse survey, and power engagement tools.
- *Performance Management:* The high-performing teams with performance feedback, and reviews, are efficiently delivered in the work.

- *Employee Development:* Enlarge and retain the employees with personalized solutions for continual development.

ELMO Software Limited

About the Company: HROnboard founded in 2013, is headquartered in Melbourne. The company is engaged in offering new HR solutions, with hassle-free experiences. In 2018, the HROnboard company was acquired by *ELMO Software Limited* (Marketing, 2018).

Solutions Offered: HROnboard makes effortless software that easily connects the new employees with the organization's culture and team, the transitioning employees, and the employees leaving the firm (HROnboard, 2013).

SINGAPORE

The HR leaders in Singapore are increasingly embracing AI technology, wherein, nearly 98 percent of the professionals are incorporating AI tools within the software or platforms, and approximately 80 percent of the leaders are forecasting a rise in AI over the projected period (Walters, 2023). The impact of the implementation of the technology largely depends upon the level of work and decision-making. The seamless technology leap provides an enriched and streamlined experience at the workplace to all employees. However, in Singapore, while many leaders focus on leveraging AI, few of them are concerned with its ethical response in the industry (Tan, 2023). Hence, AI governance not only depends upon compliance, but it is also pivotal to cultivate an ecosystem, that enriches the results with enhanced human collaboration in Singapore.

An example of a market player implementing automation and artificial intelligence in the human resource systems in Singapore is:

Ideatory Pte. Ltd

About the Company: Impress.ai, registered as Ideatory Pte.Ltd, was founded in 2017. Headquartered in Singapore, the company offers a self-service, no-code platform, emphasizing on accelerating and simplifying different parts of the recruitment flow. Impress.ai operates in nearly 5 locations with approximately 50 government and enterprise clients across the world (Pte, 2017).

Solutions Offered: The company delivers solutions based on intelligent automation and AI to cater to the challenges being faced in terms of the hiring processes and understanding the candidate experience in the system. Impress.ai provides an end-to-end recruitment platform to automate the hiring processes. This platform enables the recruiting teams to control the process and find the most suitable candidates for the profile seamlessly. The platform is driven by intelligent automation and simplifies the entire recruitment process from screening, sourcing, engaging, and gauging the candidates.

CHINA

The concepts of HR analytics and AI have the potential to transform the way businesses manage their employees in China. Harnessing the influence of data-driven insights and AI-based algorithms enables organizations to reveal significant insights into succession planning, training needs, employee engagement, and employee performance. The incorporation of AI tools in businesses across the regions of China offers enhanced decision-making, recruitment processes, and customized employee experiences, with minimal bias.

However, in China, it becomes essential for organizations to cater to ethical considerations, navigate cultural nuances, and adhere to local policies and regulations. Hence, effective exploitation of human resource analytics and artificial intelligence, concerning specific contexts in China, enables firms to optimize their strategies, create a positive environment, and boost business growth (HROne, n.d.).

An example of a market player incorporating artificial intelligence in human resource systems in China is:

HROne Co

About the Company: HROne, founded in 2005, is a fully licensed and private Foreign Enterprises Service Company (FESCo), headquartered in China. The company operates in the cities of Guangzhou, Shanghai, Beijing, and Shenzhen. The company comprises of HR operations specialists, labor dispute lawyers, and HR experts (HROne, HROne Co.,, 2022).

Solutions Offered: HROne offers an inclusive range of HR services in terms of recruitment, payroll, employer of record, HR outsourcing, and HR legal advisory.

LATEST TRENDS OF ARTIFICIAL INTELLIGENCE IN HUMAN RESOURCES

Artificial intelligence is poised to change the future of the human resources segment, in terms of talent, skills, roles, and workplace. With continual advancements in technology, the prospects of AI are promising over the forecast period. Optimizing investments and creating internal talent marketplaces in the existing systems, not only are expected to promote the hybrid model of work but also make the concept of AI the top priority among businesses in the industries (Zielinski, 2023).

Shortly, the concept of generative AI has the potential to streamline and supplement performance management and human resources (Hancock, 2023). Generative AI is a data-trained technology, that emphasizes on using prompts to generate content and is witnessing significant traction among organizations. The technology is anticipated to reshape the systems in ways such as:

- Pulling on the skills needed to be efficacious in the job, and
- Candidate personalization

The HR professionals strongly emphasize on the inclusion of AI solutions such as generative AI, based on a structured approach and framework.

Differentiating reality from myth: The first phase in evaluating Generative AI is to differentiate reality from any myths and subsequently eradicate any presumptions. The technology lead is expected to work with the compliance, legal, IT, and industry experts to comprehend the factual potential of the technology, and accordingly produce the reports.

Establish the benefits and potential of AI for human resources: The second phase includes the HR leaders generating the factual benefits of AI and, designing the potential use cases to the goals of an organization. It also emphasizes the ways AI is expected to allay any functional issues/challenges and cater to the goals by empowering individuals to perform activities seamlessly.

Evaluate and score alongside the success metrics: The third phase comprises evaluating and scoring the AI solutions contrary to the major success metrics, to decide the process of implementation. Every organization involves different metrics, however, a few of the major areas of discussion include vendor landscape, workforce readiness, governance, and ethics and risks.

Generative AI has revolutionized human resources into a planned function in terms of experience and productivity enhancements, dramatically increased self-service platforms, data-driven inclusive talent ecosystem, and customized delivery of services (Bedard, 2023).

Hence, with the changing AI-based HR landscape, it becomes essential for professionals to thoroughly understand the impact and capabilities of the technologies, and accordingly strategize their business models (Gartner, 2023).

CHALLENGES OF IMPLEMENTING ARTIFICIAL INTELLIGENCE IN HUMAN RESOURCES

Artificial intelligence technology cannot be considered a substitute for human involvement in businesses. Integration of AI in human resources is expected to include a few pitfalls, overcoming which has become a necessity (Pavlou, 2022). These include:

Rising risks to cybersecurity: Chatbots are anticipated to be the apt option for streamlining the transactional processes in HR systems. However, usage of these also poses an easy target for hackers. Hence, sharing sensitive company or personal information becomes open to theft or cyberattacks.

Involvement of humans: AI considerably plays a significant role in presenting and evaluating the decision-making processes, however, at times it does not play a viable role in the cases of non-technical, and important nuances, wherein, human intervention becomes of utmost importance.

Perpetuating bias in recruiting processes: The inclusion of AI technology to categorize the candidates is expected to unintentionally eliminate the well-qualified and deserving candidates, and generate biases. This can be attributed to the fact that, if implicit bias is included in the initial parameters, it drops in the results attained.

Machine-generated errors: At times, over-dependency on AI, poses to be incorrect. This can be due to errors in programming or misinterpretation of data during the analysis period.

CONCLUSION

The amalgamation of artificial intelligence with HRM practices is substantially altering the way companies are hiring, managing, engaging, and analyzing their workforce. Adoption of these technologies leads to the efficacious organization of work in international and national organizations, focusing on the prospects for the employees in terms of problem-solving, decision-making, and resource utilization (Budhwar, 2022).

The technology contributes immediate value to the recruitment processes and the HR systems by forecasting the talent needs and requirements within any specific department of a company. It offers an aptitude to influence the insight-driven estimates that are proficiently used to gather and evaluate data around the openings and team requisite from different departments, thereby, helping the teams to substantially line up their recruitment needs (Maskey, 2022).

The usage of artificial intelligence empowers decision-making based on behavioural patterns and historical data more accurately (Sanyaolu, December

2022). Incorporating AI in human resources is expected to address the plethora of challenges. Key players are thereby emphasizing on developing strategies and frameworks that integrate research on the applications of artificial intelligence and offer a cohesive base to explore the same.

The forthcoming AI-powered HR systems are anticipated to be successful only through the amalgamation of machines and humans, thereby, posing as a vital factor in weeding out any machine-led discrepancies and issues, while keeping the involvement of the "humans" in the HR systems intact.

REFERENCES

Amar, J. R. (2022, November 1). *Smart scheduling: How to solve workforce-planning Challenges with AI*. McKinsey.

Amos, Z. (2022, February 4). *Hive Life, Business and Techbusiness News*. Retrieved from How HR Technology Is Transforming APAC Businesses: https://hivelife.com/hr-technology/

AmpC. (2009). Retrieved from Culture Amp: https://www.cultureamp.com/

Avila, O. (2023, February). *The Future of AI on Employee Benefits*. Retrieved from KPMG: https://kpmg.com/ae/en/home/insights/2023/02/the-future-of-ai-on-employee-benefits.html

Bedard, J. L. (2023, August 24). *Boston Consulting Group*. Retrieved from How Generative AI Will Transform HR: https://www.bcg.com/publications/2023/transforming-human-resources-using-generative-ai

Bhardwaj, A. (2020, August 18). *Startup Talky*. Retrieved from Big Mistakes Companies Make While Training Their Employees: https://startuptalky.com/7-big-mistakes-while-training-employees/?_gl=1*1160n0z*_ga*WjdpLTMyb00yU2dBdXlfUnJGZDBIbFFYNUE4TVZsb2ZSNVI3dlBhaWNCT1NOQy1vbTBxbHpIOW4wVExveG92RA

Budhwar, P. M., Malik, A., De Silva, M. T. T., & Thevisuthan, P. (2022). Artificial Intelligence – Challenges and Opportunities for International HRM: A Review And Research Agenda. *International Journal of Human Resource Management, 33*(6), 1065–1097. doi:10.1080/09585192.2022.2035161

Burgess, L. (2023, July 31). *Capterra Inc. Retrieved from Are SMEs Leveraging AI in HR To Help With Decision-Making Processes?* https://www.capterra.com.au/blog/4107/study-on-the-future-of-ai-in-hr-australia#:~:text=of%20this%20article.-,One%20in%20five%20Australian%20SMEs%20use%20AI%20in%20HR,and%20personalising%20employee%20training%20programs

BusinessLine. (2018, October 8). *The Hindu Businessline: Economy. HR Consulting Firm Mercer Buys Indian Start-up Mettl for ₹250 crore*. Retrieved from HR Consulting Firm Mercer Buys Indian Start-up Mettl for ₹250 crore: https://www.thehindubusinessline.com/companies/hr-consulting-firm-mercer-buys-indian-start-up-mettl-for-250-crore/article25156969.ece

Circle, V. (2023, August 22). *Vantage Circle: human resource management*. Retrieved from Role of AI in HR: A Complete Guide: https://blog.vantagecircle.com/ai-in-hr/

Dutta, B. (2022, September 9). *Artificial Intelligence*. Retrieved from Top 8 AI-powered tools for Human Resources: https://www.analyticssteps.com/blogs/top-8-ai-powered-tools-human-resources

EDGE. (2012). *EDGE*. Retrieved from https://getedge.ai/

Gartner. (2023). *Gartner*. Retrieved from AI in HR: A Guide to Implementing AI in Your HR Organization: https://www.gartner.com/en/human-resources/topics/artificial-intelligence-in-hr

Gautam, A. (2019, June 28). *SHRM*. Retrieved from Artificial Intelligence and Employee Engagement: Connecting the dots: https://blog.shrm.org/sasia/blog/artificial-intelligence-and-employee-engagement-connecting-the-dots

Ghosh, S. (2023). *PwC*. Retrieved from AI: Possibilities of Transforming the Workplace: https://www.pwc.in/consulting/transformation-consulting/artificial-intelligence.html

Goel, S. (2021, April 25). *ETHR World*. Retrieved from How AI Can Be A Game Changer in HR Functions: https://hr.economictimes.indiatimes.com/news/trends/ai-in-hr/how-ai-can-be-a-game-changer-in-hr-functions/82245378

Hancock, B. S. (2023, July 10). *McKinsey*. Retrieved from How Generative AI Could Support—Not Replace—Human Resources: https://www.mckinsey.com/capabilities/people-and-organizational-performance/our-insights/the-organization-blog/how-generative-ai-could-support-not-replace-human-resources

Harshman, R. (2021, December 16). *Automation. Demand for Automation is Rising: Asia Pacific Needs to Prepare for a Hybrid Human-Digital Workforce*. Retrieved from Demand for Automation is Rising: Asia Pacific Needs to Prepare for a Hybrid Human-Digital Workforce.

HROnboard. (2013). Retrieved from HROnboard: https://hronboard.me/about/

HROne. (2022). Retrieved from HROne Co.: https://www.hrone.com/about-us/

HROne. (n.d.). HROne Co. Retrieved from 2005: https://www.hrone.com/blog/ai-and-hr-analytics-in-china/

Hupfer, S. (2020, March 3). Deloitte Insights. *Talent and Workforce Effects in the Age of AI*, p. 2.

Instahyre. (2014). *Instahyre*. Retrieved from https://www.instahyre.com/

Mackenzie, K. (2023). *How is AI used in human resources? 7 ways it helps HR*. Retrieved from Workable Technology Limited: https://resources.workable.com/tutorial/artificial-intelligence-in-human-resources

MarketingH. (2018). Retrieved from HROnboard: https://hronboard.me/blog/hronboard-acquired-by-elmo-software/

Maskey, S. (2022, March 23). *Forbes Technology Council*. Retrieved from How AI Is Primed To Disrupt HR And Recruiting: https://www.forbes.com/sites/forbestechcouncil/2022/03/23/how-ai-is-primed-to-disrupt-hr-and-recruiting/?sh=11c1b5b41078

Mehrotra, S. a. (2022). Recruitment Through AI in Selected Indian Companies. Metamorphosis. *Journal of Management Research*, *21*(1), 31–39.

Mercer, L. L. C. (2009). *Mercer LLC*. Retrieved from https://mettl.com/en/about/

Nuttall, K. S. (2023). *Deloitte*. Retrieved from Generation AI: Ready or Not, Here We Come!: https://www.deloitte.com/au/en/services/consulting/analysis/generation-ai-ready-or-not.html?id=au:2ps:3gl:4con-daegenerationairereport2023-2023:6con:20230905:paid_search_2&utm_source=google&utm_medium=cpc&utm_campaign=con-daegenerationairereport2023-2023&ut

Occean, P. S. (2017, February 27). *Digital HR: Platforms, people, and work*. Retrieved from 2017 Global Human Capital Trends: https://www.deloitte.com/global/en/our-thinking/insights/topics/talent/human-capital-trends/digital-transformation-in-hr.html

Pavlou, C. (2022, May). *efront*. Retrieved from AI in HR: The Good, The Bad, And The Ugly: https://www.efrontlearning.com/blog/2022/05/ai-in-hr.html

Pte, I. (2017). *Ideatory Pte*. Retrieved from https://impress.ai/about-us/

Sanyaolu, E. a. (2022). *Role of Artificial Intelligence in Human Resource Management: Overview of its Benefits and Challenges*. Academic Press.

Shu, C. (2021, July 29). *TechCrunch*. Retrieved from Employee Engagement Platform Culture Amp Raises $100M at a $1.5B Valuation: https://techcrunch.com/2021/07/29/employee-engagement-platform-culture-amp-raises-100m-at-a-1-5b-valuation/

Tan, J. (2023, August 18). *HRM Asia*. Retrieved from AI's Dual Impact on Singapore's HR Landscape: https://hrmasia.com/ais-dual-impact-on-singapores-hr-landscape/

Walters, J. (2023, September 6). *HR technology*. Retrieved from Singapore's HR Leaders Embracing AI: Survey: https://www.hcamag.com/asia/specialisation/hr-technology/singapores-hr-leaders-embracing-ai-survey/458641

Xref. (2013). Retrieved from Xref: https://www.xref.com/company/about-us

Zavvy. (2023, June 9). *AI in HR Examples: 9 Companies Successfully Using AI Innovation in Key People Processes*. Retrieved from Zavvy: https://www.zavvy.io/blog/ai-in-hr-examples

Zielinski, D. (2023, January 10). *SHRM*. Retrieved from 2023 HR Technology Trends: Talent Marketplaces, Expanding AI and Optimizing Existing Systems: https://www.shrm.org/resourcesandtools/hr-topics/technology/pages/2023-hr-technology-trends.aspx

Chapter 4
Critical Role of HR Professionals in the Adoption and Integration of AI in HRM

Atia Aftab
University of Management and Technology, Lahore, Pakistan

Komal Khalid
https://orcid.org/0000-0001-7220-6962
King Abdulaziz University, Jeddah, Saudi Arabia

ABSTRACT

In this chapter, HR professionals are spotlighted as pivotal players in integrating artificial intelligence (AI) into human resource management (HRM). Drawing inspiration from literary figures, they champion a culture of continuous learning and adaptation, ensuring that AI adoption complements rather than replaces human capabilities. Ethical leadership, inclusivity, and collaboration underpin their strategies, while a profound emphasis is placed on preserving the essence of human connection. They navigate the complexities of AI-driven decision-making, emphasizing data-driven insights and agile innovation. By fostering a symbiotic relationship between humans and AI, HR professionals elevate HRM, harmonizing technology with the organization's strategic vision. This chapter underscores HR's transformative role in marrying AI's potential with human-centric values.

DOI: 10.4018/979-8-3693-0039-8.ch004

BACKGROUND

In the intricate tapestry of today's business arena, the confluence of AI with HRM stands out as a defining juncture, marking a significant transformation in organizational paradigms. The meteoric rise of AI technologies signals not only an era of unprecedented innovation (Sun, 2021) but also an era of immense responsibility for HR practitioners. Especially within the vast and diverse ecosystem of Asian businesses, the merger of AI and HRM is a dance of harmonization, demanding a delicate balance between efficiency, ethics, and human intuition. Asian corporate landscapes, rich in culture and tradition, are currently at the cusp of a paradigmatic shift. The fusion of AI's computational might with HR's human-centric focus promises to reshape the contours of talent management, organizational strategy, and workplace dynamics. Through the pages of this chapter, we embark on a meticulous journey, dissecting the intricate nuances of this fusion and highlighting the pivotal role of HR professionals in championing the seamless integration of AI into their conventional responsibilities.

At the very heart of our mission, we believe that education can enhance an individual's self-efficacy (Farrukh et al., 2021). Our expedition is guided by a profound desire to dissect and understand the myriad ways through which AI is reshaping HRM in the Asian context (Trong Tuan, 2013). By exploring technological innovation, evolving workforce expectations, and organizational transformations, our narrative aim is to underscore the pioneering role of HR professionals in this digital renaissance. Informed by rigorous academic research and punctuated with real-world insights (Chai et al., 2021), we endeavor to provide a holistic view of the promise and challenges of AI-enhanced HR practices.

With the precision of masterful storytellers, we navigate this intersection where AI's algorithmic logic meets HRM's human touch. Inspired by luminaries like Steve Browne, Ben Eubanks, and Jim Stroud, our exploration transcends mere facts, weaving together a narrative that is as thought-provoking as it is informative, beckoning readers to reflect upon the future of work and the transformative power of AI within HRM.

THE EVOLUTION OF HRM IN THE AGE OF AI

In the grand tableau of organizational development, we witness the twilight of traditional HRM. As the amber hues of this age-old practice begin to fade, a brilliant horizon, illuminated by the shimmering lights of technology and AI, emerges. The transition of HR professionals from the confines of archaic administrative roles to the dynamic, agile, and strategic purveyors of human potential is a testament to AI's transformative touch (Yalenios & d'Armagnac, 2023). This journey, punctuated by AI's disruptive innovation (Lee et al., 2019), has catalyzed HR's evolution, propelling them from backroom operational roles to the strategic epicenter of organizations.

Delving into the annals of HRM, we find its embryonic stages firmly embedded in the industrial era (Dunn, 1990). These were times when HR's primary mandate revolved around the tangible and tactile: hiring, training, compensating, and often, firefighting. They crafted systems, ensured smooth administrative processes, managed the ebb and flow of grievances, and meticulously ensured that the company remained compliant with the legal labyrinth of labor laws. As we navigate through this historical lens, several studies have highlighted the importance of leadership (Farrukh et al., 2023), indicating how pivotal leaders were in shaping these foundational HR functions. Though indispensable, the HR professionals of yore were often seen as peripheral players in the grand organizational orchestra with limited influence.

However, with the ushering in of the digital age, the narrative began to shift dramatically. AI's entrance into the corporate arena was not just an addition but a revolution, infusing HRM with tools and insights previously unimagined. No longer was HR confined to its siloed existence. Powered by AI's data analytics, predictive modeling, and cognitive computing, HRM transformed. The once administrative-centric department became a strategic ally, wielding influence and insight. Integrating AI tools and platforms allowed HR professionals to anticipate talent needs (Chowdhury et al., 2023), forecast workforce trends, enhance employee engagement, and play a pivotal role in shaping the organization's direction and future. This rejuvenation, instigated by AI, signified more than just technological integration. It denoted the reimagining and repositioning of HRM, where human empathy synergized with artificial intellect, and HR professionals emerged not just as managers but as visionaries, leading the charge in sculpting the future contours of organizational excellence.

BENEFITS OF THIS SYMBIOTIC ALLIANCE BETWEEN AI AND HRM

The harmonious confluence of AI and HRM has ushered in many transformative benefits for organizations (Mer & Virdi, 2023). By leveraging AI's unyielding computational capabilities, HR functions have become markedly swifter and more precise, allowing for a streamlined operational flow. In talent acquisition, predictive analytics hones recruitment, enabling AI to sift through expansive data volumes and pinpoint exemplary candidates, bypassing inherent human prejudices and diversifying the talent reservoir (Tiwari et al., 2023). With AI shouldering a considerable chunk of traditional HR tasks—like resume vetting, interview orchestration, and benefits administration—the human side of HR can ascend to loftier strategic vistas, emphasizing talent cultivation, fostering robust employee engagement, and architecting a vibrant organizational ethos.

Silent Conductor

Within the intricate tapestry of performance management, AI emerges not just as a tool (Cellier, 2001) but as a silent yet formidable conductor, orchestrating a symphony of unbiased appraisals and fostering a culture of meritocracy. This conductor, though silent, is profoundly eloquent in its operations. Whereas traditional performance evaluations often teetered on the edge of human biases, integrating AI-driven algorithms ensures a paradigm shift towards more objective, transparent, and comprehensive assessments. These algorithms meticulously parse through vast swathes of data, collating patterns and generating insights that were previously imperceptible to the human eye. Such in-depth analyses offer a magnified view of an employee's strengths, areas of improvement, and potential growth avenues. By doing so, AI ensures that the evaluations do not merely become an annual ritual but evolve into a constructive feedback mechanism that resonates with employees, motivating them to pursue excellence.

Furthermore, this technological maestro has an uncanny ability to predict future performance trajectories, enabling organizations to tailor their talent development strategies with unprecedented precision. This prescience, rooted in AI's prowess, empowers organizations to proactively address skill gaps, identify high-potential talent, and craft bespoke career paths that align with organizational goals and individual aspirations. The age-old challenge of subjectivity, which once clouded the waters of performance management, is gradually dissipating, replaced by the clear, data-driven insights offered by AI. As this silent conductor continues to wave its baton, it promises a future where performance management becomes an enlightening journey of growth, understanding, and genuine appreciation rather than a mere administrative chore.

Empathetic Companions

Today, business rivalry is highly intense, and the business milieu is highly uncertain (Rafiq et al., 2023). This elevates the significance of ensuring that every facet of an organization, especially employee engagement, is optimized for adaptability and responsiveness. Empathetic AI-driven companions have emerged as beacons in the expansive domain of employee engagement, a realm often shrouded in complexities and subtleties (Sonik & Colarossi, 2020). Traditionally, gauging the pulse of employee sentiments and feelings was a herculean task, relying on intermittent feedback sessions, annual surveys, or nuanced interpersonal interactions. However, the dawn of AI, in these trying times, has revolutionized this dynamic. Chatbots, with their incessant availability, have metamorphosed into reliable confidantes for employees. Unlike their human counterparts, these digital entities are bereft of biases, always available, and proficiently programmed to respond immediately to employee queries, concerns, and feelings. Through conversational AI, employees, especially those in vast or remote teams, find an avenue to voice their thoughts, seek assistance, and even acquire guidance on intricate work-related challenges.

Moving beyond the realm of chatbots, the advent of sentiment analysis tools has added another layer of sophistication to understanding the workforce's emotional landscape. Just as solid waste generation has risen due to rapid population growth and urbanization, requiring innovative solutions (Rafiq et al., 2023), the complexities of employee emotions in today's diversified workplaces have similarly demanded advanced tools. These AI-powered sentiment analysis instruments, by meticulously sifting through vast amounts of textual data, can decode the underlying embedded emotions. Whether it is the content of an email, feedback on internal forums, or interactions on collaboration platforms, these tools provide a granular understanding of employees' prevailing mood and outlook. This heightened sensitivity to employee sentiments ensures that organizations can preemptively address potential issues, be it feelings of detachment, burnout, or discontent. The timely interventions facilitated by these AI insights help cultivate a more nurturing and responsive work environment (Daugherty & Wilson, 2018). Thus, through chatbots and sentiment analysis, AI serves not just as an operational aid but as a compassionate companion (LaGrandeur, 2015), fostering deeper connections, enhancing support structures, and amplifying a sense of belonging and well-being among the workforce.

Challenges for Transformation

The journey towards integrating AI within HRM, although shimmering with promise, is interspersed with inherent challenges that necessitate thoughtful deliberation. Predominantly, the specter of technological unemployment looms large (Chomanski, 2019). The cacophony of voices that predict AI rendering human roles obsolete engenders apprehension and skepticism. Furthermore, maintaining high-caliber employees has become a difficult issue for today's businesses (Rafiq et al., 2022), making the role of HR even more crucial. For many HR professionals, this generates an existential quandary: How do they strike a judicious equilibrium between leveraging AI's computational might and preserving the irreplaceable nuances of the human touch? The answer lies in the understanding that AI is not a replacement (Chomanski, 2019) but rather a powerful tool that augments human capabilities. HR's role, historically centered around human capital, requires them to ensure that technology acts as a lever, enhancing human potential rather than sidelining it (Chomanski, 2019).

Moreover, the digital age ushers in intricate dilemmas related to data privacy. As AI systems voraciously devour data to generate insights, the ethical dimensions of data handling come to the fore. Organizational researchers focused on HRM often grapple with securing a competitive advantage (Aman et al., 2023), emphasizing the necessity to treat every bite of information with reverence. Whether about an employee's professional trajectory or personal preferences, each piece of data is sacrosanct, meriting utmost discretion. In this digital realm, HR professionals, in their evolved avatar, must don the mantle of data custodians, ensuring rigorous compliance with data protection regulations. This heightened emphasis on privacy and security compels them to be vigilant, ushering in an era where technological proficiency is inextricably linked with ethical stewardship.

However, the technological marvel that AI represents is not infallible (Charlesworth, 2014). Instances where even the most advanced algorithms go awry are not uncommon. Embedded biases, if unchecked, can inadvertently propagate disparities, undermining the principles of equity and inclusivity. As concerns over sustainability are well recognized and encouraged by UNDP (Aman et al., 2022), the thrust on creating ethical AI frameworks that prioritize inclusivity and equity becomes even more paramount. Herein lies another pivotal role for HR professionals: to act as sentinels, ceaselessly monitoring, refining, and guiding AI systems. This ensures that the tools remain aligned with organizational values, fostering a culture of fairness. As the contours of HRM evolve in the digital age, the narrative is increasingly shaped by HR professionals who, equipped with AI's arsenal, weave tales of organizational triumphs, ensuring that the fusion of technology and human insight culminates in an era of unparalleled success and prosperity.

The Role of HR Professionals in AI Adoption

In today's rapidly changing and hectic entrepreneurial environment (Ren et al., 2019), coupled with a fiercely competitive business landscape due to increased market rivalry and changeable market dynamics, a company's success is typically determined by the quality of its goods and services. This tenet holds especially true in the dynamic sphere of HRM, where the potent gales of AI are redefining the very fabric of traditional practices. Beyond mere administrative functions, today's HR landscape requires an agile blend of human intuition and technological prowess (Gibbons, 2015). Central to this evolution are the HR professionals, visionaries equipped with the empathy of seasoned human resource veterans, and the technological literacy of the modern age. Their dual responsibility is paramount: to harness AI's prodigious capabilities while ensuring its seamless integration into the human-centric core of HR. As architects of this new age, their expertise becomes the beacon that illuminates the pathway to harmoniously blending AI-driven efficiencies with the quintessential human touch that defines HRM.

Key Responsibilities of HR Professionals in Driving the Adoption of AI In HRM

In an era punctuated by rapid technological evolution and heightened awareness of environmental issues (Jin et al., 2023)—where consumers worldwide pay greater attention—HR professionals emerge not merely as guardians of traditional human resource values but as navigators charting the course into a brave new world. The clarion call of the age beckons them to embrace AI, not with trepidation as a harbinger of disruption, but with optimism, seeing it as an unprecedented tool to catalyze organizational growth. Their vision extends beyond surface-level applications, probing deeper to ascertain the myriad facets of the organization where AI can act as a lever, optimizing processes, enhancing productivity, and fundamentally transforming how businesses operate.

However, vision without execution remains an ephemeral dream. This is where the multifaceted role of HR professionals becomes even more pronounced. In the same vein that access to finance refers to the access and use of financial products (Bhutta et al., 2021; Mushtaq et al., 2023), implementing AI in HRM signifies the practical application and utilization of technology in human-centric processes. As strategic architects, HR professionals are tasked with drawing up blueprints for AI's seamless integration, ensuring every cog and wheel of the organization moves in harmonious synchronization with this digital dynamo. This involves analyzing extant HR processes, identifying bottlenecks, and conceptualizing (Rupp et al., 2017) AI-driven solutions that amplify efficiencies while preserving the human touch. Simultaneously, as cultural stewards, they must inculcate a mindset of continual learning within the workforce, facilitating smooth transitions and championing innovations that not only propel the organization forward but also amplify the holistic experience of each employee. It is a journey of melding the technological with the human, and in this saga, HR professionals stand as the linchpins holding the narrative together.

Involvement In Identifying Relevant AI Solutions and Technologies for HR Functions

In today's complex organizational milieu, HR professionals have transcended their traditional confines, evolving into strategic technologists in the pursuit of elevating HR functions (Kim et al., 2021). Their mission is no longer confined to merely managing human assets but extends to identifying and implementing the most apt AI-driven solutions tailored to specific organizational needs. The intricacies of each HR function, from recruitment to retention, demand a keen understanding of the operational nuances. However, more than this, a true cognizance of the myriad opportunities AI brings to the fore is required. By immersing themselves in the confluence of human resource needs and technological possibilities, HR professionals demonstrate an unparalleled aptitude for sifting through the vast expanse of AI technologies available in the market. Their objective? To pinpoint those transformative solutions that can be seamlessly interwoven into the HR tapestry, ensuring the optimization of processes and the amplification of human potential.

The quest, however, is not embarked upon in isolation. A symbiotic relationship forms at this juncture, where HR professionals collaborate intensely with AI specialists, forging a confluence of human expertise and artificial intelligence (Kim et al., 2021). This synergy, a fusion of the wisdom inherent in HR practices and the cutting-edge advancements of AI, cultivates an environment of innovation. It is in this collaborative crucible that breakthrough solutions emerge - be it through AI-powered talent pipelines that redefine recruitment, analytics models that forecast workforce trends, or tools that capture the pulse of employee sentiments in real-time. The HR professional's proactive involvement in this venture ensures not just the selection of the right tools but also their alignment with the core values and overarching goals of the organization (Hays, 2019). In essence, they act as the bridge between the promise of AI and its pragmatic application in the HR domain, anchoring the future of work in a foundation of technological astuteness and human-centricity.

Highlighting The Importance of HR Professionals in Ensuring Ethical and Responsible AI Implementation in HRM Practices

In the expansive theater of modern HRM, AI presents transformative capabilities, but its immense power necessitates careful, ethical orchestration. HR professionals, known traditionally as the stewards of human potential, now find themselves shouldering an expanded responsibility (Ulrich et al., 2017). They are not just adopters of technological marvels but are the moral compasses guiding its implementation. The potency of AI's influence on HRM, from recruitment algorithms to predictive analytics for employee development, hinges on its responsible and unbiased utilization. HR professionals, drawing from a reservoir of ethical knowledge and inspired by luminaries in the domain, are tasked with formulating rigorous guidelines. These guidelines are designed not only to preempt the inadvertent biases AI might perpetuate but also to ensure that every AI-infused decision mirrors the organization's core principles of fairness, equity, and inclusivity.

Beyond the abstract realm of ethics, HR professionals delve into the tangible world of data. In an age where data is the new currency, its protection becomes paramount (Peterson et al., 2023). The convergence of HRM and AI invariably results in vast repositories of employee data being processed and analyzed. HR professionals, recognizing the sanctity of this information, become the vanguards of data privacy and security. With meticulous precision, they navigate the intricate labyrinth of data regulations, establishing robust protocols that shield sensitive employee data from potential breaches and unauthorized access. Their commitment to this cause reinforces the trust employees place in the organization, ensuring that the transformative journey of AI in HRM is anchored in a foundation of unwavering security and integrity.

When we envisage the role of HR professionals in this AI-augmented HRM epoch, the imagery that emerges is that of a maestro conducting a grand symphony (Peterson et al., 2023). Each movement, each note played, is a testament to their refined sensibilities - an intricate blend of technological acumen, ethical stewardship, and a deep-seated commitment to human values. Drawing insights from distinguished HR thinkers like Steve Browne, Ben Eubanks, and Jim Stroud, these professionals do not merely implement AI; they shape its narrative, weaving it seamlessly into the organization's broader tapestry. Through their discerning guidance, AI's adoption becomes a harmonious ballet of technology, ethics, and human-centric innovation, setting the stage for an era of unparalleled organizational success and holistic employee well-being.

Embracing a Culture of Learning and Adaptation

The intricate dance of AI adoption within an organization extends far beyond the mere integration of technology; it is inextricably linked with the metamorphosis of its people and their mindsets. For HR professionals standing at the crossroads of this transformation, the challenges are manifold. However, they draw strength from the foundational belief that the introduction of AI is not a terminal destination but a perpetual voyage of discovery (Ivanova, 2019). Channeling this understanding, they ardently champion a renewed culture within organizations - a culture deeply rooted in the tenets of learning and adaptation. This is not a transient initiative but a sustained effort, ensuring that every member of the organization sees AI not as a threat to their existence but as a catalyst, propelling them towards new horizons of personal and professional growth.

In their quest to foster this new-age organizational ethos, HR professionals delve deep into the reservoir of human knowledge – literature (Ivanova, 2019). The timeless wisdom encapsulated within the pages of renowned works serves as their guiding star. These literary treasures, penned by visionaries from various epochs, reverberate with themes of adaptability, resilience, and the indomitable spirit of humanity in the face of change. Leveraging these insights, HR professionals craft narratives that resonate deeply with employees, urging them to perceive the AI-driven transformation not as a storm to weather but as an adventure to undertake. They harness the power of stories, metaphors, and allegories, echoing the sentiments of iconic authors, to underscore the irrefutable value of being malleable in thought and resilient in action.

Moreover, the role of HR professionals is more than just inspiring the workforce. They are the navigators, guiding the ship through the tumultuous seas of technological disruption (Ivanova, 2019). To equip the crew - the employees - for this voyage, they foster an environment that celebrates curiosity, rewards the quest for knowledge, and prioritizes skill development. By establishing continuous learning modules, facilitating workshops, and providing access to resources that demystify AI, they ensure that the workforce is not merely reactive to change but actively anticipates and adapts to it. In doing so, they sculpt a legion of professionals, each armed with knowledge, adaptability, and an unquenchable thirst for growth, ensuring the organization not only survives the waves of change but rides them with unmatched prowess and dexterity.

Fostering Human-Machine Synergy

The journey of AI integration into HRM, helmed by visionary HR professionals, is paved with profound understanding and unwavering commitment. They steadfastly negate misconceptions that depict AI as a looming threat, waiting to render human roles redundant. Inspired by timeless literary works (Topol, 2019), HR leaders paint a vivid tapestry where AI is not an antagonist but a co-star in the grand narrative of organizational success. In this reimagined paradigm, humans are not diminished but are exalted, with AI serving as a tool that magnifies human attributes. The unique emotional intelligence, empathy, and intuition inherent in humans are juxtaposed with AI's precision, efficiency, and relentless computational power. Here, the message is clear: the union of human intuition with AI's capabilities births an unmatched force capable of reshaping industries and sculpting new horizons.

Standing at this transformative juncture, HR professionals do not just facilitate this union; they are its chief architects. Their role involves meticulously crafting an environment where the human workforce does not perceive AI as an external entity but as an integral part of their professional ensemble (Johnson & Verdicchio, 2017). By evoking powerful themes from celebrated literature that emphasize unity, collaboration, and mutual growth, they establish AI as a reliable comrade in every employee's journey. They envision a workspace where AI unburdens individuals from repetitive, manual tasks, granting them the liberty to pursue more creative and strategic endeavors. This not only enhances job satisfaction but catalyzes an organizational culture pulsating with innovation, creativity, and boundless possibilities. As the story unfolds, with HR professionals as its seasoned narrators, the future emerges as a vibrant tapestry of human-machine synergy, promising unparalleled growth and collective fulfillment.

Preserving the Essence of Human Connection

In the realm of HRM, with AI becoming an ever-pervasive force, the emphasis placed by HR professionals on preserving genuine human connections becomes paramount. Guided by insights from literature, they believe that, while technology can vastly amplify capabilities, it is the intangible essence of empathy, compassion, and genuine interactions that truly anchors an organization. By championing this belief, these visionaries ensure that AI in HRM acts as an enhancer of human potential and not as a barrier (Tariq et al., 2021). The literary wisdom they draw upon, reminiscent of works by luminaries like Steve Browne, Ben Eubanks, and Jim Stroud, reiterates that the crux of human resources will always lie in the 'human' rather than the 'resources'.

Thus, with a blend of technology and literary insights, these HR professionals delicately balance AI's efficiency with the invaluable warmth of human connection. Their strategies meticulously weave AI into the HRM fabric, ensuring it accentuates individuality, inclusivity, and personal touch. The outcome of this delicate orchestration envisions an AI-augmented HRM where employees feel valued, understood, and deeply connected. This vision heralds a future for Asian organizations where the intricate dance of technology and humanity crafts a narrative of innovation, understanding, and unparalleled success.

Harmonizing HRM With Organizational Strategy

The harmonization of HRM with organizational strategy is an art form where HR professionals become the painters of a grand canvas, drawing inspiration from both the realm of literature and the pragmatic world of business. By channeling their inner literary acumen, these visionaries approach HRM as a tale to be told. Every decision, every strategy, and every AI integration is a chapter that should align with the overarching plot: the organization's mission, vision, and core values. Their unique vantage point, enriched by a blend of storytelling prowess and strategic insight, enables them to ensure that the AI-driven evolution of HRM becomes an integral part of the business storyline, rather than an isolated subplot.

Indeed, just as today, marketing is considered an important field (Dastane & Haba, 2023; Fernandez et al., 2023; Zaki et al., 2023) that intricately shape the perception and value of brands, HR professionals, akin to the literary greats, craft worlds and weave characters into their intricate HRM designs. They meticulously design an HRM framework that seamlessly integrates with the organizational narrative. Delving deeply into understanding the company's ethos, they recognize that each business has unique challenges and aspirations. Armed with this knowledge, they tailor AI solutions that not only address immediate HR needs but also serve broader strategic objectives. In doing so, they transform HRM from a mere support function to a core strategic partner, firmly underscoring its pivotal role in shaping the company's future trajectory.

Emulating the foresight demonstrated by many revered authors, HR professionals look beyond the ephemeral and envision a future where HRM and organizational strategy move in lockstep (Tariq et al., 2021). This vision encompasses an ecosystem where AI tools and solutions amplify the human elements of HRM, ensuring adaptability, growth, and alignment with ever-evolving business goals. By anchoring their strategies in both the wisdom of literary classics and the practicalities of modern business dynamics, they set the stage for an HRM narrative that is both timeless and forward-looking, a testament to their role as the architects of an organization's evolving story.

Advocates of Ethical AI Leadership

In today's complex landscape, where AI's influence permeates various facets of the business world, HR professionals rise as the torchbearers of ethical AI leadership (Ronquillo et al., 2021). Inspired by the moral compass displayed in classical literature, these custodians of organizational culture internalize a deep sense of responsibility. They understand that the deployment of AI within HRM is not just a functional transformation but carries with it profound ethical implications. Thus, akin to the steadfast characters in time-honored tales who uphold principles against all odds, HR professionals champion a cause: ensuring that AI's integration aligns with the noblest of ethical standards. This commitment entails more than just token gestures; it's a comprehensive undertaking to embed integrity, fairness, and responsibility into the very DNA of AI-driven HR processes.

Guided by this literary-inspired ethos, HR professionals delve into the intricacies of AI ethics. Their journey navigates the intricate terrains of data privacy, ensuring that employees' personal and sensitive information remains shielded from unwarranted access or breaches. Moreover, with a discerning eye, they critically evaluate AI systems for algorithmic fairness, ensuring that inadvertent biases or skewed algorithms do not perpetuate discrimination or inequality. Their pursuit continues; venturing into AI governance, they lay down robust frameworks and guidelines. By doing so, they not only prevent potential missteps but also create an environment where AI flourishes responsibly, reinforcing the trust between the organization, its employees, and the broader society. Drawing parallels with the sagacious narratives of celebrated authors, HR professionals are the vigilant guardians, ensuring that the tale of AI in HRM remains one of honor, responsibility, and unwavering ethical commitment.

AI integration in HRM is about people, processes, and change management, not just technology. HR professionals are at the center of these elements, ensuring AI's promise is realized without jeopardizing ethical standards or the human touch. HR professionals must navigate the ethical waters of AI integration, particularly in areas such as automated recruitment, where bias can be introduced inadvertently. They should be capable of performing algorithmic audits and ensuring fairness. The objective is not to substitute humans but rather to augment their capabilities. HR professionals must ensure that AI systems are developed and deployed to supplement, rather than supplant, human workers (Daugherty & Wilson, 2018). With the progression of AI technologies, HR professionals must stay updated on the most recent advancements. This is crucial to ensure they and their organization's workforce possess the essential skills and knowledge required (Schwartz et al., 2020).

Empowering the Workforce Through AI Knowledge

The swift incorporation of artificial intelligence (AI) technologies across different sectors is fundamentally altering the composition of the labor force. The World Economic Forum report forecasts that by 2025, automation and rapid technological advancements will eliminate 85 million jobs worldwide. Nevertheless, the rise of 97 million novel positions that integrate human, digital, and machine capabilities (World Economic Forum, 2020) also brings forth advantageous prospects. To guarantee that workforce is prepared for the future opportunities, it is imperative to provide the workforce with AI expertise.

As the protagonists of AI adoption, HR professionals strive to equip their workforce with the knowledge and proficiency to navigate this transformative landscape (Ronquillo et al., 2021). Embracing the didactic prowess of renowned authors, they don the role of educators, offering workshops, training sessions, and resources to familiarize employees with AI technologies and their applications (Kaushal & Ghalawat, 2023).

In this educational odyssey, HR professionals unlock the true potential of AI adoption by nurturing a tech-savvy workforce. Their commitment to fostering a culture of learning not only empowers employees to embrace AI with confidence but fosters a community of innovation where curiosity and experimentation thrive. As the chapters of AI adoption unfold within Asian organizations, HR professionals assume the role of eloquent narrators, deftly crafting a story of technological revolution, ethical leadership, and human-centricity. Drawing inspiration from literary giants like

Steve Browne, Ben Eubanks, and Jim Stroud, their prose is infused with a passion for organizational excellence and an unwavering commitment to human flourishing.

Utilizing AI knowledge encompasses more than mere technical competencies. It involves comprehending the fundamental principles, capabilities, ethical implications, and constraints of AI. To enable a workforce to make informed decisions and to ensure that AI-driven solutions are not only ethical and transparent but also effective, a comprehensive knowledge base is required (Lee et al., 2020). Offering consistent AI training and workshops can greatly enhance the skills and abilities of the workforce. Organizations that provide AI-based training to their employees are expected to increase productivity by 20%. These training sessions serve the purpose of clarifying the concept of AI and can be customized to suit job positions, guaranteeing relevance, and optimizing advantages. Partnerships between businesses and educational institutions can advance this objective. Universities and industry leaders can collaboratively develop specialized artificial intelligence courses that address specific challenges in real-world industries (Davenport & Ronanki, 2018).

In the ever-evolving saga of AI and HRM, HR professionals, true to their literary spirit, craft a narrative of transformation that transcends boundaries and elevates the human experience. Like a timeless masterpiece, their role in AI adoption resonates as a symphony of wisdom, ethics, and progress, leaving an indelible mark on the pages of history.

Evolving as Agile Innovators

In this ever-changing landscape of AI integration, HR professionals embrace the essence of literary inspiration as they metamorphose into agile innovators (Kaur et al., 2021). Guided by the wisdom of authors who extol the virtues of adaptability and ingenuity, they remain open to novel possibilities and unconventional ideas.

With the agility of wordsmiths, they navigate the complexities of AI adoption, experimenting with diverse approaches to enhance HRM practices continually. In this dynamic environment, they exhibit the flexibility to recalibrate strategies (Baldegger et al., 2020), pivot when necessary, and seize opportunities for innovation. Their quest for continuous improvement becomes an evergreen theme as they strive to unravel new frontiers of AI-driven HRM that propel organizations to unprecedented heights.

CONCLUSION

As we stand on the cusp of an AI-driven future, the imperative of ethical AI leadership has never been more crucial. HR professionals, serving as the bedrock of this transformative era, intertwine technological promise with moral responsibility.

In their hands lies the power to steer the course of AI in HRM with purpose, compassion, and vision. Their advocacy for responsible AI practices ensures that as we embrace the innovations of tomorrow, we remain anchored to the enduring values that define our collective humanity.

REFERENCES

Aman, A., Rafiq, M., & Dastane, O. (2023). A cross-cultural comparison of work engagement in the relationships between trust climate – Job performance and turnover intention: Focusing China and Pakistan. *Heliyon*, *9*(9), e19534. doi:10.1016/j.heliyon.2023.e19534 PMID:37809562

Aman, A., Rafiq, M., Dastane, O., & Sabir, A. A. (2022). Green corridor: A critical perspective and development of research agenda. *Frontiers in Environmental Science*, *10*, 982473. Advance online publication. doi:10.3389/fenvs.2022.982473

Baldegger, R., Caon, M., & Sadiku, K. (2020). Correlation between entrepreneurial orientation and implementation of AI in human resources management (HRM). *Technology Innovation Management Review*, *10*(4), 72–79. doi:10.22215/timreview/1348

Bhutta, U., Martins, J. N., Mata, M. N., Raza, A., Dantas, R. M., Correia, A. B., & Rafiq, M. (2021). Intellectual Structure and Evolution of Accounting Conservatism Research: Past Trends and Future Research Suggestions. *International Journal of Financial Studies*, *9*(3), 35. doi:10.3390/ijfs9030035

Cellier, F. E. (2001). *Discrete event modeling and simulation technologies: A tapestry of systems and AI-based theories and methodologies*. Springer Science & Business Media.

Chai, K. E., Lines, R. L., Gucciardi, D. F., & Ng, L. (2021). Research Screener: A machine learning tool to semi-automate abstract screening for systematic reviews. *Systematic Reviews*, *10*(1), 1–13. doi:10.118613643-021-01635-3 PMID:33795003

Charlesworth, A. (2014). *The comprehensibility theorem and the foundations of artificial intelligence*. Minds and Machines. doi:10.100711023-014-9349-3

Chomanski, B. (2019). Massive technological unemployment without redistribution: A case for cautious optimism. *Science and Engineering Ethics*, *25*(5), 1389–1407. doi:10.100711948-018-0070-0 PMID:30357558

Chowdhury, S., Dey, P., Joel-Edgar, S., Bhattacharya, S., Rodriguez-Espindola, O., Abadie, A., & Truong, L. (2023). Unlocking the value of artificial intelligence in human resource management through AI capability framework. *Human Resource Management Review*, *33*(1), 100899. doi:10.1016/j.hrmr.2022.100899

Dastane, O., & Haba, H. F. (2023). The Landscape of Digital Natives Research: A Bibliometric and Science Mapping Analysis. *FIIB Business Review*. doi:10.1177/23197145221137960

Daugherty, P. R., & Wilson, H. J. (2018). *Human+ machine: Reimagining work in the age of AI*. Harvard Business Press.

Davenport, T. H., & Ronanki, R. (2018). Artificial Intelligence for the Real World. *Harvard Business Review*, *96*(1), 108–116.

Dunn, S. (1990). Root metaphor in the old and new industrial relations. *British Journal of Industrial Relations*, *28*(1), 1–31. doi:10.1111/j.1467-8543.1990.tb00350.x

Farrukh, M., Raza, A., & Rafiq, M. (2023). Environmentally specific authentic leadership and team green creative behavior based on cognitive-affective path systems. *International Journal of Contemporary Hospitality Management*, *35*(10), 3662–3680. doi:10.1108/IJCHM-04-2022-0530

Farrukh, M., Raza, A., Sajid, M., Rafiq, M., Hameed, R., & Ali, T. (2021). Entrepreneurial intentions: The relevance of nature and nurture. *Education + Training*, *63*(7/8), 1195–1212. doi:10.1108/ET-01-2021-0028

Fernandez, D., Dastane, O., Omar Zaki, H., & Aman, A. (2023). Robotic process automation: bibliometric reflection and future opportunities. *European Journal of Innovation Management*. doi:10.1108/EJIM-10-2022-0570

Gibbons, P. (2015). *The science of successful organizational change: How leaders set strategy, change behavior, and create an agile culture*. FT Press.

Hays, S. W. (2019). Changing roles and duties within government's human resources profession: contemporary models and challenges. In *Handbook of Public Management Practice and Reform* (pp. 205–223). Routledge.

Ivanova, M. (2019). Robots, artificial intelligence, and service automation in travel agencies and tourist information centers. In *Robots, artificial intelligence, and service automation in travel, tourism and hospitality* (pp. 221–237). Emerald Publishing Limited. doi:10.1108/978-1-78756-687-320191011

Jin, J., Rafiq, M., Hayat, N., Yang, Q., & Al Mamun, A. (2023). Discovering the Adoption of Eco-Friendly Furniture Among Chinese Customers. In N. Mansour & L. M. Bujosa Vadell (Eds.), *Finance, Accounting, and Law in the Digital Age: The Impact of Technology and Innovation in the Financial Services Sector* (pp. 273–283). Springer International Publishing. doi:10.1007/978-3-031-27296-7_25

Johnson, D. G., & Verdicchio, M. (2017). Reframing AI discourse. *Minds and Machines*, *27*(4), 575–590. doi:10.100711023-017-9417-6

Kaur, M., Rekha, A., & Resmi, A. (2021). Research landscape of artificial intelligence in human resource management: A bibliometric overview. In *Artificial Intelligence and Speech Technology* (pp. 255–262). CRC Press. doi:10.1201/9781003150664-29

Kaushal, N., & Ghalawat, S. (2023). Research perspective of artificial intelligence and HRM: A bibliometric study. *International Journal of Business Innovation and Research*, *31*(2), 168–196. doi:10.1504/IJBIR.2023.131432

Kim, S., Wang, Y., & Boon, C. (2021). Sixty years of research on technology and human resource management: Looking back and looking forward. *Human Resource Management*, *60*(1), 229–247. doi:10.1002/hrm.22049

LaGrandeur, K. (2015). Emotion, artificial intelligence, and ethics. *Beyond artificial intelligence: The disappearing human-machine divide*, 97-109.

Lee, J., Cho, H., Kim, Y., & Kim, J. (2020). Fostering AI literacy through educational policies: Current trends and recommendations. *Computers & Education*, *150*, 103841.

Lee, J., Suh, T., Roy, D., & Baucus, M. (2019). Emerging technology and business model innovation: The case of artificial intelligence. *Journal of Open Innovation*, *5*(3), 44. doi:10.3390/joitmc5030044

Mer, A., & Virdi, A. S. (2023). Navigating the paradigm shift in HRM practices through the lens of artificial intelligence: A post-pandemic perspective. *The Adoption and Effect of Artificial Intelligence on Human Resources Management, Part A*, 123-154.

Mushtaq, R., Dastane, O., Rafiq, M., & Başar, B. D. (2023). Women financial inclusion research: A bibliometric and network analysis. *International Journal of Social Economics*, *50*(8), 1169–1185. doi:10.1108/IJSE-06-2022-0438

Peterson, J., Tahssain-Gay, L., Salvetat, D., Perez, F., & Hennekam, S. (2023). How managers approach data analytics: A typology through a Resource Orchestration perspective. *Management Decision*, *61*(5), 1225–1243. doi:10.1108/MD-03-2022-0316

Rafiq, M., Dastane, O., & Mushtaq, R. (2023). Waste reduction as ethical behavior: A bibliometric analysis and development of future agenda. *Journal of Global Responsibility*, *14*(3), 360–379. doi:10.1108/JGR-09-2022-0098

Rafiq, M., Farrukh, M., Attiq, S., Shahzad, F., & Khan, I. (2023). Linking job crafting, innovation performance, and career satisfaction: The mediating role of work engagement. *Work (Reading, Mass.)*, *75*(3), 877–886. doi:10.3233/WOR-211363 PMID:36683474

Rafiq, M., Jafar, R. M. S., Ahmad, W., Dastane, O., & Sial, M. A. (2022). Job Embeddedness: Cross-cultural Comparison Between China and Pakistan During COVID-19 Pandemic. *Vision (Basel)*. doi:10.1177/09722629221129980

Ren, T. JIN, X., Rafiq, M., Chin, T., & Lee, C.-H. (2019). Moderation of Housing-related Factors on Psychological Capital–Job Embeddedness Association. *Frontiers in Psychology*. Advance online publication. doi:10.3389/fpsyg.2019.01618 PMID:31649569

Ronquillo, C. E., Peltonen, L. M., Pruinelli, L., Chu, C. H., Bakken, S., Beduschi, A., ... Michalowski, M. (2021). Artificial intelligence in nursing: Priorities and opportunities from an international invitational think-tank of the Nursing and Artificial Intelligence Leadership Collaborative. *Journal of Advanced Nursing*, *77*(9), 3707–3717. doi:10.1111/jan.14855 PMID:34003504

Rupp, D. E., Shapiro, D. L., Folger, R., Skarlicki, D. P., & Shao, R. (2017). A critical analysis of the conceptualization and measurement of organizational justice: Is it time for reassessment? *The Academy of Management Annals*, *11*(2), 919–959. doi:10.5465/annals.2014.0051

Schwartz, J. (2020). *The social enterprise at work: Paradox as a path forward.* Deloitte Insights.

Sonik, D., & Colarossi, A. (2020). *Becoming Artificial: A Philosophical Exploration Into Artificial Intelligence and What it Means to be Human* (Vol. 73). Andrews UK Limited.

Sun, X. (2021). 5G joint artificial intelligence technology in the innovation and reform of university English education. *Wireless Communications and Mobile Computing*, *2021*, 1–10. doi:10.1155/2021/2460916

Tariq, M. U., Poulin, M., & Abonamah, A. A. (2021). Achieving operational excellence through artificial intelligence: Driving forces and barriers. *Frontiers in Psychology*, *12*, 686624. doi:10.3389/fpsyg.2021.686624 PMID:34305744

Tiwari, P. C., Pal, R., Chaudhary, M. J., & Nath, R. (2023). Artificial intelligence revolutionizing drug development: Exploring opportunities and challenges. *Drug Development Research*, ddr.22115. doi:10.1002/ddr.22115 PMID:37712494

Topol, E. (2019). *Deep medicine: how artificial intelligence can make healthcare human again.*

Trong Tuan, L. (2013). Competitive intelligence and other levers of brand performance. *Journal of Strategic Marketing*, *21*(3), 217–239. doi:10.1080/0965254X.2013.765501

Ulrich, D., Kryscynski, D., Ulrich, M., & Brockbank, W. (2017). *Competencies for HR professionals who deliver outcomes*. Academic Press.

World Economic Forum. (2020). *The Future of Jobs Report 2020*. Geneva: World Economic Forum.

Yalenios, J., & d'Armagnac, S. (2023). Work transformation and the HR ecosystem dynamics: A longitudinal case study of HRM disruption in the era of the fourth industrial revolution. *Human Resource Management*, *62*(1), 55–77. doi:10.1002/hrm.22114

Zaki, H. O., Fernandez, D., Dastane, O., Aman, A., & Sanusi, S. (2023). Virtual reality in digital marketing: Research agenda based on bibliometric reflection. *Marketing Intelligence & Planning*, *41*(4), 505–524. doi:10.1108/MIP-12-2022-0568

Chapter 5
Revolutionizing Work:
The Influence of Artificial Intelligence on Employee Experience

Pradnya Bhatkulkar
UNA-Brands, Singapore

ABSTRACT

The chapter offers a thorough review of the vital factors to take into account when integrating artificial intelligence (AI) into the employee experience. The urgent need to provide HR teams with a profound awareness of AI's potential and its revolutionary influence on the HR sector is one of the primary issues that are underlined. Recognizing the breadth and depth of AI capabilities and appreciating how these capabilities will influence future HR practices are important components of this understanding. It's crucial for HR professionals to develop their AI skills because this technology will fundamentally alter how HR is conducted, not just as a trendy buzzword. The chapter's conclusion underlines that AI is an essential element of HR that has the potential to greatly influence the field's future. HR workers can open up a world of opportunities by embracing AI and play a crucial role in leading the firm to success in a quickly changing business environment.

INTRODUCTION

In the ever-changing environment of modern technology, Artificial Intelligence (AI) stands out as a flexible tool with the potential to transform the way we process information, analyse data, and use the insights produced from it to improve decision-making. Its ubiquitous effect is visible in all aspects of life. AI's tremendous impact

DOI: 10.4018/979-8-3693-0039-8.ch005

on the future of work is evident. It claims to boost productivity and provide firms with a competitive advantage. This transition affects both the nature of employment and the physical landscape of the workplace (Aggarwal, 2021). Machines are increasingly capable of performing activities previously designated for human hands, and they can even flourish in fields beyond human capabilities. However, it is vital to highlight that the advent of AI does not imply the demise of human labour. Instead, it acts as a catalyst for innovation, opening up new opportunities for growth (Fernandez et al., 2023). It is positioned to create new job opportunities and has the potential to reinvent the employee experience, initiating a paradigm shift in this process. In this context, it is warranted that HR must adapt to these revolutionary experiences by leveraging the power of AI throughout the employee life cycle, from recruitment through onboarding and development. Employee expectations continue to rise as technology advances at a dizzying speed. Our grasp of these shifting dynamics is based on extensive research that demonstrates how an organization's approach to personnel management has a significant impact on overall performance (Sharma & Tiwari, 2023).

In HRM one of the major challenges businesses encounter when it comes to influencing the employee experience is the burden of repetitive tasks. Employees often find themselves repeatedly performing routine tasks, which not only can be monotonous but also hinder their overall job satisfaction. Additionally, there's a notable absence of a readily available help center that can assist employees around the clock. This lack of support can lead to frustration when employees need assistance or information urgently, negatively impacting their experience within the organization. Moreover, personalization of the employee experience is a challenge companies face. Each employee is unique, with distinct needs, preferences, and aspirations. To create a truly engaging and fulfilling work environment, managers must find ways to tailor the experience to each individual, promoting a sense of belonging and alignment with organizational goals. Learning and development recommendations are also crucial; employees require guidance and resources to continually improve their skills and advance their careers within the company. Furthermore, there's a pressing need for optimizing talent management. Identifying and nurturing talent within the organization is essential for long-term success, but this often remains an under-addressed issue. Effective internal communication is another challenge, as miscommunication or a lack of communication can lead to misunderstandings, decreased morale, and decreased productivity. Lastly, personalization of benefits and rewards is a vital aspect of the employee experience, as one-size-fits-all approaches may not resonate with every employee, and tailoring these offerings can significantly improve job satisfaction and retention. Addressing these challenges will be instrumental in elevating the overall employee experience and fostering a more productive and satisfied workforce.

The objective of this chapter is to narrate the influence of AI on employee experience and suggest implications for managers. The chapter employs a general review method and narrates AI's impact specifically on HRM functions that affect employee experience. The chapter's aim is to provide practical recommendations rather than theory implications which can be considered as the scope of this chapter. The chapter offers a thorough review of the vital factors to take into account when integrating artificial intelligence (AI) into the employee experience within the gambit of HRM.

HRM AND THE EMPLOYEE EXPERIENCE

Since its commencement, HRM have travelled a remarkable path. HR has gone a long way from its beginnings as a purely administrative function with roots in personnel management to become a strategic powerhouse with a key role in the success of an organization. In the past, HR was mostly involved with administrative tasks like managing payroll and keeping track of employee information. However, HR has experienced a tremendous metamorphosis as a result of the changing dynamics of the workforce (Xue et al., 2023). Currently, HR professionals are responsible for managing employee data as well as fostering organizational culture, hiring talent, managing performance, fostering learning and development, resolving conflicts, and fostering employee engagement. Multiple reasons, like as globalization, changing employee expectations, and rising technology, have fueled this change. When one look further, one sees that HR is always changing to meet the needs of enterprises and workers in the modern workplace (Rafiq et al., 2022). As its potential for better decision-making is unlocked, AI is already reshaping HR. AI has the ability to examine large amounts of data and identify patterns and trends that may escape human observation. As a result, HR teams are better able to understand employee performance, engagement, and retention. AI-driven systems may automate repetitive processes like organizing interviews and screening resumes, freeing up HR personnel to concentrate on more strategic tasks and developing employee relationships. Furthermore, AI can eliminate prejudices in the hiring process by using algorithms that are fair and unbiased. HR departments can use AI to improve their operations' efficiency, accuracy, and fairness (Rezzani, Caputo, & Cortese, 2020).

The existing, intuitive-based decision-making process can give way to an evidence-based strategy in HR departments. AI enables HR to make well-informed decisions about employee hiring, training, and promotion. Utilizing AI technology guarantees justice and eliminates biases in HR procedures, resulting in a workforce that is more varied and inclusive. AI can also help detect potential skill gaps and forecast future employment requirements (Raisch & Krakowski, 2021). AI offers priceless insights into the talents and competences that will be in high demand in the future by evaluating historical data and industry patterns. This foresight helps HR departments to pro-actively create training programs and hire individuals with the appropriate capabilities, ensuring the company maintains its competitiveness in a continuously changing business environment. AI has the ability to significantly advance and improve our professional endeavors. It has the power to improve employee experiences and produce truly remarkable ones. AI is positioned to leave its impact on a wide range of sectors, including healthcare, advertising, finance, legal, education, and now even the structure of the workplace (Paesano, 2021).

Employees have experienced conversations with chatbots for tasks like reserving hotel rooms or ordering books from services like Amazon and Walmart. As one become increasingly accustomed to employing chatbots in our personal lives, we naturally expect their integration into the workplace. They'll assist us in various capacities, such as aiding in job searches, addressing frequently asked HR-related queries, and even providing coaching and mentoring. Chatbots are ushering in a digital transformation of HR processes, enabling employees to access HR solutions from virtually anywhere. By leveraging AI within HR, we are poised to cultivate a more seamless employee experience, one that is not only agile but also tailored to individual needs. The influence of AI and chatbots extends well beyond mere convenience; they are revolutionizing both the candidate and employee experiences, marking a transformative shift in the way we engage with HR functions (Zaki et al., 2023).

AI TECHNOLOGIES AND THE EMPLOYEE EXPERIENCE

AI has the potential to make significant contributions to employee well-being by alleviating the mounting pressures individuals face in their professional lives (Lee et al., 2019). Moreover, AI can enable individuals to direct their focus towards more stimulating and engaging aspects of their work. Surprisingly, despite its name, AI does not possess independent thought and excels in tasks that involve repetition. A compelling example of this is found in the field of HR. Recent research emphasizes that HR teams have frequently expressed their struggle with limited time and resources to be as strategic as they desire. If one were to approach these professionals with a solution that can alleviate administrative burdens, allowing them to dedicate more time to strategic thinking and collaborative brainstorming, they would readily embrace the opportunity (Aman et al., 2023). Following are various aspects that would get impacted or are already being impact by AI technology and in turn influencing employee experience.

AI-Powered Recruitment Tools

AI is excellent at managing talent, too. It examines employee performance and identifies patterns and trends. This enables HR to identify areas for improvement in individuals and provide the appropriate training. This not only improves each individual's performance at their work but also aids in the expansion and success of the entire company. Additionally, chatbots powered by AI are able to perform the first interviews with job candidates. They elicit answers to predefined questions and evaluate them. This not only speeds up the employment process, but also guarantees that the selection process is fair and impartial. These chatbots are made to evaluate applicants purely on the basis of their credentials and responses, removing any possibility of bias or discrimination. In this way, AI-driven recruitment tools are improving the effectiveness and fairness of the hiring process which is preferred by digital natives (Dastane & Haba, 2023; Haba et al., 2023).

The field of recruiting and selection has been significantly impacted by AI, which has improved and streamlined the employment process. By automatically scanning resumes, identifying possible candidates, and conducting preliminary evaluations, AI systems play a crucial part. As an example, AI-driven chatbots interact with job candidates in real-time. These chatbots elicit relevant information about the business and ask pertinent queries (Gupta & Bhatia, 2023). This not only saves time, but also guarantees that every applicant has a fair and uniform experience. AI helps HR managers manage vast amounts of candidate data in addition to automating initial screening. AI can identify patterns and trends in candidate profiles using machine learning algorithms, providing crucial information for HR decision-makers. For instance, AI may assess a candidate's educational background, professional background, and skill set to determine how well they might suit the organization. As a result, HR professionals can choose candidates more intelligently and based on facts, which is advantageous for both the employer and the job candidates.

Employee Engagement

Additionally, AI has the capacity to analyse employee data in order to identify recurrent trends and changes linked to employees' performance, job satisfaction, and length of tenure with the organization. HR professionals can gain important insights from this data on the elements that contribute to employees' success and job satisfaction. They can then use this information to develop plans that will improve the organization's overall performance (Dastane, 2020).

AI solutions can be a huge help in ensuring that staff members feel engaged and motivated to continue with their organization. Let's further explain this: Chatbots and other AI tools can serve as virtual assistants for employees. They can provide answers to frequently asked inquiries, current information on corporate policies, and help with new hire orientation. It's like always having a helpful coworker at hand (Enholm et al., 2022).

Employee Contentment

Employees are typically happier when they use chatbots to quickly and accurately obtain information. And they're more inclined to stick with the business if they're content. Additionally, it enables HR experts to focus on more crucial issues. Predicting Employee Turnover: AI can analyze employee data to find trends that could indicate a worker is considering quitting their position. Predictive analytics are used to do this. AI systems, for instance, can monitor factors such as how well people are performing their duties, if they are happy with their work, and what feedback they are providing. HR can intervene and take action to keep them on board if there are indications that they might depart. Simply put, AI technologies may assist employees by providing them with answers to their queries and making them happy, as well as assist businesses in retaining their important staff members by identifying those who may quit and taking measures to keep them on board (Getchell et al., 2022).

Learning and Development

AI is not limited to hiring employees. Additionally, it can be useful for improving employee learning and preserving their happiness. Think of having AI-powered chatbots. By customizing training materials to each employee's particular needs and preferences, these chatbots may provide them with a personalized learning experience. Not only does this increase the effectiveness of learning, but it also increases employee happiness and job engagement (Dastane, Fandos-Roig, & Sánchez-García, 2023). AI has the potential to have a significant impact on organizational training and development. It enables employees to have individualized and flexible learning experiences. This implies that tools with AI capabilities can design customized training programs for every employee. For instance, AI-powered chatbots can present training materials in a conversational fashion, allowing staff members to ask questions and receive prompt answers. This increases employee engagement, improves training effectiveness, and shortens the time needed for conventional classroom-style training. AI isn't solely used for content distribution, either. Additionally, it can aid in assessing worker performance and locating areas in which more education or training is required. AI algorithms can identify areas where employees may need additional training by examining a variety of data sources, including performance reviews, training records, and project results. By using a data-driven strategy, HR professionals can tailor training courses to each individual, ensuring that they are equipped with the particular knowledge and abilities required to succeed in their positions. In conclusion, AI has transformed HR operations by streamlining procedures, raising employee morale, and boosting the efficiency of training and development initiatives. AI's power to revolutionize HR practices will only increase as the technology develops, making HR operations even more effective and strategic (Dastane & Haba, 2023).

AI AND THE FUTURE OF EMPLOYMENT

The Significance of AI-HRM Intersection

An essential component of contemporary HR is the connection between AI and the employee experience. Once skilled workers join the workforce, HR departments can better support employee engagement and retention by identifying critical factors that contribute to job satisfaction and proactively addressing potential problems thanks to the integration of big data and AI (Manuti, A., & Monachino, 2020). IBM, for example, uses predictive analytics to identify workers who may be at risk of leaving the organization, allowing for proactive retention strategies. The amazing result of this strategy is that AI can forecast with 95% accuracy, saving a whopping $300 million in costs associated with staff retention. HR departments can analyze employee data, including survey results, performance reviews, and other relevant indicators, to identify patterns and trends that provide a deep understanding of employee engagement and satisfaction (Pizzoferrato, 2023). With this information, HR can make more focused efforts to increase retention and guarantee that workers are happy and productive (Canhoto & Clear, 2020).

In the past, HR teams relied on reactive measures and manually examined employee feedback, performance information, and relevant KPIs to obtain insights into work happiness. Nonetheless, HR departments may now detect such problems before they become serious and take proactive measures to address them thanks to the integration of big data and AI. In this sense, technology turns into a vital instrument for attracting and keeping top personnel as well as improving the general performance of the company. AI helps with career development and succession planning, which involves finding and developing staff members who have the ability to take on leadership or high-level positions inside the company (Mishra & Singh, 2022). Interestingly, Unilever uses AI-enabled technologies to identify high-potential workers and direct their advancement toward leadership roles. Their AI-powered "Flex Experiences" examine employee performance, ability, and prospective data to find possibilities for career advancement inside the company. Additionally, by identifying workers who are likely to thrive in leadership positions, this technology provides specialized training and development opportunities to get them ready for bigger roles down the road.

AI algorithms can efficiently identify workers with the abilities and capacity to take on new, diverse, or leadership roles by evaluating data like as work history, career goals, and employee performance. This strategy encourages internal hiring, increases employee satisfaction, and guarantees a smooth transition in the event that important personnel retire or leave the organization. AI's contribution to onboarding is equally significant. By offering individualized training and tools, it can improve the onboarding process for new hires (Loureiro et al., 2021). Businesses such as Oracle have effectively included AI-driven digital assistants into their onboarding protocols, facilitating onboarding around-the-clock and streamlining the entire process. New hires can get step-by-step help from the Oracle Digital Assistant with anything from filling out new hire paperwork to setting up benefits. New hires can use it as a resource to access corporate information and ask inquiries. In the end, our user-friendly application promotes a smooth and satisfying onboarding process for new hires.

Big data and artificial intelligence (AI) are essentially revolutionizing a number of HR operations, including hiring, employee engagement, compliance, and workplace safety. By utilizing these tools, HR departments may identify possible hazards and opportunities, gain insightful knowledge about employee behavior, and make data-driven decisions that improve performance. HR departments may streamline processes, cut expenses, and make sure they draw and keep top personnel by utilizing technology. HR departments be flexible and ready to respond to the changing needs of their companies by integrating AI and big data (Cărbune, 2022).

Using AI to Enhance Employee Experience

Organizations may improve and personalize the employee experience by utilizing the potential of AI-driven tools. For instance, AI-driven chatbots can improve communication, provide immediate support and information, and encourage a sense of community among staff members. Additionally, AI can help businesses customise their learning and development programs to fit each employee's needs and provide them with personalized recommendations and feedback. AI can also be a key factor in encouraging employee wellbeing. AI can help businesses discover possible areas of concern and execute focused wellness initiatives by analyzing employee well-being data. This not only improves the well-being and pleasure of workers, but it also raises levels of engagement and productivity (Goralski & Tan, 2020). Various facets related to the same are discussed below.

Smarter Decisions

By offering them real-time information and predictions, AI empowers HR professionals to make wiser decisions. For instance, AI systems can analyze employee data to look for trends and make predictions about the future. This assists HR professionals in identifying possible issues early and developing strategies to increase employee happiness and retention. AI also contributes to more equitable and inclusive workplaces. Information regarding the employees' histories and performance at work are taken into consideration. AI can assist businesses in resolving any unfairness and ensuring that everyone is treated equitably. Everyone benefits from a better environment, and the company looks good to talented individuals. By analyzing data from both inside and outside the firm, AI also aids in future planning. It determines the abilities the business will require as well as how to attract and retain the best candidates. The company may accomplish its objectives and maintain its position as a market leader in this way.

Enhanced Effectiveness and Productivity

AI technology performs time-consuming, repetitive jobs. This enables HR professionals to concentrate on crucial planning-related tasks. Not only does it save time, but it also improves and expedites work. AI solutions, for instance, can aid with interview preparation, offer job seekers individualized advise, and ease the transition for new hires. Additionally, AI streamlines the hiring procedure. With AI, businesses can swiftly sift through a large volume of resumes and identify the best applicants depending on their requirements. This expedites hiring and aids HR in selecting the best candidates.

AI is excellent at managing talent, too. It examines employee performance and identifies patterns and trends. This enables HR to identify areas for improvement in individuals and provide the appropriate training. This not only improves each individual's performance at their work but also aids in the expansion and success of the entire company.

Figure 1. AI and employee experience

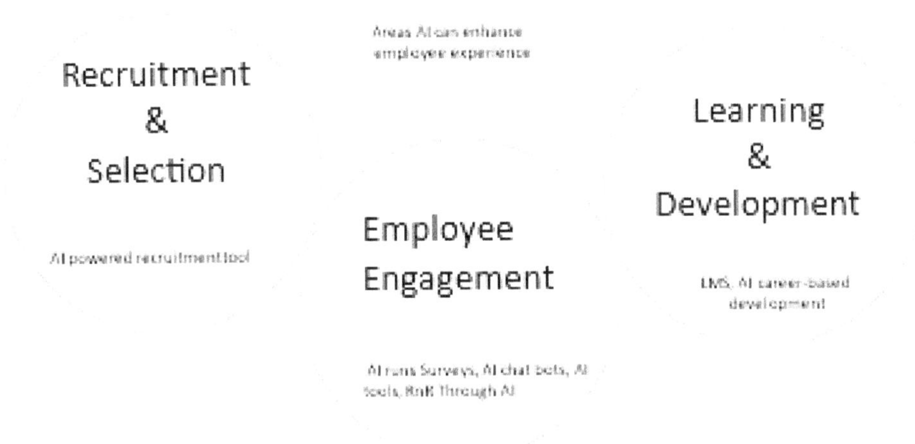

IMPLICATIONS AND RECOMMENDATIONS

The integration of AI into employee experience and HR management is fundamentally reshaping the operational landscape of businesses. It opens doors to a host of opportunities aimed at enhancing overall performance and organizational agility (Dastane, Aman & Satar, 2023). To effectively harness the power of AI for the benefit of employees, consider the following insights and recommendations:

Automate the Mundane

AI can be seamlessly integrated into virtually any business process to automate routine and mundane tasks. This automation creates space for employees to engage in more high-value, strategic work.

Eliminate Endless Emails

While chatbots are a familiar sight in many organizations, a considerable number have yet to embrace this technology for a range of reasons. However, for those with the capability to do so, AI (AI) can serve as a potent chatbot, proficiently addressing common daily inquiries posed by employees, such as: “How can I enroll in benefits?” “Where can I access my paycheck?” “How do I check my PTO balance?” Now, picture this: What if you could reclaim up to two hours a day (or perhaps even more) for your

HR operations team by enabling the chatbot to handle these routine questions? This newfound time could be dedicated to high-value projects like process optimization. As an added benefit, employees equipped with a chatbot wouldn't have to wait for responses from team members to resolve their queries.

Adoption of AI-Powered Analytics

In the ever-evolving landscape, more data analytics organizations are embracing A.I.-driven tools capable of swiftly analyzing vast datasets spanning multiple systems. These tools yield invaluable insights within seconds, steering the focus towards unraveling the compelling narratives concealed within employee data, rather than dedicating excessive time to data retrieval. The outcome? Enhanced reporting capabilities and the delivery of comprehensive metrics to leadership, enabling the construction of compelling business cases for HR initiatives. In essence, A.I. acts as a time-saver, streamlining operations, and enabling HR teams to concentrate on maximizing their employees' potential, ultimately resulting in superior employee experiences.

Improving Precision and Mitigating Bias

It's essential to acknowledge that while A.I. excels at identifying issues, the human touch remains indispensable for resolution. However, generative A.I. takes the lead by identifying and highlighting these issues at an accelerated pace and often with heightened accuracy compared to human efforts alone.

Elevating Employee Motivation

Enhancing motivation is a pivotal aspect of AI in the workplace. AI-driven engagement analysis is a technology that delves into the realm of social media content within an organization. This innovative tool can dissect unstructured data from annual and pulse surveys, as well as the conversations circulating on social media. It has the capacity to swiftly analyze hundreds of thousands of comments, pinpointing recurring themes in a matter of hours. However, for the sake of safeguarding data privacy, it is advisable to restrict this analysis to information within a corporate firewall, ensuring that sensitive data remains protected.

Enhanced Compensation Planning

When it comes to making compensation decisions, a multitude of factors need to be meticulously considered. Beyond just performance, these factors encompass the market rate for specific skills, the level of demand for these skills, and whether it's more appropriate to reward exceptional performance through base pay or bonuses. Crafting an optimal base pay structure that aligns with this comprehensive perspective demands an intricate understanding of employee skill sets, the prevailing market rates for those skills, and the trajectory of skill demand. In this context, there exists a wealth of data points to evaluate, far surpassing the capacity of a human to analyze without the assistance of advanced analytics. The introduction of AI-based compensation support brings transformative potential to the table. It can drastically reduce the countless hours spent preparing for compensation cycles, condensing this effort into a mere fraction of the time while offering decision-making guidance that delves into an extensive array of variables, surpassing traditional methods. Moreover, AI's approach to compensation decision-making underscores the significance of skills as a primary determinant. By doing so, it significantly mitigates the likelihood of biases seeping into the compensation process, ensuring a fair and objective approach.

Skill Development

In the realm of learning, AI has the potential to revolutionize skill development at both individual and organizational levels. An area that holds significant promise is the application of AI for tagging learning content. Traditionally, when learners interacted with a learning management system, their content experience was heavily reliant on the metadata provided by content developers. This metadata guided them to the relevant materials. AI-driven tagging augments learning resources, including images and documents within learning management systems, with enriched metadata. This enhancement enables learners to efficiently locate and access training content repeatedly.

AI-Enhanced Learning

Open Learning Platform: This platform seamlessly integrates employee and learning data from various sources, consolidating all pertinent content for access from any device. It fosters learning flexibility, allowing individuals to engage in learning from any location and at any time. Employee-Specific Experience: AI provides tailored learning recommendations based on an individual's job role, business group, skill set, and personal learning history. This personalization encourages continuous employee development and skill growth. Content Channels: Learning content is thoughtfully organized to cater to diverse needs and interests, simplifying content exploration and aligning with ongoing development aligned with business objectives. By rendering learning easily accessible when and where it's needed, AI significantly contributes to the acquisition of strategic skills within organizations.

Moreover, AI can create a comprehensive overview of an organization's learning initiatives through a learning dashboard. These dashboards offer insights into the progress made in addressing identified skill gaps. The learning history of individual employees can even serve as an indicator of their propensity to learn. As the shelf-life of skills rapidly diminishes, this inclination to learn is becoming just as crucial as one's current skill set (Banavar, n.d.).

Informed Skill Profiling

In the ever-evolving business landscape, understanding the skills possessed by employees and their proficiency levels is a fundamental requirement. While one approach involves employee self-assessments, these assessments often suffer from issues like over-rating and under-rating of expertise. These discrepancies occur due to the limited time managers have to meticulously audit these self-ratings. Manual assessment processes can swiftly become outdated, often devolving into mere check-the-box exercises. Enter AI, which offers a transformative solution by enabling the inference of skills through the scraping of employees' internal digital presence. This data can be sourced from various outlets such as resumes, sales records, and digital badges. Once skill profiles are generated, they can be shared with employees and managers for validation. AI-based skills inference serves as a valuable tool to uncover the 'hidden gems' within an organization—those individuals possessing skills that were previously unknown. On a broader scale, organizations can create skill heatmaps that juxtapose the skills present within the business against those that are needed. These heatmaps offer insights that pave the way for intervention plans, allowing organizations to rapidly address skill gaps and align their workforce with evolving demands.

Access to Career Coaching

Career development and coaching are potent tools for cultivating more meaningful work experiences for employees, ultimately resulting in heightened productivity and fortifying succession pipelines for businesses. Typically, career coaching is a high-touch, time-intensive, and costly endeavor. Consequently, it has predominantly been offered to individuals who were either underperforming or those deemed to possess high potential, warranting significant investment. However, the prospect of extending this opportunity for employee career development to all members of the organization promises manifold benefits. This inclusivity is likely to bolster the motivation and engagement of employees across the board, thereby enhancing overall employee job performance. In the process, the organization stands to gain significantly, experiencing an overall upsurge in workforce productivity and a more robust succession plan.

Enhancing Employee Interaction

Enter the chatbot – an application adept at comprehending natural language and engaging users in human-like conversations. Chatbots emerge as one of the most versatile AI technologies applicable, finding deployment in numerous facets of HR operations. What's striking about chatbots is their affordability in design and quick adaptability. Their implementation can be efficiently managed by non-technical HR personnel, thanks to the readily available user-friendly application programming interfaces (APIs). For organizations looking to integrate AI into their HR function, chatbots serve as a natural starting point. If your HR procedures frequently trigger inquiries from employees, a chatbot can be readily deployed, based on a well-structured frequently asked questions (FAQ) list pertaining to HR processes. Chatbots epitomize how AI can substantially enhance the employee experience by providing real-time answers round the clock. Furthermore, they continually evolve through feedback, improving the quality of responses. It's prudent to involve communications experts in chatbot design to fine-tune word choices and tone, thereby enhancing personalization and user engagement.

Employee Verification

In many industries, verifying an employee's background is a very important part of the hiring process. However, the traditional methods of doing this take a lot of time, involve a ton of paperwork, and sometimes you can't be sure if the information is genuine. In the future, AI systems might be able to connect with other companies, making these background checks much faster. This means that HR teams can check an employee's past performance without having to contact their previous employers or read recommendation letters. Traditional referral and verification processes aren't always completely accurate and may not reflect a person's true skills and abilities. With AI verification, it's a win-win for both the employer and the employee, and it also saves a lot of time. The employer knows what they're getting, and the employee gets a quicker turnaround time to their job application.

Boost Retention of the Organization

Most companies want to keep their employees for a long time because it saves money and allows employees to grow along with the company. Organizations can use AI systems to monitor what employees do at work, like their emails and internet usage.

The AI compares this to their usual behavior to see if the employee is content or considering switching jobs. AI not only helps retain employees but can also address their concerns promptly. Some people might worry that AI is invasive, but this method isn't entirely new. In the past, there were apps that tracked what employees did on their computers, but they only provided basic reports. With AI, these new apps can analyze all the data to get a better understanding of the situation and take necessary actions to improve employee retention within the organization.

Ethical Issues in AI Implementation

While AI brings about positive effects on employee productivity, speed, and efficiency, it regrettably has the potential to result in substantial job losses and unemployment, especially in sectors where labour-intensive jobs are predominant, particularly in developing countries. As one tries to make things automatic, easy, and productive, we might be giving away something important: our privacy. Using AI for watching people, keeping an eye on employees, and collecting data has made us open to problems. Some worries about privacy and protecting data come from gathering and using personal information. Most AI depends on personal data, and making sure it's clear how it works is a big concern. Leaders of an organization should always choose to be clear about how they use AI, especially if it's used to watch employees or make decisions that affect them directly. Also doing regular audits isn't just about keeping track of what might happen. It's also a chance to make your AI plans better, so they match with what your business is all about—the things it wants to achieve, how it sees the future, and especially its core values.

Limitation and Future Research Avenue

The theoretical contribution in this chapter is somewhat limited, as it predominantly relies on a general review of existing literature. It does not employ a systematic literature review (SLR) or quantitative analysis, which may be considered a methodological limitation. The scope of the chapter is also quite narrow, focusing primarily on the employee experience within the context of AI. However, it is important to note that future research could expand this analysis to investigate how AI impacts various other facets beyond just employees' experiences. The chapter, in its current form, does not delve into the potential negative implications of AI on employee experiences, often referred to as the "dark side" of AI. Exploring these adverse effects could offer a more comprehensive understanding of the subject matter. Furthermore, the chapter lacks specificity regarding the types of AI being discussed. It is important to distinguish between different AI technologies, such as generative AI and others, as they can have varying implications for the employee experience. Elaborating on the specific types of AI involved in the analysis can provide a more nuanced and precise discussion of the subject matter.

CONCLUSION

AI holds immense potential in shaping how businesses approach the employee experience and strive to enhance it. However, as we embrace this text-driven future, it is imperative to remain acutely aware of the challenges that come with it. Ethical considerations, data privacy, and security, along with the imperative need to upskill HR professionals, loom as focal areas of attention. Effectively navigating these challenges is pivotal to realizing the full potential of AI in HR. The journey of AI in HR is a captivating one, and we find ourselves still in the early stages of its development. With the continuous advancement of technology, this journey will persist in evolving and transforming as we adapt to these changes. The role of HR is poised to become more strategic, impactful, and integral to organizational success than ever before. Comprehending and harnessing AI technology will not only enhance HR operations but also play a pivotal role in shaping the future of work and the workplace. The future has arrived, and it's time for HR to step boldly into this transformative landscape.

REFERENCES

Aggarwal, K. (2021). *The impact of company characteristics on human resource disclosure index: A study on Service sector companies in India.* FIIB Business Review. doi:10.1177/23197145211010871

Aman, A., Rafiq, M., & Dastane, O. (2023). A cross-cultural comparison of work engagement in the relationships between trust climate–Job performance and turnover intention: Focusing China and Pakistan. *Heliyon*, *9*(9), e19534. doi:10.1016/j.heliyon.2023.e19534 PMID:37809562

Antonija Bozickovic, Service Desk Institute. (n.d.). *Five Ethical Issues of AI in the Modern Workplace.* Retrieved from https://www.servicedeskinstitute.com/five-ethical-issues-of-ai-in-the-modern-workplace/

Canhoto, A. I., & Clear, F. (2020). Artificial intelligence and machine learning as business tools: A framework for diagnosing value destruction potential. *Business Horizons*, *63*(2), 183–193. doi:10.1016/j.bushor.2019.11.003

Cărbune, N. (2022). Human resources management and training of highperforming managers. In Competitiveness and sustainable development (pp. 130-132). doi:10.52326/csd2022.22

Career Coach Institute Website. (2010). *Defining coaching*. Retrieved from http://www.careercoachinstitute.com/about-us.html

Dastane, D. O. (2020). Impact of leadership styles on employee performance: A moderating role of gender. *Australian Journal of Business and Management Research*, *5*(12), 27–52. doi:10.52283/NSWRCA.AJBMR.20200512A03

Dastane, O., Aman, A., Satar, B. M., & Safie, N. (Eds.). (2023). *Digital Natives as a Disruptive Force in Asian Businesses and Societies*. IGI Global. doi:10.4018/978-1-6684-6782-4

Dastane, O., Fandos-Roig, J. C., & Sánchez-García, J. (2023). It's free! Still, would I learn? Unearthing perceived value of education apps for better entrepreneurial decisions. *Management Decision*. Advance online publication. doi:10.1108/MD-09-2022-1292

Dastane, O., & Haba, H. F. (2023). The landscape of digital natives research: a bibliometric and science mapping analysis. *FIIB Business Review*.

Dastane, O., & Haba, H. F. (2023). What drives mobile MOOC's continuous intention? A theory of perceived value perspective. *The International Journal of Information and Learning Technology*, *40*(2), 148–163. doi:10.1108/IJILT-04-2022-0087

Enholm, I. M., Papagiannidis, E., Mikalef, P., & Krogstie, J. (2022). Artificial intelligence and business value: A literature review. *Information Systems Frontiers*, *24*(5), 1709–1734. doi:10.100710796-021-10186-w

Fernandez, D., Dastane, O., Omar Zaki, H., & Aman, A. (2023). Robotic process automation: Bibliometric reflection and future opportunities. *European Journal of Innovation Management*. Advance online publication. doi:10.1108/EJIM-10-2022-0570

Getchell, K. M., Carradini, S., Cardon, P. W., Fleischmann, C., Ma, H., Aritz, J., & Stapp, J. (2022). Artificial intelligence in business communication: The changing landscape of research and teaching. *Business and Professional Communication Quarterly*, *85*(1), 7–33. doi:10.1177/23294906221074311

Goralski, M. A., & Tan, T. K. (2020). Artificial intelligence and sustainable development. *International Journal of Management Education*, *18*(1), 100330. doi:10.1016/j.ijme.2019.100330

Gupta, S. K., & Bhatia, N. (2023). *A Decade of Trend in the Employee Turnover Intention Study in India: A Systematic Review and Recommendation*. FIIB Business Review. doi:10.1177/23197145231158907

Haba, H. F., Bredillet, C., & Dastane, O. (2022). Green consumer research: Trends and way forward based on bibliometric analysis. *Cleaner and Responsible Consumption*, 100089.

Lee, J., Suh, T., Roy, D., & Baucus, M. (2019). Emerging technology and business model innovation: The case of artificial intelligence. *Journal of Open Innovation*, *5*(3), 44. doi:10.3390/joitmc5030044

Loureiro, S. M. C., Guerreiro, J., & Tussyadiah, I. (2021). Artificial intelligence in business: State of the art and future research agenda. *Journal of Business Research*, *129*, 911–926. doi:10.1016/j.jbusres.2020.11.001

Manuti, A., & Monachino, D. (2020). Managing knowledge at the time of artificial intelligence: An explorative study with knowledge workers. *East European Journal of Psycholinguistics*, *7*(2). Advance online publication. doi:10.29038/eejpl.2020.7.2.man

Mishra, V., & Singh, J. (2022). *Health Technology Assessment of Telemedicine Interventions in Diabetes Management: Evidence from UAE*. FIIB Business Review. doi:10.1177/23197145221130651

Paesano, A. (2021). Artificial intelligence and creative activities inside organizational behavior. *The International Journal of Organizational Analysis*.

Pizzoferrato, A. (2023). European Legislation and AI information systems applicable to HRM. In Law, Technology and Labour (pp. 179-185). Università di Bologna.

Rafiq, M., Jafar, R. M. S., Ahmad, W., Dastane, O., & Sial, M. A. (2022). Job Embeddedness: Cross-cultural Comparison Between China and Pakistan During COVID-19 Pandemic. *Vision (Basel)*.

Raisch, S., & Krakowski, S. (2021). Artificial intelligence and management: The automation–augmentation paradox. *Academy of Management Review*, *46*(1), 192–210. doi:10.5465/amr.2018.0072

Rezzani, A., Caputo, A., & Cortese, C. G. (2020). An analysis of the literature about the application of Artificial Intelligence to the Recruitment and Personnel Selection. *Bollettino di Psicologia Applicata*, 25–33.

Sharma, S., & Tiwari, V. (2023). Modelling the Impact of Emotional Intelligence, Career Success and Happiness on Turnover Intention Among Managerial-level Employees in the Information Technology Industry. *FIIB Business Review*, *12*(3), 279–293. doi:10.1177/23197145221121082

Xue, X., Rafiq, M., Meng, F., & Peerzadah, S. A. (2023). 21st anniversary of job embeddedness: A retrospection and future research agenda. *Work*, (Preprint), 1-15.

Zaki, H. O., Fernandez, D., Dastane, O., Aman, A., & Sanusi, S. (2023). Virtual reality in digital marketing: Research agenda based on bibliometric reflection. *Marketing Intelligence & Planning*, *41*(4), 505–524. doi:10.1108/MIP-12-2022-0568

KEY TERMS AND DEFINITIONS

Career Coaching: Career coaching is when a coach and an employee work one-on-one to help reach career goals and full potential. Career coaches help with career planning, career changes, career advice, and other career decisions (Miles, 2023).

Compensation Planning: A compensation plan (also known as a comp plan) is a set of guidelines for employees' salaries, bonuses, and equity. It gives current and prospective employees a clear view of their employment package—which gives your company an advantage as you're hiring (Steinfeld, 2022).

Employee Engagement: Employee engagement is the emotional commitment the employee has to the organization and its goals (Kruse, 2012).

Employee Experience: The employee experience is defined as the cumulative assessment of an employee's interaction with your company and its people (Lute, 2022).

Chapter 6
A Bibliometric Analysis of Artificial Intelligence and Human Resource Management Studies

Azizan Bin Morshidi
https://orcid.org/0000-0001-7786-0322
Universiti Malaysia Sabah, Malaysia

Nurhizam Safie Mohd Satar
https://orcid.org/0000-0003-3389-3936
Universiti Kebangsaan Malaysia, Malaysia

Azueryn Annatassia Dania Aqeela Azizan
University of New South Wales, Australia

Rizal Zamani Idris
Universiti Malaysia Sabah, Malaysia

Rafiq Idris
Universiti Malaysia Sabah, Malaysia

Mohammad Shaukhi Md Radzi
Universiti Malaysia Sabah, Malaysia

Sitinurbayu Mohd Yusoff
https://orcid.org/0000-0003-1024-9443
Universiti Malaysia Sabah, Malaysia

Fauzie Sarjono
https://orcid.org/0000-0002-8583-0622
Universiti Malaysia Sabah, Malaysia

ABSTRACT

The pervasiveness of artificial intelligence (AI) within contemporary organisations is an undeniable phenomenon. The primary objective of this chapter is to undertake a meticulous bibliometric analysis of the scholarly literature that investigates the interconnected exploration of the utilisation and ramifications of artificial intelligence (AI) within the realm of human resource management (HRM). The researchers consulted the valued scientific database Scopus, which proved to be a fount of

DOI: 10.4018/979-8-3693-0039-8.ch006

knowledge. Ninety-one documents were initially retrieved and meticulously chosen for the analysis. The data underwent processing through the esteemed Bibliometrix software and the sophisticated Biblioshiny application tool. The results evince that the application of artificial intelligence (AI) to human resource management (HRM) constitutes an emerging domain of inquiry, characterised by a continuous and unwavering expansion and a promising trajectory for the future. Finally, the discourse examined the comparative themes that emerged before and after the advent of the COVID-19 pandemic.

INTRODUCTION

Artificial intelligence (AI), which is more widely known, is one of the most important technological advances that is changing the way people work. According to academic standards, it is important to recognise the possible impacts of artificial intelligence (AI) development (Tambe et al., 2019). Undoubtedly, the widespread use of AI has the potential to eliminate large parts of many jobs, worsening the growing problem of social imbalance. It could also have positive effects, such as making jobs better or adding jobs instead of completely replacing them. When combining these ideas, it is reasonable to say that artificial intelligence (AI) will have a huge impact on the future of human resource management (HRM). The use of AI in human resource management has great potential and can lead to many interesting results (Radonjić et al., 2022).

Given the multi-disciplinary nature of AI-HRM, it surpasses the conventional confines of traditional HRM. The dissemination of AI-infused HR solutions is contingent upon technological advancements, while the application and implications of these tools require the integration of viewpoints garnered from the social sciences. Scholars from a variety of disciplines have made essential contributions to artificial intelligence and human resource management (Brynjolfsson & McAfee, 2017). In the field of computer science, researchers have developed artificial intelligence (AI) algorithms to address and resolve human resource management (HRM) quandaries. While there is a substantial body of research on the intersection of artificial intelligence and human resource management (AI-HRM) across diverse disciplines, it is worth noting that each discipline has approached this subject from a distinct perspective, with little regard to the combination of interdisciplinary insight. While various departments across multiple organisations have embraced and integrated artificial intelligence (AI)-based tools into their operational frameworks, it is regrettable to note that the esteemed Human Resources (HR) department, as explained by Vrontis et al. (2022), has hitherto encountered impediments to successfully implementing these tools.

While reading academic literature, one comes across an abundance of works that explore the field of AI-HRM research (Tambe et al., 2019). However, it is important to note that the majority of these articles revolved around the fundamental concept of subject matter. Our study focused on a rigorous investigation of bibliometric analysis, with the goal of uncovering the intricate tapestry of research trends and the cryptic terrain of the unknown (Prikshat et al., 2023). Therefore, it is critical to provide a thorough explanation spanning a clear trajectory of the current research environment and emerging paradigms in the field of artificial intelligence and human resource management convergence.

In light of the current paradigm, it is evident that COVID-19 no longer poses the same level of risk to the majority of the population as it did during its early stages (Mer & Virdi, 2023). The perception of the pandemic's end is due in part to political and economic forces (Khalifa et al., 2022). Despite the widespread impact of the pandemic on academic research (Morshidi et al., 2022), no comprehensive bibliometric assessment of COVID-19 and AI-HRM has been conducted prior to, during, or after the pandemic (Mer & Virdi, 2023; Abdul Rahman et al., 2022). To address this gap in knowledge, the present study aims to conduct a bibliometric analysis of AI-HRM studies spanning the pandemic period. Therefore, the main goal of this study is to answer the following research questions (RQ) to show how previous research has gone into the field of Artificial Intelligence in Human Resource Management (AI-HRM) during the periods, while also looking at the latest developments in this rapidly changing field on a global level.

Research Question 1: What are the current states and trends of publications of the AI-HRM studies?

Research Question 2. What are the highly cited documents in AI-HRM research?

Research Question 3. Who are the most productive contributors in AI-HRM in terms of source titles, authors, institutions, and countries.

Research Question 4. What are the important keywords in the AI-HRM prior and post

COVID-19 pandemic?

Research Question 5. What are the themes involved in the AI-HRM prior and post COVID-19 pandemic?

LITERATURE REVIEW

Artificial Intelligence

Artificial intelligence (AI) is the use of technology to do something that normally requires a certain amount of knowledge. According to Palos-Sánchez et al. (2022), this also refers to the skill level of technologically trained systems that are on par with human performance. This is also a good way to describe artificial intelligence: it is a great example of intellectual ability because it can adapt to its surroundings and work hard to reach its goals. The topic at hand is the difference between the observable cognitive skills of computers and humans naturally occurring intellectual abilities. Artificial intelligence is different from regular software systems because it can perform complex calculations quickly, use complex methods, and handle huge amounts of high-quality combined data (Jia et al., 2018). Since its beginning, technology has become the most important thing in business and has had a huge impact (Fernandes Franca et al., 2023). It first appeared in 1956 and was a major turning point in its early use and development. There have been many recent advances and breakthroughs in information technology (IT). Among these, artificial intelligence (AI) is a key discovery that heralds a new age of possibilities (Chowdhury et al., 2023). Digital technologies have completely changed the way we do our jobs, leading to a huge shift and huge progress in business management (da Silva et al., 2022).

Analytical, human-inspired, and humanised artificial systems (Panda et al., 2023) are three separate categories within a wide area of artificial intelligence (AI). Analytical artificial intelligence (AI) systems have a unique feature that works in tandem with cognitive intelligence, making them helpful in constructing a cognitive representation of the complex world of business (Jia et al., 2018). Using machine learning algorithms, analytical artificial intelligence has the potential to provide insights into previous encounters while also facilitating the process of making informed decisions in the future (Chowdhury et al., 2023; Kaur et al., 2021). The field of human-inspired artificial intelligence involves the synthesis of cognitive and emotional intelligence, with the interaction of these capacities profoundly shaping the decision-making environment. Artificial intelligence (AI) that has been "humanised" has many skills, such as cognitive, emotional, and social intelligence (Radonjić et al., 2022). When interacting with external factors, the system shows an amazing ability to be self-aware and self-conscious. People who study computer science believe that this new method is a cutting-edge tool for the next generation of technological progress.

Artificial Intelligence and Human Resource Management

In computer science, the concept of artificial intelligence (AI) has spread over the last few decades (Tambe et al., 2019). However, it has only been in the last few years that this concept has become important. It is now seen as a useful and effective tool in business and industry, especially for jobs related to human resource management (HRM). Currently, AI is used in all parts of businesses, especially in HR management (Kiran et al., 2019; Kiran et al., 2023), for example. Artificial intelligence (AI) has replaced the most important part of human interaction, and has made many important tasks in human resource management (HRM) more efficient. These tasks included screening, hiring, onboarding, interviewing, aligning HR activities, and managing performance. Giraud et al. (2022) state that using this method in a useful and effective way leads to big improvements and greater success in the field of skilled and wanted human resource management.

Artificial intelligence (AI) systems have been used for a long time and in many different areas. However, it has only been in the last few years that this technology has made big steps forward and has been widely used in many different types of organisations (Hussain et al., 2019). Despite the fact that artificial intelligence systems have been around for decades, the idea in question needs a single, clear definition. To fully understand the complicated world of artificial intelligence, it is best to use a method that involves breaking down or categorising individual lexical units. This makes it easier to understand the deeper meanings of each word (Qamar et al. 2021).

Artificial Intelligence in Human Resource Management Practices

As technology changes rapidly and steadily around the world, it is clear that businesses and other industries are eager to use the creativity of AI systems, mostly because they are so effective and improve workflow in so many ways. An important change in the business world has occurred because of the widespread use of artificial intelligence (AI) technology in many specialised areas, such as human resource management (HRM) (Malik et al., 2020; Radonjić et al., 2022). One cannot say enough about how important and helpful this is for the effective management of HR. According to careful analysis and results from numerous studies conducted by different businesses and industries, it is clear that using artificial intelligence has huge potential to lead to improvements in caregiving, cost-cutting, and the effective and important management of human resources in the business world (Qamar et al., 2021). This covers many different areas such as hiring practices, job evaluations, performance reviews, human resource planning, employee training, and even predicting the job market. Using artificial intelligence to manage human resources has become popular among multinational companies worldwide (Chowdhury et al., 2023) because it provides access to a wide range of benefits.

After significant study and discovery, many prominent human resource (HR) practitioners agree that conventional recruitment methods have distinct benefits (Tambe et al., 2019). This classic recruitment technique encourages meaningful connections and creates special bonds with prospects. Facilitating human interaction improves information flow and reduces miscommunication (Votto et al., 2021). This technology also promotes intellectual discourse, fostering collaboration between talent acquisition professionals and jobseekers (Garg et al., 2018). Touch and emotional awareness are essential to life. The comfort that people receive from familiarity proves this. According to Vrontis et al. (2022), the traditional recruitment procedure has been validated. Formal interviews have long been a valuable method for identifying and choosing talented individuals. This implies that these practices are based on well-established ideas and significant studies, and have a rich historical context. Furthermore, it emphasises the importance of validating the results and outcomes to ensure credibility and reliability. Based on this premise, employers can acquire a plethora of information and execute the utmost discernment and curation, thereby instilling a sense of assurance that said recruitment will yield the desired advantages or optimal outcomes in the future (Naseri and Elliott, 2011). While many professionals have articulated their perspectives in support of conventional approaches to recruitment, extolling the benefits and inherent advantages of the process, it is imperative to acknowledge the existence of an alternative line of reasoning. A contingent of these professionals has espoused a proclivity for a paradigm shift or transformative alteration in the recruitment process, as they have discerned certain drawbacks or disadvantages associated with it (Bulut & Batur Dinler, 2023).

Numerous experts agree that the standard recruitment process has drawbacks that make it ineffective. According to Kshetri (2020), the traditional technique involves a lengthy recruitment process that takes time for both businesses and candidates. Traditional recruiting is time-consuming and uses outdated methods (Basu et al. 2023). An alternative view is that the traditional recruiting process is inefficient and gives recruiters little time to make good decisions (Malik et al., 2023). Experts agree that with this traditional method, recruiters rarely have enough time to communicate with applicants (Chowdhury et al., 2020).

Furthermore, during this complex approach, applicants' curriculum vitae are constantly preserved within the database following their sad expulsion from a specific vocational posture. Regrettably, these individuals are frequently condemned to obscurity and their potential for alternate careers is largely overlooked (Bankins, 2021). Instead, at their discretion, recruiters choose to explore other candidates for every new post or occupation (Panda et al. 2023). Consequently, recruiters may focus primarily on hiring people with such expertise, overlooking other deserving applicants who have gained work experience in alternative businesses or institutions of comparable renown (Arora et al., 2021; Rodgers et al., 2023). In light of the significant drawbacks inherent in the traditional approach to recruitment, organisations have increasingly embraced the use of artificial intelligence (AI) in recent times to enhance and achieve optimal human resource management (HRM) functions (Vishwakarma & Singh, 2023).

A comprehensive comparison of the conventional recruitment procedure with the integration of artificial intelligence techniques in human resource management shows that while many companies have adopted AI software for candidate interviews and overall recruitment processes as a novel and captivating technology, there is still a long way to go before this approach can be strategically implemented (Kaur et al., 2021). Numerous esteemed professionals have attested that employment screening relies heavily on candidate applications both directly submitted and online (Berhil et al. 2019). Some software applications pre-screen candidates using personality traits to determine whether they have the qualifications, experience, and skills needed for a job (Malik et al., 2020). Additionally, artificial intelligence technology seamlessly provides the organisation with all necessary inputs or information for the identification and appointment of the most qualified candidate for a specific position or employment opportunity during prescreening and selection. According to esteemed human resources practitioners, artificial intelligence (AI) is a transformative technological marvel that combines disparate elements to provide a large pool of qualified candidates and a precise ranking system (Bulut & Batur Dinler, 2023).

This rating algorithm helps to identify the best candidates for a job. This helps the company understand the AI software's feelings and observations about candidates' aptitude and attributes using the collected data and their analysis and evaluation to find the best candidates for the job. This helps businesses find the best applicant for their posts. According to some human resource specialists, artificial intelligence learns how firms choose the best individuals from many applicants. Additionally, some professionals have admitted to using AI technology to communicate with candidates for available positions (Zirar et al., 2023). However, some researchers have used similar AI programs for alternate communications. Chatbots can provide various types of applicant information to companies. This includes original data, prior experience, and other pertinent facts. These items were then transformed into a well-prepared curriculum vitae or résumé and a well-written job application, which were rigorously scrutinised by artificial intelligence software (Rodgers et al., 2023).

According to many esteemed human resources practitioners, artificial intelligence (AI) technology could provide a comprehensive synopsis of each prospective candidate after the interview or even after the entire recruitment process. This unique approach may reveal candidates' best qualities and areas of weakness in relation to their job's requirements. This approach may justify non-selection and candidate selection (Delecraz et al. 2022). It also allows applicants to ask further questions, even if they are unsure about the selection conclusion. This statement describes the benefits of AI (Chowdhury et al. 2023). Therefore, many human resource experts strongly support and use the stated strategies for not only human resource management, but also other tedious and administrative chores. Artificial intelligence can speed up such activities, saving business time and money (Vrontis et al., 2022). In this way, any employee can fix the problem without help from experienced workers.

BIBLIOMETRIC ANALYSIS METHOD

It is of utmost importance to meticulously examine The methodology employed in any research endeavour. As per the scholarly work of Zhang et al. (2021), it is evident that the use of the bibliometric approach is a fitting methodology for monitoring and presenting the statistical comprehension pertaining to a specific term or concept that has been disseminated within the realm of artificial intelligence (AI) and human resource management (HRM). The use of bibliometric analysis methodology empowers the scholarly investigator to meticulously scrutinise and meticulously document a repository of metadata information, thereby facilitating a comprehensive understanding of the propagation and diffusion of knowledge to the esteemed readership (Kaur et al., 2021). This proposition finds further validation in a recent bibliometric investigation conducted within the domains of AI and HRM. The "bibliometric" nomenclature connotes the statistical elucidation of published articles within a distinct domain or discipline, accentuating and documenting the specific concepts, studies, trends, methodologies, keywords, citations, and sources of scientific publications. The use of bibliometric analysis to conduct a literature review has gained considerable traction within the academic community. This methodological approach enables researchers to delve deeper into their respective fields of study by employing science-mapping techniques on relevant publication databases (Abdul Rahman et al., 2022). This observation is congruent with the findings of a comprehensive survey of scholarly works utilising targeted online databases, most notably the esteemed Scopus database, employing a rigorous methodology of bibliometric analysis (Ahmi, 2022). This meticulous approach facilitated the accumulation of a substantial corpus of publications and pertinent articles, thereby enhancing the robustness and comprehensiveness of this study. Scopus database, in its remarkable capacity, bestows upon its users unparalleled flexibility to traverse a myriad of bibliographic domains with utmost ease and finesse.

Defining Keywords

The use of appropriate keywords in the execution of a bibliometric review is imperative. In accordance with the study's defined objectives, the researcher employed the following query master keywords: artificial intelligence and human resource management. Meticulous researchers possess the capacity to discover a myriad of permutations, relevance, and combinations of the aforementioned keywords, thereby exhibiting a profound understanding of the subject matter at hand.

Henceforth, we conclude the exploration within the scope of the article title domain by employing the following query: (TITLE ((artificial intelligence OR AI OR digital* OR robot*)) AND TITLE((human resource management OR HRM))).

The use of a title search string will ensure a solid result pertaining to the keyword search (Ahmi, 2022).

Search Strategy

Utilising the online Scopus database, this academic study avails of a vast reservoir of published documents pertaining to the scope of AI-HRM. The Scopus online database was deliberately selected as the primary source of information for this study because it is widely recognised as a preeminent repository of citations and abstracts in the domains of technology, social science, business, and management, encompassing the intricate scopes of AI and HRM (Haba et al, 2022). It is worth noting that the entirety of the peer-reviewed articles that grace the pages of this esteemed Scopus online database emanates exclusively from highly reputable and esteemed academic publishers, namely, Elsevier, Emerald, Inderscience, Springer, and the Taylor and Francis Group (Kafi et al., 2023).

The decision to utilise solely the Scopus database was based on several key considerations that contributed to the robustness and reliability of the analysis. First, Scopus is widely recognised for its extensive scholarly literature encompassing a comprehensive range of academic disciplines and research domains. The inclusivity of reputable journals, conferences, and patents from diverse fields ensures a holistic view of the scientific landscape, enabling us to capture a comprehensive overview of scholarly outputs related to the research area (Dastane and Haba, 2023).

Second, Scopus is renowned for its meticulous indexing process, which ensures the inclusion of high-quality peer-reviewed publications. This feature is crucial in maintaining the integrity and credibility of bibliometric analysis, as it reduces the likelihood of inadvertently including low-quality or non-peer-reviewed sources that might skew the findings (Zaki et al, 2023).

Moreover, the user-friendly interface and robust search functionalities provided by Scopus facilitated the efficient and effective retrieval of relevant scholarly publications, enabling authors to conduct a thorough and exhaustive analysis within the scope of the research objectives (Fernandez et al., 2023).

While the authors acknowledge the presence of other notable databases, such as Web of Science and Google Scholar, each database has its own strengths and limitations. In this study, the authors carefully evaluated the specific requirements of the research objectives and determined that Scopus was best aligned with the selected criteria for comprehensive coverage, data integrity, and efficient accessibility (Ahmi, 2022).

The authors trust that their rationale for selecting Scopus as the primary database for bibliometric analysis is evident. Figure 1 serves as an illustrative representation of the intricately delineated steps encompassing the search strategy employed in this scholarly investigation as well as the meticulously outlined steps pertaining to the execution of bibliometric analysis.

Data Analysis Tools

To achieve the research objective and offer a thorough elucidation of the research questions posited in this study, we employed Biblioshiny, an outstanding application meticulously tailored for the Bibliometrix R package, to diligently carry out the bibliometric analysis (Aria & Cuccurullo, 2017). The foremost aim of this endeavour, characterised by an unwavering commitment, is to expedite the intricate undertaking of scientific bibliometric analysis. Figure 2 illustrates the multifarious stages and scrupulous analyses that have been pursued diligently throughout the trajectory of this sophisticated enquiry. The analyses expounded within this scholarly investigation have been systematically classified into two discernible categories: descriptive analysis and network analysis. The aforementioned analytical methodologies have predominantly been utilised to tackle the research questions (RQs) put forth in the earlier section of this chapter.

Figure 1. Flow diagram of the search strategy
Source: Ahmi (2022) and Morshidi et al. (2022)

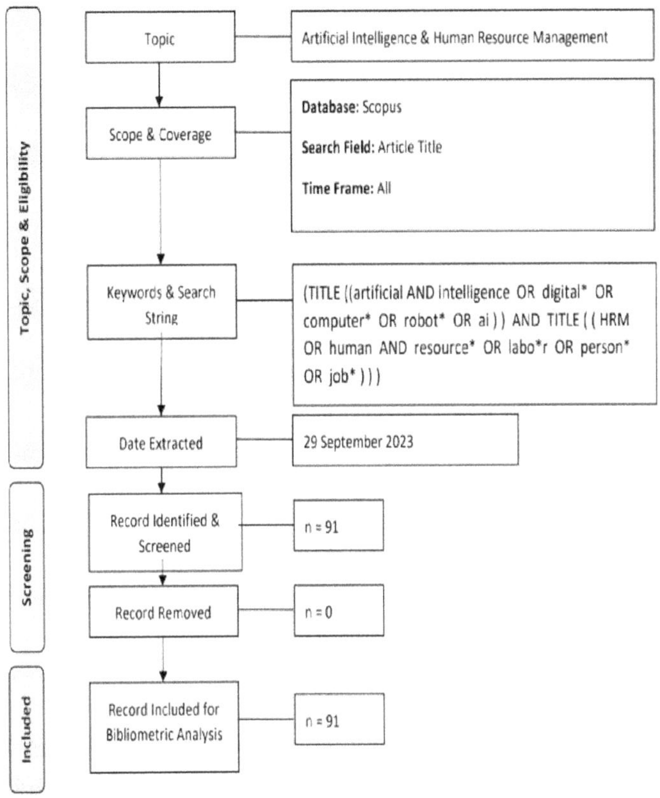

Figure 2. Detail steps for bibliometric analysis using Bibliometrix and Biblioshiny
Sources: Authors (guided by Kafi et al., 2023; Ahmi, 2022)

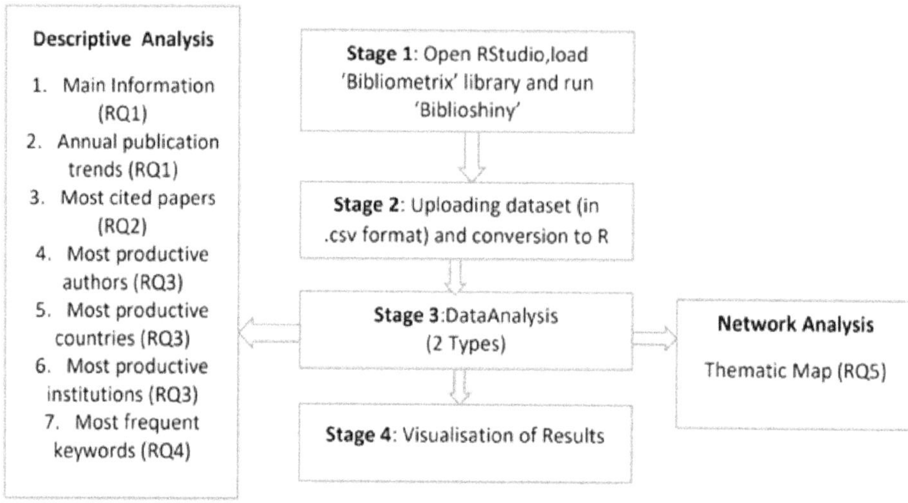

ANALYSIS AND RESULTS

This section delves into the research profile of AI-HRM, expounding upon the sources of publication spanning the years 2015 to 2023. The aforementioned encompasses a comprehensive compilation of data pertaining to the present condition of scholarly publications, prevailing research patterns, highly cited documents, authors of prolific output, nations and institutions of origin, sources of publication, and keywords employed by the authors.

Main Information

The inception of scholarly discourse pertaining to the intersection of AI and the domains of human resource management can be traced back to 2015, as evidenced by a seminal publication that covered the esteemed Scopus database. The corpus of scholarly publications exhibits a commendable surge, evincing a remarkable annual growth rate of 51.67%

Table 1. Main information about selected documents

Description	Results
MAIN INFORMATION ABOUT DATA	
Timespan	2015:2023
Sources (Journals, Books, etc)	72
Documents	91
Annual Growth Rate %	51.67
Document Average Age	1.48
Average citations per doc	11.29
References	1
DOCUMENT CONTENTS	
Keywords Plus (ID)	272
Author's Keywords (DE)	167
AUTHORS	
Authors	246
Authors of single-authored docs	22
AUTHORS COLLABORATION	
Single-authored docs	23
Co-Authors per Doc	2.95
International co-authorships %	24.18
DOCUMENT TYPES	
Article	37
Book	2
Book chapter	16
Conference paper	32
Erratum	1
Retracted	1
Review	2

Annual Publication Trends

The annual publication trends from 2015 to 2023 are presented in Table 2 and Figure 3. They show the total number of publications, the total number of citations, citations per document, and citations per year. From this bibliometric study, we can see that 2022 and 2023 have the most publications in the field of AI-HRM, with a total of 22 and 27 works, respectively. Because of the post COVID-19 pandemic, there may be a surge in academic publications.

Table 2. Annual publications trends

Year	TP	TC	C/D	C/Y	Citable Years
2015	1	75	75	8.33	9
2018	2	81	40.5	6.75	6
2019	3	339	113	22.6	5
2020	13	122	9.38	2.35	4
2021	22	155	7.05	2.35	3
2022	22	204	9.27	4.64	2
2023	27	51	1.82	1.82	1
Total	90	1027	181.02		

Figure 3. Growth and publication impact per year

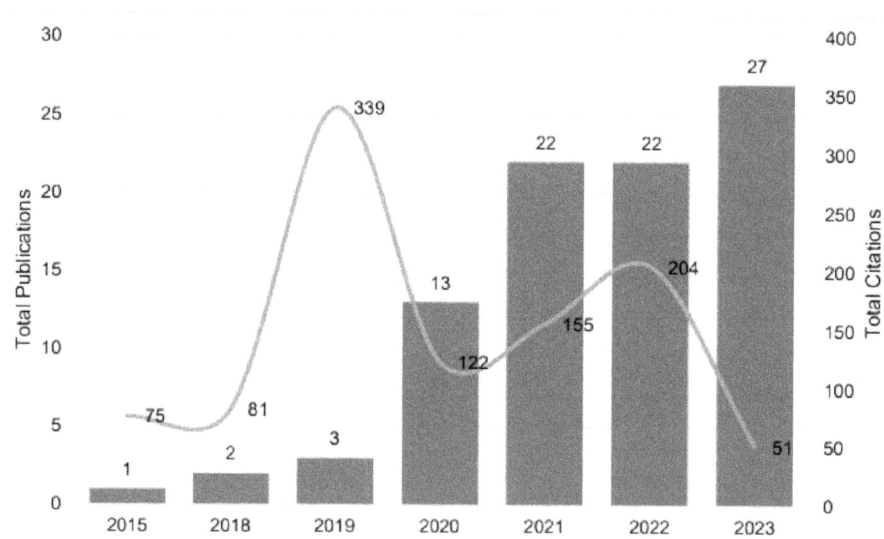

Most Cited Papers

Table 3 shows the articles that garnered the highest number of citations, both on a global scale and within the academic community. The preeminent scholarly publication serves as an arbiter of the article's prominence in the academic sphere. In a broader context, global citations serve as a manifestation of the recurring citation rate on an annual basis, specifically in instances where data retrieval has taken place. The preeminent scholarly work authored by Tembe et al. (2019), boasting an impressive citation count of 294, delves into the intricate scope of AI-HRM. While perusing the scholarly landscape, one cannot help but be captivated by the intellectual prowess exhibited in academic discourse. It is with great pleasure that authors draw your esteemed attention to the second most-cited article by the erudite Vrontis et al. (2022). This seminal work, adorned with staggering 166 citations, delves into the intricate AI-HRM complexities, shedding light on the multifaceted challenges that beset this noble endeavour. In a similar vein, authors encourage readers to cast your discerning gaze upon the third most-cited article, crafted by Strohmeier and Piazza in 2015. This scholarly masterpiece, adorned with no fewer than 75 citations, signifies early academic ventures in the AI-HRM field. These intellectual endeavours serve as testaments to the indomitable spirit of human enquiry, as we strive to comprehend and address the complexities of the AI-HRM world.

Table 3. Top 20 highly cited documents

No.	Author(s)	Title	Source Title	TC	C/Y
1	Tambe P.; Cappelli P.; Yakubovich V. (2019)	Artificial intelligence in human resources management: Challenges and A path forward	California Management Review	294	58.80
2	Vrontis D.; Christofi M.; Pereira V.; Tarba S.; Makrides A.; Trichina E. (2022)	Artificial intelligence, robotics, advanced technologies and human resource management: a systematic review	International Journal of Human Resource Management	166	83.00
3	Strohmeier S.; Piazza F. (2015)	Artificial intelligence techniques in human resource management—A conceptual exploration	Intelligent Systems Reference Library	75	8.33
4	Jia Q.; Guo Y.; Li R.; Li Y.; Chen Y. (2018)	A conceptual artificial intelligence application framework in human resource management	Proceedings of the International Conference on Electronic Business (ICEB)	64	10.67
5	Abdeldayem M.M.; Aldulaimi S.H. (2020)	Trends and opportunities of artificial intelligence in human resource management: Aspirations for public sector in Bahrain	International Journal of Scientific and Technology Research	55	13.75
6	Votto A.M.; Valecha R.; Najafirad P.; Rao H.R. (2021)	Artificial Intelligence in Tactical Human Resource Management: A Systematic Literature Review	International Journal of Information Management Data Insights	45	15.00
7	Berhil S.; Benlahmar H.; Labani N. (2019)	A review paper on artificial intelligence at the service of human resources management	Indonesian Journal of Electrical Engineering and Computer Science	37	7.40
8	Qamar Y.; Agrawal R.K.; Samad T.A.; Chiappetta Jabbour C.J. (2021)	When technology meets people: the interplay of artificial intelligence and human resource management	Journal of Enterprise Information Management	31	10.33
9	Chowdhury S.; Dey P.; Joel-Edgar S.; Bhattacharya S.; Rodriguez-Espindola O.; Abadie A.; Truong L. (2023)	Unlocking the value of artificial intelligence in human resource management through AI capability framework	Human Resource Management Review	31	31.00
10	Kshetri N. (2020)	Evolving uses of artificial intelligence in human resource management in emerging economies in the global South: some preliminary evidence	Management Research Review	21	5.25
11	Garg V.; Srivastav S.; Gupta A. (2018)	Application of Artificial Intelligence for Sustaining Green Human Resource Management	2018 International Conference on Automation and Computational Engineering, ICACE 2018	17	2.83
12	Arora M.; Prakash A.; Mittal A.; Singh S. (2021)	HR Analytics and Artificial Intelligence-Transforming Human Resource Management	2021 International Conference on Decision Aid Sciences and Application, DASA 2021	14	4.67
13	Qi L.; Yao K. (2021) RETRACTED IN 2023	Artificial intelligence enterprise human resource management system based on FPGA high performance computer hardware	Microprocessors and Microsystems	13	4.33
14	Bankins S. (2021)	The ethical use of artificial intelligence in human resource management: a decision-making framework	Ethics and Information Technology	13	4.33

continued on following page

Table 3. Continued

No.	Author(s)	Title	Source Title	TC	C/Y
15	Rodgers W.; Murray J.M.; Stefanidis A.; Degbey W.Y.; Tarba S.Y. (2023)	An artificial intelligence algorithmic approach to ethical decision-making in human resource management processes	Human Resource Management Review	11	11.00
16	Palos-Sánchez P.R.; Baena-Luna P.; Badicu A.; Infante-Moro J.C. (2022)	Artificial Intelligence and Human Resources Management: A Bibliometric Analysis	Applied Artificial Intelligence	11	5.50
17	Tewari I.; Pant M. (2020)	Artificial Intelligence Reshaping Human Resource Management: A Review	Proceedings of IEEE International Conference on Advent Trends in Multidisciplinary Research and Innovation, ICATMRI 2020	11	2.75
18	Aldulaimi S.H.; Abdeldayem M.M.; Mowafak B.M.; Abdulaziz M.M. (2021)	Experimental perspective of artificial intelligence technology in human resources management	Studies in Computational Intelligence	8	2.67
19	Caldés R.G. (2019)	Big data and artificial intelligence in public sector human resource management; [Big data e inteligencia artificial en la gestión de los recursos humanos del sector público]	Revista Catalana de Dret Public	8	1.60
20	Song Y.; Wu R. (2021)	Analysing human-computer interaction behaviour in human resource management system based on artificial intelligence technology	Knowledge Management Research and Practice	8	2.67

Most Productive Authors

Table 4 presents a comprehensive overview of the previous authors in terms of productivity. It showcases esteemed individuals who have made significant contributions to the field, delineating their total publication count, the number of papers that have garnered citations, the cumulative citation count, the h index, and the year in which their publication journey commenced. In accordance with the data shown in Table 4, Hamdan, A emerged as a preeminent luminary within the AI-HRM field. The sheer magnitude of his scholarly output is nothing short of remarkable, as evidenced by the prodigious tally of the three articles. Subsequently, we encounter the scholarly contributions of Prereira V, who has also authored a commendable assemblage of three articles, and Ghosh S, whose work boasts a respectable compilation of two documents.

Table 4. Most productive authors

Author's Name	TP	NCP	TC	h-Index	g-Index	PYS	m-Index
Hamdan, A.	3	0	0	0	1	2023	0.000
Pereira, V.	3	2	168	2	1	2022	1.000
Ghosh, S.	2	0	0	0	1	2023	0.000
Temsamani, Y.K.	2	2	7	2	0	2021	0.667
Pandey, A.	2	0	0	0	1	2023	0.000
Aldulaimi, S.H.	2	2	63	2	0	2020	0.500
Garg, V.	2	2	19	2	0	2018	0.333
Chilamkurti, N.	2	0	0	0	1	2023	0.000
Votto, A.M.	2	1	45	1	1	2021	0.333
Chowdhury, S.	2	2	33	2	0	2023	2.000
Notes: TP = Total Publications; NCP=Number of cited papers; TC= Total Citations; PYS= Publication year start							

Most Productive Countries

Table 5 displays a comprehensive list of the 20 nations that have demonstrated productivity in terms of publishing papers, with a minimum threshold of two publications. The nations that have demonstrated the highest levels of scholarly output in the AI-HRM field include India, China, the United States, the United Kingdom, Bahrain, Morocco, Australia, France, Italy, Bangladesh, Canada, Germany, Spain, Cyprus, and Malaysia.

Table 5. Top countries which published two or more documents

Country	Frequency	%
India	70	76.92
China	46	50.55
UK	24	26.37
USA	24	26.37
Bahrain	16	17.58
Morocco	8	8.79
Australia	6	6.59
France	6	6.59
Italy	6	6.59
Bangladesh	5	5.49
Canada	5	5.49
Germany	5	5.49
Spain	5	5.49
Cyprus	4	4.40
Malaysia	4	4.40
Saudi Arabia	4	4.40
Finland	3	3.30
Indonesia	3	3.30
United Arab Emirates	3	3.30
Netherlands	2	2.20

Most Productive Institutions

Similarly, researchers employed Biblioshiny as a tool for extracting institutions with the highest level of productivity. According to the quantity of publications produced by each organisation, Table 6 provides a thorough overview of the affiliations or institutions that have shown the highest levels of productivity. To enhance clarity, the table includes the top 22 affiliations. According to Table 6, Amity University and Applied Science University (ASU) emerged as the leading institutions in terms of productivity in the field of AI-HRM. With eight noteworthy total of 8 publications, both universities demonstrate a strong commitment to debating and disseminating knowledge on this subject matter.

Table 6. Top institutions which published two or more documents

Institution	TP	%
Amity University	4	4.40%
Applied Science University	4	4.40%
Ahlia University	3	3.30%
University of Birmingham	3	3.30%
University of Business and Technology	3	3.30%
La Trobe University	2	2.20%
Shiv Nadar Institution of Eminence deemed to be University	2	2.20%
Universitat Oberta de Catalunya	2	2.20%
Aston University	2	2.20%
GITAM University	2	2.20%
Vaasan Yliopisto	2	2.20%
TBS Business School	2	2.20%
College of Business and Finance	2	2.20%
The University of Texas at San Antonio	2	2.20%
The University of North Carolina at Greensboro	2	2.20%
Hohai University	2	2.20%
Mohammed V University in Rabat	2	2.20%
Maharaja Agrasen Institute of Technology	2	2.20%
Aston Business School	2	2.20%
School of Management Fudan University	2	2.20%
Galgotias University	2	2.20%
Birmingham Business School	2	2.20%

Most Productive Source Titles

The corpus of scholarly work comprises 91 articles disseminated across various esteemed academic journals. The analysis of publication sources was conducted based on the acquired data and is displayed in Table 7. To promote simplicity, we shall proceed to present the particulars of the foremost decadal periodicals, ensuring that each journal boasts a minimum of two published articles. The empirical data presented in Table 7, which are situated below, unequivocally demonstrate that Disruptive Artificial Intelligence and Sustainable Human Resource Management: Impacts and Innovations - The Future of HR, a publication curated by the esteemed IEEE Xplore, boasts the most substantial corpus of scholarly articles. This preeminent journal, distinguished by its unwavering commitment to the advancement of knowledge in the scope of AI-HRM, has amassed an impressive aggregate of five meticulously crafted publications. Subsequent literary works encompass the esteemed Lunk Notes in Networks and Systems, as well as the illustrious Journal of Physics: Conference Series. A comprehensive depiction of the evolution of journal productivity over the years is presented in Table 7.

Table 7. Most productive source titles

Source Title	TP	NCP	h-Index	g-Index	Citable Year	PYS	m-Index
Disruptive Artificial Intelligence and Sustainable Human Resource Management: Impacts and Innovations - The Future of HR	5	0	0	0	1	2023	0.00
Lecture Notes in Networks and Systems	4	4	1	1	2	2022	0.50
Journal of Physics: Conference Series	4	4	2	2	4	2020	0.50
Studies in Computational Intelligence	3	3	1	2	3	2021	0.33
Artificial Intelligence Techniques in Human Resource Management	3	1	0	0	1	2023	0.00
Mathematical Problems in Engineering	2	2	1	2	3	2021	0.33
Human Resource Management Review	2	2	2	2	1	2023	2.00
Lecture Notes in Electrical Engineering	2	2	1	1	4	2020	0.25
International Journal of Scientific and Technology Research	2	0	2	2	4	2020	0.50
Notes: TP=Total Publications; NCP=Number of Cited Papers; TC=Total citations; PYS= Publication Start Year							

Most Frequent Keywords

In this bibliometric study, the researchers meticulously examined the prevailing methodologies utilised in the domain of AI-HRM. The objective was to conduct a comparative analysis, thereby shedding light on various approaches commonly employed in this field. In the current investigation, Table 8 provides a comprehensive overview of the frequently employed terms, along with their corresponding lists of keywords. The following presentation, denoted as Table 8, shows the author's keywords and indexed keywords of the preeminent 10 authors. It is worth noting that these keywords manifested on more than two occasions.

Table 8. Top keywords

Author's Keywords	Occurrences	Indexed Keywords	Occurrences
Artificial Intelligence	65	Human Resource Management	88
Human Resource Management	52	Artificial Intelligence	56
Machine Learning	7	Information Management	29
Recruitment and Selection	5	Resource Allocation	29
Big Data	4	Natural Resources Management	27
Hr Analytics	4	Management	12
Organisational Resources	4	Decision Making	8
Ai	3	Performance Appraisal	7
Deep Learning	3	Personnel Training	7
Hrm	3	Big Data	6
Information Technology	3	Competition	6
Potential Benefits	3	Deep Learning	6
Public Sector	3	Training And Development	6
Sustainability	3	Employment	5
Systematic Literature Review	3	Hospital Information System	5
Augmented Intelligence	2	Machine Learning	5
Autonomous Ai	2	Organizational Management	5
Chatbots	2	Competitive Advantage	4
Covid 19	2	Decision Support Systems	4
Data Analysis	2	Digital Storage	4
Data Mining	2	Intelligent Decision-Support Systems	4
Decision-Making	2	Sustainable Development	4
Emerging Technologies	2	Article	3
Ethics	2	Compensation (Personnel)	3
Fourth Industrial Revolution	2	Data Handling	3

Thematic Themes

Figures 4 and 5 depict the thematic maps both before and after the onset of the COVID-19 pandemic, respectively. Figure 4 depicts the pre-pandemic locations of these themes. Themes of high centrality and density are commonly seen and extensively discussed in the existing literature, making them the focal point of AI-HRM research. The predominant focus within this quadrant pertains to the AI-HRM domain. The only three themes pertaining to this map were human resource management, artificial intelligence, and natural resource management. In contrast, Figure 5 illustrates the spatial arrangement of thematic elements pertaining to AI-HRM in the context of the COVID-19 pandemic. It is evident that the topics of AI-HRM have emerged as fundamental and overarching issues in contemporary AI-HRM research. The utilisation of digital transformation, ethical technology issues, and sustainable development have become emerging issues to be studied. Training and development, personnel compensation, and competitive advantage have been seen as prominent focal points, whereas machine learning and marketing-related aspects are identified as niche areas of interest. The developing trend in the discipline embarks on research undertaking in AI-HRM, as seen in the lower-left quadrant of Figure 5.

Figure 4. Thematic map (before COVID-19)

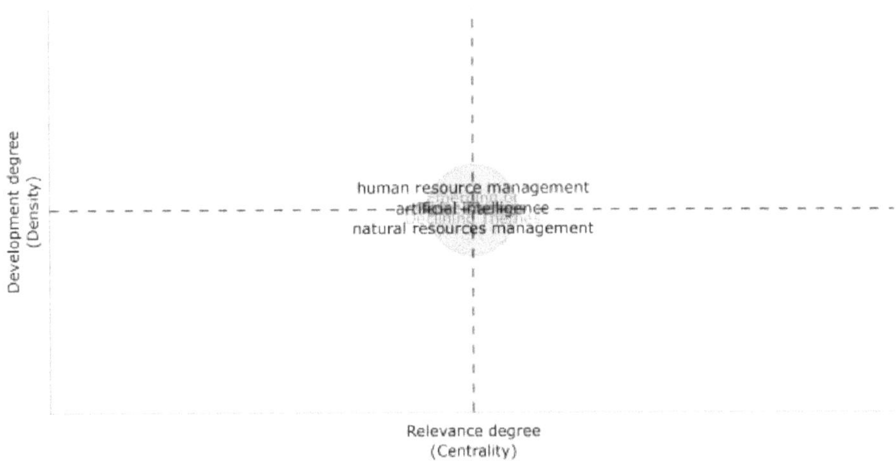

Figure 5. Thematic map (after COVID-19)

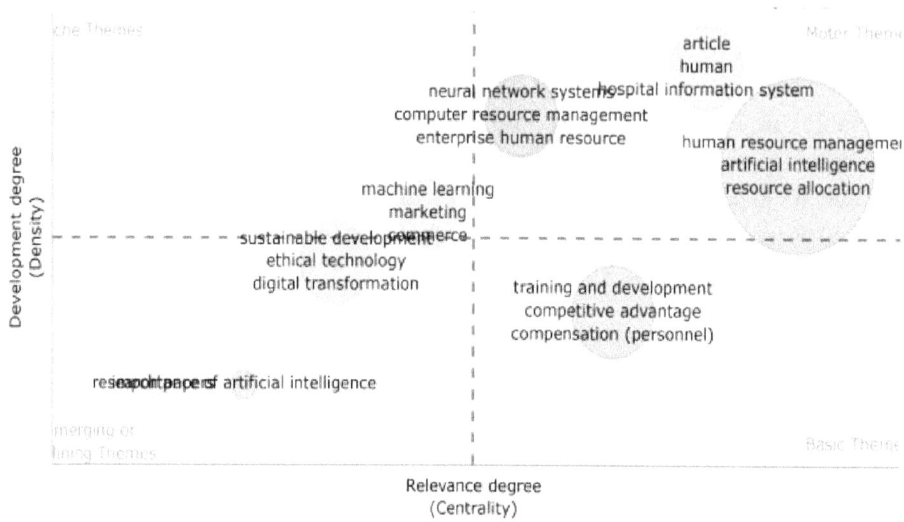

DISCUSSION

This comprehensive bibliometric analysis delves into the field of AI-HRM research, encompassing the temporal dimensions preceding, during, and subsequent to the COVID-19 pandemic. Evidently, the authors have successfully addressed the gap in the literature by conducting a bibliometric analysis of the AI-HRM trend prior to, during, and after the pandemic. This investigation revealed a remarkable proliferation of scholarly publications pertaining to this domain. This is because interest in the field is rapidly growing. Consequently, this surge in research output necessitates heightened impetus for further investigations in the realm of AI-HRM. The discourse surrounding noteworthy contributions proffered by preceding erudite scholars has been meticulously examined and expounded throughout the course of the past nine years.

The advent of artificial intelligence (AI) has resulted in profound metamorphosis within the realm of human resource management (HRM) across diverse organisational landscapes. The concept of AI-mediated Human Resource Management (HRM) entails the utilisation of artificial intelligence systems and tools to aid or supplant human HR professionals in the execution of diverse HR tasks. These tasks encompass but are not limited to recruitment, training, performance evaluation, compensation, and fostering employee engagement. The utilisation of artificial intelligence in the realm of human resource management holds immense potential for both employers and employees, as it bestows upon them a plethora of advantageous outcomes. These include, but are not limited to, cost reduction, efficiency amplification, accuracy refinement, fairness elevation, and innovation cultivation (Mer & Virdi, 2023).

While the antecedent investigations and associated lexemes scrutinised do indeed evince the salience of AI-HRM enquiry, it is incumbent upon us, in light of the COVID-19 pandemic, to discern that forthcoming erudites may adopt a more discerning stance vis-à-vis the extant discourse. This is particularly germane when considering the research constellations that warrant due attention to ameliorate the conspicuous gaps that presently exist. In the realm of AI-HRM scholarship, it is imperative for scholars to comprehensively analyse their respective domains and academic endeavours, taking into account the multifaceted viewpoints of various stakeholders, most notably esteemed HRM practitioners and dedicated employees (Allal-Chérif et al., 2021). Within the context of the pandemic era, an intriguing matter of consequence arises in relation to the convergence of artificial intelligence and human resource management. Specifically, a notable deficiency emerges in the scholarly exploration of this subject matter, namely, the dearth of policy perspectives. An analysis pertaining to the effective governance of prospective technological misconduct mandates a thorough exploration of the government's function and the nation's policy within a particular jurisdiction.

From a more practical perspective, the primary catalysts behind the adoption of AI-mediated Human Resource Management (HRM) in the contemporary workplace can be attributed to three key factors: the escalating need for skilled personnel, the evolving characteristics of work, and the progression of technological advancements. The escalating need for talent arises from the burgeoning disparity in skills, advancing age of the workforce, and intensifying global contest for skilled individuals (Malik et al. 2020). Artificial Intelligence (AI) has the potential to engender a myriad of legal and ethical quandaries, encompassing concerns surrounding data protection, privacy preservation, bias mitigation, discrimination prevention, liability attribution, and the imperative of obtaining informed consent (Kaur et al., 2021).

In its quest for advancement and sophistication, artificial intelligence ought to demonstrate a profound reverence for the fundamental principles of human dignity, autonomy, and diversity. These principles, which lie at the core of our societal fabric, demand unwavering acknowledgement and adherence from the realm of AI (Budhwar et al., 2023). By embracing and upholding these principles, AI can truly transcend its technological origins and become a force that not only augments human capabilities but also fosters a Furthermore, the concept of collaboration in the realm of artificial intelligence entails the imperative that its development and implementation should be undertaken in a manner that embraces the active engagement and consultation of all pertinent stakeholders. These stakeholders encompass a wide array of entities, including but not limited to employers, employees, labour unions, customers, suppliers, regulatory bodies, and society at large. The imperative of artificial intelligence (AI) extends beyond its technical advantages and functional capabilities. It is incumbent on AI to cultivate an environment that nurtures trust, facilitates effective communication, and promotes harmonious cooperation among all stakeholders involved (Brynjolfsson & McAfee, 2017). Third, innovation necessitates the presence of a lucid and well-defined human resource management (HRM) vision, purpose, and strategy that serves as an impetus for the advancement of artificial intelligence (AI). It is imperative that artificial intelligence (AI) systems are not only developed with technical proficiency but also with a keen awareness of the organisational goals, values, and culture they are intended to serve. This alignment between AI and the aforementioned aspects is of utmost importance, as it ensures that the deployment and utilisation of AI technologies are in harmony with the overarching objectives and principles of the organisation at hand.

A key challenge that employers face is maintaining compliance with regulations and reporting requirements. Automations can help by gathering and organizing data, streamlining compliance checks, ensuring policies and rules are followed, and creating accurate reports. This helps to lower the risk of failing to accurately follow regulations, make HR more transparent, and create an agility layer to more easily deal with changing requirements. Automations can also ensure accuracy and eliminate human errors, streamline payroll and timekeeping procedures, assist with employee onboarding and offboarding, and improve training and development programs. To embrace AI, one should think of it as another human brain and learn to relinquish control.

CONCLUSION

In summary, this chapter discusses the growth of research in the field of Artificial Intelligence in Human Resource Management (AI-HRM) before, during, and after the COVID-19 pandemic. The use of artificial intelligence in HRM has the potential to bring advantages to both employers and employees. However, there is a lack of policy perspectives in scholarly research on the governance of AI-mediated HRM. The primary drivers of AI-HRM adoption are the escalating need for skilled personnel, the evolving nature of work, and technological advancements. The development of AI-HRM must also embrace principles of human dignity, autonomy, and diversity, and involve active engagement of stakeholders.

REFERENCES

Abdul Rahman, N. A., Ahmi, A., Jraisat, L., & Upadhyay, A. (2022). Examining the trend of humanitarian supply chain studies: Pre, during and post COVID-19 pandemic. *Journal of Humanitarian Logistics and Supply Chain Management, 12*(4), 594–617. doi:10.1108/JHLSCM-01-2022-0012

Ahmi, A. (2022). *Bibliometric Analysis using R for Non-Coders: A practical handbook in conducting bibliometric analysis studies using Biblioshiny for Bibliometrix R package.* Academic Press.

Aldulaimi, S. H., Abdeldayem, M. M., Mowafak, B. M., & Abdulaziz, M. M. (2021). Experimental perspective of artificial intelligence technology in human resources management. *Studies in Computational Intelligence, 954*, 487–511. doi:10.1007/978-3-030-72080-3_26

Allal-Chérif, O., Yela Aránega, A., & Castaño Sánchez, R. (2021). Intelligent recruitment: How to identify, select, and retain talents from around the world using artificial intelligence. *Technological Forecasting and Social Change, 169*(January), 120822. Advance online publication. doi:10.1016/j.techfore.2021.120822

Anayat, S. (2023). Human resources management after industry 4.0: Blending AI and HRM. *Strategic Human Resource Management in the Hospitality Industry: A Digitalized Economic Paradigm,* 97–115. doi:10.4018/978-1-6684-7494-5.ch005

Aria, M., & Cuccurullo, C. (2017). bibliometrix: An R-tool for comprehensive science mapping analysis. *Journal of Informetrics, 11*(4), 959–975. doi:10.1016/j.joi.2017.08.007

Arora, M., Prakash, A., Mittal, A., & Singh, S. (2021). HR Analytics and Artificial Intelligence-Transforming Human Resource Management. *2021 International Conference on Decision Aid Sciences and Application, DASA 2021*, 288–293. 10.1109/DASA53625.2021.9682325

Avrahami, D., Pessach, D., Singer, G., & Chalutz Ben-Gal, H. (2022). A human resources analytics and machine-learning examination of turnover: Implications for theory and practice. *International Journal of Manpower, 43*(6), 1405–1424. doi:10.1108/IJM-12-2020-0548

Bankar, S., & Shukla, K. (2023). Performance Management and Artificial Intelligence: A Futuristic Conceptual Framework. In Contemporary Studies of Risks in Emerging Technology, Part B (pp. 341–360). Emerald Publishing Limited. doi:10.1108/978-1-80455-566-820231019

Bankins, S. (2021). The ethical use of artificial intelligence in human resource management: A decision-making framework. *Ethics and Information Technology, 23*(4), 841–845. doi:10.100710676-021-09619-6

Basu, S., Majumdar, B., Mukherjee, K., Munjal, S., & Palaksha, C. (2023). Artificial Intelligence–HRM Interactions and Outcomes: A Systematic Review and Causal Configurational Explanation. *Human Resource Management Review, 33*(1), 100893. doi:10.1016/j.hrmr.2022.100893

Berhil, S., Benlahmar, H., & Labani, N. (2019). A review paper on artificial intelligence at the service of human resources management. *Indonesian Journal of Electrical Engineering and Computer Science, 18*(1), 32–40. doi:10.11591/ijeecs.v18.i1.pp32-40

Brynjolfsson, B. Y. E., & McAfee, A. (2017). Artificial Intelligence for Real. *Harvard Business Review,* (1), 1–31. https://starlab-alliance.com/wp-content/uploads/2017/09/AI-Article.pdf

Budhwar, P., Chowdhury, S., Wood, G., Aguinis, H., Bamber, G. J., Beltran, J. R., Boselie, P., Lee Cooke, F., Decker, S., DeNisi, A., Dey, P. K., Guest, D., Knoblich, A. J., Malik, A., Paauwe, J., Papagiannidis, S., Patel, C., Pereira, V., Ren, S., ... Varma, A. (2023). Human resource management in the age of generative artificial intelligence: Perspectives and research directions on ChatGPT. *Human Resource Management Journal, 33*(3), 606–659. doi:10.1111/1748-8583.12524

Bulut, A., & Batur Dinler, Ö. (2023). The Effect of Industry 4.0 and Artificial Intelligence on Human Resource Management. *Uluslararası Doğu Anadolu Fen Mühendislik ve Tasarım Dergisi, 5*(2), 143–166. doi:10.47898/ijeased.1306881

Caldes, R. (2019). Big data and artificial intelligence in public sector human resource management. *Rev. Catalana Dret Pub., 58*(9).

Chowdhury, S., Dey, P., Joel-Edgar, S., Bhattacharya, S., Rodriguez-Espindola, O., Abadie, A., & Truong, L. (2020). Unlocking the value of artificial intelligence in human resource management through AI capability framework. *Human Resource Management Review, 33*(1), 100899. doi:10.1016/j.hrmr.2022.100899

Chowdhury, S., Dey, P., Joel-Edgar, S., Bhattacharya, S., Rodriguez-Espindola, O., Abadie, A., & Truong, L. (2023). Unlocking the value of artificial intelligence in human resource management through AI capability framework. *Human Resource Management Review, 33*(1), 100899. doi:10.1016/j.hrmr.2022.100899 da Silva, L. B. P., Soltovski, R., Pontes, J., Treinta, F. T., Leitão, P., Mosconi, E., de Resende, L. M. M., & Yoshino, R. T. (2022). Human resources management 4.0: Literature review and trends. *Computers & Industrial Engineering, 168*(March), 108111. Advance online publication. doi:10.1016/j.cie.2022.108111

Dastane, O., & Haba, H. F. (2023). The Landscape of Digital Natives Research: A Bibliometric and Science Mapping Analysis. *FIIB Business Review, 0*(0). Advance online publication. doi:10.1177/23197145221137960

Delecraz, S., Eltarr, L., Becuwe, M., Bouxin, H., Boutin, N., & Oullier, O. (2022). Responsible Artificial Intelligence in Human Resources Technology: An innovative inclusive and fair by design matching algorithm for job recruitment purposes. *Journal of Responsible Technology, 11*(November), 100041. doi:10.1016/j.jrt.2022.100041

Fernandez, D., Dastane, O., Omar Zaki, H., & Aman, A. (2023). Robotic process automation: Bibliometric reflection and future opportunities. *European Journal of Innovation Management*. Advance online publication. doi:10.1108/EJIM-10-2022-0570

Garg, V., Srivastav, S., & Gupta, A. (2018). Application of Artificial Intelligence for Sustaining Green Human Resource Management. *2018 International Conference on Automation and Computational Engineering, ICACE 2018,* 113–116. 10.1109/ICACE.2018.8686988

Giraud, L., Zaher, A., Hernandez, S., & Akram, A. A. (2022). The impacts of artificial intelligence on managerial skills. *Journal of Decision Systems*, 1–34. doi:10.1080/12460125.2022.2069537

Haba, H. F., Bredillet, C., & Dastane, O. (2022). Green consumer research: Trends and way forward based on bibliometric analysis. *Cleaner and Responsible Consumption*, 100089.

He, T., Sun, Z., Shi, Q., Zhu, M., Wang, H., Wang, J., Wen, F., & Lee, C. (2019). Self-Powered Intuitive Control Interface Towards Diversified Gaming, AI, and Online Shopping Applications. *2019 20th International Conference on Solid-State Sensors, Actuators and Microsystems and Eurosensors XXXIII, TRANSDUCERS 2019 and EUROSENSORS XXXIII*, 2452–2455. 10.1109/TRANSDUCERS.2019.8808310

Horodyski, P. (2023). Applicants' perception of artificial intelligence in the recruitment process. *Computers in Human Behavior Reports, 11*(January), 100303. doi:10.1016/j.chbr.2023.100303

Huang, X., Yang, F., Zheng, J., Feng, C., & Zhang, L. (2023). Personalized human resource management via HR analytics and artificial intelligence: Theory and implications. *Asia Pacific Management Review*, (4), 598–610. Advance online publication. doi:10.1016/j.apmrv.2023.04.004

Hussain, A., Mkpojiogu, E. O. C., Abubakar, H., & Hassan, H. M. (2019). A mobile usability test assessment of an online shopping application. *Journal of Computational and Theoretical Nanoscience*, *16*(5–6), 2511–2516. doi:10.1166/jctn.2019.7923

Jacob Fernandes França, T., São Mamede, H., Pereira Barroso, J. M., & Pereira Duarte dos Santos, V. M. (2023). Artificial intelligence applied to potential assessment and talent identification in an organisational context. *Heliyon*, *9*(4), e14694. Advance online publication. doi:10.1016/j.heliyon.2023.e14694 PMID:37035361

Jatobá, M., Santos, J., Gutierriz, I., Moscon, D., Fernandes, P. O., & Teixeira, J. P. (2019). Evolution of Artificial Intelligence Research in Human Resources. *Procedia Computer Science*, *164*, 137–142. doi:10.1016/j.procs.2019.12.165

Jia, Q., Guo, Y., Li, R., Li, Y., & Chen, Y. (2018). A conceptual artificial intelligence application framework in human resource management. *Proceedings of the International Conference on Electronic Business (ICEB),* 106–114.

Kafi, A., Zainuddin, N., Saifudin, A. M., Shahron, S. A., Razalli, M. R., Musa, S., & Ahmi, A. (2023). Meta-analysis of food supply chain: Pre, during and post COVID-19 pandemic. *Agriculture & Food Security*, *12*(1), 1–22. doi:10.118640066-023-00425-5 PMID:36883120

Kaur, M., Rekha, A., & Resmi, A. (2021). Research landscape of artificial intelligence in human resource management: A bibliometric overview. In R. Yadav, R. Yadav, & S. B. Gupta (Eds.), *Artificial Intelligence and Speech Technology* (pp. 463–477). doi:10.1201/9781003150664-29

Khalifa, M., Al Baz, M., & Muttar, A. K. (2022). The Impact of Applying Artificial Intelligence on Human Resources Crisis Management: An Analytical Study on COVID19. *Information Sciences Letters*, *11*(1), 269–276. doi:10.18576/isl/110127

Kiran, P. R., Chaubey, A., & Shastri, R. K. (2023). Role of HR analytics and attrition on organisational performance: A literature review leveraging the SCM-TBFO framework. *Benchmarking*. Advance online publication. doi:10.1108/BIJ-06-2023-0412

Kshetri, N. (2020). Evolving uses of artificial intelligence in human resource management in emerging economies in the global South: Some preliminary evidence. *Management Research Review*, *44*(7), 970–990. doi:10.1108/MRR-03-2020-0168

Malik, A., Budhwar, P., & Kazmi, B. A. (2023). Artificial intelligence (AI)-assisted HRM: Towards an extended strategic framework. *Human Resource Management Review*, *33*(1), 100940. Advance online publication. doi:10.1016/j.hrmr.2022.100940

Malik, A., Budhwar, P., & Srikanth, N. R. (2020). Gig Economy, 4IR and Artificial Intelligence: Rethinking Strategic HRM. In Human & Technological Resource Management (HTRM): New Insights into Revolution 4.0 (pp. 75–88). Emerald Publishing Limited. doi:10.1108/978-1-83867-223-220201005

Mer, A., & Srivastava, A. (2023). Employee Engagement in the New Normal: Artificial Intelligence as a Buzzword or a Game Changer? In The Adoption and Effect of Artificial Intelligence on Human Resources Management, Part A (pp. 15–46). Emerald Publishing Limited. doi:10.1108/978-1-80382-027-920231002

Mer, A., & Virdi, A. S. (2023). Navigating the Paradigm Shift in HRM Practices Through the Lens of Artificial Intelligence: A Post-pandemic Perspective. In P. Tyagi, N. Chilamkurti, S. Grima, K. Sood, & B. Balusamy (Eds.), *The Adoption and Effect of Artificial Intelligence on Human Resources Management, Part A* (pp. 123–154). Emerald Publishing Limited. doi:10.1108/978-1-80382-027-920231007

Morshidi, A., b, K. Y. S., Yussof, K. M., Idris, R. Z., Idris, R., & Abas, A. (2022). Online work adjustment in the sustainable development context during COVID-19 pandemic: A systematic literature review. *International Journal of Work Innovation*, *3*(3), 269–288. doi:10.1504/IJWI.2022.127668

Muralidhar, S., Bharadwaj, A., & Bhat, K. P. (2022). Artificial intelligence and human resource management: A conceptual study. *BOHR International Journal of Advances in Management Research*, *2*(1), 72–80. doi:10.54646/bijamr.2023.20

Naseri, M. B., & Elliott, G. (2011). Role of demographics, social connectedness and prior internet experience in adoption of online shopping: Applications for direct marketing. *Journal of Targeting. Measurement and Analysis for Marketing*, *19*(2), 69–84. doi:10.1057/jt.2011.9

Palos-Sánchez, P. R., Baena-Luna, P., Badicu, A., & Infante-Moro, J. C. (2022). Artificial Intelligence and Human Resources Management: A Bibliometric Analysis. *Applied Artificial Intelligence*, *36*(1), 2145631. Advance online publication. doi:10.1080/08839514.2022.2145631

Pan, Y., & Froese, F. J. (2023). An interdisciplinary review of AI and HRM: Challenges and future directions. *Human Resource Management Review*, *33*(1), 100924. Advance online publication. doi:10.1016/j.hrmr.2022.100924

Panda, G., Dash, M. K., Samadhiya, A., Kumar, A., & Mulat-weldemeskel, E. (2023). Artificial intelligence as an enabler resiliency : past literature, present debate and future research directions. *International Journal of Industrial Engineering and Operations Management*. doi:10.1108/IJIEOM-05-2023-0047

Prikshat, V., Islam, M., Patel, P., Malik, A., Budhwar, P., & Gupta, S. (2023). AI-Augmented HRM: Literature review and a proposed multilevel framework for future research. *Technological Forecasting and Social Change*, *193*(April), 122645. doi:10.1016/j.techfore.2023.122645

Qamar, Y., Agrawal, R. K., Samad, T. A., & Jabbour, C. J. C. (2021). When technology meets people: The interplay of artificial intelligence and human resource management. *Journal of Enterprise Information Management*, *34*(4), 1339–1370. doi:10.1108/JEIM-11-2020-0436

Radonjić, A., Duarte, H., & Pereira, N. (2021, June). (2022). Artificial intelligence and HRM: HR managers' perspective on decisiveness and challenges. *European Management Journal*. Advance online publication. doi:10.1016/j.emj.2022.07.001

Rodgers, W., Murray, J. M., Stefanidis, A., Degbey, W. Y., & Tarba, S. Y. (2023). An artificial intelligence algorithmic approach to ethical decision-making in human resource management processes. *Human Resource Management Review*, *33*(1), 100925. doi:10.1016/j.hrmr.2022.100925

Safara, F. (2022). A Computational Model to Predict Consumer Behaviour During COVID-19 Pandemic. *Computational Economics*, *59*(4), 1525–1538. doi:10.100710614-020-10069-3 PMID:33169049

Singh, A., Kanaujia, A., Singh, V. K., & Vinuesa, R. (2023). Artificial intelligence for Sustainable Development Goals: Bibliometric patterns and concept evolution trajectories. *Sustainable Development (Bradford)*, (May), 1–31. doi:10.1002d.2706

Song, Y., & Wu, R. (2021). Analysing human-computer interaction behaviour in human resource management system based on artificial intelligence technology. *Knowledge Management Research and Practice*, *00*(00), 1–10. doi:10.1080/14778238.2021.1955630

Tambe, P., Yakubovich, V., & Cappelli, P. (2019, February). Artificial Intelligence in Human Resources Management: Challenges and a Path Forward. *California Management Review*, *61*(4), 15–42. doi:10.1177/0008125619867910

Varma, A., Dawkins, C., & Chaudhuri, K. (2023). Artificial intelligence and people management: A critical assessment through the ethical lens. *Human Resource Management Review*, *33*(1), 100923. doi:10.1016/j.hrmr.2022.100923

Vishwakarma, L. P., & Singh, R. K. (2023). An Analysis of the Challenges to Human Resource in Implementing Artificial Intelligence. In The Adoption and Effect of Artificial Intelligence on Human Resources Management, Part B (pp. 81–109). Emerald Publishing Limited. doi:10.1108/978-1-80455-662-720230006

Votto, A. M., Valecha, R., Najafirad, P., & Rao, H. R. (2021). Artificial Intelligence in Tactical Human Resource Management: A Systematic Literature Review. *International Journal of Information Management Data Insights*, *1*(2), 100047. doi:10.1016/j.jjimei.2021.100047

Vrontis, D., Christofi, M., Pereira, V., Tarba, S., Makrides, A., & Trichina, E. (2022). Artificial intelligence, robotics, advanced technologies and human resource management: A systematic review. *International Journal of Human Resource Management*, *33*(6), 1237–1266. doi:10.1080/09585192.2020.1871398

Zaki, H. O., Fernandez, D., Dastane, O., Aman, A., & Sanusi, S. (2023). Virtual reality in digital marketing: Research agenda based on bibliometric reflection. *Marketing Intelligence & Planning*, *41*(4), 505–524. doi:10.1108/MIP-12-2022-0568

Zhang, Y., Xu, S., Zhang, L., & Yang, M. (2021). Big data and human resource management research: An integrative review and new directions for future research. *Journal of Business Research*, *133*(April), 34–50. doi:10.1016/j.jbusres.2021.04.019

Zhang, Y., Zhang, M., Li, J., Liu, G., Yang, M. M., & Liu, S. (2021). A bibliometric review of a decade of research: Big data in business research – Setting a research agenda. *Journal of Business Research*, *131*(December), 374–390. doi:10.1016/j.jbusres.2020.11.004

Zirar, A., Ali, S. I., & Islam, N. (2023). Worker and workplace Artificial Intelligence (AI) coexistence: Emerging themes and research agenda. *Technovation*, *124*(June), 102747. doi:10.1016/j.technovation.2023.102747

Chapter 7
Benefits and Challenges Regarding the Adoption of HRM4.0 in Public Universities of Malaysia

Saeed Mohammed Qurtas Barzani
Universiti Utara Malaysia, Malaysia

Muhammad Imran
Universiti Utara Malaysia, Malaysia

Irfan Hameed
UCSI University, Malaysia & International University of Rabat, Morocco

ABSTRACT

The main purpose of this study is to explain the benefits and challenges of adopting HRM4.0 in public universities in Malaysia. Past studies stressed that the public universities of Malaysia are lacking in advanced HRM practices such as use of HRM 4.0. The semi-structured interviews have been conducted in the HR departments of six public sector universities in Malaysia. The findings of the study revealed five factors affecting the use of HRM 4.0 in HR departments of public universities, namely its advantages, system quality and usability, quick decision-making process, user satisfaction, and subjective norms. At the same time, the performance and productivity of the HR departments are positively related to the use of HRM 4.0. This study mainly focuses on the perceived modeling structure of HRM4.0 to assess the contributory factors and challenges that have an impact on the productivity of HRM4.0 in Malaysian public universities.

DOI: 10.4018/979-8-3693-0039-8.ch007

1. INTRODUCTION

According to the World Economic Forum (2020), 84% of respondents would accelerate the digitalization of work (such as video conferencing and remote working), and 50% would accelerate the automation of jobs, hence increasing the usage of digital technology. According to a survey conducted by Deloitte (Da Silva et al., 2022), just 33 percent of employees are prepared for technology advancements, particularly remote work, which poses a big challenge for HRM 4.0. This viewpoint is predicted to present challenges for the workforce. Further, the concept of HRM 4.0 was developed to help HR professionals understand how the changes brought about by the Industry would affect HRM 4.0 practices (Waris et al., 2022). Human resource management (HRM) has been given a new lease on life thanks to the use of Industry 4.0 technologies, which have made the field more nimble, safeguarded workers' well-being before entering the workforce, and unlocked the untapped human potential. Hence, HRM 4.0 must create a digital culture of digital workers who are trained in digital technology and have the necessary skills to increase productivity (Liboni et al., 2019).

The HRM 4.0 paradigm shift has far-reaching effects on how we educate our future workers and shape our industries (Malik et al., 2020). People will be able to showcase their abilities in ways that are more meaningful if they learn to engage in activities that demand more strategic planning, coordination, and originality and fewer simple, mindless tasks (Sima et al., 2020). Hence, human labor and individual analysis can be replaced by automated processes, and enormous amounts of data can be analyzed rapidly, intelligently, and precisely (Li et al., 2022). Pio et al., (2020), also demonstrated that Industries functioning in the information age utilize the digital technology developed by HRM 4.0. HRM duties benefit greatly from the incorporation of such technology into the management procedure.

Formerly time-consuming and laborious tasks like reviewing resumes and selecting candidates with the highest likelihood of meeting job requirements can now be automated with the help of big data and AI (Waris et al., 2021). Key performance indicators (KPIs) can help artificial intelligence (AI) evaluate workers and signal promotions, which were traditionally determined by a worker's tenure in a post and training requirements (Wang et al., 2022). Using AI as a management and learning system enables features like career plan development, which seeks to determine the best methods for fostering the growth, qualification, and motivation of the staff.

Despite the widespread adoption of HRM 4.0 software, it's crucial to be aware of how Industry is influenced by HRM 4.0 practices and how this, in turn, may affect employees and other key players in the labor market, such as schools, agencies that handle hiring and placement, and businesses that provide in-house training. Despite the research on HRM in the context of HRM 4.0, we still don't fully understand how

HRM 4.0 affects the development of HRM and how people management adapts to the problems that arise when smart technologies are used. So, research is needed to confirm HRM 4.0 trends by considering how digital technologies are being used in the business world. Our goal in writing this paper is to investigate the following:

RQs: Discuss the difficulties and opportunities presented by implementing HRM 4.0 at Malaysia's public universities.

The researcher's goal is to make a theoretical contribution to HRM 4.0 research in the context of public sector universities of Malaysia by deploying HRM 4.0 for new paths to be taken by the HRM 4.0 field and its practitioners, as well as by academia and their employees, in order to meet the challenges posed by the Fourth Industrial Revolution. The most important HRM 4.0 developments and their interconnections need to be explored further to make a theoretical framework (Imran et al., 2019). So, the purpose of this research is to reveal developments in HRM, competencies, strategies, and digitalisation-related facets. HRM4.0 also helps a lot with organizing and developing talent strategies, which are important for managing the workforce well.

Tracking the health and well-being of employees in the organization through the use of wearable devices such as the Internet of Things and developing talent strategies that are more suitable for employee well-being Intelligent artificial intelligence technology is not only used for organizational performance planning, tracking, and evaluation but also provides accurate and objective data based on organizational needs. Personalization and immediate feedback on employee performance are also auxiliary functions, better meeting the needs of high performers, providing effective personalized training for low performers, and improving the combat effectiveness of the entire organization (Hameed et al., 2019; Puhovichova & Jankelova, 2020).

The technology of the workplace faces the challenge of revising traditional HR practices to be able to adapt to and support the new employee-organization relationship. In the new relationship, employees are not limited to fixed workplaces and formal working hours; instead, they can work with people inside and outside the organization across organizational boundaries (Colbert et al., 2016). Intelligent technology continues to expand the way and scope of HRM 4.0 and provides new solutions. There is a more direct relationship between employees, HRM 4.0, and the organization (Isari et al., 2019). It supports a more flexible work environment and promotes friendly consideration of people's habits and attitudes towards contact (Hecklau et al., 2016). In the people-oriented nature of Industry 4.0, HRM 4.0 should become an organizational unit and promote its socially sustainable implementation (Hecklau et al., 2016).

The counterpart of digitalization in the academic sector is digitalization, which affects all parts of teaching and running a university, The traditional relationship between a teacher and a student has changed a lot in universities around the world (Telukdarie & Munsamy, 2019). Due to the increasing volume of the Internet and updated information, the traditional definition of teachers/educators/academics/professors may need to be redefined. In addition, the adoption of Industry 4.0 is changing the teaching skill requirements of education practitioners as their responsibilities change; hence, the reform of universities is imperative. The support and implementation measures of the corresponding environment are another problem that needs to be solved.

Higher education is at a crossroads as environmental, financial, and social problems pose challenges to the teaching effect of the theory used in the operation practice and curriculum content. The practice and technology of IR4.0 can meet the challenges of higher education universities to a large extent (Telukdarie & Munsamy, 2019). The structure of traditional universities is divided into three levels: strategy, operation, and control. Specifically, the strategic activities determine the objectives of the existence and development of the university, with teaching, research, and innovation as its objectives. Strategic functions have multiple dimensions such as HRM 4.0, research and innovation, teaching, financial management, institutional planning and resource management, marketing management, information technology, quality management, and student service.

The operational function is a sustainable activity for achieving the objectives of the strategic function (Telukdarie & Munsamy, 2019). Universities play the role of science communication through research and education (Hameed et al., 2022). HR, represented by university teaching and knowledge employment, enables many new projects in various countries to come into being and be implemented in practice. Their main focus is the deepening and application of professional knowledge namely the innovation, management, organization, management, and motivation of scientific work (Shobaki et al., 2017). Since HRM 4.0 revolution will have a significant impact on the way people live and work, many countries including Malaysia want to keep up with the pace and join the Industrial Community (Halili et al., 2021).

Malaysia is also making efforts to promote the transformation of its society from a labor-driven economy to a knowledge-based society. The Malaysian Minister of Higher Education has strategically planned a higher education system in accordance with the 2015-2025 Higher Education Plan for Education and the global movement of the Industrial Revolution of HRM 4.0 (Halili et al., 2021). The field of education, especially higher education, has always been the driving force of social change as it plays the role of transmission and transformation in cutting-edge knowledge and application practice.

Malaysian public universities are responsible for making contributions to the country's economic development because of the vast government authoritative culture. In order to maintain relevance to current needs, universities must continue to develop and meet environmental and social needs. The environment provided by universities plays an important role in providing students with the abilities required by Industry 4.0 (Kamarul Bahrin et al., 2016). In HRM4.0, creativity is emphasized such as in the introduction of new products and services. HRM 4.0 also brings many challenges to the education industry, such as the introduction and use of various advanced learning tools, multiple types of opportunities for education, and the knowledge and basic skills that everyone needs to survive in this digital era (Halili et al., 2021). Therefore, the main purpose of this paper is to explore and investigate ways to influence Malaysian public universities in the global context to embrace HRM 4.0. Towards that end, this study firstly conducts a critical review of literature on HRM4.0, and then emphasizes on how the HRD of public universities understand the benefits and challenges of HRM 4.0.

In general, HRM is one of those fields that never really gets boring. meantime, the majority of businesses had to overcome a variety of challenges before they could gain any benefits. These challenges usually have to be solved by people and people are not perfect (Pillai & Srivastava, 2022). Therefore, we have good days and bad days. People we love and people that are right in our 'allergy zone'. Companies need good people in HR, one must ensure that they have the right staff, at the right place, at the right time. In addition, HRM 4.0 is involved in any problem that requires a change in people or company culture (Da Silva et al., 2022). Sometimes the things we develop for the good of our personnel and our company will end up working out the opposite way, and then it's up to us to figure out why and to fix the situation. Therefore, it may be necessary to examine the adoption of HRM 4.0 in developing countries such as Malaysia (Ab Rahman & Ismail, 2018).

The rapid development of the information industry has affected the technology application of relevant departments in Malaysian public universities (Zain et al., 2005). Such institutions are leading institutions that adopt modern systems and concepts in various fields to achieve the same competitive advantage academically and practically (Al-Kumaim et al., 2021). There is a lot of work to be done, and a lot of challenges to be overcome by the HRM departments (Bondarouk et al., 2017). According to the survey conducted by Digi, the surveyed organizations and companies showed some specific reasons for not adopting the digital HR platform at present, including high cost (44%), small organization size (28%), low efficiency of task integration systems (17%), and staff's concern about work redundancy (Saleh et al., 2022). Many of the factors listed above do affect and hinder the effective implementation of HRM4.0 in the actual application environment. Therefore, many project reports that attempted to implement HRM 4.0 have not been effective in doing so.

Concurrently, the main exploratory factor in many organizations is to reduce the stress in various departments due to many internal and external factors; therefore, the problem that is going to be addressed in this research is to explore the benefits and challenges of using HRM 4.0. in public universities in Malaysia.

2. LITERATURE REVIEW

2.1 Use of Industry 4.0 in Human Resource Management

According to Pillai and Sivathanu (2020), the concept of HRM4.0 has been termed smart HR4.0 and coined in response to subsequent technical advancements that cannot be classified as electronic HRM (e-HRM). It entails the creation of a 4.0 environment that stimulates the development of new tools and procedures for the HR department while fundamentally challenging the present style of operation (Isari et al., 2019). HRM4.0 can alter end-to-end HR processes spanning all elements of talent onboarding, talent development, and talent off-boarding(Sivathanu & Pillai, 2018). HRM4.0, as it is known, materializes the industry strategy for filling in the gaps surrounding dynamic skills so as to adapt and thrive in the 4.0 market, merging real and virtual global information and IT management expertise (Hecklau et al., 2016). The multiple terms used to describe Industry 4.0 are lexically helpful for learners and relevant practitioners to understand and become familiar with the expected changes in management and the market that may result. These predictable changes are being applied and solved in different industries and fields (Liboni et al., 2019).

According to Dhanpat et al., (2020), technology, management, and soft skills are crucial for maintaining or creating an organization's competitive advantage in the Industry 4.0 era. Girisha (2020) pointed out that HRM4.0, through its technological advantages, typically digital and intelligent, has had an impact on HR performance. The new technological process of HR includes e-recruitment, e-selection, e-training, and development. HR4.0 means integrating the strategic objectives of the enterprise into the behavior of the employees of the organization using integrated and flexible technologies to remain consistent (Panos & Bellou, 2016).

In addition, Kristoff et al. (2018) predicted that the organizational application or adoption of HR4.0 will lead to a trend of hierarchical flattening, which enables HR to improve accuracy and efficiency, thus improving the performance of the entire organization. Ras et al. (2017) pointed out that organizations using HR4.0 have tried to use AI technology to evaluate employee performance, which helps in providing timely and more accurate performance feedback to employees. HR4.0 must be intelligent so as to acquire growing skills and capabilities to manage the new generation of employees who are increasingly becoming the main pillar of the workforce (Liboni et al., 2019).

2.2 Benefits of Human Resource Management 4.0

HRM4.0 is required by firms that promote industrial transmission 4.0 (Sae-Lim & Jermsittiparsert, 2019). HRM4.0 is required to handle industrial problems. Various technologies such as the Internet of Things, big data analytics, and artificial intelligence boost HR activities, thus improving HR teams and performance (Sivathanu & Pillai, 2018). HR4.0 helps different companies in implementing a more strategic role in the entire organization's growth (Watthanabut, 2019). That flexibility is meaningful when it is upward and positive. HR4.0 assists several firms in bringing talent on board, which invariably results in increased corporate performance (Watthanabut, 2019) HRM4.0 also helps in the development of talent for businesses; in the past, many firms had adopted the sophisticated HR4.0 strategic method to improve

HR process performance (Sivathanu & Pillai, 2018).

HRM4.0 is referred to as a transition agent in the organization, and it is intended to assist employees in accepting unavoidable adjustments and using potential methods to build value for their companies (Tamminga & Parham, 2018). This is supported by Olsen and Tomlin (2020) who made it clear that digitalization, as supported by high-tech, not only reduces the operating costs of the organization, renders the working environment flexible, and improves the quality and speed of work, but also reduces the possible tension between stakeholders thus improving the work performance of employees and organizations. Similarly, Lager and Milojkovic (2018) found that digitalization promotes and improves employees' participation in organizational activities. Meanwhile, Fedorova et al. (2019)) found that digitalization reduces and simplifies daily work tasks and human errors, and improves employees' work accuracy and performance.

2.3 Digital HR Old Vs New Rules (Varadaraj & Al Wadi, 2021)

Isari et al. (2019) showed that HRM4.0 may become a key factor in changing thinking. It can support new business models and improve employees' new digital (not yet digital) labor skills. HRM4.0 encourages and supports continuous learning and the development of capabilities that meet the requirements of the market and strategic partners, as well as the skills retraining process required by the contemporary environment. In order to promote cooperation and innovation, HRM4.0 should collaborate with educational institutions at all levels such as universities, high schools, and professional associations, harness their advantages, and manage the labor force with diversified backgrounds and the arrangement of multiple types of employment posts to achieve organizational goals. In response to the defects of 4.0, the HRD experiences the least side effects through prevention in advance.

Mushfiqur et al. (2018) insisted that the approach between HR strategy and HR system needs to be consistent to achieve the effect of less input and more output. Typically, the purpose is to save budget and time and to obtain HR information or conditional information more easily and safely. The improvement of communication and efficiency will help improve the quality of services provided by the HR department, and strengthen the ability, knowledge, and skills of employees. All these will lead to more efficient use of HR in practice, and HRM practice will in turn lead to better organizational and employee performance. Due to the trend of the new technology environment, the way of working is also driven by digitalization. The practice of intelligent HRM needs to be continuously learned, designed, and implemented. HRM4.0 may have a greater impact on organizational performance and objectives in actual work scenarios and play a greater role (Imperatori et al., 2020). The digital HR rules are given in Table 1.

Table 1. Digital HR rules

Old Rules	New Roles
1. The HR department focuses on design and harmonization to create standard HR practices.	HR department focuses on optimizing, employers' productivity, teamwork, engagement, and career growth.
2. HR selects a cloud-based vendor and implements out-of-the-box practices to create scale.	HR builds innovative, company-specific programs, and leverages the platform of scale.
3. The HR Centre of Excellence focuses on process design and process excellence.	HR Centre focuses on excellence leverages, AI, chat, app, and other advanced technology.
4. HR focuses on self-service as a way to scale service and support.	HR focuses on enablement to help people to get work done in a more effective way.
5. HR programs are designed for scale and consistency around the world.	HR programs target employees' segments, personal and specific groups.

2.4 The Role of Human Resource Management 4.0 in Universities

The university, which is a branch of the educational system, has a wide range of duties that it must fulfill in order to help society achieve its aspirations for expansion and development; the objectives, however, cannot be adequately met without proper coordination in all university activities (Abraham & Bariyaa, 2020). The university must therefore make sure that the appropriate resources are obtained and managed in order to achieve its goals and objectives as well as those of the wider society (Abraham & Bariyaa, 2020). HRM4.0 refers to the practice of using electronic platforms for managing an organization's HR components, which include both skilled and unskilled labor.

According to Shah et al. (2020), HRM4.0 focuses on implementing HRM strategies, policies, and practices in businesses via the deliberate and direct support of, and full use of, web-based channels. Mahfod et al. (2017) agreed that HRM4.0 is frequently referred to as HR information systems (HRIS), virtual HRM, HR intranet, web-based HRM, and HR portals; it is, therefore, the use of technical tools and other communication technologies to manage an organization's HR for the sake of organizational efficiency and effectiveness, as well as long-term goal accomplishment. The HR department may end up playing a key role in assisting employees, managers, and the emerging digital (and not yet digital) workforce in adopting a 4.0 attitude (Imperatori et al., 2020). It must facilitate ongoing learning, creation (and identification) of appropriate competencies, and re-skilling procedures that are now required (Imperatori et al., 2020).

The HR department should accomplish this by developing novel forms of partnerships and open innovation initiatives in conjunction with educational institutions including universities and professional associations, and by managing a more mixed-race and diverse workforce and various employment arrangements. Additionally, the HR department has a significant potential role in mitigating and controlling the negative effects of Industry 4.0, such as individual discomfort and outdated competencies, organizational stagnation and loss of control, and societal growth in unemployment and social inequality (Brisco, 2022).

The adoption of HR4.0 in Malaysian public universities makes it easier for employees from various departments within a business to collaborate in order to satisfy the needs of the organization. Explaining this concept is therefore significant for the management of an organization such as the university system since it simplifies curriculum planning, budgetary planning, infrastructural planning, and HR planning in order to fulfil the university's special demands (Abraham & Bariyaa, 2020). According to Waghmarel (2018), e-recruitment refers to publishing openings on an organization's website and allowing applicants to send their resumes electronically through email or other electronic media. This e-recruitment technology has assisted in the reduction of many of the common administrative duties associated with the recruiting process in most formal companies. Several electronic channels such as the Internet, television, radio, and mobile devices are used to promote job openings and assess competent applicants before they are deployed to regions of need. These processes are easy and fast and also save other resources when they are done electronically (Abraham & Bariyaa, 2020).

According to Kamal et al. (2016), many firms have begun to rely on e-training due to its capacity to reach large populations across different regions or nations while also lowering expenses and distributing effective information; due to its global accessibility and reach to people of many social orientations, e-training is hence viewed as the preferred learning medium. There are several virtual platforms available in the technology world of today as provided by many organizations to give their staff the information, abilities, and attitudes necessary for professionally providing services.

Formal institutions like universities can easily provide their staff with the technical, critical, and ethical skills and values required for goal achievement (Abraham & Bariyaa, 2020). Amara and Atia (2016) asserted that human resources 4.0 has multiple components such as the provision of different sources of information; discussion, analysis, and evaluation; update of information, improvement of skills, provision of training by means of new technology, and sharing of experience through media; interactive training environments; fulfillment of market demand for qualified employees and employees with special skills; and closing of social structure gaps caused by rapid and sustainable development.

Universities in the modern environment are generally trying to improve the quality of their education and teaching in pursuit of better educational results. For example, they try to create customized courses that are designed and implemented by lecturers and students at the teaching and learning ends to closely connect and focus on the characteristics of students (Bajunid & Wong, 2016). Others include the provision of training opportunities, incentive salaries, bonuses, awards, seminars, teaching activities, research, field trips, discipline teaching facilities, and many other teaching attempts at local and overseas universities which may help improve the job satisfaction of lecturers and provide opportunities for their career development (Sinniah et al., 2019).

At present, the quality and effect of education at the university level in Malaysia are closely related to the improvement of professional success and satisfaction of university teachers. Therefore, the Ministry of Higher Education of Malaysia has set a target of producing 60,000 PhD graduates by 2023. In comparison, in 2016, only 1,967 Malaysians had received doctorates. This amount reflects just 0.006% of the total population of the nation. Every year, 16.9% of Malaysians complete their PhDs. Malaysia has 17,149 PhD degree holders between 2005 and 2016 (Sinniah et al., 2019) in this ground-breaking 4.0 technology.

However, PhD instructors in Malaysia are now facing issues that may be influencing their work satisfaction, which can lead to decreased productivity, absenteeism, failure to satisfy student demands, and other issues (Richardson & Wong, 2018). According to the Pollian Educational Poll, 51.7% of academic staff at universities and colleges plan to look for new positions rather than stay in their current jobs. When employees feel this way, it can have a detrimental impact on the higher education industry's turnover rate which in turn can reduce the number of students in institutions or schools (Zahid Noor, 2015). According to Iwu et al., (2016), despite their reputation as producers of key skills, universities are likely to be worst hit. This is due to a multitude of variables including money, management, and inadequate user integration as well as inadequate financial assistance and difficulties in collecting a large amount of previous paperwork.

Malaysian public universities are facing a difficult scenario due to a scarcity of HR with the necessary skill sets for institutions to remain relevant, viable, and competitive (Baharom, 2019). Public universities are among the organizations that have taken a step back and rethought new methods of talent management considering these new criteria. Malaysia's public universities are gradually realizing the importance of comprehending the nature of their business, where their strategic orientation lies, and what skills and qualifications are required in their workforce in order to accomplish goals and objectives (Baharom, 2019). Public universities face the challenge of attracting and recruiting the necessary candidates, developing, and shaping their HR4.0, and making sure their investments pay off on top of retaining good people after determining the tasks that need to be carried out by their HR (Baharom, 2019).

3. METHODOLOGY

A qualitative method is adopted in this study to achieve the research objectives. In-depth and relevant information, views, and experiences on HRM4.0 from the respondents were acquired through the setting of open questions and text expression. The qualitative research method is a form of inductive research that constructs relevant concepts, assumptions, or theories through the collected data. This process is contrary to deductive research in which the assumptions are tested as empirical research (Ab Rahman & Ismail, 2018). In addition, qualitative research is a specific interpretation of a phenomenon or an event at the starting point. Therefore, the data collected are usually rich and have both breadth and depth, which can better explain the complexity of the phenomenon studied. To sum up, the purpose of qualitative research is not to draw a general and representative conclusion, but to emphasize the uniqueness of each case and compare it with broader theories (See Table 3.1).

3.1 Advantages and Disadvantages of Qualitative Research

Bertaux (1981), explained that when researchers have reached a point where the data obtained from the first few respondents show many similarities, they could stop the interview. In other words, when the answers given by the respondents seem to be consistently the same, the saturation point has been reached. The six participants selected from the HR departments of the six Malaysian public universities were asked to answer the pre-set questions according to the participants' understanding of HR4.0. Due to the large number of universities in Malaysia, it is difficult for the researcher to use all as it is not feasible both economically and practically. As this study adopts the qualitative analysis method, four universities from four states were selected as the research objects. The managers of the HR departments in the selected public universities were interviewed to obtain and collect data.

The following are the screening criteria when selecting the public universities:

1. A public university with a complete HR department.
2. It has relevant agreements with government agencies and has obtained investments to promote its HR information system activities.
3. Public universities with experience in implementing HR digitalization in the HR department of the university.

3.2 Profile of the Study Respondents

In the first section semi-structured interviews conducted and are recorded by using iPhone 13's "voice notes" app. In the beginning, all the data was assembled in a raw form. By selecting four public universities the researcher put his effort into getting more data from the several public universities but due to unforeseen reasons and a busy schedule unable to get the vast variety. Therefore, the researcher made a plan to conduct interviews only with those respondents who were ready to be a part of this subjective research., A positive relationship between the researcher and the respondents is crucial in ensuring that the interviews are completed in real-time recognition. To gain valid and reliable data, the researcher followed the suggestion given by Wilkinson and Kao, (2019).

It also applied principles like selecting a relatively quiet setting, highlighting the reasons for the interviewee to make sure that all the respondents positively respond to the interview questions, and making them satisfied that all the collected responses will be confidential. The researcher also explains the pre-designed plan of the interview before interviewing to deliver the proper knowledge for the sake of the interview, specifying the duration of the interview, informing the respondents of the researcher's contact information, asking the informants about any hazy issues before the interview, and using an audio or visual recorder. The profile is given in Table 2.

Table 2. Respondents profile

NO.	Position/Department	Gender	Qualifications	Experience
R1	Manager/HR Department	Male	Master	6 years
R2	Manager/HR Department	Male	Master	5 years
R3	Manager/HR Department	Male	Degree	3 years
R4	Manager/HR Department	Male	Master	5 years
R5	Manager/HR Department	Female	Master	7 years
R6	Manager/HR Department	Male	Master	4 years

The interview protocol includes the below questions:

(1) What are the motivations for implementing HRM4.0?
(2) Which elements helped your university's adoption of HRM4.0?
(3) What factors have prevented your university from implementing HRM4.0?
(4) What did you learn (about the system and implementation) throughout your university's adoption?
(5) Can you describe the organizational changes brought about by the introduction of HRM4.0 at your university?

Due to the nature of this study, the primary data collection methods were used. The researcher collected data from four public universities in Malaysia (HR departments). The primary data was gathered through interviews, which provided the researcher with greater control over the study process. In order to address the research question of this study, the researcher obtained qualitative data by conducting interviews with experts in the field of study. Also, a semi-structured interview encourages the interviewer to prepare ahead of time to steer the session. Mostly, the study focused on the benefits and challenges regarding the adoption of HRM4.0 in Malaysian public universities.

4. FINDINGS

The research results of this study show the obvious advantages of HR4.0 and the benefits it can bring to the organization, mainly improving the ability to quickly obtain reports and documents, enabling efficient human resources decision-making and daily management functions, controlling costs, and saving time. The system has the advantage of cutting-edge digital technology and can store a large amount of data to optimize and accurately recruit and train employees. In addition, the timeliness of HR4.0 is quite outstanding. This advantage is reflected in two completely different work natures, which are the key factors in promoting human resources management. Firstly, it enables the attainment of required human resources information promptly, and secondly, it helps employees complete and optimize their work in a shorter time. The HR4.0 system can help employees meet work requirements and achieve organizational goals through its powerful functions.

Another finding is that HR4.0 can help speed up the decision-making of superiors. The adoption of HR4.0 can help organizational managers gain decision-making advantages, and identify and seize development opportunities promptly, thus contributing to the healthy and sustainable development of the organization and enterprise, on top of improving organizational efficiency. Additionally, HR4.0

demonstrates systematic integration and collaborative work of internal and external hardware and software. It enables the collection of relevant information with more powerful functions and advantages and shortens information processing time to achieve organizational goals. With the advent of 4.0 technology, the responsibilities and work of human resources management are becoming more extensive, shifting from traditional personnel management. In addition, this study shows that the quality of the system used by public universities can make the traditional archiving function of human resources employee information more flexible and easier to use.

The main obstacle to promoting and implementing HR4.0 is the pressure and challenge from colleagues and peers in the field of HR. The working environment of HRD in Malaysian public universities lacks experienced HR4.0 users. This study identified the factors that hinder Malaysian universities from adopting HRM4.0; based on the interviews and observations, these include unfamiliarity with the system, high cost, and low organizational budget. The summary of findings has been presented in Table 3.

Table 3. Summary of findings

Construct	Items
Advantages of using HRM4.0 Adoption (Benefits)	1. Efficiently performing the functions of HRM. 2. Improving the ability to quickly obtain reports 3. Reducing cost and saving time 4. Cutting-edge digital technology can store a large amount of data to optimize and accurately recruit and train employees.
	5. Timelines A. It enables the attainment of required human resources information in a timely manner B. It helps employees complete and optimize their work in a shorter time
	6. Help employees meet work requirements and achieve organizational goals through its powerful functions.
	7. Speed up the decision-making
	8. The quality of the system used by public universities can make the traditional archiving function of human resources employee information more flexible and easier to use.
	9. Avoid the mistakes
Factors of HRM4.0 adoption (Challenges)	1. High cost 2. The working environment of HRD in Malaysian public universities lacks experienced HR4.0 users' Low efficiency in task integration system. unfamiliarity with the system
	3. low organizational budget

5. CONTRIBUTION OF THE STUDY

1. Updated training sessions to improve the practical ability to use HRM4.0 usage to maximize academic performance.
2. It also increases the efficiency of work concerning the ease of students' records and managing them effectively (reducing time constraints).
3. The usage of HRM4.0 rapidly enhances the capability of the administration staff on a larger scale by managing several things like student credentials.
4. It can also maximize the improved outcomes in real-time recognition such as quick access to the desirable task in an effective manner.
5. By following the subjective research work many public sector universities can achieve their desirable objectives in terms of administration in future endeavours.

5.1 Study Limitations And Suggestions for the Future Study

Firstly, the major limitation of this study is the lack of related studies using a qualitative approach, especially interviews to retrieve information from the Malaysian context. Additionally, interviews with the HR Departments are relatively costly and time-consuming due to the location of the universities in different cities and districts. The busyness of the HR managers is another difficulty for the researcher.

Secondly, the sample in this study is restricted only to public universities in Malaysia, and therefore may not be generalized to other industries. However, the results could be generalized to other types of universities such as private universities, as well as other sectors and industries in Malaysia. Thirdly, this study concentrates only on the qualitative approach conducted in interviews which does not consider other avenues for a quantitative approach such as surveys and questionnaires.

This study takes Malaysian public universities as sample selection points. Therefore, it is recommended to carry out follow-up research related to HR4.0 in private universities, government institutions at different levels, and various types of organizations such as private and public organizations, and small and multinational companies, so that industries in all fields can benefit from modern human resources management methods as quickly and safely as possible. In universities and other institutions of higher learning, the overall budget of outdated and inefficient human resources systems can be reduced with the help of modern HR4.0. When the system is used to manage the database of employees and students, faster, cheaper, and more efficient results are produced.

The results also revealed that different factors such as the relatively high maintenance cost of HR4.0 and the user's continuous training needs will directly or indirectly affect the promotion and implementation of HR4.0 in Malaysian public universities. However, this study only focuses on the structure and dimensions of the HR4.0 success model proposed by the research measurement. Future research can focus on the significance of this research and design research to measure the impact of maintenance costs and training needs.

It was also found that the HR4.0 system currently used by the HR departments of the four public universities is unsystematic and lacks continuity. The components of the system are scattered within the organization and are not effectively connected, resulting in interruptions in communication flow. It is necessary to further promote the unification of the HR4.0 system and train operators to improve the usage effect of HR4.0. Future researchers may consider establishing a unified HR4.0 system communication model in public universities.

5.2 Conclusion

This study has explored and investigated the benefits and challenges of adopting HRM4.0 in four public universities in Malaysia. Firstly, this study discusses the concept of HR digitalization. The current research explores several relevant concepts with the help of a literature review. In addition, most of them define the basic process of the organization whether it belongs to the remote or physical business environment. It may replace the traditional concept of the HR practice system and transform it into HRM4.0. The study results also illustrated that the successful Adoption of HRM4.0 may come from three levels namely the organization, technology, and people. It can also be categorized into several fields such as budget constraints, attitude, financial constraints, lack of skilled labor, management support, and user acceptance.

In addition, HRM4.0 also provides the foundation of guaranteed operational advantages and other closed relevant interests i.e., the enthusiasm and participation of employees, reduced costs and time, faster decision-making, timely and high-quality communication, rapid delivery of services, and customer satisfaction. It can also intelligently alleviate the internal stress. Therefore, research shows that HRM4.0 is an important aspect of the realization of the development goals of universities. Moreover, several other scientific and systematic studies have explored HRM4.0. Moreover, it can be observed during the recent COVID-19 pandemic, HRM4.0 was popularized and valued to a certain extent. It abandoned the weaknesses of traditional HR practices. Therefore, we encourage future research to scientifically examine more aspects of this concept, such as how it affects the work performance of users and employees. Subsequently, the infrastructure construction for the application of new technologies needs to be considered by the government and policymakers. It can promote the development of more advanced systems for new start-ups and current businesses.

REFERENCES

Ab Rahman, Z. N., & Ismail, N. (2018). Determinant Factors for Managing Innovation in the Malaysian Public Sector. *MATEC Web of Conferences, 150*, 1–5. 10.1051/matecconf/201815005042

Abraham, L. N., & Bariyaa, J. (2020). Status of Principals' ICT Usage in Secondary School Administration in Rivers State. *African Research Review*, *14*(1), 61–71. doi:10.4314/afrrev.v14i1.6

Al-Kumaim, N. H., Alhazmi, A. K., Mohammed, F., Gazem, N. A., Shabbir, M. S., & Fazea, Y. (2021). Exploring the impact of the covid-19 pandemic on university students' learning life: An integrated conceptual motivational model for sustainable and healthy online learning. *Sustainability (Basel)*, *13*(5), 1–21. doi:10.3390u13052546

Al Shobaki, M. M., Naser, S. S. A., Amuna, Y. M. A., El Talla, A., Al Shobaki, M. M., Naser, S. S. A., Amuna, Y. M. A., El, S. A., & The, T. (2017). The Efficiency of Information Technology and its Role of e- HRM in the Palestinian Universities To cite this version : HAL Id : hal-01572642 The Efficiency of Information Technology and its Role of e- HRM in the Palestinian Universities. *International Journal of Engineering and Information Systems*, *1*(5), 36–55. http://www.ijeais.org/wp-content/uploads/2017/07/IJEAIS170705.pdfThisVersionisavailableat:http://hdl.handle.net/10419/167316www.ijeais.org36

Baharom, A. (2019). Talent management: Malaysian public universities vs private industries. *Journal of Human Development and Communication*, *8*, 83–96.

Bajunid, I. A., & Wong, W. C. K. (2016). Private higher education institutions in Malaysia. In A Global Perspective on Private Higher Education. doi:10.1016/B978-0-08-100872-0.00008-2

Ben Amara, N., & Atia, L. (2016). E-Training-and-Its-Role-in-Human-Resources-Development. *Global Journal of Human Resource Management*, *4*(1), 1–12.

Bondarouk, T., Parry, E., & Furtmueller, E. (2017). Electronic HRM: Four decades of research on adoption and consequences. *International Journal of Human Resource Management*, *28*(1), 98–131. doi:10.1080/09585192.2016.1245672

Brisco, R. (2022). Understanding Industry 4.0 Digital Transformation. *Proceedings of the Design Society*, *2*, 2423–2432. doi:10.1017/pds.2022.245

Colbert, A., Yee, N., & George, G. (2016). The digital workforce and the workplace of the future. *Academy of Management Journal, 59*(3), 731–739. doi:10.5465/amj.2016.4003

da Silva, L. B. P., Soltovski, R., Pontes, J., Treinta, F. T., Leitão, P., Mosconi, E., de Resende, L. M. M., & Yoshino, R. T. (2022). Human resources management 4.0: Literature review and trends. *Computers & Industrial Engineering, 168*(March), 108111. Advance online publication. doi:10.1016/j.cie.2022.108111

Dhanpat, N., Buthelezi, Z. P., Joe, M. R., Maphela, T. V., & Shongwe, N. (2020). Industry 4.0: The role of human resource professionals. *SA Journal of Human Resource Management, 18*(May), 10. doi:10.4102ajhrm.v18i0.1302

Fedorova, A., Zarubina, A., Pikulina, Y., Moskovskikh, A., Balandina, T., & Gafurova, T. (2019). Digitalization of the Human Resource Management : Russian Companies Case. *SOCIOINT 2019- 6th International Conference on Education, Social Sciences and Humanities,* 1227–1230. https://www.ocerints.org/socioint19_e-publication/abstracts/papers/713.pdf

Girisha, M. C. (2020). E-Human Resource Management (E-Hrm) Practices in Automotive Industry in Karnataka. *Mukt Shabd Journal, 9*(4), 152–163. https://www.researchgate.net/publication/340524950

Halili, S. H., Sulaiman, S., Sulaiman, H., & Razak, R. (2021). Embracing industrial revolution 4.0 in universities. *IOP Conference Series. Materials Science and Engineering, 1088*(1), 012111. doi:10.1088/1757-899X/1088/1/012111

Hameed, I., Haq, M. A., Khan, N., & Zainab, B. (2022). Social media usage and academic performance from a cognitive loading perspective. *On the Horizon, 30*(1), 12–27. doi:10.1108/OTH-04-2021-0054

Hameed, I., Khan, A. K., Sabharwal, M., Arain, G. A., & Hameed, I. (2019). Managing successful change efforts in the public sector: An employee's readiness for change perspective. *Review of Public Personnel Administration, 39*(3), 398–421. doi:10.1177/0734371X17729869

Hecklau, F., Galeitzke, M., Flachs, S., & Kohl, H. (2016). Holistic Approach for Human Resource Management in Industry 4.0. *Procedia CIRP, 54*, 1–6. doi:10.1016/j.procir.2016.05.102

Imperatori, B., Bissola, R., Butera, F., & Bodega, D. (2020). Work and HRM in the 4.0 era: Insights and research directions. *Studi Organizzativi, 2*(2), 9–26. doi:10.3280/SO2019-002001

Imran, M., Salisu, I., Aslam, H. D., Iqbal, J., & Hameed, I. (2019). Resource and information access for SME sustainability in the era of IR 4.0: The mediating and moderating roles of innovation capability and management commitment. *Processes (Basel, Switzerland)*, *7*(4), 211. doi:10.3390/pr7040211

Isari, D., Bissola, R., & Imperatori, B. (2019). HR Devolution in the Digital Era: What Should We Expect? *Advanced Series in Management*, *23*, 41–61. doi:10.1108/S1877-636120190000023004

Iwu, C. G., Eme-ukandu, N., & Allen-ile, C. (n.d.). ADMINISTRATIO Effects of the Use of Electronic Human Resource Management (E- HRM) Within Human Resource Management (HRM) Functions at Universities 1. *Introduction and Purpose.*, *8*(1), 5–20.

Kamal, K., Alaghbari, M., & Atteia, M. (2016). E-training & employees ' performance a practical study on the ministry of education in the Kingdom of Bahrain E-Training & Employees ' Performance a Practical Study on the Ministry of Education in the Kingdom of Bahrain. *Journal of Resources Development and Management, 18*(March), 1–8.

Kamarul Bahrin, M. A., Fauzi Othman, M., Nor Azli, N. H., & Farihin Talib, M. (2016). Industry 4.0: A Review on Industrial Automation and Robotic. *Jurnal Teknologi, 78*(6–13), 137–143. www.jurnalteknologi.utm.my

Kristoff, B. H., Hoen, B. T., Adrian, L., & Stang, V. (2018). *Digitalization & hr.* Academic Press.

Lager, D., & Milojkovic, E. (2018). *Digitalization and the renewal of employee engagement surveys*. https://gupea.ub.gu.se/bitstream/handle/2077/57453/gupea_2077_57453_1.pdf?sequence=1

Li, W., Waris, I., Sun, C., Hameed, I., Bhutto, M. Y., & Ali, R. (2022). Understanding the role of corporate social responsibility and sustainable supply chain management in shaping the consumers' intention to use sharing platforms. *Frontiers in Psychology*, *13*, 970444. doi:10.3389/fpsyg.2022.970444 PMID:36072017

Liboni, L. B., Cezarino, L. O., Jabbour, C. J. C., Oliveira, B. G., & Stefanelli, N. O. (2019). Smart industry and the pathways to HRM 4.0: Implications for SCM. *Supply Chain Management*, *24*(1), 124–146. doi:10.1108/SCM-03-2018-0150

Mahfod, J., Khalifa, N. Y., & Faisal Al, M. (2017). Electronic human resource management (E-HRM) system. *International Journal of Economic Research*, *14*(15), 563–576.

Malik, S. Y., Cao, Y., Mughal, Y. H., Kundi, G. M., Mughal, M. H., & Ramayah, T. (2020). Pathways towards sustainability in organizations: Empirical evidence on the role of green human resource management practices and green intellectual capital. *Sustainability (Basel)*, *12*(8), 1–24. doi:10.3390u12083228

Mushfiqur, R., Mordi, C., Oruh, E. S., Nwagbara, U., Mordi, T., & Turner, I. M. (2018). The impacts of work-life-balance (WLB) challenges on social sustainability: The experience of Nigerian female medical doctors. *Employee Relations*, *40*(5), 868–888. doi:10.1108/ER-06-2017-0131

Noor, Z. (2015, April). Impact of Job Promotion and Job Advancement on Job Satisfaction in Universities of Kpk Province of Pakistan. *Science International (Lahore)*, *27*(2), 1499–1505.

Olsen, T. L., & Tomlin, B. (2020). Industry 4.0: Opportunities and challenges for operations management. *Manufacturing & Service Operations Management*, *22*(1), 113–122. doi:10.1287/msom.2019.0796

Panos, S., & Bellou, V. (2016). Maximizing e-HRM outcomes: A moderated mediation path. *Management Decision*, *54*(5), 1088–1109. doi:10.1108/MD-07-2015-0269

Pillai, R., & Sivathanu, B. (2020). Adoption of artificial intelligence (AI) for talent acquisition in IT/ITeS organizations. *Benchmarking*, *27*(9), 2599–2629. doi:10.1108/BIJ-04-2020-0186

Pillai, R., & Srivastava, K. B. L. (2022). Smart HRM 4.0 for achieving organizational performance: A dynamic capability view perspective. *International Journal of Productivity and Performance Management*. Advance online publication. doi:10.1108/IJPPM-04-2022-0174

Puhovichova, D., & Jankelova, N. (2020). Changes of human resource management in the context of impact of the fourth industrial revolution. *International Scientific Journal, 141*(3), 138–141. https://stumejournals.com/journals/i4/2020/3/138

Ras, E., Wild, F., Stahl, C., & Baudet, A. (2017). Bridging the skills gap of workers in industry 4.0 by human performance augmentation tools - Challenges and roadmap. *ACM International Conference Proceeding Series, Part F1285*, 428–432. 10.1145/3056540.3076192

Richardson, C., & Wong, H. W. (2018). Expatriate academics in Malaysia: Motivation, adjustment, and retention. *Journal of Management Development*, *37*(3), 299–308. doi:10.1108/JMD-12-2017-0421

Sae-Lim, P., & Jermsittiparsert, K. (2019). Is the fourth industrial revolution a panacea? Risks toward the fourth industrial revolution: Evidence in the Thai economy. *International Journal of Innovation. Creativity and Change*, *5*(2), 732–752.

Saleh, A., Al-Shameri, A. S., Sarah, S., & Omar, B. (2022). *HR Digitalization as a Critical HR practice to Navigate through Covid-19 for the Improvement of the Employee Job Performance: Review Paper*. Academic Press.

Shah, N., Michael, F., & Chalu, H. (2020). E-HRM and Motivation: A Case of Manufacturing Companies in Tanzania. *East African Journal of Business and Economics*, *2*(1), 53–71. doi:10.37284/eajbe.2.1.241

Sinniah, S., Mohamed, R. K. M. H., Mior, W. R., Harith, A., Izni, W. N., & Rawshdeh, Z. A. (2019). Talent retention in private universities of Malaysia. *International Journal of Engineering and Advanced Technology, 8*(6), 233–239. doi:10.35940/ijeat.F1038.0986S319

Sivathanu, B., & Pillai, R. (2018). Smart HR 4.0 – how industry 4.0 is disrupting HR. *Human Resource Management International Digest*, *26*(4), 7–11. doi:10.1108/HRMID-04-2018-0059

Tamminga, J., & Parham, S. (2018). The Adaptation of the Logistic Industry to the Fourth Industrial Revolution: The Role of Human Resource Management. *Journal of Business Management & Social Sciences Research*, *7*(9), 179–191. https://www.researchgate.net/publication/327531057

Telukdarie, A., & Munsamy, M. (2019). Digitization of Higher Education Institutions. *IEEE International Conference on Industrial Engineering and Engineering Management, December*, 716–721. 10.1109/IEEM44572.2019.8978701

Varadaraj, D. A., & Al Wadi, D. B. M. (2021). A Study on Contribution of Digital Human Resource Management towards Organizational Performance. *The International Journal of Management Science and Business Administration*, *7*(5), 43–51. doi:10.18775/ijmsba.1849-5664-5419.2014.75.1004

WaghmarelS. (2018). A Study of E-Recruitment: From the Perspective of Job Applicants. doi:10.13140/RG.2.2.17695.61605

Wang, X., Waris, I., Bhutto, M. Y., Sun, H., & Hameed, I. (2022). Green initiatives and environmental concern foster environmental sustainability: A study based on the use of reusable drink cups. *International Journal of Environmental Research and Public Health*, *19*(15), 9259. doi:10.3390/ijerph19159259 PMID:35954613

Waris, I., Barkat, W., Ahmed, A., & Hameed, I. (2022). Fostering sustainable businesses: Understanding sustainability-driven entrepreneurial intention among university students in Pakistan. *Social Responsibility Journal*, *18*(8), 1409–1426. doi:10.1108/SRJ-10-2020-0399

Waris, I., Farooq, M., Hameed, I., & Shahab, A. (2021). Promoting sustainable ventures among university students in Pakistan: An empirical study based on the theory of planned behavior. *On the Horizon*, *29*(1), 1–16. doi:10.1108/OTH-10-2020-0035

Watthanabut, B. (2019). From HR 4.0 to better supply chain flexibility: Role of talent on boarding and a development in Thailand. *International Journal of Supply Chain Management*, *8*(5), 804–815.

Wilkinson, J. E., & Kao, C. P. (2019). Aspects of socio-emotional learning in Taiwan's pre-schools: An exploratory study of teachers' perspectives. *International Journal of Child Care and Education Policy*, *13*(1), 1–17. doi:10.118640723-019-0057-6

Zain, M., Rose, R. C., Abdullah, I., & Masrom, M. (2005). The relationship between information technology acceptance and organizational agility in Malaysia. *Information & Management*, *42*(6), 829–839. doi:10.1016/j.im.2004.09.001

Chapter 8
Artificial Intelligence and Green Human Resource Management:
Navigating the Challenges

Fazeelat Masood
https://orcid.org/0000-0003-1487-6882
Bahria University, Pakistan

Naveed R. Khan
UCSI University, Malaysia

Erum Masood
Bahria University, Pakistan

ABSTRACT

Artificial intelligence (AI) refers to developing computer systems that can perform tasks that typically require human intelligence, such as learning, problem-solving, and decision-making. Green HRM, on the other hand, is a holistic approach to managing human resources that considers the environmental impact of an organization's operations. The AI-green HRM integration has the potential to create a powerful synergy that can help organizations become more sustainable. For example, AI can be used to analyze data and identify areas of an organization where energy and resources are being wasted. This information can then be used to develop and implement more sustainable practices. First, this chapter generates insights into the significance of AI-Green HRM integration. Second, this chapter illustrates challenges faced by organizations in the adoption of AI in endorsing green HRM practices. Third, this chapter concludes the managerial implications of AI-Green HRM for organizations, in particular the Malaysian context.

DOI: 10.4018/979-8-3693-0039-8.ch008

INTRODUCTION

Early waves of industrialization were attributed to the concerns of global warming (Bradu et al., 2022; Sharma et al., 2022). A significant increase in climatic change and warming trends did pose global threats, such as wildfires, hot waves, and droughts, which caused a mountable loss to the global economy. Gradually, concerns for cleaner production policies and environmental protection stimulated organizations to be environmentally aware while meeting the demands of the market & consumers and the law (Pham et al., 2020). In the face of environmental degradation, humanity is inclined towards sustainability under the banner of *satisfying the needs of the present generation without comprising the rights/needs of the future generations* (Ogbeibu et al., 2023). The adoption of sustainability became ubiquitous within business (DesJardins, 2016), thereby creating an *environment-sustainability bandwagon* where organizations seemed responsible for sustainable outcomes addressing the socio-environmental effects of their business decisions (Ababneh, 2021). This bandwagon effect advocated changes in the organizational stance on the adequate adaptation of environmental practices. The need to address global concerns about nature and natural resources in an environmentally protective manner has marked the era of the digit-globe (digitalized globalization).

With the fourth industrial revolution (IR 4.0), humanity has progressed towards technology embedded lives (Yong et al., 2022). IR 4.0 has created a new world of enormous possibilities for humanity, the planet they inhibit and its resources (Ogbeibu et al., 2023). Smart technologies such as artificial intelligence (AI), the blockchain, and the internet of things (IoT) are transforming the governance system, manufacturing and production processes and the entire management system (Bradu et al., 2022). These technologies have brought large-scale changes across organizations and industries with production automation and digitalized industrial processes (Ababneh, 2021). Thereby, endorsing sustainability 4.0 through renewable energy and resource efficiency (Javaid et al., 2022). Following these trends, by 2025, organizations plan to move 60% of their IT estate to cloud (Baig et al., 2023).

Recently, the IR 4.0 driven sustainability has been the center of research (Bradu et al., 2022; Hassoun et al., 2022; Javaid et al., 2022; Polas et al., 2022). Adding fuel to the fire is the United Nations (UN) 2030 Agenda of sustainable development goals (SDGs). For sustainable development of the planet, its resources and societies, the UN has proposed 17 SDGs aiming at global sustainability concerns that seek contributions from both ends, i.e., businesses and the government (Yong et al., 2022). Among these goals, SDG # 12 i.e., responsible consumption and production signifies the role of the business community in achieving sustainable development. Under SDG # 12, Target 12.6 promotes sustainable business by encouraging organizations towards the adoption of sustainable practices and sustainability-data inclusive reporting (UN, 2023). Organizations such as Atmonia (Iceland), Mittemitte (Germany), Phenix (France), Armadioverde (Italy), Leko Labs (Luxembourg), Ducky (Norway), Karma (Sweden), Effa (Ukraine), and Notpla (UK) are endorsing Target 12.6 by integrating sustainability and environmental goals into business strategy and policies (Valuer, 2022). With a growing number of organizations, industries, and nations adopting and endorsing sustainable business initiatives, a *green bandwagon effect* has emerged (S. Ahmad, 2015). Ababneh (2021), however, argued that there's more to it than meets the eye.

At organizational level, focus on sustainability inclusive strategy alone may not guarantee the efficient accomplishment of such environmental goals. Rather, attention needs to be paid to the human factor as individuals' cognitive judgment, attitudes, social values, and dedication are connotative to environmental behavior (Ababneh, 2021; Song & Wu, 2021). This calls for inquiry into why and how human involvement in the environmental discourse can help realize sustainability goals. In response, green human resource management (GHRM) has surfaced as a promising notion in advancing organization and employee-level environment-related outcomes. Emerging as a new research stream, green HRM helps understand the human aspect of enhancing sustainability in organizations (Pham et al., 2020).

The current era has witnessed a paradigm shift in the organizational approach to manage business resources and practices (Gupta, 2021). Among these resources, people are the critical asset for yielding the sustainability mantra of an organization. Given the current environmental pressures, organizations are focusing on the green aspect of managing their human resource (Pham et al., 2020). Green HRM is a holistic approach to managing human resources that takes into account the environmental impact of an organization's operations (Muster & Schrader, 2011). According to Renwick et al. (2008), green HRM contributes to environmental management by aligning employees with the environmental strategy of an organization via employee relations, performance appraisal and management, training and development, and reward systems. In this endeavor of creating a green persona, organizations are increasingly borrowing support from IR 4.0 green innovation technologies (GITs) such as AI, machine learning and data science. Organizations adopt AI technology to create value and competitive advantage to which human resource is critical. Among AI technology's value recipients, employees are the focus of recent surge in debates surrounding AI and HRM scholars. These debates are mainly centered on the themes related to merits and demerits of AI adoption to HRM systems and practices (Nam et al., 2021; Pham et al., 2020; Tambe et al., 2019; Yong et al., 2022).

Apparently, application of AI to organizations and people-related matters is on the rise. Recent scholarly works have been focused on the opportunities and challenges of adopting AI in healthcare (Abouelmehdi et al., 2018; Al Badi et al., 2022; Sun & Medaglia, 2019), hotel industry (Nam et al., 2021), construction industry (Regona et al., 2022), banking industry (Rahman et al., 2021), agriculture (Lazim et al., 2020), and manufacturing (M. F. Ahmad et al., 2022). These scholarly works mainly explore AI adoption and related issues at industry-level; hence, the scope of identified challenges is rather broad and generic to people-related issues. Tambe et al. (2019) point this as a situation different from HR issues when applying AI technologies. Addressing Tambe et al.'s (2019) concerns, this chapter aims to (i) describe the role of AI technology and AI-based systems in green HRM (ii) discuss challenges faced by organizations in AI adoption to HR practices and related issues (iii) highlight the managerial implications of AI-enabled green HRM.

GLOBAL SCENARIO OF ARTIFICIAL INTELLIGENCE (AI)

In 2018, McKinsey's report recognized AI as a power to transform the work and workplace by automating business processes and systems while addressing moonshot societal challenges. AI technology is defined as a device with the ability to perceive its surroundings i.e., environment and act in a way that maximizes its chances of success at a specific goal (Sun & Medaglia, 2019). As a family of technologies, AI has shown potential to boost the economic activity. Popular AI technologies include natural language processing (NLP), machine learning, virtual assistants, computer vision and robotic process automation (Bughin et al., 2018). With growing scholarly research, three types of AI conceptualizations have emerged; these include artificial narrow intelligence (ANI), artificial general intelligence (AGI), and artificial super intelligence (ASI) (Regona et al., 2022). However, organizations' understanding of the AI technology and the type of tasks it can help perform is crucial to AI adoption (Davenport & Ronanki, 2018).

By 2030, AI will emerge as a game changer contributing up to $ 15.7trillion to the global economy; out of which, $ 9.1trillion will account for consumption side effects and $ 6.6trillion will result from increased productivity (PWC, 2020). 70% of the global AI-driven economic gain will amount up to $ 10.7trillion concentrated in China and North America (see Figure 1).

Figure 1. Region-wise economic impact of AI technology
Source: Adopted from PWC (2020, p. 9)

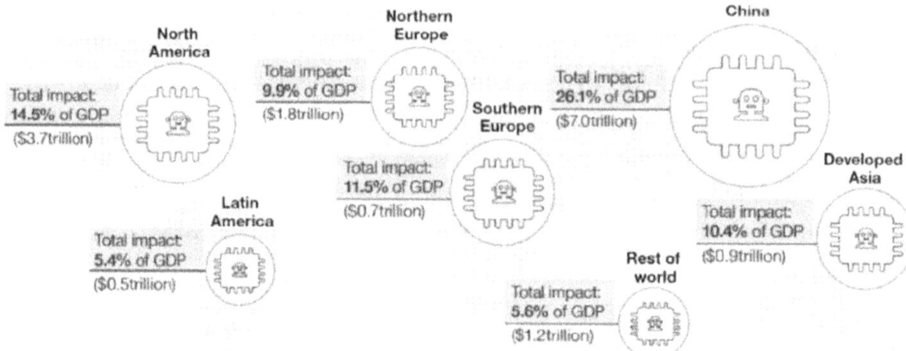

AI and related technologies have gained momentum in public and private sector organizations from automotive, healthcare, financial, construction, and agriculture (Omar et al., 2017; Rahman et al., 2021; Regona et al., 2022; Sun & Medaglia, 2019). From real world data, PWC create AI impact index across a few industries with growing AI diffusion. Among industries, healthcare and automotive rank highest on PWC's (2020) AI impact indicator with 37% potential AI consumption impact (see Figure 2). Among various reasons, companies choose to adopt AI to make current products better while only 22% of the surveyed executives intent to adopt AI to reduce head count (Davenport & Ronanki, 2018).

Figure 2. AI impact by sector
Source: Adopted from PricewaterhouseCoopers (2020)

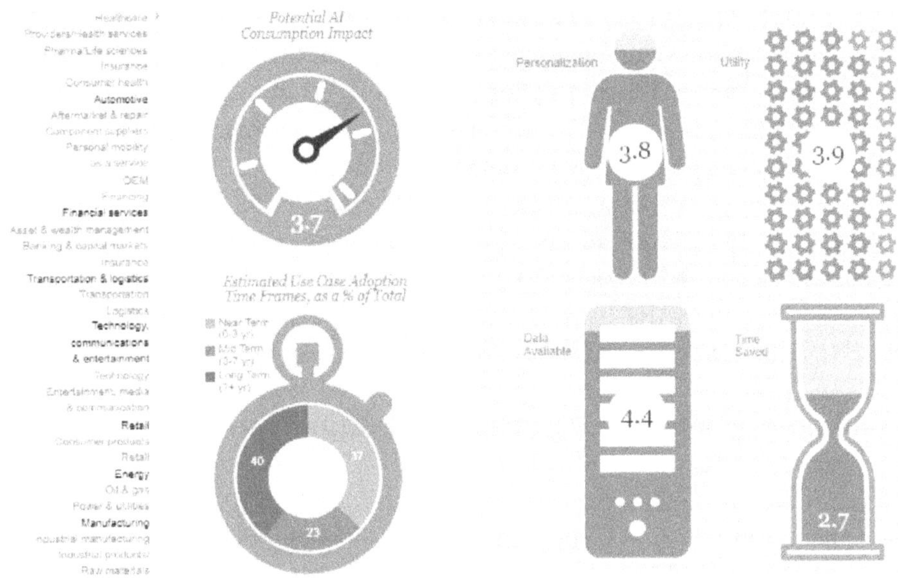

Gradually, Asian economies such as China, South Korea, India, Malaysia, and Japan are realizing the power of AI. To size the revolutionary AI opportunity, Asian countries are joining the race for promoting technological and economic development in the domestic markets. Responding to AI emergence as a new focus of international competition, China is taking a look at its resources (be natural, human or intelligence) and their inter-relationships (Yang, 2019). In 2017, Chinese government initiated a development plan for new generation AI with the social and technical protocols to be carefully considered to ensure the creation of reliable and trustable AI technology. Later in 2019, Chinese Ministry of Science and Technology (MOST) established a National Governance Committee which was tasked with the release of governance principles for developing responsible AI (W. Wu et al., 2020). China has introduced the New Generation AI Development Plan 2015-2030 that serves as a blueprint of AI ecosystem in China (F. Wu et al., 2020). Following a top-down approach, Chinese tend to view AI as a tool for progress; however, recent years have seen a shift in the Chinese popular culture AI-robots as partners rather than tools to development. In South Korea, human-AI interaction put humans as the top priority and machines in a support role (Gal, 2020).

Likewise, AI is emerging as a priority area in Indian policy development. In 2018, Indian Union Government approved 100% increase in funding toward skill development, training and research in AI and related technologies. Under the banner of Digital India, Union Government is providing digital infrastructure to ensure the development of AI technology made in and made to work for India (Marda, 2018). In 2021, Malaysian government formulated national policy on IR 4.0 to promote sustainable development and digitization in the country (Yong et al., 2022). Malaysia's Government Transformation Programme (GTP) is encouraging the use of AI in private agencies and government delivery systems (Samsurijan et al., 2022). By 2030, Malaysian government is aiming for productivity boost by 30% across all sectors. To achieve this, Malaysian government has initiated AI Roadmap (AIRmap) (Mansor, 2021). In Malaysia, recent AI-enabled projects include Stethee Pro (an AI-enabled stethoscope), Malaysia's first AI legal aid center and Simultaneous artificial response and action (SARA - an AI-enabled fashion technology), and Supahands' DIANE (Digital Innovation Assistant for kNowledge Engineering).

AI Technology and its Organizational Significance

Branching out from the field of computer science, AI follows a process of intelligent transformation in which machines are enabled to imitate human behaviors and rational thinking. In this process of thinking and behaving like a human, AI technology intelligentizes the data by identifying, organizing, synthesizing, and then understanding and operating (Song & Wu, 2021). A key attribute of AI technology is to automate human tasks which are time consuming, repetitive, and mechanical in nature but not complex (Ramachandran et al., 2022). AI technology utilizes computer algorithms such as machine learning algorithms to create computer intelligence enabling machines to do work as humans do. These algorithms use induction and synthesis principles to make machines learn and update the knowledge system on a continuous basis. Thereby, allowing machines to diagnose, reason, and make decisions (Song & Wu, 2021).

Globally, per day use of AI embedded technologies by business enterprises and consumers has increased exponentially. For example, Google search engine offering search options tailored to one's search histories, Amazon recommending its users a personalized product, website chatbot (AI assistant) interacting with website users/visitors, and Alexa providing weather updates and suggesting use of umbrella (Baer, 2023). A survey of HR Leaders and global businesses reported that 58% of organizations mainly use AI to improve quality and consistency, 26% to improve productivity, and 16% to improve insights (see Figure 3).

Figure 3. Leading use of AI in organizations
Source: Adopted from Statista (2020)

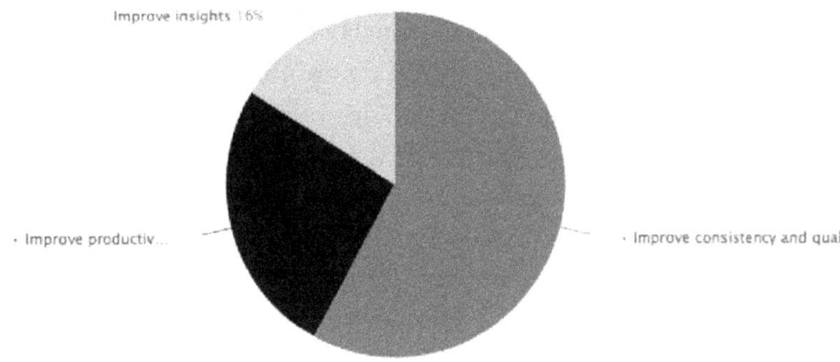

According to a research, more than 50% of organizations report that their business has adopted AI in at least one way (Baig et al., 2023). Common ways in which AI technology is used in the workplace include employee and customer-related data collection, software-aided trainings, use of chatbots, use of computer algorithms to process job applications, and forecast employee retention and hiring success rate (Oracle, 2019). AI can be utilized to forecast the future demand of the products and services, thus reducing the waste of resources and overproduction. Additionally, AI enables organizations to automate various HR processes, such as recruiting and performance evaluation, which can help organizations save time and resources.

GREEN HUMAN RESOURCE MANAGEMENT (GHRM)

Growing stakeholder pressures are urging organizations to engage in environmentally sustainable practices. In doing so, business enterprises are seeking green sources of competitive advantage; a popular source to which is the greening of traditional business models. Such green initiatives are the key to green HRM practices (Hameed et al., 2020). Green HRM is an HR aspect of ecological/environmental management (Renwick et al., 2008). The concept is about greening the HRM practices in a competitive and functional aspect to promote the critical use of people (human resource) in achieving the environmental goals that contribute to environmental sustainability (Jackson et al., 2011). To put it simply, green HRM encompasses everything that relates to the creation of awareness, promotion of adoption and execution of HR practices in a sustainable manner (Benevene & Buonomo, 2020).

Green HRM refers to the use of HRM policies, practices, and philosophies to encourage sustainable use of business resources while preventing environmental concerns within the organization (Zoogah, 2011). Kramar (2014) describe green HRM as a set of activities aimed at enhancing positive environment-related outcomes. It encourages the use of HRM policies to manage the environment within an organization (Sharma et al., 2022). Under green HRM, organizations systematically align their traditional HRM practices (such as training & development, reward systems, and recruitment) with the green policies to meet the environmental goals of the business (S. Ahmad, 2015). Green HRM promotes individuals' involvement to ensure the sustainable use of organizational resources to attain the environmental sustainability objectives (Ari et al., 2020). This indicates that employee behaviors are critical to green HRM practices in achieving the green objectives and environmental sustainability policies of organizations (Hameed et al., 2020).

According to Renwick et al. (2013), green HRM is composed of three components that include (i) *green abilities* - organizations develop green abilities of employees by recruiting and selected talented people, providing them trainings in environmental knowledge, and promoting green leadership (ii) *green employees* – organizations may use green performance appraisal and link pay and rewards with the environmental management, and (iii) *green opportunities* - organizations empowering and encouraging wider employee engagement in green initiatives and environmental management may see improved employee involvement in eco-sustainable behaviors. Using Ability-Motivation-Opportunity (AMO) framework, Ari et al. (2020) proposed that HR initiatives promote effective performance outcomes via triggering employees' motivation to do work while enhancing their abilities. Under this theoretical framework, employees are motivated to engage in environmentally friendly practices when there are visible signs of managerial investment in green practices that develop employees' environment-related skills, abilities, and knowledge (Ari et al., 2020).

Green HRM is increasingly becoming an essential factor for successful execution of environmental management practices. Following supplies-values fit theory, Dumont et al. (2017) found green HRM effect on employees' in-role and extra-role green behaviors channeling through psychological processes. Hameed et al. (2020) found that green HRM practices affect employees' green citizenship behavior when they are empowered. Green empowerment makes employees more obliged and responsible towards green initiatives. In a way, green empowerment channels the indirect effect of green HRM on employees' organizational citizenship behavior toward environment. In a study of Malaysian manufacturing employees, Fang et al. (2022) found green culture and green innovation as mechanisms to explain the green HRM effect on environmental performance.

Role of AI Technology in Green HRM

Parallel to technological advancement, organizations seem to enter a common enterprise progress via continually adjusting to the waves of change. With time, however, many management problems are emerging from these adjustments. For instance, in the current business enterprise model, material and human resources are less supportive of the diversified internal business, as a result, organizations are facing overburdening management costs, lowering organizational flexibility and slower pace of development. Similarly, growing number of couriers and packages has flared the management costs of logistics businesses (Song & Wu, 2021). These business examples solidify the case for adopting a competent HRM model as the traditional HRM approaches seem less applicable to the modern enterprise. This urgent need of the businesses is partially addressed by the adoption of green HRM practices and partially by green innovation technologies (GITs). Among various GITs, AI is a buzz word (Song & Wu, 2021). AI technology is changing the world of HR by shifting the focus from paper-based processes to paper-less practices. In doing so, AI technology is lending a hand to streamline and automate day-to-day and routine HR tasks (Prikshat et al., 2023). For example, OpenAI's Chat GPT ca play the role of HR assistant to address employees' low-level queries such as how to update emergency contact details on daily basis. By delegating tedious administrative works, HR may focus on the organization's strategic direction. Chat GPT can also help organizations in data management and recruitment process.

In the race of attaining a sustainable competitive advantage, AI technology has become the key; yet its application is limited to a fewer organization. This, according to Gupta (2021), is partly attributable to the fear of job loss (machines replacing humans) and partly to the inability of people to manage such applications. In Malaysian context, the HR ministry has raised concerns over possible job market recession; according to an estimate, growing popularity and adoption of AI may create job loss of nearly 4.5million Malaysians (Tilo, 2023). Although people show concerns about potential job loss but they are warming up to AI as 53% of the respondents showed enthusiasm about having a robot co-worker (Oracle, 2019). This people-robot trust factor was observed to be higher in India (90%), China (88%), and lower in USA (57%) and UK (54%). In Oracle's (2019) survey of more than 8,000 HR professionals, 50% of the participants stated that they use some form of AI at work.

Adoption of AI technology can help organizations attain green practices by reducing human effort and improving work efficiency. This notion is exemplified by an application AskDexter that handles HR functions such as addressing employee queries about company policies and leaves. This application provides information about job opportunities; it also allows job seekers in aligning their skills with the job requirements (Gupta, 2021). For job seekers, Jobscan is another tool that not only facilitates the job seekers but also partners with leading career service organizations and higher education institutions (HEIs) such as University of Michigan, Temple University, Rutgers, Outplacement Australia, Mass Hire, Work Source, and WSG (Workforce Singapore) to improve employee outcomes (Jobscan, 2023). Also, companies such as KPMG, NASA, Microsoft, and Amazon use application tracking system (ATS), which is a human resource software that automates the hiring process and efficiently manages the recruitment process from job posting to onboarding (Baes, 2022). Below the case of FriendHRM explains growing use of HR software solutions among Malaysian organizations (FriendHRM, 2023).

Case Study

FriendHRM, An HRM software solution to Malaysian human resource management

FriendHRM is a made-in-Malaysia software gaining popularity among Malaysian HR managers and businesses. Published by Prometheus Tech, FriendHRM is a free online application that Malaysian organizations can use to manage their employees effectively regardless of business size. FriendHRM is an HR software that streamlines HR processes, automates recruitment and onboarding processes, manages employee data and tracks time off requests.

Rohana Mohammed, a business user of FriendHRM state "As a small business owner, I was having some tough time to manage my growing team's HR needs. I was spending hours each week managing paperwork, scheduling interviews, and tracking employee data. That's when I decided to invest in FriendHRM HR software, and it has been a game-changer for my business. FriendHRM has helped me automate many of our HR processes, saving me time and allowing me to focus on other important aspects of my business. I especially appreciate the onboarding and Task management features, which have made it easy to onboard new employees and track their progress. Overall, I highly recommend FriendHRM HR software to any small business owner looking to streamline their HR processes and grow their team" (FriendHRM, 2023, p. n.d.).

The software promotes team collaboration through better management of human resource, attendance, payroll, leave, shift, and task and sales. Among Malaysian organizations, FriendHRM is growing in popularity to analyze work flows, meet HR needs, and improve work efficiency.

Current role of AI technology in HR systems and practices seem to provide a vivid example of how organizations can achieve Renwick et al.'s (2013) green HRM. With AI technology, IT companies are developing applications to facilitate the HR functions of recruitment & selection, training & development (R&D), and person-job fit. HR planning has a tedious job of assigning the right person to the right job which is made easier with AI technologies (Prikshat et al., 2023). For green recruitment & selection, organizations use AI technology to screen candidate resumes and choose a suitable one who matches the job requirement. For instance, professional e-platforms such as Job-Builder and Indeed increasingly reply on intelligence tools to automate the candidate sourcing under recruitment function. This can be explained with Beamery, a data-mining algorithm based software that optimizes the process of candidate sourcing. A good side to AI supported green recruitment & selection is improved work efficiency, lowering burden of personnel and streamlining of what the organizations require and whom they hire. However, a downside to AI-supported green practice is as highlighted by Stahl (2021) that automated technologies have caused up to 60% cut down in the jobs of recruiters. Although COVID-19 pandemic caused socio-economic havoc, it also surprisingly promoted digitization of various HR practices. For instance, physical interview protocols are replaced with face-to-face interface meets. Applications such as MS Teams, Skype, and Zoom are enabling recruiters and interviewees to meet in a virtual environment. It not only expedites the recruitment process but also saves travel costs for interviewees and venue arrangements and other related management costs to the organizations.

Likewise, the use of such tech-supported portals has played an important role in the greening of employee abilities via green T&D practices. Literature suggests the effective role of AI in employees' training and development. AI systems can help organizations develop and maintain electronic inventory of employees that can facilitate the process of searching for an appropriate candidate within the organization. These systems can also help employees manage their prospective careers (Prikshat et al., 2023). AI can be used to analyze employee data and identify areas where employees may need training or development to become more environmentally conscious. Today, numerous organizations across various industries are using Zoom, MS Teams, Google Meet platform and Google Classroom to train their employees. Adoption of these technologies has not only changed the physical time-space aspect of training & development but also reduced the related management costs (such as resources and time). Maity (2019) advocates the use of AI in identifying and facilitating the training needs of employees. Bites AI, an application leveraging the power of AI technology, helps with the training & development of frontline workers. This application creates content capsules comprising of microlearning units; each unit has an AI-generated quiz, video, summary card and a discussion board (Worcman, 2023).

Greening employees is the second component of Renwick et al.'s (2013) green HRM. This component is achieved when organizations motivate green employees through performance appraisal and reward systems. However, Mercer's (2019) global survey of 1,154 HR leaders showed that 70% of companies seek to improve the link between performance management and talent-related decisions such as succession planning, development, and promotions. Unchanged from last five years, only 2% of the surveyed companies believe that their performance management system is offering the desired value (Mercer, 2019). AI technology offers a solution to this HR problem by monitoring employee activities and tracking key performance indicators (KPIs). Use of AI in performance management systems can help promote data-based decision making via supporting data analysis, generating metrics, and suggesting improvements/adjustments (Soni, 2023).

According to Ari et al. (2020), employees exhibit pro-environmental behaviors (PEBs) when management invests in green HRM practices. The use of AI technology in performance appraisal and management helps organizations in motivating employees to adopt green behaviors. For example, robust use of data analytics automates the process of manual assessment and reviews; it offers real-time assessments using accurate and up-to-date data (Soni, 2023). Moreover, AI can be applied in smart monitoring of the employee's work patterns, identifying the areas where they are wasting energy and resources, thus implementing the policies and mechanisms to reduce the wastage (Gupta, 2021). Since AI systems maintain record of employees' personal details along with any changes in their beneficiary, marital status, or dependents; hence, AI systems can easily track employee data. Thus, AI adoption in the payroll system enables HR managers to efficiently handle HR payroll and related activities (Prikshat et al., 2023).

Renwick et al.'s (2013) last component of green HRM is creating green opportunities. This brings forth application of AI in employee engagement. AI can be used to analyze employee engagement data and identify patterns that indicate a lack of commitment to sustainability. This information can then be used to develop strategies to improve employee engagement, such as providing training and development opportunities or creating incentives for employees who demonstrate a commitment to sustainability.

AI-Green HRM Implications for Malaysian Organizations

In Malaysia, organizations are gradually using AI and AI-enabled software and tools that not only improves the HR functioning but also upskills employees for value-added jobs. Findings of a survey of 12 Malaysian companies showed the growing use of AI in recruitment, HR shared service operations, reporting and analytics, talent management, learning and development, and self-service assistance (Sithambaram & Tajudeen, 2023).

AI and Green HRM can help Malaysian firms improve ESG (Environmental, Social, and Governance) by providing data-driven insights and automating various HR processes while also considering environmental sustainability. For example, AI can be used to analyze large amounts of data to identify areas where the company can reduce its carbon footprint, increase energy efficiency, and implement sustainable workplace practices. AI can also help track ESG metrics and provide regular reports on the company's performance.

Green HRM can help improve ESG by implementing policies and practices that promote sustainable development and environmentally responsible behavior.

This includes reducing the company's carbon footprint, promoting telecommuting and flexible work arrangements, and encouraging sustainable travel practices. Additionally, Green HRM can ensure that ESG considerations are integrated into the company's recruitment, performance management, and compensation processes.

By combining the power of AI and Green HRM, Malaysian firms can better understand and address ESG challenges while also considering the environmental impact of their operations and practices. This can improve their reputation, attract, and retain talent, and achieve long-term sustainability.

CHALLENGES IN ADOPTING AI-ENABLED GREEN HRM

Two decades of evidence from various companies, industries, and countries support the notion that AI technology has the potential to create value for organizations, employees, and customers in a smart way (Chowdhury et al., 2023). On one hand, AI is changing the way of living; on the other hand, it is assisting organizations in streamlining their business processes, boosting efficiency, lowering management & production costs, and increasing productivity (Tewari & Pant, 2020). Among recent debates on the topic, AI integration with HRM practices has earned sincere scholarly interest (Budhwar et al., 2022; Malik et al., 2020; Prikshat et al., 2023). Where researchers are reviewing and explicating the merits of AI-enabled HRM practices for organizations (Chowdhury et al., 2023; Prikshat et al., 2023); there are others debating its fruitfulness and challenges for organizations and its employees (Tambe et al., 2019; Tewari & Pant, 2020).

AI-enabled HRM has changed the way organizations are hiring, managing, and engaging their employees. Today, AI-enabled HR applications such as GustoHR, CloudHR, SAP SuccessFactors, CakeHR, ZohoPeople, BambooHR, and OnPay are widely used by organizations for various HR-related matters (Prikshat et al., 2023). Growing use of such applications has not only created opportunities for green HRM and redefined the role of HR professionals but also raised concerns among employees about its efficacy and future role in the organization. Though the integration of AI and Green HRM looks fascinating, there are many challenges in implementing AI in Green HRM at organizational level. As observed by Tambe et al. (2019), AI adoption in HR is likely to be prone to challenges ranging from conceptual to practical understanding of such AI-HR duo. The reason being when data analytics is applied to man-matters, it may conflict with what society views as important in making people-related sequential decisions. For example, use of AI technology in hiring function may ease and speed up matching employee attributes with job performance; however, such algorithm-based approach may lead to distorted hiring decisions as job performance is a biased indicator itself. This notion was exemplified with the Amazon hiring problems back in 2018 (Tambe et al., 2019).

In Malaysia, lack of awareness about the economic potential of AI & related GITs and limited access to capital discourages Malaysian firms from AI adoption. Also, lack AI education, training, and human capital in AI and robotics has slowed down the adoption of AI among Malaysian organizations (M. F. Ahmad et al., 2022). Among various related concerns, below discussed are a few significant challenges to AI-enabled green HRM practices.

Lack of Awareness About AI and Green HRM

At firm level, strategic management and employees need to be on the same page to successfully attain green HRM practices. Incoherence between the top management and employees about what entails green HRM and how it can benefit the employees and the firm is a challenge. Adding to this ambiguity, is the adoption of AI technology to facilitate green HR practices without creating awareness about how AI-enabled green HRM practices and decisions will affect employees. For example, Budhwar et al. (2022) found that there is lack of transparency in how organizations utilize AI technology provided output to make decisions about employees. As a result, expected effects of AI-enabled green HRM remain unrealized due to negligence in the initiation and execution of eco-friendly HRM practices. Also, when employees are unable to understand the procedure followed in AI-based decisions or are unable to accept AI-based decisions; they are likely to engage in adversarial behaviors (Tambe et al., 2019). Poor communication between organizations and employees on which AI technologies are being used and how AI-system makes employee-related decisions can only worsen the situation. Wilson et al. (2017) signify the need for open communication with employees to ensure prompt use of AI-enabled practices. Failure to do so will give rise to challenge 2 and 3 as described below.

Lack of Understanding and Expertise

Adopting AI in green HRM is challenged with the lack of understanding and expertise among organizations. This is a twin challenge as expertise required in AI adoption relate to both (i) updated skills and capabilities of IT experts providing IT services within the organization and (ii) IT users i.e., management and employees, who rely on these technologies and information technology (IT) assisted systems to perform their routine tasks. There may be a lack of expertise within organizations to effectively implement and manage AI systems. Also, many companies may not fully understand the capabilities of AI or how it can be applied to HRM, and as a result, may be hesitant to invest in the technology. At firm-level, the financial aspect of adopting AI is another factor that disrupts the process of AI adoption. Therefore, insufficient understanding of how AI technology can help solve business issues is a potential challenge to AI adoption (Chatterjee, 2020). First, organizations need to have a clear understanding of the strategic role that AI technology will play in the business then communicate the same to IT department and HR users of AI-enabled systems.

Resistance to Change

Lack of transparency and poor communication are the common factors causing resistance to change within organizations (Malik et al., 2020). Employees may be resistant to the implementation of new technology and may be unwilling to change the way they work. This can make it difficult for organizations to effectively implement and utilize AI systems. This is likely to happen when employees and management are unfamiliar with the AI technology and its role in promoting green culture in the organization (Nam et al., 2021). At employee-level, adoption of AI intends to ease the HR jobs by managing predictable and routine tasks, but it also worries employees about losing job. This fear of job loss may provoke employee resistance unless organizations make people understand that AI and such green technologies are to support routine works rather than to replace people. To this, emphasize the need to develop a better human-AI configuration so employees lower their guard against AI by seeing it as a technology that compliments rather than competing with humans (Budhwar et al., 2022). For instance, Sithambaram & Tajudeen (2023) found that AI adoption in HRM does not lead to lowering number of head counts rather it enables employees to better prepare for more value-added jobs. It is another technology-assisted way to upskill one's employees. At management-level, financial justification factor may convince or unconvince managers to welcome AI adoption. As a result, organizations are facing issues of negative employee attitudes and increasing intents of turnover (Prikshat et al., 2023). Additionally, it can also be difficult for organizations to communicate the benefits of AI to employees and gain their buy-in. Resistance to change will lower employee commitment to AI and green practices.

Ethical, Legal and Security Concerns

Recent survey statistics indicate ethical use of AI in HR practices as one of the major challenges in the technology adoption (see Figure 4). Privacy refers to the way employee data is used and governed while security is about the data protection against stealth for destructive means (Abouelmehdi et al., 2018). 42% of the surveyed

Malaysian HR Leaders agreed that employee privacy is a major concern in AI-powered HR practices (Sofiah, 2023). Organizations endorsing AI-enabled green HRM need to take their employees in confidence about what data is collected, why it is collected and how it is used to make informed and morally responsible decisions (Prikshat et al., 2023). Otherwise, data privacy and security concerns may challenge the adoption of AI-enabled green HRM practices. As AI systems often rely on large amounts of data, organizations must ensure that this data is collected, stored, and used in compliance with relevant data privacy laws and regulations. If not, legality issues of AI adoption may raise employee concerns about data and information used by AI systems to make employee-related decisions (Nam et al., 2021). It will also add to ethical concerns of employees about transparency, integrity and reliability of AI systems used by organizations to make HR decisions; thereby, lack of trust may create potential challenges for AI adoption (Al Badi et al., 2022). Additionally, organizations must ensure that the AI systems they implement are secure to prevent data breaches and unauthorized access. Adopting AI in green HRM is not a simple task and requires a well-structured approach. Organizations need to understand the capabilities and limitations of AI, and make sure that the data is used in compliance with the data privacy laws.

Figure 4. Use of AI in one's current role
Source: Adopted from Sofiah (2023)

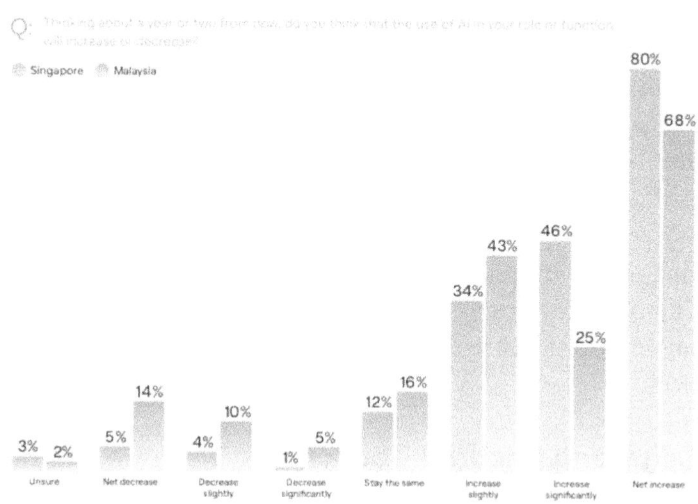

According to Tambe et al. (2019), complexity of HR outcomes makes it a unique case for observing and gradually addressing the AI adoption challenges. HR issues such as employee dismissal are relatively rare events having serious social and ethical concerns; predicting such outcomes using data science may not suffice rather give birth to new challenges. Therefore, organizations planning to adopt AI in the execution of HR practices need to be wary of the HR areas where AI can be adopted and to what extent and pace of change shall be followed to ensure a successful AI-HRM configuration.

MANAGERIAL IMPLICATIONS OF AI-GREEN HRM ADOPTION

In the light of discussion from earlier sections, this section is centered on the managerial implications that adoption of AI in Green HRM may have for organizations. Emphasis will be made on the managerial implications that such adoption has for Malaysian organizations while addressing third objective of this chapter.

First, the key managerial implications to address the challenges of adopting AI in green HRM is to develop a clear communication strategy. This should include clear explanations of the benefits of AI for the organization and for the environment, as well as how the technology will be implemented and used. This will help to gain the buy-in and support of employees and address any concerns they may have about the technology.

The second important managerial implication is to provide employee training and development opportunities. Employees need to be educated and trained on how to use and benefit from the AI systems implemented in the organization. Additionally, providing employees with development opportunities that focus on sustainability and environmental awareness can help to promote environmentally friendly behavior and improve employee engagement. This can be done through workshops, seminars, webinars, and e-learning opportunities.

Lastly, adopting AI in green HRM also implies that organizations must ensure that they are compliant with all relevant laws and regulations regarding data privacy, security, and environmental protection. This includes putting in place governance mechanisms to ensure that the data used in AI systems is collected, stored, and used in compliance with the laws and regulations. Additionally, organizations should also have in place regular auditing and monitoring mechanisms to ensure compliance and address any issues that may arise.

CONCLUSION

Addressing the sustainability goal about responsible consumption and production, organizations are shifting their focus towards green technologies and green practices across the globe. Under this effect, the green revolution is changing the business approach to food processing, production, retailing, and services. At the organizational level, AI applications to various business areas such as accounting, production, and IT have received considerable attention. However, AI-HRM integration to manage people has triggered a new stream of research focused on exploring, reviewing, and explicating the AI adoption effects on firm-level and individual outcomes and related HRM practices. Adding to the agenda are the organizational measures to promote AI-enabled green HRM practices. Although AI adoption helps facilitates greening employees and creating green opportunities but ignorance to potential issues of resistance to change and lack of awareness may hinder its usefulness.

In conclusion, AI and green HRM are two important and rapidly evolving areas of business that have the potential to significantly impact organizations and society. The intersection of these two areas has the potential to create a powerful synergy that can help organizations become more efficient and sustainable. By utilizing AI to analyze data and identify areas where resources are being wasted, organizations can develop and implement more sustainable practices. Additionally, by using AI to automate various HR processes and improve employee engagement, organizations can save time and resources while promoting environmentally friendly behavior among employees.

REFERENCES

Ababneh, O. M. A. (2021). How do green HRM practices affect employees' green behaviors? The role of employee engagement and personality attributes. *Journal of Environmental Planning and Management*, *64*(7), 1204–1226. doi:10.1080/09640568.2020.1814708

Abouelmehdi, K., Beni-Hessane, A., & Khaloufi, H. (2018). Big healthcare data: Preserving security and privacy. *Journal of Big Data*, *5*(1), 1. doi:10.118640537-017-0110-7

Ahmad, M. F., Husin, N. A. A., Ahmad, A. N. A., Abdullah, H., Wei, C. S., & Nawi, M. N. M. (2022). Digital Transformation: An Exploring Barriers and Challenges Practice of Artificial Intelligence in Manufacturing Firms in Malaysia. *Journal of Advanced Research in Applied Sciences and Engineering Technology*, *29*(1), 1. Advance online publication. doi:10.37934/araset.29.1.110117

Ahmad, S. (2015). Green Human Resource Management: Policies and practices. *Cogent Business & Management*, *2*(1), 1030817. doi:10.1080/23311975.2015.1030817

Al Badi, F. K., Alhosani, K. A., Jabeen, F., Stachowicz-Stanusch, A., Shehzad, N., & Amann, W. (2022). Challenges of AI Adoption in the UAE Healthcare. *Vision (Basel), 26*(2), 193–207. doi:10.1177/0972262920988398

Ari, E., Karatepe, O. M., Rezapouraghdam, H., & Avci, T. (2020). A Conceptual Model for Green Human Resource Management: Indicators, Differential Pathways, and Multiple Pro-Environmental Outcomes. *Sustainability (Basel), 12*(17), 7089. doi:10.3390u12177089

Baer, S. (2023, March 28). Council Post: How To Incorporate Artificial Intelligence Into Learning And Development. *Forbes*. https://www.forbes.com/sites/forbeshumanresourcescouncil/2023/03/28/how-to-incorporate-artificial-intelligence-into-learning-and-development/

Baes, H. (2022, August 18). *Applicant Tracking Systems: The Ultimate Guide for Job Seekers in 2022*. Jobscan. https://www.jobscan.co/applicant-tracking-systems/

Baig, A., Brown, J. S., & Forrest, W. HV, V., Hjartar, K., & Yee, L. (2023, January 6). Where Is Tech Going in 2023? *Harvard Business Review*. https://hbr.org/2023/01/where-is-tech-going-in-2023

Benevene, P., & Buonomo, I. (2020). Green Human Resource Management: An Evidence-Based Systematic Literature Review. *Sustainability (Basel), 12*(15), 15. Advance online publication. doi:10.3390u12155974

Bradu, P., Biswas, A., Nair, C., Sreevalsakumar, S., Patil, M., Kannampuzha, S., Mukherjee, A. G., Wanjari, U. R., Renu, K., Vellingiri, B., & Gopalakrishnan, A. V. (2022). Recent advances in green technology and Industrial Revolution 4.0 for a sustainable future. *Environmental Science and Pollution Research International*. Advance online publication. doi:10.100711356-022-20024-4 PMID:35397034

Budhwar, P., Malik, A., De Silva, M. T. T., & Thevisuthan, P. (2022). Artificial intelligence – challenges and opportunities for international HRM: A review and research agenda. *International Journal of Human Resource Management, 33*(6), 1065–1097. doi:10.1080/09585192.2022.2035161

Bughin, J., Seong, J., Manyika, J., Chui, M., & Joshi, R. (2018). *Notes from the AI Frontier | Modeling the Impact of AI on the World Economy*. McKinsey Discussion Paper. https://www.mckinsey.com/featured-insights/artificial-intelligence/notes-from-the-AI-frontier-modeling-the-impact-of-ai-on-the-world-economy

Chatterjee, S. (2020). AI strategy of India: Policy framework, adoption challenges and actions for government. *Transforming Government: People Transforming Government, 14*(5), 757–775. doi:10.1108/TG-05-2019-0031

Chowdhury, S., Dey, P., Joel-Edgar, S., Bhattacharya, S., Rodriguez-Espindola, O., Abadie, A., & Truong, L. (2023). Unlocking the value of artificial intelligence in human resource management through AI capability framework. *Human Resource Management Review*, *33*(1), 100899. doi:10.1016/j.hrmr.2022.100899

Davenport, T. H., & Ronanki, R. (2018). Don't start with moon shots. *Harvard Business Review*, 108–116.

DesJardins, J. (2016). Is it Time to Jump off the Sustainability Bandwagon? *Business Ethics Quarterly*, *26*(1), 117–135. doi:10.1017/beq.2016.12

Dumont, J., Shen, J., & Deng, X. (2017). Effects of Green HRM Practices on Employee Workplace Green Behavior: The Role of Psychological Green Climate and Employee Green Values. *Human Resource Management*, *56*(4), 613–627. doi:10.1002/hrm.21792

Fang, L., Shi, S., Gao, J., & Li, X. (2022). The mediating role of green innovation and green culture in the relationship between green human resource management and environmental performance. *PLoS One*, *17*(9), e0274820. doi:10.1371/journal.pone.0274820 PMID:36173966

Friend, H. R. M. (2023). *FriendHRM- Best Online CRM, HR management software in Malaysia*. FriendHRM. https://www.friendhrm.com

Gal, D. (2020). Perspectives and Approaches in AI Ethics: East Asia. In M. D. Dubber, F. Pasquale, & S. Das (Eds.), *The Oxford Handbook of Ethics of AI* (pp. 606–624). Oxford University Press. doi:10.1093/oxfordhb/9780190067397.013.39

Gupta, M. (2021). The Role of Artificial Intelligence in Adopting Green HRM Practices. In G. Rana, A. Khang, R. Sharma, A. K. Goel, & A. K. Dubey (Eds.), *Reinventing Manufacturing and Business Processes Through Artificial Intelligence* (1st ed.). CRC Press. doi:10.1201/9781003145011-1

Hameed, Z., Khan, I. U., Islam, T., Sheikh, Z., & Naeem, R. M. (2020). Do green HRM practices influence employees' environmental performance? *International Journal of Manpower*, *41*(7), 1061–1079. doi:10.1108/IJM-08-2019-0407

Hassoun, A., Prieto, M. A., Carpena, M., Bouzembrak, Y., Marvin, H. J. P., Pallarés, N., Barba, F. J., Punia Bangar, S., Chaudhary, V., Ibrahim, S., & Bono, G. (2022). Exploring the role of green and Industry 4.0 technologies in achieving sustainable development goals in food sectors. *Food Research International*, *162*, 112068. doi:10.1016/j.foodres.2022.112068 PMID:36461323

Jackson, S. E., Renwick, D. W. S., Jabbour, C. J. C., & Muller-Camen, M. (2011). State-of-the-Art and Future Directions for Green Human Resource Management: Introduction to the Special Issue. *German Journal of Human Resource Management*, *25*(2), 99–116. doi:10.1177/239700221102500203

Javaid, M., Haleem, A., Pratap Singh, R., Khan, S., & Suman, R. (2022). Sustainability 4.0 and its applications in the field of manufacturing. *Internet of Things and Cyber-Physical Systems*, *2*, 82–90. doi:10.1016/j.iotcps.2022.06.001

Jobscan. (2023). *About Us*. Jobscan. https://www.jobscan.co/about/

Kramar, R. (2014). Beyond strategic human resource management: Is sustainable human resource management the next approach? *International Journal of Human Resource Management*, *25*(8), 1069–1089. doi:10.1080/09585192.2013.816863

Lazim, R. M., Nawi, N. M., Masroon, M. H., Abdullah, N., & Iskandar, M. C. M. (2020). Adoption of IR4.0 into Agricultural Sector in Malaysia: Potential and Challenges. *Advances in Agricultural and Food Research Journal*, *1*(2), 2. Advance online publication. doi:10.36877/aafrj.a0000140

Maity, S. (2019). Identifying opportunities for artificial intelligence in the evolution of training and development practices. *Journal of Management Development*, *38*(8), 651–663. doi:10.1108/JMD-03-2019-0069

Malik, A., Srikanth, N., & Budhwar, P. (2020). Chapter 4: Digitisation, Artificial Intelligence (AI) and HRM. In J. Crawshaw, P. Budhwar, & A. Davis (Eds.), *Human Resource Management: Strategic and International Perspectives* (3rd ed., pp. 88–111). SAGE.

Mansor, D. (2021, August 30). How Malaysia Can Navigate Its Future Economy With AI – Microsoft Malaysia News Center. *Microsoft Malaysia News Center*. https://news.microsoft.com/en-my/2021/08/30/how-malaysia-can-navigate-its-future-economy-with-ai/

Marda, V. (2018). Artificial intelligence policy in India: A framework for engaging the limits of data-driven decision-making. *Philosophical Transactions. Series A, Mathematical, Physical, and Engineering Sciences*, *376*(2133), 1–19. doi:10.1098/rsta.2018.0087 PMID:30323001

McKinsey. (2018). *AI, Automation, and the Future of Work: Ten Things to Solve for*. McKinsey Global Institute. http://dln.jaipuria.ac.in:8080/jspui/bitstream/123456789/1335/1/MGI-Briefing-Note-AI-automation-and-the-future-of-work_June2018.pdf

Mercer. (2019). *Mercer's 2019 Global Performance Management Survey*. Marsh & McLennan Companies. https://www.imercer.com/uploads/common/HTML/LandingPages/AnalyticalHub/june2019-mercer-2019-global-performance-management-survey-executive-summary.pdf

Muster, V., & Schrader, U. (2011). Green Work-Life Balance: A New Perspective for Green HRM. *German Journal of Human Resource Management: Zeitschrift Für Personalforschung*, *25*(2), 140–156. doi:10.1177/239700221102500205

Nam, K., Dutt, C. S., Chathoth, P., Daghfous, A., & Khan, M. S. (2021). The adoption of artificial intelligence and robotics in the hotel industry: Prospects and challenges. *Electronic Markets*, *31*(3), 553–574. doi:10.100712525-020-00442-3

Ogbeibu, S., Emelifeonwu, J., Pereira, V., Oseghale, R., Gaskin, J., Sivarajah, U., & Gunasekaran, A. (2023). Demystifying the roles of organisational smart technology, artificial intelligence, robotics and algorithms capability: A strategy for green human resource management and environmental sustainability. *Business Strategy and the Environment*, 1–20. doi:10.1002/bse.3495

Omar, S. A., Hasbolah, F., & Zainudin, U. M. (2017). The Diffusion of Artificial Intelligence in Governance of Public Listed Companies in Malaysia. *International Journal of Business Economics and Law*, *14*(2), 1–9.

Oracle. (2019). *Oracle | From Fear to Enthusiasm* (Global Study 2019 Oracle and Future Workplace AI@Work). Oracle. https://www.oracle.com/webfolder/s/assets/ebook/ai-work/index.html?source=:ow:ms:pt:RC_PDMK191009P00032:LPD400002437&intcmp=:ow:ms:pt:RC_PDMK191009P00032:LPD400002437

Pham, N. T., Hoang, H. T., & Phan, Q. P. T. (2020). Green human resource management: A comprehensive review and future research agenda. *International Journal of Manpower*, *41*(7), 845–878. doi:10.1108/IJM-07-2019-0350

Polas, M. R. H., Afshar Jahanshahi, A., Kabir, A. I., Sohel-Uz-Zaman, A. S., Osman, A. R., & Karim, R. (2022). Artificial Intelligence, Blockchain Technology, and Risk-Taking Behavior in the 4.0IR Metaverse Era: Evidence from Bangladesh-Based SMEs. *Journal of Open Innovation*, *8*(3), 168. doi:10.3390/joitmc8030168

PricewaterhouseCoopers. (2020). *PwC's Global Artificial Intelligence Study: Sizing the prize*. PwC. https://www.pwc.com/gx/en/issues/data-and-analytics/publications/artificial-intelligence-study.html

Prikshat, V., Malik, A., & Budhwar, P. (2023). AI-augmented HRM: Antecedents, assimilation and multilevel consequences. *Human Resource Management Review*, *33*(1), 100860. doi:10.1016/j.hrmr.2021.100860

PWC. (2020). *Sizing the prize | What's the real value of AI for your business and how can you capitalise?* [PWC's Global AI Study]. PWC. https://www.pwc.com/gx/en/issues/analytics/assets/pwc-ai-analysis-sizing-the-prize-report.pdf?source=:ow:ms:pt:RC_PDMK191009P00032:LPD400002437

Rahman, M., Ming, T. H., Baigh, T. A., & Sarker, M. (2021). Adoption of artificial intelligence in banking services: An empirical analysis. *International Journal of Emerging Markets*. doi:10.1108/IJOEM-06-2020-0724

Ramachandran, K. K., Apsara Saleth Mary, A., Hawladar, S., Asokk, D., Bhaskar, B., & Pitroda, J. R. (2022). Machine learning and role of artificial intelligence in optimizing work performance and employee behavior. *Materials Today: Proceedings*, *51*, 2327–2331. doi:10.1016/j.matpr.2021.11.544

Regona, M., Yigitcanlar, T., Xia, B., & Li, R. Y. M. (2022). Opportunities and Adoption Challenges of AI in the Construction Industry: A PRISMA Review. *Journal of Open Innovation*, *8*(1), 45. doi:10.3390/joitmc8010045

Renwick, D., Redman, T., & Maguire, S. (2008). *Green HRM: A review, process model, and research agenda*. University of Sheffield Management School. https://onlinelibrary.wiley.com/doi/abs/10.1111/j.1468-2370.2011.00328.x

Renwick, D. W. S., Redman, T., & Maguire, S. (2013). Green Human Resource Management: A Review and Research Agenda*. *International Journal of Management Reviews*, *15*(1), 1–14. doi:10.1111/j.1468-2370.2011.00328.x

Samsurijan, M. S., Ebekozien, A., Nor, A. N. A., Shaed, M. M., & Radin, B. R. F. (2022). Artificial intelligence in urban services in Malaysia: A review. *PSU Research Review*. doi:10.1108/PRR-07-2021-0034

Sharma, C., Sakhuja, S., & Nijjer, S. (2022). Recent trends of green human resource management: Text mining and network analysis. *Environmental Science and Pollution Research International*, *29*(56), 84916–84935. doi:10.100711356-022-21471-9 PMID:35790632

Sithambaram, R. A., & Tajudeen, F. P. (2023). Impact of Artificial Intelligence in Human Resource Management: A Qualitative Study in the Malaysian Context. *Asia Pacific Journal of Human Resources*, *61*(4), 821–844. doi:10.1111/1744-7941.12356

Sofiah, A. (2023, August 24). *More than half of HR leaders surveyed in Singapore and Malaysia share concerns about the ethical use of AI*. Human Resources Online. https://www.humanresourcesonline.net/more-than-half-of-hr-leaders-surveyed-in-singapore-and-malaysia-share-concerns-about-the-ethical-use-of-ai

Song, Y., & Wu, R. (2021). Analysing human-computer interaction behaviour in human resource management system based on artificial intelligence technology. *Knowledge Management Research and Practice*, 1–10. doi:10.1080/14778238.2021.1955630

Soni, H. (2023, February 1). *10 Areas AI Impacts Performance Management Practices*. About Leaders. https://aboutleaders.com/performance-management-practices/

Stahl, A. (2021, October 3). How AI Will Impact The Future Of Work And Life. *Forbes*. https://www.forbes.com/sites/ashleystahl/2021/03/10/how-ai-will-impact-the-future-of-work-and-life/

Statista. (2020). *Global business and HR leaders use of AI to assist workers 2020*. Statista. https://www.statista.com/statistics/1120120/global-business-and-hr-leaders-use-of-ai-to-assist-workers/

Sun, T. Q., & Medaglia, R. (2019). Mapping the challenges of Artificial Intelligence in the public sector: Evidence from public healthcare. *Government Information Quarterly*, *36*(2), 368–383. doi:10.1016/j.giq.2018.09.008

Tambe, P., Cappelli, P., & Yakubovich, V. (2019). Artificial Intelligence in Human Resources Management: Challenges and a Path Forward. *California Management Review*, *61*(4), 15–42. doi:10.1177/0008125619867910

Tewari, I., & Pant, M. (2020). Artificial Intelligence Reshaping Human Resource Management: A Review. *2020 IEEE International Conference on Advent Trends in Multidisciplinary Research and Innovation (ICATMRI)*, 1–4. 10.1109/ICATMRI51801.2020.9398420

Tilo, D. (2023, June 28). HR minister: Malaysia needs to retrain 50% of workforce amid AI rise. *Human Resources Director (HRD)*. https://www.hcamag.com/asia/specialisation/learning-development/hr-minister-malaysia-needs-to-retrain-50-of-workforce-amid-ai-rise/450731

UN. (2023). *12.6 Sustainability Reporting (Businesses)* [SDG 12 Data and Progress]. SDG 12 Hub. https://sdg12hub.org/sdg-12-hub/see-progress-on-sdg-12-by-target/126-sustainability-reporting-businesses

Valuer. (2022). *Innovative Companies & SDG 12: Responsible Consumption and Production*. https://www.valuer.ai/blog/aligning-business-with-sdg-12-by-collaborating-with-startups

Wilson, H. J., Daugherty, P. R., & Morini-Bianzino, N. (2017). The jobs that artificial intelligence will create. *MIT Sloan Management Review*, *58*(4), 14–16.

Worcman, V. (2023, February 9). *How Bites AI is Unleashing Employee Training and Development*. Bites. https://mybites.io/blog/employee-training-powered-by-ai/

Wu, F., Lu, C., Zhu, M., Chen, H., Zhu, J., Yu, K., Li, L., Li, M., Chen, Q., Li, X., Cao, X., Wang, Z., Zha, Z., Zhuang, Y., & Pan, Y. (2020). Towards a new generation of artificial intelligence in China. *Nature Machine Intelligence*, *2*(6), 6. Advance online publication. doi:10.103842256-020-0183-4

Wu, W., Huang, T., & Gong, K. (2020). Ethical Principles and Governance Technology Development of AI in China. *Engineering (Beijing)*, *6*(3), 302–309. doi:10.1016/j.eng.2019.12.015

Yang, X. (2019). Accelerated Move for AI Education in China. *ECNU Review of Education*, *2*(3), 347–352. doi:10.1177/2096531119878590

Yong, J. Y., Yusliza, M. Y., Ramayah, T., Farooq, K., & Tanveer, M. I. (2022). Accentuating the interconnection between green intellectual capital, green human resource management and sustainability. *Benchmarking: An International Journal*, 1463–5771. doi:10.1108/BIJ-11-2021-0641

Zoogah, D. B. (2011). The Dynamics of Green HRM Behaviors: A Cognitive Social Information Processing Approach. *German Journal of Human Resource Management*, *25*(2), 117–139. doi:10.1177/239700221102500204

Chapter 9
AI-Powered Employee Experience:
Strategies and Best Practices

Dwijendra Nath Dwivedi
https://orcid.org/0000-0001-7662-415X
Krakow University of Economics, Poland

Ghanashyama Mahanty
https://orcid.org/0000-0002-6560-2825
Utkal University, India

ABSTRACT

AI has become an indispensable tool for businesses seeking to enhance the employee experience. Businesses that implement it can increase employee satisfaction, enhance customer service, and decrease cost per employee served – ultimately adding significant business value. Artificial intelligence instruments can improve employee experiences across several areas: recruitment, onboarding, training, and performance management. Furthermore, this use case will profoundly impact customer experiences overall.

1. INTRODUCTION

The COVID-19 pandemic has forever changed the relationship between employees and firms. Intensified war for talent, snowballing employee attrition, demand for a high degree of autonomy, widespread employee burnout and mental health issues,

DOI: 10.4018/979-8-3693-0039-8.ch009

and demand for lucrative financial and non-financial compensations make workforce management more difficult.

These changing global conditions in the workspace put human capital leaders under tremendous stress to find ways and means to deliver the best to win the talent war. Authors feel that during the COVID-19 pandemic, managing employees has been as tricky as managing business P&L. Businesses thriving in today's dynamic environment require happy and dedicated employees.

Given the complexity of the problem, what would be a better tool than emerging AI for providing an end-to-end solution starting from recruitment to winning back employees? AI tools make it easier than ever for companies to engage and motivate their staff members. AI tools simplify processes like recruitment, performance management, and productivity monitoring. They eliminate human bias while helping companies address employee issues through transparent feedback channels. Staff satisfaction depends on demonstrating care, support and authenticity. AI capabilities can assist this by automating processes, reducing escalation rates and giving employees all the data they require for effective job performance. We can use dynamic AI agents can also uncover employee sentiment through real-time surveys and provide coaching for more remarkable performance.

Employees who enjoy their work experience tend to remain motivated and perform better. AI tools can improve employee experiences by helping companies identify and retain top talent, customize learning experiences for individual learners, automate administrative tasks efficiently, and facilitate data-driven decision making. AI can also help and enable employees to search for part-time projects that meet their skillsets and career goals. These AI engines would enable the company to utilize their benched workforce while simultaneously decreasing burnout and rework for overworked resources.

As soon as a company hires new employees, it is imperative that they feel welcomed into the organization. This is particularly important in larger organizations where it may be challenging for managers and HR to create personal connections between all employees. AI-powered technologies can assist by offering personalized experiences, improving communication channels, and supporting data-driven decision-making processes. AI chatbots can aid the hiring process in several ways. From screening resumes and scheduling interviews to answering frequently asked questions and automating initial candidate interactions - AI bots provide an efficient means of streamlining initial candidate interactions while saving time and decreasing the workload for hiring teams. AI can also enhance employee experiences by simplifying processes, eliminating repetitive tasks and offering personalized learning and development opportunities. AI-powered learning management systems can automatically track employee progress while giving customized feedback based on each employee's strengths and weaknesses, helping improve performance while increasing job satisfaction; virtual assistants also use AI technology to manage workload and stay organized.

Reaching professional goals is vital to many employees, and artificial Intelligence can simplify this task. AI tools can assist an employee who feels ready for promotion within their company by identifying opportunities and offering training courses to prepare them for a new role - making the transition much smoother for the employee. As work environments shift, personalized employee experiences become ever more crucial. Artificial Intelligence helps businesses craft a seamless employee journey that boosts productivity and overall business performance. AI-powered employee experience engine can also enable employees to easily celebrate promotions on digital recognition sites or pages that are easy to customize each time and personalize. Furthermore, personalized coaching for employees who may still need to be ready to advance helps motivate them in their current roles while encouraging them toward personal and professional development. It also creates more satisfaction in work by eliminating monotonous, repetitive tasks while offering more efficient workflow solutions for employees.

2. LITERATURE STUDY

Cao et al. (2018) conducted extensive user research to identify the needs and problems of contemporary office workers. He created a Cognitive Hub that provides AI-based services to improve work experience and the well-being of office workers. Hosseini et al.(2023) sketched a set of ethical guidelines for introducing experimental technologies into workplaces. Drage & Mackereth (2022) claims that using AI technology to make the recruitment process racial and gender-neutral is very misleading. They made several recommendations to AI HR firms, their firms and policy makers to make the process more sound and objective.

Mantello & Ho (2023) interrogate the growing importance of technology centre automated human management processes and its implication towards the Global workforce. While emotional recognition technologies are aiding human capital management, they argue that priority should be given to people-centred managerial decisions. Pillai et al. (2023) conducted an interesting study by surveying 1130 employees on their adoption and experience using an employee chatbot. The research briefly summarises the "reasons for" and "reasons against" adopting AI-enabled employee chatbots. Naqvi et al. (2023) study focuses on the cause and effect of employee experience in a large fashion retail brand in India. One key observation of the study is that AI-powered HR bots can substantially improve the employee experience.

Johnson et al. (2020) found eHRM and AI can potentially transform how the hospitality and tourism industry recruits and selects employees. They cautioned that these tools, policies and procedures much be made aware and well-received by employees before you roll those in the organization. Black et al. (2020) outlined the reasons underlying the development of AI-enabled recruiting systems evolved from nice to talk about to necessary to utilize. Also, it recommended in the competitive digital world how human resources managers take full advantage of the tool. Hmoud & László (2019) talks of about the emerging trend of using Ai in the human resources management process. It highlights the importance AI will in automating the repeating tasks such as sourcing, screening and early interview by making the recruitment process more cost-effective and efficient. Albert (2019) provides a comprehensive review of AI applications used in the employee recruitment and selection domain. Also, the study conducts a piece of primary research to find out the areas where AI-enabled tools can play an important role. Abdelhay (2023) found that with AI and robotics, firms can increasingly be able to handle tasks like hiring and onboarding new employees, as well as data collection, analysis, and management. Tschang & Mezquita (2020) give a perspective of how AI, alongside other emerging technologies, can substantially augment capabilities and, in turn, create enormous economies of scale and scope of the firms that believe and employ those. John W. Murphy et. al. (2021) focused on key points that is the need to produce a responsible technology, so that employees are not further overworked and manipulated. David R. Fineman et al. (2021)I dentified eight factors as important to creating a successful people analytics program. Anna Lena et al. (2022) systematically reviewed the literature on the ethicality of AI-enabled recruiting. Purva Grover et al. (2020) provided guidelines for managers for AI applications in different components of Operation management.

3. EMPLOYEE LIFE CYCLE IN AN ORGANIZATION

Employee Life Cycle in an organization refers to the process of recruiting, training and developing employees in an organization. This model helps organizations build an engaged workforce which helps achieve their goals. Understanding this model is critical for HR teams looking to maximize each stage of recruitment and offboarding for more engaging employee experiences while decreasing turnover rates.

Figure 1. Employee life cycle
Source: Author

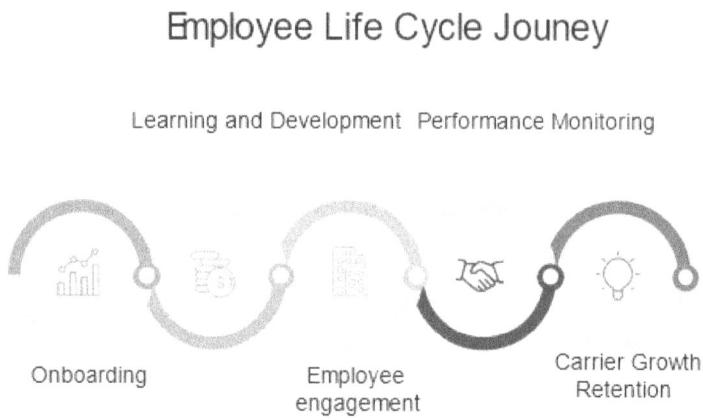

3.1 Onboarding

Beginning a new job is exciting and daunting for the employee and company. On one side, they need to familiarize themselves with coworkers and the environment of the office to adjust more quickly, while on the other side, employees must understand their responsibilities and expectations for this particular role. At this stage, the objective is to maximize an employee's experience so they feel more valued and satisfied at work - this can help improve productivity while decreasing turnover rates. At this stage, various metrics are used to monitor performance: average employee tenure or the percentage of new hires who leave within their first year are both important performance measures. Another metric to use is the employee net promoter score which indicates how likely employees are to recommend a company to a friend. If these metrics seem problematic, reevaluating how expectations are set with new hires needs to be investigated.

3.2 Learning and Development

At this stage, employees acquire the skills they need to do their jobs more efficiently and effectively, learn about the company culture, and become productive team members. Employee life cycle management plays a vital role in this stage as it helps boost productivity and morale among staff members. Companies often prioritize recruitment and onboarding when creating an employee lifecycle optimization strategy for their business; all stages of the employee life cycle should be considered to ensure positive employee experiences from start to finish. Doing this can increase retention rates and create an overall more contented workforce.

3.3 Performance Monitoring

Consistent employee performance monitoring is vitally important to any business, enabling managers to provide instantaneous feedback and assist their staff members in developing their skills. Monitoring also identifies any potential issues or predicts employee turnover; encourages external learning activities like seminars and conferences to keep team members engaged with their work while developing their careers further

3.4 Carrier Growth Retention

Much goes into an employee's journey through their life cycle, from recruitment and attraction through performance monitoring, learning & development and carrier growth retention phases before leaving through separation or alumni. HR teams have ample opportunities to enhance employees' experiences throughout their employment experience.

Therefore, retention is one of the key aspects of the employee lifecycle for any organization - keeping existing employees for longer will reduce hiring and training costs; retaining staff for longer is key! To retain employees more effectively, it's essential to understand what makes employees happy and how we can enhance company culture to promote retention - obtaining feedback from current and past staff through surveys is a good place to start. Keeping more current workers happy by offering flexible work arrangements, student loan repayment assistance, or wellness programs may also save costs. Many ways exist to assess employee experiences, from conducting regular employee engagement surveys and reviewing attrition and productivity rates to taking an in-depth view of each stage of an employee lifecycle - each stage should be reviewed so that one can optimize employee experiences with business and improve them accordingly.

4. USE CASES WITH A PROFOUND IMPACT ON CUSTOMER EXPERIENCES OVERALL

3.1 Personalized Learning and Development

Personalized learning is a training method that tailors curriculum and instruction specific to the learner's needs and learning style. It's a type of education that allows employees to acquire new skills when and how they're needed - an effective strategy for increasing employee engagement and retention and driving productivity and business expansion. Personalized learning differs from traditional classroom instruction by not necessitating lecturing from educators; rather, students work on projects tailored to their interests or learning styles, and the educator becomes more of a coach and mentor, helping the child acquire all the knowledge needed for success.

Teachers are then freed up to focus more on the social and emotional aspects of education and provide extra assistance to struggling students to help them catch up sooner. Personalized learning provides students with an experience that is both flexible and collaborative, enabling them to collaborate on group projects together - an activity which can teach valuable communication and leadership skills.

Students also better understand how they can apply their newfound knowledge in real-life situations, such as starting a business or running marketing campaigns. With real-time, real-peer collaboration on projects and instructor guidance, this form of education offers students invaluable knowledge that they can use immediately in real-life situations. As technology and job markets rapidly shift, employees must quickly develop the latest in-demand skills. Organizations are turning to artificial intelligence (AI)-enhanced L&D programs to help employees upskill or reskill more efficiently. AI can tailor learning content to each employee by analyzing activity, progress and challenges they are facing to recommend training materials that will best benefit them. It makes learning more efficient and effective - both critical to success. Personalized learning offers numerous financial advantages over traditional methods. By using AI to personalize the learning experience for each person, customized learning saves resources while improving employee satisfaction.

3.2 Improved Recruitment Process

Artificial Intelligence-powered recruitment software can help find applicants and automate the entire recruitment process from sourcing to resume screening, saving recruiters and hiring managers time and energy in dealing with administrative tasks. It frees them up for more strategic activities that drive real business results while eliminating administrative tasks from their daily duties. AI-powered recruitment software assists HR teams with finding suitable candidates and can automate candidate scoring and feedback to aid better hiring decisions. It reduces time spent screening applicants, scheduling interviews, coordinating with colleagues within the team, and ultimately increasing productivity during recruitment processes.

Recruitment optimization can be an invaluable way of increasing employee retention rates and fostering organizational diversity. When used effectively, AI can effectively combat human biases that may sway hiring decisions and result in bad hires. Numerous companies are already taking steps to use AI for recruitment purposes. This artificial intelligence-powered tool uses machine learning technology to identify qualified applicants by asking questions about experience and qualifications. Artificial intelligence can also help facilitate recruitment by analyzing existing candidate pools and uncovering profiles that might have gone overlooked. Such candidates tend to fit better with company culture and will likely remain employed at organizations more permanently than others. While AI may help eliminate bias from the hiring process, it relies heavily on data to learn how to screen resumes and shortlist candidates effectively. Furthermore, its design must be free from bias and regularly monitored to keep any harmful discrimination and bias at bay.

3.3 Employee Engagement

Employee engagement refers to the psychological connection employees feel between themselves, their jobs, organizations and coworkers - an essential aspect of organizational success. Engaged workers tend to be happier and more productive than disengaged ones. Companies seeking to engage employees must foster an environment in which employees feel empowered and encouraged to thrive, including cultivating leaders and teams dedicated to placing people first, building an ethical culture within teams, and promoting an atmosphere of collaboration. Employers utilize various tools to gauge employee engagement, such as surveys and reward and recognition programs. These measures allow employers to define employee engagement before assessing it to monitor it over time and make strategic improvements for employee wellbeing.

3.4 Performance Management

Performance management is an integral component of human resource management strategies for any organization, helping managers and employees understand how their work contributes to reaching company goals. Furthermore, this allows managers to track employee performance while giving constructive feedback. AI-powered performance review systems have become an indispensable resource in helping managers collect and assess employee performance data, provide objective assessments of performance, identify areas for improvement and offer tailored coaching and feedback services to their staffs' careers and foster a healthier and more productive workforce.

Companies are transitioning away from annual assessments towards continuous evaluation models for performance management. This model allows managers and employees to regularly meet to provide feedback on a particular task or project while helping managers identify if they're creating environments that encourage peak team performance. With AI-powered performance reviews, HR teams can collect data from various sources before using this insight to inform hiring, development, and retention decisions - ultimately leading to more informed choices about retaining talent or identifying leadership candidates. AI-powered performance reviews also use data collected to predict burnout and lower employee attrition risk, enabling HR teams to mobilize benched resources effectively without overworking them. AI-powered software can also assist HR professionals by automating routine HR tasks, such as processing paperwork and answering inquiries, freeing up resources to focus on more strategic endeavours like expanding employee bases or improving business results. As businesses become ever-more competitive, organizations realize the necessity of offering customized employee experiences is more essential than ever before. Leveraging emerging technologies such as artificial intelligence (AI) and virtual reality training solutions, organizations can create personalized employee journeys that foster success while equipping employees with all of the tools necessary for their success. Establishing effective performance management techniques is crucial to maintaining employee engagement and productivity levels at optimal levels across industries, yet only 6% of CEOs are happy with their organization's appraisal systems.

3.5 Well-Being and Health

AI engines can provide personalized recommendations for stress reduction, exercise, and healthy habits. AI-powered tools can also support mental health by offering virtual counselling or connecting employees with appropriate resources. HR teams can harness AI to HR's advantage by employing devices that interpret employee feedback and sentiment analysis. While traditional employee surveys use static questions to collect data, AI-powered solutions can use open-ended queries to uncover what employees desire from their work experience.

3.6 Collaboration and Communication

AI can enhance collaboration by providing intelligent tools for knowledge sharing, document management, and project coordination. It can analyze communication patterns to identify potential bottlenecks or areas for improvement. AI can also facilitate language translation, enabling seamless communication across diverse teams. Employees expect a tailored experience across their lives, including at work. Unfortunately, as companies scale, it becomes more challenging for HR and leadership teams to stay connected with employees and ensure they feel known and supported; that's where AI comes in and can make a significant difference.

3.7 Improved Employee Retention

AI-enabled tools can assist HR teams with identifying patterns in employee data that predict which employees might leave, so they can take proactive steps to prevent resignations. AI can not only assist the recruitment process but can also play an essential role in employee retention by enabling recruiters to be more proactive and focus on relationship-building with candidates - which is particularly valuable when hiring long-term relationships, such as marketing or sales positions that involve building long-term bonds with candidates - thus enriching candidate experiences as well as positioning them for future advancement within an organization.

3.8 Intelligent Remote Working

Modern AI tools offer many features to make remote work as efficient and effective as possible, including streamlining repetitive tasks, eliminating manual errors and providing advanced business intelligence. Automated workflows and forecasting tools help manage resources and shift scheduling more effectively, using predictive analytics software to identify peak times and allocate staff accordingly. Artificial intelligence tools in call centres can automate escalation processes and reduce agent workload, freeing them up to focus on more challenging and emotionally charged aspects of their jobs. Furthermore, AI supports a more diverse and flexible workplace by improving remote working policies, practices, and procedures. AI can provide employees with invaluable career development opportunities by suggesting internal job applications that align with their skills and interests or courses and training programs designed to hone them further - helping keep employees happy, productive and loyal to their employers.

3.9 Fairer Promotions

Employees want to feel that their company cares for them, leading to a shift from traditional engagement metrics to employee experience metrics. AI tools may assist companies in improving the process of recognition, rewards and performance management. These tools can assist employers and employees by eliminating bias from hiring and promotion processes and making identifying internal talent candidates for new roles easier. Furthermore, these programs may suggest courses or training programs tailored to employees' professional development goals. Dynamic AI agents use natural language processing (NLP) and machine learning to understand an employee's sentiment in real-time and respond accordingly. Businesses will continue to adopt AI technologies soon to enhance employee experiences and strengthen HR functions,

3.10 Diversity and Equality

While AI can make employees happier by eliminating repetitive, time-consuming tasks and freeing them up to focus on more complex work, its deployment must be carefully considered to prevent issues like bias again gender, ethnicity, income and other social and demographic profiles.

AI companies have begun creating diversity and equality tools that analyze algorithms used by software applications.

3.11 Business Continuity

AI-powered employee experience solutions boost productivity and morale and aid business continuity by giving employees access to tools such as predictive analytics solutions, automated processes, and more in an emergency situation. Furthermore, these technologies empower workers to take more control over their work without needing approval from a manager first. As the COVID-19 pandemic unfolded, some organizations were forced to reconsider their business continuity strategy. No longer is it enough for HR managers to develop and implement contingency plans for issues like fire drills or IT outages - they must consider what could happen if their entire work environment becomes disrupted. Employees can no longer physically come into the office. What happens, for example, if an employee is assigned to make client visits but feels unsafe due to coronavirus? Or what if some customers request email visits instead due to safety concerns? HR managers need to carefully consider these scenarios when developing emergency preparedness strategies with new policies. Many companies invest significant effort and time in crafting and testing business continuity plans, yet these can become outdated and redundant over time. It is wise to convene an annual tabletop review meeting with all relevant parties involved in reviewing them, to avoid severe business failure.

3.12 Reputational Risk

Businesses today are placing increased focus on employee experience. After all, unhappy employees cannot provide an outstanding customer experience - and turnover rates can be costly. AI-powered tools and technologies can improve employee experiences in numerous ways, such as automating routine tasks to offering personalized learning and development opportunities. They can also help businesses monitor staff performance more efficiently and reduce time spent on tedious administrative tasks while creating a healthier work-life balance for staff members. Automated systems can assist customer service agents during peak periods or seasonal rushes in eliminating tedious, repetitive transactions like answering customer delivery status questions, which is often frustrating for customer service agents. By removing this task for them, employees have more time and capacity to focus on more complex matters and provide emotional support to their customers. An AI platform could identify skills most essential to a company and devise a program to hone them, showing employees that the company cares for their growth and success, thus increasing employee satisfaction and loyalty. However, businesses must use AI-powered technologies carefully. Employees must understand how and why data is collected to ensure they feel at ease using this new technology and that its systems do not try to discriminate against them.

3.13 Employee Ethics

AI may sound futuristic, but it has already become essential to every part of our lives. From using autocorrect on our phones to ordering food via AI services - AI is becoming an integral part of life. AI technology also plays an essential role in the workplace by automating tedious tasks and meeting employee needs more effectively than ever. However, AI raises ethical considerations that need to be considered for employee engagement. If not designed or utilized correctly, AI tools could become biased and unfair in their application - thus prompting organizations to establish clear guidelines, policies and training around their ethical use. Employees must be made aware of how AI will impact their work, as well as clear policies regarding the ethical use of this new technology. One way to facilitate this is to provide employees with a forum to actively discuss AI in the organization, share experiences and voice any concerns, questions or ideas regarding how AI could be implemented more successfully for an improved workplace experience. Furthermore, regularly monitoring AI systems for bias and fairness evaluation. This may mean reviewing training data, validating decisions made by AI systems or even comparing the performance of different groups within the organization.

5. KEY CONSIDERATIONS WHILE IMPLEMENTING AI FOR EMPLOYEE ENGAGEMENTS

HR leaders prioritize increasing employee engagement as one of their top goals, yet with AI's proliferation, it has become more challenging than ever to understand what to expect and how best to leverage this technology for engagement purposes. Luckily some best practices can help HR managers get the most out of their AI engagement solutions. To ensure the success of AI engagement initiatives, we must start off with clear goals in mind. Doing this will allow us to determine key metrics that can measure impact and provide insight into how AI tools for engagement perform. Furthermore, aligning AI engagement initiatives with deeper organizational KPIs will ensure that the AI platform would support overall business goals, from lowering turnover rates to increasing productivity.

One key consideration for AI engagement tools could be ease of use and adoption by the workforce. A user-friendly tool with positive experiences should be easily adaptable by all workers in the organization. A pilot program may help test this theory; otherwise, it might prove challenging to drive adoption across the entire organization. As more global organizations make AI part of their operations, companies must take a proactive approach to ensure their AI engagement tools are effective and up to date. To do so, companies should promote open discussion among employees regarding the development and evaluation processes of these tools, as this will ensure they are used ethically, with consideration given to privacy and bias issues.

AI tools for employee engagement are helping HR teams provide more tailored work experiences to increase employee satisfaction and retention. AI can identify which employees have the ability, based on both hard and soft skills as well as motivational factors, to move into leadership positions; then recommend learning opportunities that will help them grow into those roles - thus meeting career goals more easily. AI can assist the team's productivity by identifying bottlenecks and inefficiencies in scheduling meetings, such as suggesting better times based on calendar availability. It frees up time so the teams can focus on other projects while increasing productivity. AI can also provide insight into what employees think and feel through chatbots and other internal communication platforms, allowing managers to quickly address critical issues that may arise in the workplace. AI tools offer many advantages to employee engagement efforts, but it's essential to remember that not all AI solutions are created equal. Some may be more dependable and effective than others.

6. CONCLUSION

People are critical to the organization. The pandemic has changed the world of work, and employees are demanding more pay, higher flexibility, and superior work-life balance. These pose an intricate and complex challenge for business leaders to manage the future workforce better. When the Global workforce world changed, one could no longer manage people in the old way.

Fortunately, the new technologies are reshaping the workspace. The higher digitization and data allowed one to dive deep into specific areas of the employee life cycle to understand employee pain points and help us put appropriate policies and procedures to work on superior employee engagement programs. The AI capabilities help streamline internal communication by eliminating roadblocks and equipping employees with the tools they need to reach their professional goals. The one concern we need to manage is that using AI in HR may lead to biases if misused unknowingly, especially when AI systems use biased data that leads to discriminatory results. AI-trained workforce coupled with ethical AI use framework and guidelines eliminate from the decision process.

REFERENCES

Abdelhay, S. (2023) How Artificial Intelligence can affect the process of recruitment and improve the quality of new hired employees. *Resmilitaris, 13*(3), 2517-2533.

Albert, E. (2019). AI in talent acquisition: A review of AI-applications used in recruitment and selection. *Strategic HR Review, 18*(5), 215–221. doi:10.1108/SHR-04-2019-0024

Black, J. S., & Esch, P. V. (2020). AI-enabled recruiting: What is it and how should a manager use it? *Business Horizons, 63*(2), 215–226. doi:10.1016/j.bushor.2019.12.001

Cao, Y., Vasek, J., & Dusik, M. (2018). Design towards AI-powered workplace of the future. Lecture Notes in Computer Science (Including Subseries Lecture Notes in Artificial Intelligence and Lecture Notes in Bioinformatics), 10921 LNCS, 3–20. doi:10.1007/978-3-319-91125-0_1

Collins, L., Fineman, D. R., & Tsuchida, A. (2017). *People Analytics: Recalculating the Route*. Deloitte Insights. Available at https://www2.deloitte.com/insights/us/en/focus/human-capital-trends/2017/people-analytics-in-hr.html

Daugherty, P. R., Wilson, H. J., & Chowdhury, R. (2018). Using artificial intelligence to promote diversity. *MIT Sloan Management Review*.

Drage, E., & Mackereth, K. (2022). Does AI Debias Recruitment? Race, Gender, and AI's "Eradication of Difference.". *Philosophy & Technology, 35*(4), 89. Advance online publication. doi:10.100713347-022-00543-1 PMID:36246553

Dwivedi, D., Batra, S., & Pathak, Y. K. (2023). A machine learning based approach to identify key drivers for improving corporate's esg ratings. *Journal of Law and Sustainable Development, 11*(1), e0242. doi:10.37497dgs.v11i1.242

Dwivedi, D., & Ghanashyama, M. (2023). Human Creativity vs. Machine Creativity: Innovations and Challenges. Multidisciplinary Approaches. In Z. Fields (Ed.), *AI, Creativity, Innovation, and Green Collaboration* (pp. 19–28). IGI Global.

Dwivedi, D. N., Tadoori, G., & Batra, S. (2023). Impact of women leadership and ESG ratings and in organizations: A time series segmentation study. *Academy of Strategic Management Journal*, *22*(S3), 1–6.

Grover, P., Kar, A. K., & Dwivedi, Y. K. (2022). Understanding artificial intelligence adoption in operations management: Insights from the review of academic literature and social media discussions. *Annals of Operations Research*, *308*(1–2), 177–213. doi:10.100710479-020-03683-9

Hmoud, B., & László, V. (2019). Will Artificial Intelligence Take Over Human resources Recruitment And Selection. *Network Intelligence Studies*, 21-30.

Hosseini, Z., Nyholm, S., le Blanc, P. M., Preenen, P. T. Y., & Demerouti, E. (2023). Assessing the artificially intelligent workplace: An ethical framework for evaluating experimental technologies in workplace settings. *AI and Ethics*. Advance online publication. doi:10.100743681-023-00265-w PMID:36846834

Hunkenschroer, A. L., & Luetge, C. (2022). Ethics of AI-Enabled Recruiting and Selection: A Review and Research Agenda. In Journal of Business Ethics (Vol. 178, Issue 4, pp. 977–1007). Springer Science and Business Media B.V. doi:10.100710551-022-05049-6

Johnson, R.D., Stone, D.L., & Lukaszewski, K.M. (2020). *The benefits of eHRM and AI for talent acquisition*. Academic Press.

Mantello, P., & Ho, M. T. (2023). Emotional AI and the future of wellbeing in the post-pandemic workplace. *AI & Society*. Advance online publication. doi:10.100700146-023-01639-8 PMID:36776535

Murphy, J. W., & Largacha-Martínez, C. (2021). Is it possible to create a responsible AI technology to be used and understood within workplaces and unblocked CEOs' mindsets? *AI & Society*. Advance online publication. doi:10.100700146-021-01316-8

Naqvi, S. R., Sareen, P., Sharma, T., & Naqvi, A. (2023). Enhancing Employee Experience with HR Bots: A Study in Mega Company. *2023 10th International Conference on Computing for Sustainable Global Development (INDIACom)*, 227-230.

Pillai, R., Ghanghorkar, Y., Sivathanu, B., Algharabat, R. S., & Rana, N. P. (2023). Adoption of artificial intelligence (AI) based employee experience (EEX) chatbots. *Information Technology & People*. Advance online publication. doi:10.1108/ITP-04-2022-0287

Pozzi, F. A., & Dwivedi, D. (2023). ESG and IoT: Ensuring Sustainability and Social Responsibility in the Digital Age. In S. Tiwari, F. Ortiz-Rodríguez, S. Mishra, E. Vakaj, & K. Kotecha (Eds.), *Artificial Intelligence: Towards Sustainable Intelligence. AI4S 2023. Communications in Computer and Information Science* (Vol. 1907). Springer., doi:10.1007/978-3-031-47997-7_2

Tschang, F. T., & Mezquita, E. A. (2020). Artificial Intelligence as Augmenting Automation: Implications for Employment. *The Academy of Management Perspectives*.

Chapter 10
Synergizing AI and HRM:
Leveraging Business Analytics for a Future-Ready Workforce

Kamaal Allil
https://orcid.org/0000-0001-5466-6519
University of Hertfordshire, UK

ABSTRACT

This chapter explores the integration of artificial intelligence (AI) and human resource management (HRM) practices within the Asian business landscape. It offers a comprehensive examination of the evolution of AI in HRM, emphasizing the benefits and potential challenges associated with implementing AI-driven HRM strategies. The discussion highlights the importance of synergizing AI and HRM through business analytics, offering insights into how AI can enhance recruitment, retention, and employee engagement. The author delves into potential ethical, cultural, and legal issues associated with AI-driven HRM, highlighting the necessity for thoughtful and strategic implementation. Finally, the chapter proposes strategies for successfully incorporating AI in HRM, emphasizing the development of AI competencies, fostering a data-driven culture, and ensuring ethical AI deployment. The discussion provides a foundation for future research, policy development, and practical applications in AI-driven HRM, promoting a future-ready workforce in Asia.

DOI: 10.4018/979-8-3693-0039-8.ch010

1. INTRODUCTION

1.1. Background and Context

The rapid advancements in technology, particularly in the field of artificial intelligence (AI), have dramatically transformed various aspects of businesses, including human resource management (Brynjolfsson & Mitchell, 2017). AI technologies, such as machine learning, natural language processing, and cognitive computing, are increasingly being integrated into HRM practices to optimize recruitment, employee engagement, performance management, and training and development (Gélinas et al., 2022).

The Asian market has been experiencing significant growth in recent years, with many countries in the region becoming economic powerhouses. This has led to an increasing demand for a skilled workforce that can adapt to the evolving business landscape, placing human resources at the forefront of organizational success (Kim, 2012). Consequently, the integration of AI in HRM practices has gained substantial attention in the Asian context, as organizations seek innovative ways to manage and develop their human capital more effectively (Budhwar et al., 2022; Järvelä et al., 2023).

The rise of AI-driven HRM practices has also prompted a growing interest in leveraging business analytics, which involves the use of data, statistical analysis, and quantitative methods to inform decision-making processes (Sharma et al., 2014). By integrating AI-driven HRM practices with business analytics, organizations can gain deeper insights into their workforce, improve HR processes, and ultimately foster a future-ready workforce in Asia (Gélinas et al., 2022).

This edited book chapter, therefore, aims to explore the intersection of AI and HRM in the Asian context, providing valuable insights into the methodologies, theories, and applications of AI in HRM practices. The chapter will also discuss the challenges and opportunities associated with the integration of AI and HRM, highlighting the potential impact of AI on HR strategies, and offering a holistic view for policymakers and practitioners to shift their focus toward AI-driven HRM practices.

1.2. Objectives and Scope of the Chapter

The primary objectives of this edited book chapter are:

1. To provide an in-depth understanding of AI and HRM concepts, and their evolution in the context of the Asian market.

2. To explore the synergies between AI and HRM, highlighting the role of business analytics in enhancing HRM practices and fostering a future-ready workforce in Asia.
3. To discuss the challenges and risks associated with AI-driven HRM practices, including ethical considerations, data privacy, and cultural and legal implications.
4. To outline strategies for the successful implementation of AI in HRM, focusing on building AI competencies within HR departments, promoting a data-driven culture, and ensuring ethical AI deployment.

The scope of this chapter includes a comprehensive exploration of the integration of AI and HRM in Asia, with an emphasis on the potential benefits and challenges of leveraging business analytics for building a future-ready workforce. The chapter will cater to a diverse audience, including researchers, policymakers, organizational managers, advanced-level students, leaders, academicians, and government officials interested in understanding the impact of AI on HR strategies and fostering a future-ready workforce in Asia.

1.3. Significance of the Chapter

The significance of this chapter lies in its comprehensive examination of the integration of AI and HRM within the Asian context, addressing a growing need for research and understanding in this area. By providing insights into the benefits, challenges, and strategies associated with AI-driven HRM practices, this chapter contributes to the existing body of knowledge and offers valuable guidance for policymakers, practitioners, and researchers. Key aspects of significance include:

1. Filling a research gap: Although AI and HRM have been studied separately, there is a scarcity of research exploring their intersection, particularly in the context of Asia (Budhwar et al., 2022; Järvelä et al., 2023) (You, 2020). This edited book chapter seeks to bridge this gap by examining the synergies between AI and HRM, focusing on the Asian market.
2. Enhancing HRM practices: The chapter highlights the role of business analytics in optimizing HRM practices, demonstrating how data-driven decision-making can contribute to more effective and efficient HRM processes.
3. Supporting future-ready workforces: By exploring the potential impact of AI-driven HRM practices on workforce development in Asia, the chapter offers valuable insights for organizations seeking to adapt to the rapidly evolving business landscape and foster a future-ready workforce.
4. Informing policy and practice: The chapter provides a holistic view of AI-driven HRM, discussing both the benefits and challenges associated with its

implementation. This information can guide policymakers and practitioners in developing strategies and policies that support the effective integration of AI and HRM.

5. Stimulating further research: This chapter lays the groundwork for future research on the intersection of AI and HRM, opening new avenues for academic inquiry and encouraging further exploration of this dynamic and rapidly evolving field (Gélinas et al., 2022).

2. AI IN HRM: CONCEPTS AND EVOLUTION

2.1. Defining AI and HRM

Artificial Intelligence (AI) refers to the development of computer systems that can perform tasks that typically require human intelligence, such as visual perception, speech recognition, decision-making, and natural language understanding (Norvig & Russell, 2016). AI technologies often involve machine learning, deep learning, and neural networks, which enable computers to learn and adapt from experience without being explicitly programmed.

Human Resource Management (HRM) is the strategic and coherent approach to managing an organization's most valuable asset: its people. HRM involves the development and implementation of policies and practices related to personnel management, such as recruitment, training, compensation, performance evaluation, and employee relations (Armstrong & Taylor, 2023). The ultimate goal of HRM is to optimize the performance and productivity of employees to achieve organizational objectives.

2.2. Evolution of AI in HRM

The application of AI in HRM has evolved significantly over the past few decades, with the technology increasingly becoming a key component of modern HR practices. The following timeline highlights the major milestones in the evolution of AI in HRM:

Late 1990s to early 2000s: The advent of the internet and the proliferation of online job boards marked the beginning of AI's role in HRM. These platforms utilized basic AI algorithms to match job seekers with suitable job vacancies (Cascio & Montealegre, 2016).

Mid-2000s: As AI technologies advanced, HR professionals began leveraging more sophisticated tools, such as applicant tracking systems (ATS) and resume parsers, to streamline the recruitment process and improve the efficiency of candidate screening (Stone et al., 2015).

Late 2000s to early 2010s: The rise of social media and professional networking platforms, such as LinkedIn, facilitated the use of AI in talent acquisition and recruitment marketing. HR professionals utilized AI-driven analytics to identify and target potential candidates based on their online profiles and activity (Chitrao et al., 2022).

Mid-2010s onwards: Recent advancements in AI and machine learning have paved the way for the development of various HRM applications, including chatbots for candidate engagement, natural language processing (NLP) for sentiment analysis in employee feedback, and predictive analytics for workforce planning and performance management (Votto et al., 2021).

2.3. Technological Advancements and the Asian Context

The rapid growth of AI technologies in Asia has significantly impacted the HRM landscape in the region. Countries such as China, Japan, South Korea, and Singapore are leading the way in AI research and development, fostering an environment of innovation and collaboration (Lee, 2018). These technological advancements have driven the adoption of AI-driven HRM practices across various industries in Asia, with organizations increasingly leveraging AI tools to enhance their HR processes and strategies.

In the Asian context, AI-driven HRM practices have been particularly effective in addressing the region's unique labor market challenges, such as talent shortages, an aging workforce, and the need for upskilling and reskilling (Budhwar et al., 2022; Jaiswal et al., 2022). Furthermore, the increasing emphasis on digital transformation and Industry 4.0 has prompted organizations in Asia to explore the potential of AI to optimize HRM functions and improve overall business performance (Javaid et al., 2022).

In conclusion, the integration of AI into HRM has evolved significantly over time, with the technology becoming an essential component of modern HR practices. The rapid growth of AI technologies in Asia has further accelerated the adoption of AI-driven HRM practices, helping organizations in the region address their unique labor market challenges and prepare for the future of work.

3. SYNERGIZING AI AND HRM: THE ROLE OF BUSINESS ANALYTICS

3.1. AI Applications in HRM: Recruitment, Retention, and Employee Engagement

The integration of AI and HRM has led to the development of various applications that leverage business analytics to improve HR processes and outcomes. Some key AI-driven applications in HRM include:

Recruitment: AI-powered recruitment tools, such as applicant tracking systems (ATS), help streamline the hiring process by automating tasks like candidate screening, interview scheduling, and background checks (Albert, 2019; Oswal et al., 2020). AI-driven recruitment platforms also utilize machine learning algorithms to analyze large datasets and identify patterns that can predict candidate success, helping organizations make more informed hiring decisions (Pessach et al., 2020).

Retention: AI can also play a crucial role in enhancing employee retention. Predictive analytics and machine learning algorithms can analyze employee data, such as performance metrics, tenure, and feedback, to identify potential attrition risks and recommend targeted interventions (Ramachandran et al., 2022). AI-powered tools can also help organizations develop personalized career development plans and learning opportunities, fostering employee growth and satisfaction.

Employee Engagement: AI-driven HRM tools, such as chatbots and sentiment analysis software, can help improve employee engagement by facilitating communication, providing real-time feedback, and identifying areas for improvement (Votto et al., 2021). AI applications can also analyze employee engagement data to uncover trends and correlations, informing HR strategies and initiatives to enhance overall employee satisfaction and productivity.

3.2. The Power of Data-Driven Decision Making in HRM

Data-driven decision making is a critical component of modern HRM, as it enables organizations to make evidence-based decisions that align with their strategic objectives. By leveraging AI and business analytics, HR professionals can:

Improve HR processes: AI-driven analytics can help HR teams identify inefficiencies and bottlenecks in their processes, enabling them to make data-informed decisions that optimize workflows and drive better results (Marler & Boudreau, 2017).

Enhance workforce planning: AI-powered predictive analytics can help organizations forecast workforce needs, identify skills gaps, and develop targeted talent acquisition and development strategies (Shukla, 2009).

Monitor and evaluate performance: AI-driven HRM tools can help organizations track and assess employee performance more accurately and objectively, informing performance management and compensation decisions (Malik et al., 2023).

3.3. The Benefits of Integrating AI and Business Analytics in HRM

Integrating AI and business analytics in HRM offers numerous benefits for organizations, including:

Improved efficiency: AI-driven HRM tools can automate repetitive and time-consuming tasks, freeing up HR professionals to focus on more strategic and value-added activities (Albert, 2019; Oswal et al., 2020).

Enhanced decision making: AI-powered analytics can provide HR teams with deeper insights into their workforce, enabling them to make more informed decisions that align with organizational objectives (Marler & Boudreau, 2017).

Better talent acquisition and management: AI-driven recruitment and talent management tools can help organizations identify and attract top talent, develop personalized career development plans, and improve employee engagement and retention (Albert, 2019; Chitrao et al., 2022).

Greater adaptability: AI-driven HRM tools can help organizations quickly adapt to changing market conditions, evolving workforce needs, and new technologies, ensuring they remain competitive and future-ready (Votto et al., 2021).

In conclusion, synergizing AI and HRM through the integration of business analytics can lead to significant improvements in recruitment, retention, and employee engagement, while also enhancing data-driven decision-making and overall HR efficiency. By embracing AI-driven HRM practices, organizations can position themselves for success in today's rapidly changing business landscape.

4. CHALLENGES AND RISKS OF AI-DRIVEN HRM IN ASIA

4.1. Ethical Considerations and Data Privacy

As organizations increasingly integrate AI-driven HRM practices, several ethical and data privacy concerns arise. This section will discuss the key ethical considerations and data privacy challenges associated with the adoption of AI-driven HRM in Asia.

Bias and Discrimination

One of the primary ethical concerns related to AI-driven HRM is the potential for bias and discrimination in AI algorithms (Mullainathan & Spiess, 2017). AI systems learn from historical data, which may reflect existing biases present in the organization or society. If not addressed, these biases can perpetuate and even exacerbate unfair practices in recruitment, performance evaluation, and talent development (Kim, 2018).

To mitigate these risks, organizations must ensure that their AI-driven HRM systems are designed and trained to recognize and correct for potential biases. This requires ongoing monitoring and validation of AI algorithms to ensure fairness and transparency in decision-making (Barocas et al., 2019).

Data Privacy

The use of AI-driven HRM practices also raises concerns about data privacy, as these systems often rely on large volumes of personal and sensitive employee data (Kuner et al., 2017). Organizations must ensure that they are compliant with data privacy regulations, such as the European Union's General Data Protection Regulation (GDPR) and the Asia-Pacific Economic Cooperation (APEC) Privacy Framework, which outline requirements for the collection, processing, and storage of personal data (APEC, 2005; EU GDPR, 2016).

To address data privacy concerns, organizations should implement robust data protection measures, such as data anonymization, encryption, and secure storage. Additionally, they must ensure that employees are informed about the collection and use of their data and provide opportunities for employees to access, correct, or delete their personal information (Kuner et al., 2017).

In conclusion, addressing ethical considerations and data privacy challenges is crucial for the successful implementation of AI-driven HRM practices in Asia. By acknowledging these concerns and implementing appropriate measures, organizations can leverage AI-driven HRM to optimize their workforce management while maintaining ethical standards and data privacy.

4.2. Cultural and Legal Implications

The adoption of AI-driven HRM practices also presents various cultural and legal implications that organizations in Asia must navigate. This section will discuss the key cultural and legal challenges associated with implementing AI-driven HRM practices in the region.

Cultural Differences and Adaptation:

Organizations in Asia often operate across diverse cultural contexts, which can influence the effectiveness of AI-driven HRM practices. Cultural differences may impact the way employees perceive and interact with AI-driven HRM systems, affecting their acceptance and adoption of these technologies (Cachat-Rosset & Klarsfeld, 2023).

To address this challenge, organizations should consider the cultural context in which they operate when designing and implementing AI-driven HRM systems. This may involve tailoring communication strategies, user interfaces, and system features to align with local cultural norms and preferences (Cachat-Rosset & Klarsfeld, 2023; Vos & Boonstra, 2022).

Legal Compliance

The use of AI-driven HRM practices also raises legal concerns, particularly in areas such as data protection, labor law, and employment discrimination (Bodie et al., 2017). Organizations in Asia must navigate a complex and often inconsistent legal landscape, as regulations related to AI and data protection vary across different jurisdictions (Malgieri & Comandé, 2017).

To mitigate legal risks, organizations should closely monitor regulatory developments and ensure compliance with relevant laws and regulations in the countries where they operate (Bodie et al., 2017). This may involve working with legal counsel to develop policies and procedures related to AI-driven HRM practices, such as data collection and storage, algorithmic decision-making, and employee rights (Malgieri & Comandé, 2017).

In conclusion, successfully implementing AI-driven HRM practices in Asia requires organizations to address both the cultural and legal implications associated with the use of AI in human resource management. By taking a proactive approach to understanding and addressing these challenges, organizations can leverage AI-driven HRM to optimize their workforce management while remaining sensitive to cultural differences and compliant with legal requirements.

4.3. Ensuring Human-AI Collaboration

As organizations in Asia increasingly adopt AI-driven HRM practices, it becomes crucial to ensure effective collaboration between humans and AI systems. This section will discuss the key challenges associated with promoting human-AI collaboration in the context of HRM and offer suggestions for fostering a harmonious relationship between the two.

Building Trust

One of the main challenges in promoting human-AI collaboration is building trust between employees and AI-driven HRM systems (Tuncer & Ramirez, 2022). Employees may be skeptical of AI systems' ability to make fair and accurate decisions, particularly in sensitive areas such as performance evaluation, promotion, and compensation (Lee & See, 2004).

To build trust in AI-driven HRM systems, organizations should prioritize transparency and explainability in their AI algorithms, allowing employees to understand how decisions are made and ensuring that the systems are perceived as fair and unbiased (Tuncer & Ramirez, 2022). Additionally, organizations can provide training and education programs to help employees better understand the benefits and limitations of AI-driven HRM practices and build their confidence in working with these systems (Budhwar et al., 2022; Järvelä et al., 2023).

Balancing Automation and Human Expertise:

Another challenge in promoting human-AI collaboration is finding the right balance between automation and human expertise (Gabriel Szydlo et al., 2023). While AI-driven HRM practices can automate many routine tasks and enable data-driven decision-making, human expertise remains essential for interpreting complex data, understanding nuanced cultural contexts, and making strategic decisions (Budhwar et al., 2022).

To strike the right balance, organizations should view AI-driven HRM systems as complementary tools that enhance, rather than replace, human expertise (Budhwar et al., 2022; Järvelä et al., 2023). By encouraging collaboration between HR professionals and AI systems, organizations can leverage the strengths of both to optimize their human resource management practices (Budhwar et al., 2022).

In conclusion, ensuring effective human-AI collaboration is a critical aspect of successfully implementing AI-driven HRM practices in Asia. By building trust in AI systems, prioritizing transparency and explainability, and striking the right balance between automation and human expertise, organizations can foster a collaborative environment in which AI-driven HRM practices thrive and enhance overall workforce management.

5. STRATEGIES FOR SUCCESSFUL IMPLEMENTATION OF AI IN HRM

5.1. Building AI Competencies Within HR Departments

Successfully implementing AI-driven HRM practices requires organizations to build AI competencies within their HR departments. This section will discuss the key steps organizations can take to develop AI expertise among HR professionals, enabling them to effectively leverage AI-driven HRM practices.

Training and Education

The first step in building AI competencies within HR departments is to provide training and education programs for HR professionals (Budhwar et al., 2022; Järvelä et al., 2023). These programs should cover topics such as the fundamentals of AI, machine learning, and data analytics, as well as specific applications of AI in HRM, such as talent acquisition, performance management, and employee engagement (Brynjolfsson & Mitchell, 2017). By equipping HR professionals with the necessary knowledge and skills, organizations can ensure that they are prepared to work with AI-driven HRM systems effectively.

Collaboration with IT Departments and External Partners

To develop AI expertise within HR departments, organizations should also encourage collaboration between HR professionals and IT departments or external partners specializing in AI and data analytics (Gélinas et al., 2022). This collaboration can facilitate knowledge transfer, allowing HR professionals to learn from experts in AI and data analytics and enabling them to better understand the technical aspects of AI-driven HRM practices.

Creating an AI-Centric HR Culture

Developing AI competencies within HR departments also requires fostering an AI-centric culture that values data-driven decision-making and embraces technological innovation (Przegalinska & Jemielniak, 2023). Organizations should encourage HR professionals to adopt a proactive mindset towards AI-driven HRM practices, promoting a culture of experimentation and continuous learning (Przegalinska & Jemielniak, 2023). By creating an environment that supports AI adoption, organizations can facilitate the development of AI expertise within HR departments and ensure that HR professionals are well-positioned to leverage AI-driven HRM practices effectively.

In conclusion, building AI competencies within HR departments is a critical aspect of successfully implementing AI-driven HRM practices. By providing training and education programs, promoting collaboration with IT departments and external partners, and fostering an AI-centric culture, organizations can develop AI expertise among HR professionals and optimize their human resource management practices through the effective use of AI-driven HRM systems.

5.2. Promoting a Data-Driven Culture

To successfully implement AI-driven HRM practices, organizations must promote a data-driven culture that values evidence-based decision-making and embraces technological innovation. This section will discuss strategies for fostering a data-driven culture within organizations and the potential benefits of adopting such a culture in the context of AI-driven HRM.

Leadership Commitment

A critical factor in promoting a data-driven culture is securing leadership commitment to the value of data-driven decision-making and AI-driven HRM practices (Sharma et al., 2014). Top management should communicate the importance of data-driven approaches to HRM, set clear expectations, and provide resources for implementing AI-driven HRM practices. By demonstrating support for a data-driven culture, leaders can encourage HR professionals and other employees to embrace AI-driven HRM practices and the benefits they offer.

Data Accessibility and Literacy

To foster a data-driven culture, organizations must ensure that HR professionals and employees have access to relevant data and possess the necessary skills to interpret and apply the data to decision-making processes (Brynjolfsson & Mitchell, 2017). This can be achieved through training programs that teach data literacy skills, such as data visualization, statistical analysis, and critical thinking. Moreover, organizations should establish systems and processes that facilitate data access and sharing, allowing HR professionals to leverage data for improved decision-making and collaboration (Gélinas et al., 2022).

Employee Involvement

Encouraging employee involvement in the development and implementation of AI-driven HRM practices is another key aspect of promoting a data-driven culture (Budhwar et al., 2022; Järvelä et al., 2023). By involving employees in the process, organizations can ensure that AI-driven HRM practices are designed with employee needs and preferences in mind, fostering buy-in and adoption of these practices. Additionally, employee involvement can facilitate knowledge sharing and collaboration, further strengthening the data-driven culture within the organization.

In conclusion, promoting a data-driven culture is an essential strategy for successfully implementing AI-driven HRM practices. By securing leadership commitment, ensuring data accessibility and literacy, and encouraging employee involvement, organizations can foster a culture that values evidence-based decision-making and embraces AI-driven HRM practices, leading to more effective and efficient human resource management.

5.3. Ensuring Ethical AI Deployment

For the successful implementation of AI-driven HRM practices, organizations must ensure that AI systems are deployed ethically, addressing concerns related to fairness, transparency, and data privacy. This section will discuss strategies for ensuring ethical AI deployment and the importance of considering ethical dimensions in AI-driven HRM practices.

Transparency and Explainability

One key aspect of ethical AI deployment is ensuring transparency and explainability in AI algorithms and decision-making processes (Waltl & Vogl, 2018). Organizations should prioritize the development and use of AI systems that provide clear explanations for their decisions, allowing employees to understand the rationale behind these decisions and fostering trust in AI-driven HRM practices (de Fine Licht & de Fine Licht, 2020). Additionally, transparent AI systems can help organizations identify and address potential biases or inaccuracies in AI-driven HRM practices, ensuring fairness and accuracy in decision-making processes.

Data Privacy and Security

Protecting employee data privacy and security is another essential aspect of ethical AI deployment (Mittelstadt, 2019). Organizations must establish robust data protection policies and practices to ensure compliance with relevant data privacy regulations, such as the General Data Protection Regulation (GDPR) in the European Union (EU GDPR, 2016) or the Personal Data Protection Act (PDPA) in Singapore (Singapore PDPC, 2012). This may include implementing encryption methods, anonymizing data, or limiting data access to authorized personnel. By ensuring data privacy and security, organizations can build trust in AI-driven HRM practices and mitigate potential risks associated with data breaches or misuse.

Addressing Bias and Discrimination

AI-driven HRM practices have the potential to perpetuate or exacerbate biases and discrimination if not carefully designed and monitored (Cath, 2018; Delecraz et al., 2022). Organizations should actively work to identify and mitigate potential biases in AI-driven HRM practices by assessing the quality and representativeness of the data used to train AI systems, regularly auditing AI-driven HRM practices for fairness, and involving diverse stakeholders in the design and evaluation of AI systems (Cath, 2018). By addressing biases and discrimination, organizations can ensure that AI-driven HRM practices promote fairness, equity, and inclusiveness in the workplace.

In conclusion, ensuring ethical AI deployment is a crucial aspect of successfully implementing AI-driven HRM practices. By prioritizing transparency and explainability, protecting data privacy and security, and addressing biases and discrimination, organizations can deploy AI-driven HRM practices ethically and responsibly, leading to more effective and equitable human resource management.

6. CONCLUSION

6.1. Summary of Findings

This chapter provides a summary of the key findings discussed throughout the book, highlighting the significance of integrating AI-driven HRM practices with business analytics for fostering a future-ready workforce in Asia.

AI in HRM: Concepts and Evolution

The chapter began by exploring the fundamental concepts of AI and HRM and tracing the evolution of AI-driven HRM practices. The chapter highlighted the growing role of AI in HRM, particularly in the Asian context, where rapid technological advancements are transforming the way organizations manage their human resources.

Synergizing AI and HRM: The Role of Business Analytics

The chapter examined the integration of AI-driven HRM practices with business analytics, demonstrating how AI applications in HRM, such as recruitment, retention, and employee engagement, can benefit from data-driven decision-making. The synergistic relationship between AI and business analytics in HRM was shown to offer numerous benefits, including improved efficiency, more informed decision-making, and better organizational performance.

Challenges and Risks of AI-Driven HRM in Asia

The chapter also addressed the potential challenges and risks associated with AI-driven HRM practices in Asia, such as ethical considerations and data privacy concerns, cultural and legal implications, and the need for effective human-AI collaboration. By addressing these challenges, organizations can ensure the responsible and successful implementation of AI-driven HRM practices.

Strategies for Successful Implementation of AI in HRM

Finally, the chapter offered strategies for organizations looking to successfully implement AI-driven HRM practices, focusing on building AI competencies within HR departments, promoting a data-driven culture, and ensuring ethical AI deployment. By adopting these strategies, organizations can maximize the potential benefits of AI-driven HRM practices and prepare for a future where AI plays a central role in human resource management.

6.2. Future Research Directions and Policy Implications

This section outlines potential future research directions and policy implications stemming from the findings presented in this chapter, emphasizing areas where further exploration can help advance our understanding of AI-driven HRM practices and their integration with business analytics in the Asian context.

Future Research Directions

Longitudinal studies: While the chapter has provided valuable insights into the current state of AI-driven HRM practices in Asia, there is a need for longitudinal research to understand the long-term effects of these practices on organizational performance, employee well-being, and the broader labor market.

Cross-cultural comparisons: The chapter has focused primarily on the Asian context; however, future research could examine cross-cultural differences in AI-driven HRM practices and their impact on organizations and employees across different regions.

AI-driven HRM in specific industries: future research could delve into the unique challenges and opportunities associated with AI-driven HRM practices in specific industries, such as healthcare, education, or finance.

Policy Implications:

Regulatory frameworks: Policymakers should consider developing comprehensive regulatory frameworks that address ethical concerns, data privacy, and security issues related to AI-driven HRM practices. These frameworks could help ensure the responsible development and deployment of AI-driven HRM practices across organizations.

Skill development and education: Policymakers should invest in skill development and education programs that equip the workforce with the necessary skills to thrive in an AI-driven HRM environment, such as data literacy, critical thinking, and adaptability.

Collaboration between stakeholders: Policymakers should foster collaboration among various stakeholders, such as government agencies, educational institutions, industry associations, and private organizations, to facilitate the sharing of best practices, resources, and knowledge related to AI-driven HRM practices.

In conclusion, this chapter has provided valuable insights into the integration of AI-driven HRM practices with business analytics in the Asian context, offering a foundation for future research and policy development in this rapidly evolving field.

6.3. Final Remarks

This chapter has explored the intersection of AI and HRM in the Asian context, demonstrating the potential benefits of leveraging business analytics for building a future-ready workforce. Throughout the chapters, we have discussed the evolution of AI in HRM, the role of business analytics in synergizing AI and HRM practices.

We have also addressed the challenges and risks associated with AI-driven HRM practices, including ethical considerations, data privacy concerns, and cultural and legal implications. By identifying strategies for the successful implementation of AI in HRM, such as building AI competencies within HR departments, promoting a data-driven culture, and ensuring ethical AI deployment, organizations can maximize the potential benefits of AI-driven HRM practices.

This chapter serves as a starting point for researchers, policymakers, organizational managers, advanced-level students, leaders, academicians, and government officials interested in understanding the impact of AI on HR strategies and fostering a future-ready workforce in Asia. The insights provided in this book offer a foundation for future research, policy development, and practical applications in the rapidly evolving field of AI-driven HRM.

As technology continues to advance, and AI plays an increasingly central role in human resource management, it is crucial for organizations to stay ahead of the curve and proactively adapt to the changing landscape. By embracing the power of AI-driven HRM practices and integrating them with business analytics, organizations can unlock new opportunities for growth, innovation, and success in the Asian market and beyond.

REFERENCES

Albert, E. T. (2019). AI in talent acquisition: A review of AI-applications used in recruitment and selection. *Strategic HR Review*, *18*(5), 215–221. doi:10.1108/SHR-04-2019-0024

APEC. (2005). *APEC Privacy Framework*. https://www.apec.org/Publications/2005/12/APEC-Privacy-Framework

Armstrong, M., & Taylor, S. (2023). *Armstrong's Handbook of Human Resource Management Practice: A Guide to the Theory and Practice of People Management*. Kogan Page Publishers.

Barocas, S., Hardt, M., & Narayanan, A. (2019). *Fairness and Machine Learning. fairmlbook*. Academic Press.

Bodie, M. T., Cherry, M. A., McCormick, M. L., & Tang, J. (2017). The law and policy of people analytics. *U. Colo. L. Rev.*, *88*, 961. https://heinonline.org/HOL/LandingPage?handle=hein.journals/ucollr88&div=31&id=&page=

Brynjolfsson, E., & Mitchell, T. (2017). What can machine learning do? Workforce implications. *Science*, *358*(6370), 1530–1534. doi:10.1126cience.aap8062 PMID:29269459

Budhwar, P., Malik, A., De Silva, M. T., & Thevisuthan, P. (2022). Artificial intelligence–challenges and opportunities for international HRM: A review and research agenda. *International Journal of Human Resource Management*, *33*(6), 1065–1097. doi:10.1080/09585192.2022.2035161

Cachat-Rosset, G., & Klarsfeld, A. (2023). Diversity, Equity, and Inclusion in Artificial Intelligence: An Evaluation of Guidelines. *Applied Artificial Intelligence*, *37*(1), 2176618. doi:10.1080/08839514.2023.2176618

Cascio, W. F., & Montealegre, R. (2016). How Technology Is Changing Work and Organizations. *Annual Review of Organizational Psychology and Organizational Behavior, 3*(1), 349–375. doi:10.1146/annurev-orgpsych-041015-062352

Cath, C. (2018). Governing artificial intelligence: Ethical, legal and technical opportunities and challenges. *Philosophical Transactions. Series A, Mathematical, Physical, and Engineering Sciences, 376*(2133), 20180080. doi:10.1098/rsta.2018.0080 PMID:30322996

Chitrao, P., Bhoyar, P. K., Divekar, R., & Bhatt, P. (2022, February 24-26). Study on Use of Artificial Intelligence in Talent Acquisition. *2022 Interdisciplinary Research in Technology and Management (IRTM)*. doi:10.100700146-020-00960-w

Delecraz, S., Eltarr, L., Becuwe, M., Bouxin, H., Boutin, N., & Oullier, O. (2022). Responsible Artificial Intelligence in Human Resources Technology: An innovative inclusive and fair by design matching algorithm for job recruitment purposes. *Journal of Responsible Technology, 11*, 100041. doi:10.1016/j.jrt.2022.100041

EU GDPR. (2016). *General data protection regulation (GDPR)* (Regulation (EU) 2016/679 of the European Parliament and of the Council of 27 April 2016 on the protection of natural persons with regard to the processing of personal data and on the free movement of such data, and repealing Directive 95/46/EC, Issue). https://data.europa.eu/eli/reg/2016/679/oj

Gabriel Szydlo, S., Ronit, B., & Yoav, M. (2023). Human-Machine Collaboration in AI-Assisted Surgery: Balancing Autonomy and Expertise. In P. S. Dr. Stanislaw (Ed.), Artificial Intelligence in Medicine and Surgery - An Exploration of Current Trends, Potential Opportunities, and Evolving Threats. IntechOpen. doi:10.5772/intechopen.111556

Gélinas, D., Sadreddin, A., & Vahidov, R. (2022). Artificial Intelligence in Human Resources Management: A Review and Research Agenda. *Pacific Asia Journal of the Association for Information Systems, 14*(6), 1–42. doi:10.17705/1pais.14601

Jaiswal, A., Arun, C. J., & Varma, A. (2022). Rebooting employees: Upskilling for artificial intelligence in multinational corporations. *International Journal of Human Resource Management, 33*(6), 1179–1208. doi:10.1080/09585192.2021.1891114

Järvelä, S., Nguyen, A., & Hadwin, A. (2023). Human and artificial intelligence collaboration for socially shared regulation in learning. *British Journal of Educational Technology, 54*(5), 1057–1076. doi:10.1111/bjet.13325

Javaid, M.0, Haleem, A., Singh, R. P., & Suman, R. (2022). Artificial intelligence applications for industry 4.0: A literature-based study. *Journal of Industrial Integration and Management*, *7*(01), 83–111. doi:10.1142/S2424862221300040

Kim, J. (2012). Past and future of the labor force in emerging Asian economies. *Japan and the World Economy*, *24*(2), 87–100. doi:10.1016/j.japwor.2012.01.004

Kim, P. T. (2018). Big Data and artificial intelligence: New challenges for workplace equality. *U. Louisville L. Rev.*, *57*, 313.

Kuner, C., Svantesson, D. J. B., Cate, F. H., Lynskey, O., & Millard, C. (2017). Machine learning with personal data: Is data protection law smart enough to meet the challenge? *International Data Privacy Law*, *7*(1), 1–2. doi:10.1093/idpl/ipx003

Lee, J. D., & See, K. A. (2004). Trust in automation: Designing for appropriate reliance. *Human Factors*, *46*(1), 50–80. doi:10.1518/hfes.46.1.50.30392 PMID:15151155

Lee, K.-F. (2018). AI superpowers: China, Silicon Valley, and the new world order. Houghton Mifflin.

Malgieri, G., & Comandé, G. (2017). Why a Right to Legibility of Automated Decision-Making Exists in the General Data Protection Regulation. *International Data Privacy Law*, *7*(4), 243–265. doi:10.1093/idpl/ipx019

Malik, A., Budhwar, P., & Kazmi, B. A. (2023). Artificial intelligence (AI)-assisted HRM: Towards an extended strategic framework. *Human Resource Management Review*, *33*(1), 100940. doi:10.1016/j.hrmr.2022.100940

Marler, J. H., & Boudreau, J. W. (2017). An evidence-based review of HR Analytics. *International Journal of Human Resource Management*, *28*(1), 3–26. doi:10.1080/09585192.2016.1244699

Mittelstadt, B. (2019). Principles alone cannot guarantee ethical AI. *Nature Machine Intelligence*, *1*(11), 501–507. doi:10.103842256-019-0114-4

Mullainathan, S., & Spiess, J. (2017). Machine Learning: An Applied Econometric Approach. *The Journal of Economic Perspectives*, *31*(2), 87–106. doi:10.1257/jep.31.2.87

Norvig, P., & Russell, S. (2016). *Artificial intelligence: a modern approach* (Global Edition). Pearson Education Limited.

Oswal, N., Khaleeli, M., & Alarmoti, A. (2020). Recruitment in the Era of Industry 4.0: use of Artificial Intelligence in Recruitment and its impact. *PalArch's Journal of Archaeology of Egypt/Egyptology, 17*(8), 39-47.

Pessach, D., Singer, G., Avrahami, D., Chalutz Ben-Gal, H., Shmueli, E., & Ben-Gal, I. (2020). Employees recruitment: A prescriptive analytics approach via machine learning and mathematical programming. *Decision Support Systems*, *134*, 113290. doi:10.1016/j.dss.2020.113290 PMID:32501316

Przegalinska, A., & Jemielniak, D. (2023). *Strategizing AI in Business and Education*. Cambridge University Press., doi:10.1017/9781009243520

Ramachandran, K. K., Apsara Saleth Mary, A., Hawladar, S., Asokk, D., Bhaskar, B., & Pitroda, J. R. (2022). Machine learning and role of artificial intelligence in optimizing work performance and employee behavior. *Materials Today: Proceedings*, *51*, 2327–2331. doi:10.1016/j.matpr.2021.11.544

Sharma, R., Mithas, S., & Kankanhalli, A. (2014). Transforming decision-making processes: A research agenda for understanding the impact of business analytics on organisations. *European Journal of Information Systems*, *23*(4), 433–441. doi:10.1057/ejis.2014.17

Shukla, S. K. (2009). *Decision models and artificial intelligence in supporting workforce forecasting and planning*. The University of Texas at San Antonio.

Singapore, P. D. P. C. (2012). *Personal Data Protection Act 2012*. https://sso.agc.gov.sg/Act/PDPA2012

Stone, D. L., Deadrick, D. L., Lukaszewski, K. M., & Johnson, R. (2015). The influence of technology on the future of human resource management. *Human Resource Management Review*, *25*(2), 216–231. doi:10.1016/j.hrmr.2015.01.002

Tuncer, S., & Ramirez, A. (2022). Exploring the Role of Trust During Human-AI Collaboration in Managerial Decision-Making Processes. In HCI International 2022 – Late Breaking Papers: Interacting with eXtended Reality and Artificial Intelligence. doi:10.22215/etd/2022-15336

Vos, J. F. J., & Boonstra, A. (2022). The influence of cultural values on Enterprise System adoption, towards a culture – Enterprise System alignment theory. *International Journal of Information Management*, *63*, 102453. doi:10.1016/j.ijinfomgt.2021.102453

Votto, A. M., Valecha, R., Najafirad, P., & Rao, H. R. (2021). Artificial Intelligence in Tactical Human Resource Management: A Systematic Literature Review. *International Journal of Information Management Data Insights*, *1*(2), 100047. doi:10.1016/j.jjimei.2021.100047

Waltl, B., & Vogl, R. (2018). Increasing Transparency in Algorithmic- Decision-Making with Explainable AI. *Datenschutz und Datensicherheit - DuD, 42*(10), 613-617. doi:10.1007/s11623-018-1011-4

Chapter 11
Blockchain Technology in the Digital Auditing Paradigm

Aziatul Waznah Ghazali
https://orcid.org/0000-0002-1324-5248
Faculty of Economics and Management, Universiti Kebangsaan Malaysia, Malaysia

Nur Aima Shafie
Accounting Research Institute, Universiti Teknologi MARA, Malaysia

Yusarina Mat Isa
https://orcid.org/0000-0003-2587-3759
Faculty of Accountancy, Universiti Teknologi MARA, Malaysia

Zulaikha Amirah Johari
Faculty of Economics and Management, Universiti Kebangsaan Malaysia, Malaysia

Hafizah Omar Zaki
Faculty of Economics and Management, Universiti Kebangsaan Malaysia, Malaysia

Zuraidah Mohd Sanusi
Accounting Research Institute, Universiti Teknologi MARA, Malaysia

ABSTRACT

The introduction of blockchain technology has ushered in a new era in the field of auditing. This study explores the multifaceted impact of blockchain technology on auditing practices, emphasizing its potential to revolutionize audit methodologies. The fundamental principles of blockchain and its implications in the auditing domain are explored extensively. Moreover, the chapter also discusses the role of auditors in navigating the complexities of blockchain. As the digital auditing landscape evolves, blockchain emerges as a powerful tool that promises to improve the credibility of financial reporting, making it imperative for professionals, academics, and regulators.

DOI: 10.4018/979-8-3693-0039-8.ch011

I. INTRODUCTION

Blockchain first emerged as a core technology behind the well-known Bitcoin cryptocurrency[1] in 2008. Blockchain technology is motivated by its use of peer-to-peer network technology in tandem with cryptography[2]. The integration enables strangers to conduct transactions with each other without needing a conventional trusted broker, such as a bank or payment processing network. Blockchain technology will massively reduce transactional costs and decrease transaction processing time by replacing the broker and harnessing the power of peer-to-peer networks (Jiang, 2018; Sadu, 2018; Varma, 2019, Hou et al., 2023). Furthermore, blockchain will revolutionise and change a wide variety of industries, ranging from public services to private services (Mahbod & Hinton, 2019; Ng, 2019). Therefore, a variety of capital investment businesses and large companies participate in blockchain technology research and testing to reengineer irrelevant practises and business models. For example, Binance is a worldwide leading exchange for cryptocurrencies, offering a wealth of functionality, trading pairings, security, and liquidity at a minimal fee. According to Coinmarketcap.com, the volume of traded cryptocurrency on Binance was worth $2,438 million in October 2019, which came majorly from trading Bitcoin.

The increasing adoption of cryptocurrencies indicates they have the potential to disrupt how businesses operate in the near future. Given that the blockchain technology functions as a public ledger for cryptocurrencies transactions, it is likely that such technology is able to transform multiple industries, which include the auditing profession. However, there is still a lack of research studies on how this technology will assist auditors in their auditing work. Specifically, one of the main issues confronting auditors concerns how the application of blockchain in auditing will benefit auditors in discharging their functions. Blockchain technology is advancing at a faster rate than the internet, which took two decades to build and another decade to mature as a business network (Tapscott & Tapscott, 2017). Many scholars have recently highlighted the potential of blockchain in providing real-time auditing, such as the ability to speed up audit preparation, allowing auditors to focus on riskier transactions, reducing fraud risk, providing consistent document format in real-time, enabling inventory measured in real-time, saving time on document confirmation, and no longer requiring traditional sampling techniques (Abreu, Aparicio, & Costa, 2018; Bible, Raphael, Riviello, Taylor, & Valiente, 2017; Bone, 2018; Cong, Du, & Vasarhelyi, 2018; Hoelscher, 2018; Jiang, 2018; Mahbod & Hinton, 2019; Nathalie, Gauthier, Morin, & Arber, 2019; Sadu, 2018; Tysiac & Drew, 2018). Understanding the current development of technology is critical in light of the fact that particularly important considering that a blockchain system would improve audit efficiency and effectiveness. Nevertheless, it is critical that one should recognise that there is a downside to every invention discovered. Therefore, this paper discusses those benefits as well as limiting the new technology in the context of auditing.

This paper has five major contributors. First, it gives an overview of blockchain's key features, explores its possible integration into auditing, discusses the main advantages and challenges, and analyses how the application of this technology can improve audit procedures for practitioners. Second, this paper is among the first few blockchain studies to explore the potential and limitations of blockchain technology, specifically in financial statements auditing, which will be a concern for auditors before they fully utilise this technology. Thirdly, it is among the first few studies to explore current blockchain development by Big 4 audit firms, which will increase the awareness of current practitioners and academicians. Fourthly, it addresses the challenges faced by professionals in the accounting and auditing sectors while implementing audit technology based on the Technologies Acceptance Model (TAM). Such discussions and diagrams give practitioners and technology providers insight into the application of the technologies in current audit procedures and facilitate the transition of the existing audit framework into the next generation. Lastly, this paper also offers practitioners and academics potential areas that future research can explore in the auditing field with a useful source of reference contents.

The rest of this paper continues in this manner: Section II presents the outline of the blockchain background. Section III explores the potential use of blockchain in financial statement auditing. Section IV discusses the current research and development of the Big 4 audit firms (Deloitte, PwC, EY, and KPMG) in blockchain. Section V discusses the problems of blockchain adoption and deployment with future avenues for work. Section VI provides a conclusion for this paper.

II. BLOCKCHAIN BACKGROUND

The blockchain concept was used for the first time in 1999 when the technical approach for addressing timestamping of digital assets was proposed. Time-stamping is designed to track where and when a file has been produced in the article "How to time-stamp a digital document" (Haber & Stornetta, 1991). Nonetheless, in 2009, a mysterious person or collective organisation under the pseudonym of Satoshi Nakamoto began the first practical implementation of the technology by releasing the first Bitcoin cryptocurrency, which uses blockchain to monitor and validate the movement of this cryptocurrency. In his paper "Bitcoin: A Peer-To-Peer Electronic Cash System" he described the blockchain idea and bitcoin (Nakamoto, 2008). This paper describes blockchain as a modern distributed ledger technology which uses a decentralised consensus model to ensure that transactions entered into the chain can never be deleted after the network participants have verified this.

Blockchain technology has evolved well beyond bitcoin in recent years and is now being tested in many industries, particularly in the supply chain and financial sectors (Fernandez, Dastane, Omar Zaki & Aman, 2023). Yet blockchain technology needs to evolve and has not already been proved at the enterprise level. However, several audit companies have taken blockchain projects to further understand the consequences of this development. For auditing practitioners, it is important to keep up with innovations in this field. Subsequently, blockchain technology has matured and evolved through three phases (Swan, 2015). The first phase includes money transfers and facilities such as payment systems and distribution services. The second phase is a more complex layer of smart contracts than a single currency. The third phase is a blockchain consortium that encompasses cross-sectors. Figure 1 shows the evolution of the blockchain and highlights the key points of the three phases.

Figure 1. Evolution of blockchain
Source: Candusio (2018)

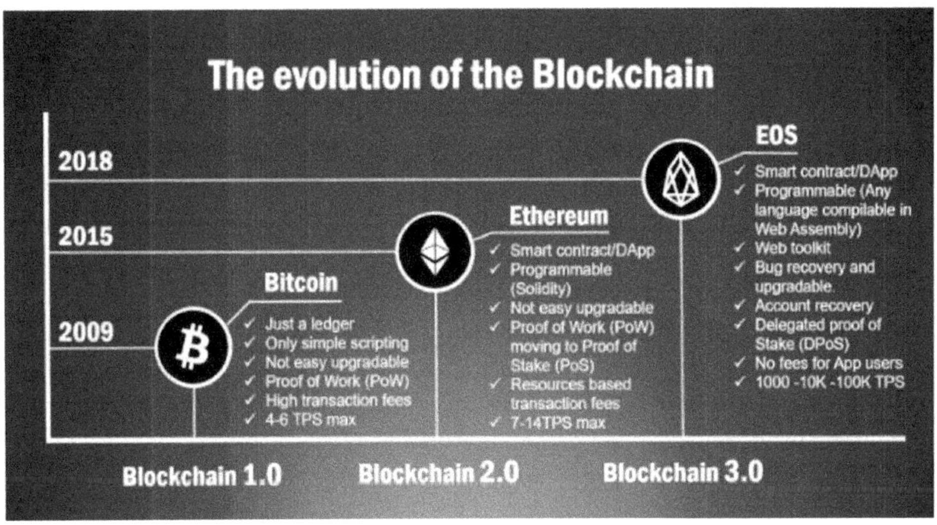

The Bitcoin blockchain has the following characteristics: (i) immutable; (ii) decentralised; (iii) consensus-driven; and (iv) Transparent (Sultan, Ruhi, & Lakhani, 2018). The Blockchain is designed to serve as a permanent transaction ledger. If a block has been added to the chain, it cannot be changed for two reasons. First, it is designed to require massive computing resources to connect a transaction or block to the chain. Second, an alteration of the block would result in the chain of hash values being wrongly authenticated. Figure 3 illustrates the process of hashing and how they bind the blocks into the chain, which makes it almost impossible for a single party to exploit any blockchain data. This will benefit auditing by reducing the risks of fraud and enabling greater reliability in transaction records.

Figure 2. Nakamoto's blockchain proposal
Source: Nakamoto (2008)

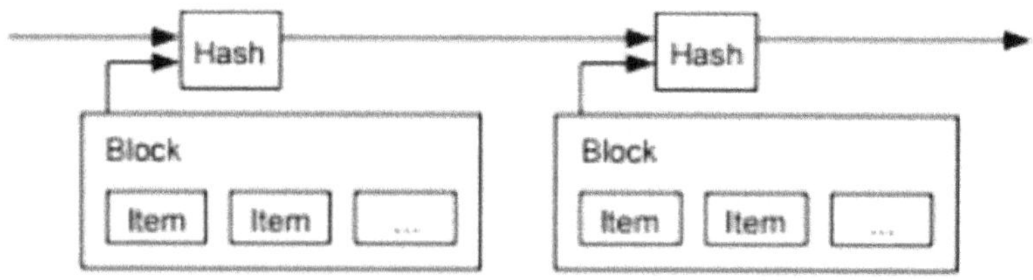

As the blockchain is decentralised over peer-to-peer, each node can engage in the proof-of-work consensus to verify transactions by contributing computational power. These blockchain nodes have access to the full ledgers. Nakamoto proposed the Proof-of-Work (PoW)[3] as the consensus for the Bitcoin blockchain, wherein nodes will continuously hash the block with an arbitrary number until a value less than the defined target is met. The block then extends the current chain after it was identified. However, the Bitcoin PoW consensus is subject to "51 per cent" attacks, in which a mining pool with 51 per cent of the mining power can create its own blocks into the blockchain or fork it to create a new independent branch that eventually diverges from the main blockchain at a later point (Baliga, 2017). This attack refers to a form of assault on a blockchain network in which an assailant acquires dominance over more than half of the network's computational capacity. The aforementioned scenario confers onto the assailant the capability to impede the functioning of the network and potentially steal funds.

Financial audits could be negatively impacted by a 51 percent attack in a number of ways, including double spending, fraud, manipulation, and loss of trust. Auditors would have trouble verifying transactions if the attacker was double-spending coins or committing fraud. Higher financial audit costs would almost definitely be the outcome of the greater risk of fraud and the challenges in verifying transactions. However, in order to mitigate the risk of a 51% attack, many measures can be implemented. These measures encompass augmenting the quantity of nodes inside the network, adopting a more robust consensus process, and implementing the use of a hardware wallet. Financial auditors can also take precautions to lessen the possibility of a 51% attack, such as using several sources of proof, keeping up with security issues, and working with a reputable audit firm. Furthermore Proof-of-Stake (PoS)[4], is an alternative consensus method used by the Ethereum blockchain to address the weakness of PoW in terms of the large amount of energy used in mining operations. Based on the current pattern, PoS is more suitable for private blockchains and PoW is more relevant for public blockchains (Abreu et al., 2018).

Transparency is another well-known feature of blockchain, as demonstrated by Bitcoin. For example, Blockchain.com provides near-real-time information such as transactions, transaction, total price, Bitcoin, Ethereum, and Bitcoin Cash complexity and hash rates to all users. Similarly, business organisations require transparency to secure stakeholder investment and build confidence between them. Additionally, Deloitte also believes that blockchain will dramatically improve business and partnership relationships, business processes, data transparency, economic productivity, and long-term sustainability (Grewal-Carr & Stephen, 2016). Increased accountability, along with the verifiable capability of the blockchain functionality, may increase shareholder interest by reducing the possibility of profit manipulation (Dai & Vasarhelyi, 2017; Yermack, 2017). Considering these characteristics of blockchain, there are numerous chances to create a more robust audit trail through the usage of this innovation in both traditional and e-commerce enterprises.

The use of blockchain technology in auditing has certain advantages and disadvantages. or instance, external auditor-created smart contracts on a blockchain will enable the implementation of audit procedures while providing stakeholders with real-time audit reports and increased transparency (Rozario & Vasarhelyi, 2018). Additionally, intelligent audit approaches can assist auditors in assessing the audit's risks. These include intelligent analytical procedures and intelligent internal control measures that perform audit tasks on the auditor's behalf automatically (Deshpande, Stewart, Lepetit, & Gunashekar, 2017). Blockchain-assisted smart auditing practises have huge potential to assist auditors in not just increasing audit efficiency but also in meeting the diverse information needs of multiple parties, beyond a qualitative audit judgement. Auditors will save significant time by virtually eliminating the requirement to examine, authenticate, validate, and substantiate processes. Indeed, statutory audits and other forms of audits may rise in popularity as organisations examine the costs and benefits of blockchain applications.

Moreover, the efficiency improvements associated with blockchain technology may enable auditors to focus their efforts on other high-risk areas, such as internal control, regulatory, or organisational audits (Hoelscher, 2018). Auditors may also be able to undertake additional work remotely as fieldwork at the client's site will be reduced. This could eventually result in the abolition or, at the very least, a radical redefinition of these occupations in the control and evaluation of activities. Gradually, blockchain is best achieved by combining the community's participants to create a common platform, which increases the difficulty of interoperability on two levels (PwC, 2018), first at the technical level, as each participant's systems must be comparable to the public blockchain, and second at the blockchain governance level, as each participant must decide on the public ledger.

Whilst blockchain created unparalleled incentives for the growth and transformation of the audit sector, it also faces a number of hurdles, including data security, talent and technology finance, business and awareness promotion, as well as practical implementation and execution (Jiang, 2018). Although several blockchain ventures have been founded and some of these have even been well developed, such as Bitcoin and Ethereum, there are still problems of interoperability between blockchain infrastructures. Meanwhile, Enterprise Resource Planning (ERP) vendors and software companies are also dealing with the problem of blockchain compatibility with enterprise information systems which sometimes include a number of functional modules (Kacina, Harler, & Rajnic, 2017). Compatibility issue hinders the exchange and transmission of information that is susceptible to programming faults or programme vulnerabilities between various software products.

Therefore, the auditor also needs to consider some risks associated with blockchain which including limitations on scalability[5], emerging threats to privacy and security. While blockchain can assert that a transaction occurred, it cannot give sufficient audit evidence pertaining to the nature of a transaction. Transactions can still be illegal, fraudulent or unauthorized regardless. As a result, a blockchain transaction cannot ascertain whether or not the contract is being carried out by connected parties. Transactions on a blockchain may also be coupled with an off-chain agreement. Apart from these technical obstacles, legal uncertainty is the primary impediment to blockchain implementation today, as PwC and Deloitte indicated in their studies(Pawczuk, Massey, & Schatsky, 2018; PwC, 2018).

In the technological era, auditors must exercise professional judgment and consider the reliability of the data. Simultaneously, auditor may need to consider and measure the efficiency of the consensus protocol used, as well as the capacity for modifying and leveraging the consensus protocol. Although not specifically addressed in auditing standards, auditors will need to assess the Digital Assets and Liabilities of management's accounting practices. The usage of blockchain technology will also necessitates auditors to determine how audit processes might be adjusted to maximised the benefits while mitigating the incremental risks.

III. BLOCKCHAIN TECHNOLOGY IN FINANCIAL STATEMENTS AUDIT

The notion of utilising blockchain technology in auditing stems from the fact that blockchain technology create precise audit trails to each transaction. Traditional audit procedures involve manual verification of transactions and balances that have been reported in the firm's financial books. These procedures are superfluous with the usage of blockchain technology, as auditors may instantly access related documents of the business transactions with external parties. From audit evidential procedures, confirmation from external parties is perceived as more reliable evidence than the firm's internally generated record. According to ISA 500 Audit Evidence, "the reliability of audit evidence is influenced by its source and by its nature, and is dependent on the individual circumstances under which it is obtained" (*ISA 500: Audit Evidence*, 2009, p. 5). Further reliable evidence can be provided by independent parties interested in publishing their financial records on a public ledger. Blockchain ledgers incorporate protocols that require relevant parties to validate transaction details as a requirement to ensure the transaction is valid and reliable as sufficient audit evidence (Perkinson & Miller, 2016; Sadu, 2018). This explanation suggests however that the blockchain must adopt beyond a single company. For a better understanding Brandon (2016) provide an illustration on how the adoption of blockchain in multi companies may affect audit procedure: Besides the ABC Company auditor, XYZ company may also have an external auditor. Such auditors, for both ABC and XYZ, may review the same transactions at the same time. If a company owned only one ledger with their vendors and debtors, then the expense and time for the audit will be reduced.

Recent research has argued that a blockchain technology in auditing will minimize audit costs by creating: (i) traceable audit trails; (ii) automated audit processes; (iii) transaction authentication; (iv) asset tracking; (v) smart contract development; and (vi) resources database and distribution network, from raw materials to intellectual property (Baron, 2017). The implementation of Blockchain will build a completely new system whereby each transaction ever made can be checked in real-time and made publicly available. The audit trail is checked by nodes using unified cryptographic validity controls. The transaction data in blockchain will demonstrate that there is potential earning management, such as revenue overestimation by channel filling or round-tripping against theft in financial reporting (Wang & Kogan, 2018). Nonetheless, once the data has been submitted and accepted, the validation of transaction information and details will be distributed into the entire network, allowing the transfer of funds from one partner to another in real-time and no longer needing the auditor to validate them (Smith, 2018).

Blockchain technology provides several significant benefits compared to traditional audit techniques. These advantages encompass: Blockchain transactions possess two key characteristics: transparency and immutability. Transparency refers to the ability to observe and comprehend the details of these transactions. Immutability, on the other hand, signifies that once a transaction is recorded on the blockchain, it becomes unalterable and cannot be erased without the collective agreement of the network participants. Implementing this measure has the potential to effectively mitigate instances of fraud and errors in the context of audits. The utilisation of blockchain technology has the potential to streamline several auditing processes, including the collection of evidence and the reconciliation of accounts, through enhanced efficiency and automation. This has the potential to allocate auditors' time towards more intricate and strategic responsibilities. Additionally, the implementation of blockchain technology has the potential to decrease auditing expenses through the elimination of intermediaries and the automation of certain auditing activities whilst at the same time exhibits a high level of security, thereby rendering it arduous for malicious actors to manipulate audit data. These more stringent auditing methods in Blockchain technology are opposed to the traditional audit procedures, as outlined in Figure 3 adapted from Appelbaum and Nehmer (2017a).

Figure 3. Audit procedures comparison of traditional manual procedures and Blockchain enabled continuous procedures
Source: Appelbaum and Nehmer (2017a)

Procedure	Tradition Method	Blockchain enable Continuous Method
Inspection of Records or Documents	Pull samples of records and trace/verify/match	Evaluate entire datasets in ERP using blockchain
Inspection of Tangible Assets	Physical inventory, walkthrough, open boxes	RFID tagging
Observation	Stand/sit with worker(s) and observe	Use blockchains or process mining to verify workflows
Inquiry	Written or oral interviews	Monitor processes and controls, identify process violators for examination
Confirmation	Verify account balance	Link data streams using blockchain applications
Recalculation	Extract and recalculate figures to verify	Monitor all data and run calculation automatically at intervals desired
Re-performance	Re-performance procedures to verify	Automatically replicate all transactions and identify exceptions
Analytical Procedure	Scanning and statistics	Filter real-time data with continuity equations and statistics

Since data contained in blockchains are accessible in real-time, traditional sampling methods used in financial statements audit may not be required. Through inspecting the whole archive using data analysis, auditors can provide better quality assurance. Therefore, conventional verification and authentication procedures view it as sufficient evidence for the audit to approve a transaction into a secure blockchain. With an expanded general ledger, the ability to change transactional or fake data is essentially minimized because the cryptographic signatures allow all parties involved in a certain transaction. A consolidated public ledger enables the auditors to view, in real-time, the transactional documents needed to conduct the audit, in addition to the more accurate and legal information, to facilitate more consistent audits. Blockchain will also reduce audit dependence for financial transactions and automate third-party authentication (Spoke, 2015).

Blockchain technology also makes it possible for auditors to conduct automated audit processes with preferences from a population instead of a sample since data held in blockchains are accessible in real-time. Blockchain provides an immutable ledger and a chance to test full transaction populations, possibly in real-time (Dai & Vasarhelyi, 2017; Sadu, 2018; Zhang, Pei, & Vasarhelyi, 2017). Therefore, using traditional sampling methods used in the financial statements may no longer be relevant. The distributed ledgers can also offer an opportunity for auditing with a stronger sense of trust more often or even constantly, provided that technology can make it tougher to alter transactions. The use of a distributed public ledger, as well as more accessible and relevant records, offers auditors the exclusive access to transactional information required for auditing in real-time and enables continuous auditing.

Furthermore, the capability to trace the ownership of the assets owned by a company as well as the previous owner of the assets can also be traced by blockchain. Blockchain is ideal for monitoring goods where consumers wish to know the roots and past owners by providing an immutable database (Nash, 2016). For example, in order to provide legitimacy in the diamond trade, Everledger Ltd uses blockchain technology (Hutt, 2016). Walmart China has collaborated with the VeChain project PwC platform to tackle food safety issues by monitoring the food supply chain (Ilija, 2019). Blockchain can be used to stop fraudulent transactions and to track them up. Since blockchain keeps a log of assets movement, a misappropriation can be easily detected (Wang & Kogan, 2018).

In addition, the evolution of blockchain and smart contract also carry advantages to auditors in conducting their audit work. Szabo explains smart contract using an analogy of a vending machine to illustrate their real-world operationalization in Figure 4 example.

Figure 4. Example of smart contract
Source: Rozario and Vasarhelyi (2018)

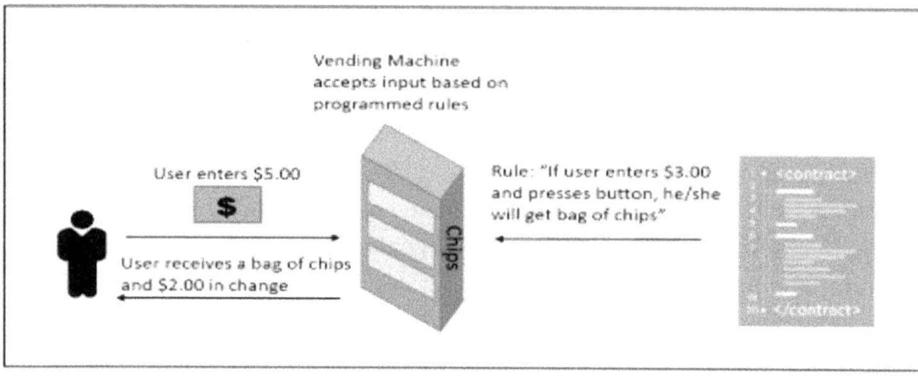

At the beginning stage, smart contract employed on a blockchain can initiate the execution of audit procedures, while offering shareholders close proximity to real-time audit reporting and greater transparency. With the second phase of blockchain, it becomes possible to implement a smart contract as the governance functions are allocated to the contributing nodes (Buterin, 2014; Dai & Vasarhelyi, 2017). The integration of these smart contract and blockchain technology creates another dimension known as blockchain smart audit procedures (Rozario & Vasarhelyi, 2018). This invention has a huge potential for helping the external auditor improve the quality of the audit and to meet the various information criteria of various parties which go further than the general opinion of the audit. Through automating contract negotiation and execution, smart contract minimizes transaction costs and make small-value transactions economically viable, the blockchain provides a commendable platform for smart contract.

It should be noted that not all the elements of financial audits can be put into blockchain smart audit procedures. Audit areas on accounting issues will be done outside the blockchain, for example, the determination of fair value assets Auditor also must ensure the client has a robust data integrity verification mechanism in place to prevent false transactions into the blockchain. Smart contract may be produced randomly and without authorisation and the expired contracts may be used in combination with new substitution smart contract. In summary, it is important to verify the mechanism as a consequence of the transactions reported in a blockchain, in order to ensure network trust and data integrity before the auditor considers it as reliable sources of information for example, transactions carried out by related parties, connected to an off-chain[6] side arrangement or inaccurately categorized in the financial statement.

IV. BLOCKCHAIN DEVELOPMENT IN BIG 4 AUDIT FIRMS FROM INTERNATIONAL CONTEXT

Undeniably, blockchain technology has attracted a lot of attention, including from the Big 4 international audit firms which are actively planning for blockchain consulting and testing service offerings. Early on in the Europe, Deloitte was the earliest Big 4 player to explore blockchain technology. Deloitte established the first blockchain lab in Dublin in May 2016. Later, Deloitte partnering with the Institute of Banking (IoB), Bank of Ireland, AIB, Ulster Bank to develop a new training framework[7] for the financial services industry focused on blockchain technology to validate the qualifications of the employees. Moreover, the audit giant also mounted a Bitcoin ATM at their Toronto workplace premises which showed the company's interest in cryptocurrencies. In fact, Deloitte has reported in collaboration with 22 other firms including Fidelity and Amazon in supporting a new blockchain acceleration program called Startup Lab. This initiative will hold seminars for blockchain companies to support them in the development of a range of skills relevant to the industry (Kuhn, 2019). Gradually, the Big Four organization has recently developed its own blockchain-based network called Blockchain in a Box which is an independent platform that is able to host blockchain-based solutions (Deloitte, 2019b).

In 2017, PwC started accepting Bitcoin as part of the billing of its services (Chaparro, 2017). Besides, PwC has also paid particular interest in stable coins and has established a partnership with Cred, a decentralized lending platform to boost the emerging U.S. dollar-sized cryptocurrencies industry. Moreover, PwC collaborated with Northern Trust, a large U.S. storage firm, which later introduced new tools for auditor which providing easy access to data stored on a proprietary ledger. Using the program, auditors can access read-only data in close proximity to real-time as securities are bought and traded between public investors and private investors while equity companies offer cash from borrowers (Castillo, 2018). PwC and VeChain (a blockchain platform) helped Walmart China establish a commodity traceability platform based on the blockchain platform roughly a year after joining the partnership (PwC, 2019b). News broke in July 2018 that PwC Switzerland was auditing Tezos which is a non-profit organization proving educational support for the smart contract and Dapp platform. This is the first time a Big Four firm has approved a large-scale blockchain enterprise as an audit partner. PwC today is arguably the most pragmatic company in cryptocurrencies and blockchain exploration.

With another audit giant in mind, EY has been investing in more crypto-related application projects than any of its competitors in the Big Four. First-generation EY Ops Chain was launched in 2017 followed by the second generation upgrades to support 20 million private network transactions daily by using blockchain technology for the incorporation of financial services into assets and the creation of a smart contract library that automates standard business processes (EY, 2019b). In fact, EY announced that a model of EY Blockchain Analyzer[8] second generation is eligible to EY employees and non-auditing clients. Later, EY Smart Contract Analyzer was developed for the public blockchain Ethereum, it is primarily designed to test and monitor token and smart contract prior to their release and once available on public blockchains (EY, 2019a).

KPMG has grown its presence in the blockchain area and has also been an alliance partner with Wall Street since 2017 (WSBA, 2017). KPMG formed an alliance with blockchain organization, Guardtime in 2019, a multinational expert in the creation of new digital products and services leveraging proprietary technology to provide clients with blockchain-enabled business processes (Guardtime, 2019). KPMG has collaborated with Microsoft, Tomia and R3 to develop a blockchain application aimed at streamlining the transactional cycle from a multi-week to a multi-day phase by saving time on payment and conflict processing, improving transparency and reducing high costs for consumers, making the expected 5G transition and the subsequent procedures as smooth as possible (Ghosh, 2019). Besides investment in blockchain-backed ventures, KPMG also researched cryptocurrencies and released a guideline in 2019 for the impact of Cryptoassets on accounting and tax. A cross-functional structure has also been developed by KPMG professionals to help companies adopt cryptocurrency as part of their business (KPMG, 2019a). Figure 5 and Table 1 shows the summary of Big 4 in blockchain development until October 2019 and the summary for the blockchain approach of the Big 4 Firm respectively.

Figure 5. Development of blockchain technology in Big 4 audit firms

Development	PwC	EY	KPMG	Deloitte
Crypto/blockchain market reports	√	√	√	√
Blockchain-based software solutions	√	√	√	√
First-hand adoption (Bitcoin acceptance, crypto ATMs)	√			√
Investments in the crypto market				

Table 1. Summary for the blockchain approach of the Big 4 firm

Big 4 Firm	Blockchain Approach
Deloitte	Focused on developing its own blockchain-based solutions, such as its Blockchain in a Box platform. Also interested in training and educating the financial services industry about blockchain technology.
PwC	Focused on using blockchain technology to improve the efficiency and accuracy of auditing and financial reporting. Also interested in using blockchain technology to develop new financial products and services.
EY	Focused on developing blockchain-based applications for a variety of industries. Also interested in using blockchain technology to improve the transparency and efficiency of business processes.
KPMG	Focused on providing blockchain consulting and testing services to its clients. Also interested in using blockchain technology to improve the efficiency and accuracy of auditing and financial reporting.

Despite all the developments of Big 4 international audit firms, it may be predictable the blockchain will influence the Big 4 audit firms in Malaysia sooner. Recently, Malaysia's Securities Commission has given full approval to Luno's offer to act as an Acknowledged Market Operator (Digital Asset Exchange) (Fong, 2019). Luno is Malaysia's first cryptocurrency exchange to get that certification. The regulator has stated that Luno has fulfilled all the conditions required and can now give Malaysians the opportunity to purchase, sell and store cryptocurrency on its website. This shows the Malaysia government also supporting the adoption of blockchain technology to create a new platform for the industrial revolution and job creation. However, there is still a lack of blockchain research in Malaysia especially in the auditing area. Therefore, this paper presents the advantages and challenges of blockchain to attract more ideas and interest in both practitioner and academician sector.

In conclusion, the Big 4 audit firms are evidently demonstrating a significant level of commitment towards the adoption and integration of blockchain technology. The firm's allocation of resources towards blockchain consulting and testing services, together with its efforts in developing blockchain-based tools and resources, indicate their conviction in the transformative potential of blockchain technology within the auditing sector. Nevertheless, it is imperative to acknowledge that blockchain technology is currently in its nascent phase of advancement. Several problems must be addressed prior to achieving widespread adoption of blockchain technology within the auditing business. Some of the difficulties that need to be addressed are: The absence of definitive regulatory advice pertaining to blockchain technology and there is also a growing demand for enhanced training and education programmes targeting auditors to acquire a deeper understanding of blockchain technology as well as a growing demand for enhanced interoperability among diverse blockchain platforms. Notwithstanding these obstacles, the Big 4 audit firms are strategically positioned to spearhead the implementation of blockchain technology inside the auditing sector. The acceleration of blockchain technology adoption in the auditing business will be facilitated by their investments in blockchain consulting and testing service offerings, together with their development of tools and resources based on blockchain.

V. DISCUSSION ON THE CHALLENGES IN ADOPTING BLOCKCHAIN TECHNOLOGY AND FUTURE RESEARCH

This paper discusses the challenges in adoption of blockchain in auditing perspective based on the Technology Acceptance Model (TAM) by Davis (1989) because the intention-based model developed specifically to address the characteristics of the technology. According to Lai (2017), in addition to forecasting, TAM aims at allowing researchers and practitioners to discern why a new technique or procedure can be acceptable or not appropriate by taking the right measures. Technology acceptance has received fairly extensive attention from researchers and practitioners of information systems (IS) (Alshurideh, Al Kurdi, & Salloum, 2019; Bach, Čeljo, & Zoroja, 2016; Handoko, Sabrina, Ayuanda, & others, 2019; Lin, 2017; Winarno, Prayitno, & Samudra, 2019; Wu & Chen, 2017). The foundation of TAM model comprised of two specific beliefs: Perceived Usefulness (PU) and Perceived Ease of Use (PEU).

Blockchain is similar to previous audit innovations in the needs of majority business implementation to optimize the technology's capacity. According to Dai and Vasarhelyi (2017), blockchain can only optimize the gain to companies through the wide adoption of the system, as adequate participants are required to ensure the ledger's stability, provide accurate transaction authentication and avoid unlawful collusion. This paper will further point out the perceived usefulness and ease of use based on the context of the audit of the financial statements. Future research opportunities are also established which solve the challenges. Many studies have acknowledged significant influences in the adoption of audit technologies from technology readiness and competence (Appelbaum & Nehmer, 2017b; Appelbaum & Smith, 2018; Chen, 2017; Dai & Vasarhelyi, 2016; Kokina, Mancha, & Pachamanova, 2017; Mansour, 2016; Yusof et al., 2018).

Perceived Usefulness

Perceived Usefulness is defined as the subjective probability that the use of blockchain technology will improve audit practices (Davis, 1989). Although blockchain has the potential to bring significant savings by increasing operational efficiency and significantly reducing audit time, there are considerable obstacles to be addressed before the technology can reach mass acceptance in the audit sector (Bible et al., 2017; Broby & Paul, 2017; Dai & Vasarhelyi, 2017; Jiang, 2018). In fact, being able to exchange information reliably and securely is a key advantage in auditing, which is characterized by an assurance service of diversifying customer areas. Blockchain technology and adopters benefit most from the engagement of their partners as a consortium (Francisco & Swanson, 2018; Korpela, Hallikas, & Dahlberg, 2017). Hence, in practice, it is only when consumer adoption reaches a critical mass that a powerful network effect is enabled that turns blockchain into embraced industry practice. Nonetheless, owing to divergent degrees of technical readiness and the immediate need to consider the mutual benefits of blockchain-based collaboration, corporate participation will be challenging at first.

Ideally, the principle behind the use of blockchain for fraud prevention is by boost data transparency and encourage third parties to verify so that transactions are legitimate and reliable (Abreu et al., 2018; Antipova, 2018; Dai, 2017; Dai, Wang, & Vasarhelyi, 2017; Giordano, 2019; Li, 2017). Nevertheless, this method may not be as successful in the real world as it ought. Of example, if a private blockchain becomes fully controlled by top managers of an organization, they can make false transactions and oblige a group of companies to allow verification, the management and oversight pledge of decentralization is reversed. Blockchain shall instead be spread among divergent, relatively independent parties including sellers, customers, investors and banks. These parties can become independent verifiers responsible for the identification of fraudulent transactions, especially external transactions. For instance, Electo et al. (2008) developed a project called Ledgerium whitepaper version 2.2 which provides a blockchain consortium for accounting and auditing application layer to allow selected parties to participate in the chain.

In addition, the transactions also checked by other parties before being added to the ledger, thus improve the transparency of the transactions and technology usability. Acceptance of a transaction into a decentralized blockchain may be sufficient proof of audit for certain claims in auditing financial statements, such as the existence of the transaction. For example, it is possible to track Bitcoin transaction on the blockchain to validate the transaction details. Nevertheless, the auditor may or may not be able to determine the item delivered when analysing data on the blockchain alone. Transactions occurring on a ledger may still be illegal, illegitimate or prohibited. Moreover, a transaction on a blockchain cannot discern between the related parties whether the transaction is being executed. This will require additional work from the auditor to isolate the transaction between clients and related parties. Further upgrades to ensure data integrity is expected to result in an improved robustness mechanism in the blockchain. One of the recommendations is to merge blockchain and ERP applications like SAP Leonardo which incorporate smart technology.

Although bringing smart contract into blockchain can simplify auditing of the financial statements and reduce the workload of auditors, they need to realize that blockchain is not the solution for every situation. This may remove many of the work-intensive and time-consuming manual data analysis and audit planning tasks for an entity's management and staff. Reduced lag time can be an opportunity to make financial reporting and audit more efficient and effective by enabling auditors and management to concentrate on more critical and complicated activities while completing routine audits in a near real-time (Bible et al., 2017). While various blockchain projects have been set up and some of them are well-established, such as Bitcoin and Ethereum, problems of interoperability within blockchain infrastructures still remain. In the form of an audit of financial statements, management will be responsible for developing internal controls to check whether the source code for a smart contract is compatible with the business logic expected. Some researchers have suggested this if organizations rely on a smart contract or smart controls to act as automated application controls, effective IT General Controls need to be in place to support reliable application processing (Huang, Hung, Yen, Chang, & Jiang, 2011; Norman, Payne, & Vendrzyk, 2009).

Perceived Ease of Use

Perceived Ease of Use refers to how convenient the future user intends the target system to be effortless (Davis, 1989). Blockchain created unparalleled incentives for the growth of the audit industry and for change. Nevertheless, the blockchain technology continues to face challenges such as cybersecurity, scalability and regulation (Accounting Today, 2017; CPAJ Staff, 2019; Hoelscher, 2018; Jiang, 2018; Rozario & Vasarhelyi, 2018; Smith, 2018). One threat is an attack on "51 per cent," or "majority rule". A user may present false data in the blocks in this attack to create a fraudulent transaction that most nodes on the blockchain accept as true. Hackers can also exploit bugs in endpoints where people interact with the network, which is when they are most likely to attack the information. Another threat is the manipulation of information in a supply chain by harnessing a blockchain's confidentiality and traceability capabilities. Generally, the production and implementation of blockchain require a robust system before the accounting companies can implement the technology to avoid any failure regarding data security breaches that may produce a high overhead for the company. Audit firms should collaborate with the e-commerce industry to develop the technology because they are connected to high-data security networks like Amazon, Alibaba, Rakuten and Groupon. According to Dai and Vasarhelyi (2017), once blockchain technology becomes widely adopted, it will continue in places where protection and security of details are of paramount concern and data scale is not overwhelming, such as e-commerce corporations.

Support for talent and technology also become a challenge to the auditor in adopting new technology like blockchain (Accounting Today, 2017; Nathalie et al., 2019; Rozario & Vasarhelyi, 2018; Sadu, 2018; Zhang, Dai, & Vasarhelyi, 2018). There are two (2) factors that the technology preparation initiative will likely impact the auditor's ease of use in blockchain, which are the financial and practical tools of the company. Firstly, the financial audit firm must decide whether they can embrace or oppose new technology. This is because the adoption of new technologies requires a tremendous amount of capital to develop and implement.

For example, with a large initial investment in the smart contract, audit processes will have to dramatically change, companies have to rebalance their staff, put and trust their information in the public domain, and convince business partners to partake in an open-share system although the information may be encrypted. Although technology can provide the auditor with a lot of utility, another concern about the user-friendliness of the system also becomes an important issue for the audit firm to remember. For instance, credentials can be compromised or stolen, and there are concerns that they may be vulnerable to programming errors or weaknesses in systems. The basic principle of increasing the ease of use of technologies must be first grasped by consumers of the new technology. Consequently, the audit firm must also mandate that the auditor develop a training program to improve their knowledge and skills before any new technology is implemented.

Furthermore, promotion and recognition of regulators also made a huge impact on the challenges of new technology adoption in auditing (Deloitte, 2019a; KPMG, 2019b; PwC, 2019a). There are many new regulatory standards that need to be implemented and many of which have not yet been enforced to simplify blockchain adoption. Legal risks, for example, stem from the lack of standards and rules for blockchain compliance in various legal regimes around the world will increase the audit firms' resistance to technology adoption. Similarly, in some off-chain transactions that result in false assurance, incorrectly legitimized transactions will lead auditors to perceive the technology is too risky to use in their daily routine.

Regulatory complexity associated with additional work for the company to adopt new technology, making it necessary for auditors to be involved from the beginning and not only after deployment when a final system needs auditing. Regulators must have a deep understanding of the technology to provide adequate advice and monitoring. This will help to prevent exploitation and misuse of blockchain and smart contract. Consequently, regulators are expected to play an essential role in the process of deployment of blockchain in the audit sector.

To conclude, due to various considerations, auditors may find blockchain technology difficult to adopt and integrate into their present processes such as, concerns about cybersecurity. Blockchain is not immune to security risks. Auditors must be on the lookout for potential flaws such as the “51 percent attack” and the exploitation of defects in user interface points with the network. Furthermore, data security is critical, and any breach could result in huge overhead expenses for audit firms. Another concern is data manipulation in supply chains. Auditors must be mindful of the possibility of hostile actors manipulating information within a supply chain that makes use of blockchain’s confidentiality and traceability characteristics. This tampering has the potential to jeopardise the integrity of the data being audited.

Additionally, adoption of blockchain technology can be resource-intensive and require a significant financial investment. This includes the creation of smart contracts, the redesign of audit processes, the reallocation of personnel, and the resolution of data sharing and trust difficulties. Even if the data is encrypted, convincing business partners to use an open-share system can be difficult. Auditors also must assess the usability of blockchain technologies. Concerns may include credential theft, the possibility of programming errors or system weaknesses, and the necessity for intensive training programmes to ensure auditors have the necessary knowledge and skills for blockchain technology. Since regulatory norms for blockchain usage are still emerging, auditors may face compliance issues. In some legal jurisdictions, the lack of defined standards and laws can lead to legal problems and resistance to technological adoption. To ensure compliance and security, regulatory complications need the involvement of auditors from the start, rather than only after deployment. Regulatory promotion and recognition are also important variables. Auditors rely on regulatory guidance and standard enforcement. To prevent exploitation and misuse of blockchain and smart contracts, regulators must completely grasp blockchain technology and give adequate advise and oversight. To maintain a secure and compliant environment, authorities must be involved in the adoption of blockchain in the audit sector.

VI. CONCLUSION

There is still a lot of uncertainty about how blockchain will affect the audit paradigm, including how quickly it will affect that. Blockchain already starts to affects auditors of those organizations that adopt blockchain in their business model and the adoption rate is expected to rise continuously. Nevertheless, blockchain technology will not in the immediate future substitute financial reporting and auditing of the financial statements. The audits are the backbone of an organization which operates efficiently and effectively in debt and equity funding, capital market participation, fusions, acquisitions, compliance with regulation and capital markets. Financial statements reflect management points, like estimates, many not readily outlined or calculated in blockchains.

The independent audit process also increases the trust of customers, which is key to the continued operation of the capital-market system. Any weakening of this trust may damage the reputation, stock price, and shareholder value of a company and may lead to fines, penalties, or asset loss. Auditors require the use of their expertise to conduct an independent audit of the records by holders of the financial statements. Such professional judgements can not be undermined by blockchains. Nonetheless, auditors must consider advancement in blockchain technology as this impacts their customers ' information systems, which in turn affect their position in the audit. In order to conduct an audit to blockchain settings, the auditors will know about blockchain technology and consult with experts.

In addition, auditors need to be mindful of the potential for enhancing data collection through their customers' adoption of blockchain technology during audit exercises. Auditors also must consider whether the blockchain technology will allow the development of automatic audit routines. Until widespread blockchain acceptance, the auditing industry shall proactively embrace and respond upon the opportunities and challenges. Auditors are inspired by their potential to grow, strengthen and build on their previously demonstrated capacity to adapt to the needs of a rapidly changing business world to track innovations in blockchain technology.

Future research could delve into potential synergies and conflicts between blockchain and artificial intelligence in the context of digital auditing. Focusing on leveraging these technologies to improve audit methodologies and trustworthiness of data would also provide valuable insights. As blockchain technology matures and becomes more ingrained in auditing practises, research in these areas will play a crucial role in influencing the future of the digital auditing paradigm, ensuring its efficacy, security, and relevance in a world that is increasingly digital and decentralised.

ACKNOWLEDGMENT

The authors would like to extend their gratitude to the Ministry of Higher Education for funding this research under the Fundamental Research Grant Scheme - Sustainability in Social Capital Outreach: Modelling Blockchain Technology for Microfinance Institution 600-RMC/FRGS 5/3 (064/2022).

REFERENCES

Abreu, P. W., Aparicio, M., & Costa, C. J. (2018). Blockchain technology in the auditing environment. *Iberian Conference on Information Systems and Technologies, CISTI,* 1–6. 10.23919/CISTI.2018.8399460

Accounting Today. (2017). Scoping out the audit of the future; A virtual roundtable of experts looks at how technology and other trends are reshaping a core service of the accounting profession. *Accounting Today, 31*(6), 6,52,53. Retrieved from https://search.proquest.com/docview/1910741844/fulltext/3D17D388739842BBPQ/1?accountid=11528

Alshurideh, M., Al Kurdi, B., & Salloum, S. A. (2019). Examining the main mobile learning system drivers effects: A mix empirical examination of both the Expectation-Confirmation Model (ECM) and the Technology Acceptance Model (TAM). *International Conference on Advanced Intelligent Systems and Informatics*, 406–417.

Antipova, T. (2018). Using blockchain technology for government auditing. *Iberian Conference on Information Systems and Technologies, CISTI,* 1–6. 10.23919/CISTI.2018.8399439

Appelbaum, D., & Nehmer, R. A. (2017a). Designing and auditing accounting systems based on blockchain and distributed ledger principles. *Feliciano School of Business*, 1–19. Retrieved from https://pdfs.semanticscholar.org/edc2/4c3ae8cb7f4f978c9353d47986168265fe03.pdf

Appelbaum, D., & Nehmer, R. A. (2017b). Using drones in internal and external audits: An exploratory framework. *Journal of Emerging Technologies in Accounting, 14*(1), 99–113. Advance online publication. doi:10.2308/jeta-51704

Appelbaum, D., & Smith, S. S. (2018). Blockchain basics and hands-on guidance: Taking the next step toward implementation and adoption. *The CPA Journal, 88*(6), 28–37. http://web-1ebscohost-1com-10000f4h3028c.han.ub.fau.de/ehost/pdfviewer/pdfviewer?vid=16&sid=fc526975-895b-430e-8f7b-c92229f39f1b%40sessionmgr4007

Bach, M. P., Čeljo, A., & Zoroja, J. (2016). Technology acceptance model for business intelligence systems: Preliminary research. *Procedia Computer Science, 100*, 995–1001. doi:10.1016/j.procs.2016.09.270

Baliga, A. (2017). *Understanding blockchain consensus models*. Whitepaper.

Baron, J. (2017). Blockchain What you need to know. *Accounting Today, 31*(11), 47.

Bible, W., Raphael, J., Riviello, M., Taylor, P., & Valiente, I. O. (2017). Blockchain technology and its potential impact on the audit and assurance profession. In *CPA Canada, AICPA & UW CISA*. Retrieved from https://www.aicpa.org/interestareas/frc/assuranceadvisoryservices/blockchain-impact-on-auditing.html%0Ahttps://www.aicpa.org/content/dam/aicpa/interestareas/frc/assuranceadvisoryservices/downloadabledocuments/blockchain-technology-and-its-potential-impact

Bone, B. Y. J. (2018). Five trends shaping digital transformation. *Internal Auditor*, (October), 19–21.

Brandon, D. (2016). The blockchain : The future of business information systems? *International Journal of the Academic Business World*, *10*(2), 33–40.

Broby, D., & Paul, G. (2017). The financial auditing of distributed ledgers, blockchain and cryptocurrencies. *Journal of Financial Transformation*.

Buterin, V. (2014). A next-generation smart contract and decentralized application platform. In *Etherum*. Retrieved from http://blockchainlab.com/pdf/Ethereum_white_paper-a_next_generation_smart_contract_and_decentralized_application_platform-vitalik-buterin.pdf

Chaparro, F. (2017). *A 'Big Four' accounting firm is accepting bitcoin payments*. Retrieved November 30, 2017, from Business Insider US website: https://www.businessinsider.my/a-big-four-accounting-firm-is-accepting-bitcoin-payments-2017-11/?r=US&IR=T

Chen, L. (2017). Continuous Delivery: Overcoming adoption challenges. *Journal of Systems and Software*, *128*, 72–86. doi:10.1016/j.jss.2017.02.013

Cong, Y., Du, H., & Vasarhelyi, M. A. (2018). Technological disruption in accounting and auditing. *Journal of Emerging Technologies in Accounting*, *15*(2), 1–10. doi:10.2308/jeta-10640

Dai, J. (2017). *Three essays on audit technology: Audit 4.0, blockchain, and audit app* (Rutgers University). Retrieved from https://rucore.libraries.rutgers.edu/rutgers-lib/55154/PDF/1/

Dai, J., & Vasarhelyi, M. A. (2016). Imagineering audit 4.0. *Journal of Emerging Technologies in Accounting*, *13*(1), 1–15. Advance online publication. doi:10.2308/jeta-10494

Dai, J., & Vasarhelyi, M. A. (2017). Toward blockchain-based accounting and assurance. *Journal of Information Systems*, *31*(3), 5–21. doi:10.2308/isys-51804

Dai, J., Wang, Y., & Vasarhelyi, M. A. (2017). Blockchain: An emerging solution for fraud. *The CPA Journal*, *87*(6), 12–14. http://esc-web.lib.cbs.dk/login?url=http://search.ebscohost.com/login.aspx?direct=true&db=bth&AN=123973389&site=ehost-live&scope=site

Dastane, O., Omar Zaki, H. & Aman, A. (2023). Robotic process automation: bibliometric reflection and future opportunities. *European Journal of Innovation Management*. doi:10.1108/EJIM-10-2022-0570

Davis, F. D. (1989). Perceived usefulness, perceived ease of use, and user acceptance of information technology. *Management Information Systems Quarterly*, *13*(3), 319–339. doi:10.2307/249008

del Castillo, M. (2018). *Northern trust, PwC launch 'Instant' blockchain audits*. Retrieved March 19, 2018, from Coindesk.com website: https://www.coindesk.com/northern-trust-and-pwc-launch-instant-blockchain-audits

Deloitte. (2019a). Deloitte's 2019 global blockchain survey. Deloitte Insights.

Deloitte. (2019b). *Deloitte debuts ' Blockchain In a Box ' (BIAB)*. Retrieved from https://www2.deloitte.com/us/en/pages/about-deloitte/articles/press-releases/blockchain-in-a-box.html

Deloitte. (2019c). *Irish banking industry first in Europe in building new education platform based on blockchain*. Retrieved from https://www2.deloitte.com/ie/en/pages/technology/articles/Irish_banking_industry_first_in_Europe_in_building_new_education_platform_based_on_blockchain.html

Deshpande, A., Stewart, K., Lepetit, L., & Gunashekar, S. (2017). *Distributed Ledger Technologies/Blockchain: Challenges, opportunities and the prospects for standards. British Standards Institution*. BSI. doi:10.7249/RR2223

Electo, C. I., Golash, R., & Ma, K. (2008). Ledgerium Whitepaper. In *Ledgerium* [Version 2.2]. Retrieved from https://whitepaper.ledgerium.io/ledgerium-foundation

EY. (2019a). *EY launches smart contract testing service for blockchain clients*. Retrieved April 16, 2019, from https://www.ey.com/en_gl/news/2019/04/ey-launches-smart-contract-testing-service-for-blockchain-clients

EY. (2019b). *EY Ops Chain industrializes the blockchain at scale for enterprises*. Retrieved April 16, 2019, from https://www.ey.com/en_gl/news/2019/04/ey-ops-chain-industrializes-the-blockchain-at-scale-for-enterprises

EY. (2019c). *Multimillion-dollar investment in EY Blockchain Analyzer delivers new upgrades for blockchain and cryptocurrency audit and tax services*. Retrieved April 16, 2019, from https://www.ey.com/en_gl/news/2019/04/multimillion-dollar-investment-in-ey-blockchain-analyzer-delivers-new-upgrades-for-blockchain-and-cryptocurrency-audit-and-tax-services

Fong, V. (2019). *Luno Is The First Cryptocurrency Exchange to Receive Full Approval in Malaysia*. Retrieved October 22, 2019, from https://fintechnews.my/21843/blockchain/luno-becomes-first-cryptocurrency-exchange-to-receive-full-approval-in-malaysia/

Francisco, K., & Swanson, D. (2018). The supply chain has no clothes: Technology adoption of blockchain for supply chain transparency. *Logistics*. doi:10.3390/logistics2010002

Ghosh, A. (2019). *How blockchain is streamlining settlements between telecom companies*. Retrieved from KPMG website: https://info.kpmg.us/news-perspectives/technology-innovation/blockchain-streamlining-settlements-between-telecom-companies.html

Giordano, A. (2019). Accountants embrace distributed ledgers. *Global Finance*, *33*(3), 72–72.

Grewal-Carr, V., & Stephen, M. (2016). *Blockchain enigma. Paradox. Opportunity*. Deloitte.

Guardtime. (2019). *KPMG forms strategic alliance with Guardtime*. Retrieved from https://guardtime.com/blog/kpmg-forms-strategic-alliance-with-guardtime

Haber, S., & Stornetta, W. S. (1991). *How to time-stamp a digital document*. Lecture Notes in Computer Science. Including Subseries Lecture Notes in Artificial Intelligence and Lecture Notes in Bioinformatics. doi:10.1007/3-540-38424-3_32

Handoko, B. L., Sabrina, S., Ayuanda, N., & ... (2019). Admission of information technology in external audit profession: Impact of organizational, social and individual factors. *2019 International Conference on Information Management and Technology (ICIMTech), 1*, 36–41. 10.1109/ICIMTech.2019.8843720

Hoelscher, J. (2018). Taking the lead on blockchain. *Internal Auditor*, (February), 19–21. Retrieved from https://search.proquest.com/docview/1680732671?accountid=12492%0Ahttps://sfx.mit.edu/sfx_local?url_ver=Z39.88-2004&rft_val_fmt=info:ofi/fmt:kev:mtx:journal&genre=unknown&sid=ProQ:ProQ%3Aabicomplete&atitle=Risk+Watch&title=Independent+Banker&issn=00193674&

Hou, R., Ye, X., Zaki, H. B. O., & Omar, N. A. B. (2023). Marketing Decision Support System Based on Data Mining Technology. *Applied Sciences (Basel, Switzerland), 13*(7), 4315. doi:10.3390/app13074315

Huang, S. M., Hung, W. H., Yen, D. C., Chang, I. C., & Jiang, D. (2011). Building the evaluation model of the IT general control for CPAs under enterprise risk management. *Decision Support Systems, 50*(4), 692–701. Advance online publication. doi:10.1016/j.dss.2010.08.015

Hutt, R. (2016). Beyond bitcoin: 4 surprising uses for blockchain. *World Economic Forum.*

Ilija, M. (2019). *The Chinese branch of Walmart and Vechain team up on PwC blockchain safety platform.* Retrieved from https://cryptomaniaks.com/walmart-china-vechain-pwc-blockchain-food-safety

ISA 500: Audit Evidence. (2009). doi:10.4324/9781315762395-4

Jiang, X. (2018). The application of blockchain in auditing. *2nd International Conference on Education Science and Economic Management (ICESEM 2018), 184*(January), 1018–1023. 10.2991/icpel-18.2018.10

Kacina, J., Harler, M. C., & Rajnic, M. (2017). *SophiaTX Whitepaper The Blockchain for Business.* Retrieved from https://www.sophiatx.com/storage/web/SophiaTX_Whitepaper_v1.9.pdf

Kokina, J., Mancha, R., & Pachamanova, D. (2017). Blockchain emergent industry adoption and implications for accounting. *Journal of Emerging Technologies in Accounting, 14*(2), 91–100. doi:10.2308/jeta-51911

Korpela, K., Hallikas, J., & Dahlberg, T. (2017). Digital supply chain transformation toward blockchain integration. *Proceedings of the 50th Hawaii International Conference on System Sciences.* 10.24251/HICSS.2017.506

KPMG. (2019a). *Accounting for cryptoassets – What's the impact on your financial statements?* Author.

KPMG. (2019b). *Ten key regulatory challenges of 2019.* Retrieved from https://assets.kpmg/content/dam/kpmg/us/pdf/2018/12/ten-key-regulatory-challenges-pov-v5-web.pdf

Kuhn, D. (2019). *Amazon, Deloitte, Fidelity partner with IDEO CoLab on blockchain accelerator.* Retrieved July 11, 2019, from Coindesk website: https://www.coindesk.com/amazon-deloitte-messari-partner-with-ideo-colab-on-blockchain-startup-accelerator

Lai, P. (2017). The literature review of technology adoption models and theories for the novelty technology. *Journal of Information Systems and Technology Management*, *14*(1), 21–38. doi:10.4301/S1807-17752017000100002

Li, Z. (2017). Will blockchain change the audit? *China-USA Business Review*, *16*(6), 294–298. doi:10.17265/1537-1514/2017.06.006

Lin, H.-C. (2017). Nurses' satisfaction with using nursing information systems from technology acceptance model and information systems success model perspectives: a reductionist approach. *CIN: Computers, Informatics. Nursing*, *35*(2), 91–99. PMID:27618401

Mahbod, R., & Hinton, D. (2019). Blockchain the future of the auditing and assurance profession. *Armed Forces Comptroller*, *64*(1), 23–27.

Mansour, E. M. (2016). Factors affecting the adoption of Computer Assisted Audit Techniques in audit process: Findings from Jordan. *Business and Economic Review*, *6*(1), 248–271. doi:10.5296/ber.v6i1.8996

Murray, J. (2018). The Coming World of Blockchain: A Primer for Accountants and Auditors. *The CPA Journal*.

Nakamoto, S. (2008). *Bitcoin: A peer-to-peer electronic cash system*. Retrieved from http://www.academia.edu/download/54517945/Bitcoin_paper_Original_2.pdf

Nash, K. S. (2016). IBM pushes blockchain into the supply chain. *The Wall Street Journal*.

Nathalie, B., Gauthier, M., Morin, J.-H., & Arber, S. (2019). The Potential Impact of Blockchain Technology on Audit Practice. *Journal of Strategic Innovation and Sustainability*, *14*(2), 35–59. doi:10.33423/jsis.v14i2.1370

Ng, C. (2019). Blockchain in the Accounting Curriculum. *Pennsylvania CPA Journal, 90*(1), 14–15. Retrieved from http://eds.a.ebscohost.com/eds/Citations/FullTextLinkClick?sid=e1bbad5a-8886-4460-aecb-cce09bbdbc59@sessionmgr4007&vid=6&id=pdfFullText

Norman, C. S., Payne, M. D., & Vendrzyk, V. P. (2009). Assessing information technology general control risk: An instructional case. *Issues in Accounting Education*, *24*(1), 63–76. Advance online publication. doi:10.2308/iace.2009.24.1.63

Pawczuk, L., Massey, R., & Schatsky, D. (2018). Breaking blockchain open Deloitte's 2018 global blockchain survey. Deloitte. doi:10.1002/ejoc.201200111

Perkinson, J., & Miller, R. (2016). Unimpeachable blockchains: Could blockchain revolutionise the accounting profession? In Acuity (Vol. 3). Academic Press.

PwC. (2018). Blockchain is here. What's your next move? In *PwC's Global Blockchain Survey 2018*. Retrieved from https://www.pwc.com/gx/en/issues/blockchain/blockchain-in-business.html?WT.mc_id=CT11-PL1000-DM2-TR1-LS4-ND30-TTA5-CN_US-GX-xLoSBlockchain-StratITForecast&_cldee=a3BvbWFsbGV5QGdtYWlsLmNvbQ%3D%3D&eq=CT11-PL1000-DM2-CN_US-GX-xLoSBlockchain-StratITForecast&e

PWC. (2018). Blockchain is here. What's your next move? In PwC's Global Blockchain Survey 2018.

PwC. (2019a). *Financial Service Technology 2020*. Retrieved from https://www.pwc.com/gx/en/financial-services/assets/pdf/technology2020-and-beyond.pdf

PwC. (2019b). *PwC and VeChain help Walmart China build its Blockchain Traceability System*. Retrieved June 25, 2019, from PwC website: https://www.pwccn.com/en/press-room/press-releases/pr-250619.html

Rozario, A. M., & Vasarhelyi, M. A. (2018). Auditing with Smart Contracts. *The International Journal of Digital Accounting Research, 18*(December), 1–27. doi:10.4192/1577-8517-v18_1

Sadu, I. (2018). Auditing blockchain. *Internal Auditor*, *75*(6), 17–19.

Smith, S. S. (2018). Blockchain augmented audit – benefits and challenges for accounting professionals. *Journal of Theoretical Accounting Research*, *14*(1), 117–138. http://search.ebscohost.com/login.aspx?direct=true&AuthType=cookie,ip,shib,uid&db=bsu&AN=131747318&lang=pt-br&site=eds-live&authtype=sso

Spoke, M. (2015). *How blockchain tech will change auditing for good.* Retrieved from Coindesk.com website: https://www.coindesk.com/blockchains-and-the-future-of-audit

Staff, C. P. A. J. (2019). Auditing implications of blockchain and cybersecurity: Certified Public Accountant. *The CPA Journal*, *89*, 38–39. http://eds.a.ebscohost.com/eds/Citations/FullTextLinkClick?sid=e1bbad5a-8886-4460-aecb-cce09bbdbc59@sessionmgr4007&vid=8&id=pdfFullText

Sultan, K., Ruhi, U., & Lakhani, R. (2018). Conceptualizing Blockchains: Characteristics & Applications. *11th IADIS International Conference. Information Systems*, *2018*, 49–57. https://arxiv.org/abs/1806.03693

Swan, M. (2015). Blockchain: Blueprint for a new economy. In Climate Change 2013 - The Physical Science Basis. doi:10.1017/CBO9781107415324.004

Tapscott, D., & Tapscott, A. (2017). How blockchain will change organizations. *MIT Sloan Management Review*, *58*(2), 10. doi:10.7551/mitpress/11645.003.0010

Tysiac, K., & Drew, J. (2018). Accounting firms: The next generation. *Journal of Accountancy*, *225*(6), 26–32. http://web.b.ebscohost.com.ezproxy.ub.gu.se/ehost/pdfviewer/pdfviewer?vid=1&sid=d1eed4fe-a91b-49a5-85ab-238e241ec257%40pdc-v-sessmgr05

Varma, J. R. (2019). Blockchain in Finance. *Vikalpa*, *44*(1), 1–11. doi:10.1177/0256090919839897

Wang, Y., & Kogan, A. (2018). Designing confidentiality-preserving Blockchain-based transaction processing systems. *International Journal of Accounting Information Systems*, *30*, 1–18. Advance online publication. doi:10.1016/j.accinf.2018.06.001

Winarno, B. H., Prayitno, E., & Samudra, S. T. (2019). Continuance intention to use MOOCs: Integrating the Technology Acceptance Model (TAM) and Task Technology Fit (TTF) model. *Journal of International Conference Proceedings*, *2*(2), 46–49. doi:10.32535/jicp.v2i2.601

WSBA. (2017). *Wall Street blockchain alliance adds KPMG as corporate member*. Retrieved from https://www.wsba.co/uploads/3/7/9/4/3794101/wsbafinal11-15.pdf

Wu, B., & Chen, X. (2017). Continuance intention to use MOOCs: Integrating the technology acceptance model (TAM) and task technology fit (TTF) model. *Computers in Human Behavior*, *67*, 221–232. doi:10.1016/j.chb.2016.10.028

Yermack, D. (2017). Corporate governance and blockchains. *Review of Finance*, rfw074. Advance online publication. doi:10.1093/rof/rfw074

Yusof, H., Farhana Mior Badrul Munir, M., Zolkaply, Z., Jing, L. C., Yu Hao, C., Swee Ying, D., … Kok Leong, T. (2018). Behavioral intention to adopt blockchain technology: Viewpoint of the banking institutions in Malaysia. *International Journal of Advanced Scientific Research and Management*, *3*(10), 1–6. Retrieved from www.ijasrm.com

Zhang, C., Dai, J., & Vasarhelyi, M. A. (2018). The impact of disruptive technologies on accounting and audiiting education. *The CPA Journal*, *88*(9), 20–26.

Zhang, L., Pei, D., & Vasarhelyi, M. A. (2017). Toward a new business reporting model. *Journal of Emerging Technologies in Accounting*, *14*(2), 1–15. doi:10.2308/jeta-10570

ENDNOTES

1. Bitcoin is a peer-to-peer version of electronic cash, also known as the first cryptocurrency as coined by Satoshi Nakamato.
2. See, (Nakamoto, 2008)
3. See, (Baliga, 2017).
4. See, (Baliga, 2017).
5. Scalability occur as demand rises, when certain transactions took days to verified. Block can contain only a limited number of data as transactions need to wait in a queue to be placed in the next block if demand grows too large (Murray, 2018).
6. Transactions that take place not in public blockchain, but in the wallet provider's proprietary ledger between members of the same wallet network.
7. The European financial services industry's first portal facilitates authentication, monitoring, direct access and control of regulatory and other professional trainings, academic certificates and lifelong learning credentials. (Deloitte, 2019c).
8. A business application that is usable at any time, allowing financial reporting, criminal audits, transaction tracking and tax estimates, serving EY teams and clients through accounting, tax and transaction advisory services globally (EY, 2019c).

Chapter 12
AI in Market Research:
Transformative Customer Insights – A Systematic Review

Manisha Paliwal
https://orcid.org/0000-0002-4439-4457
Sri Balaji University, Pune, India

Nishita Chatradhi
https://orcid.org/0000-0002-3744-3820
Sri Balaji University, Pune, India

ABSTRACT

This systematic review examines the role of artificial intelligence (AI) in market research and its impact on customer insights. While existing research has extensively explored AI's influence on marketing, education, and customer experience, a noticeable gap remains in understanding AI's role in reshaping the market research industry. This study aims to fill that gap by focusing on the unexplored territory of AI-driven market research and customer insights. The review follows a structured methodology, analyzing relevant research articles published between 2000 and 2023 using the TCCM framework. The findings demonstrate AI's significant impact on customer experiences, market segmentation, and personalized services across various industries. By embracing AI's capabilities, businesses can thrive in the data-driven and competitive landscape, forging lasting connections with their target audiences and driving success in the dynamic world of business.

DOI: 10.4018/979-8-3693-0039-8.ch012

1. INTRODUCTION

Artificial intelligence (AI) is a rapidly expanding field, and many academics are now investigating how AI will affect the marketing industry. Market researchers are investigating how AI can improve the consumer experience in order to increase customer loyalty and, by extension, profits. With over $5 billion invested in AI startups in just the last two years, the field is poised to revolutionize marketing and commerce worldwide (Insights, 2018; Rangaswamy et al., 2020). When AI performs mundane, repetitive tasks, consumers benefit from lower prices, a wider variety of service channels, new discoveries, and more room for human creativity and ingenuity (Smart Insights, 2018; Haenlein & Kaplan, 2019). Because of long-term margin pressures, shorter strategy cycles, and higher customer expectations, businesses are increasingly adopting AI technologies supported by data analytics. This alters how businesses interact with their customers and has the potential to increase brand loyalty (Evans, 2019). AI advancements, in particular, may help businesses gain a better understanding of their customers' preferences (Evans, 2019). Businesses that strategically implement AI technologies at various touch points with the customer experience stand to gain significantly and increase customer satisfaction (Shakir & Ramzan, 2021).

1.1 AI and Market Research

The introduction of AI into market research has sparked a slew of new lines of inquiry, including the use of AI to power robotics (Lu et al., 2020; Wirtz et al., 2018); AI-led market research and sales strategies; and an investigation into how AI-enabled delivery can result in greater value for customers. Despite this lengthy list, there is little agreement among market researchers about how AI technologies should be used in the future (Rosca et al., 2018).

For a long time, market research has been an essential tool for businesses, allowing them to better understand their customers, assess the competition, and make informed decisions (Schmidt et al., 2023). In the past, manual data collection, pen and paper surveys, focus groups, and statistical analysis were all standard tools for conducting market research. Although these techniques provided useful insights, they were time-consuming to implement and consumed a lot of resources while failing to account for the nuances of consumer behaviour. the AI era, in which cutting-edge technology has given market research new life. Researchers have been able to systematically uncover previously hidden patterns and insights into consumer preferences and market dynamics with the advent of cutting-edge AI algorithms and techniques (Shakil et al., 2023; Schmidt et al., 2023). Using AI, market researchers can speed up their work and improve their accuracy. The incorporation of AI into market research represents a watershed moment, providing market researchers with unprecedented tools and capabilities that were previously unimaginable (Wilson-Nash et al 2020).

While a plethora of research has been dedicated to exploring AI's impact on marketing(Nordin et al 2019; Mustak et al., 2021; Kashyap et al 2021; Zaki et al., 2023), marketing strategies (Mikalef et a., 2023), education, digital marketing(Gigante et al., 2023; Khalifa et al., 2021), and customer experience, there remains a noticeable gap in understanding how AI is reshaping the market research industry and driving AI-driven customer insights. It is within this context that the authors of this chapter embark on a critical examination, seeking to shed light on the transformative potential of AI in market research.

1.2 AI, Market Research and HRM

AI and market research have enhanced HRM (Ransbotham et al., 2020). AI-driven market research has transformed talent acquisition. AI algorithms quickly identify top candidates based on skills, qualifications, and experience in automated resume screening. Human decision-making biases are reduced and HR professionals save time. AI can also analyze social media and online behaviour to determine an applicant's fit with an organization, improving hiring decisions. IBM and Unilever have increased profits and hiring efficiency by using AI (Malik et al., 2022).

Any company needs motivated and engaged workers. HRM uses AI-powered market research tools to track employee sentiment and engagement in real time (Duan et al., 2019). These tools assess morale using employee feedback, surveys, and natural language conversations. Anticipating issues helps HR address concerns and boost employee satisfaction. Glint and Qualtrics provide HR professionals with robust platforms for such initiatives. A market research AI could assist HR departments in personalising employee development programmes (Margherita, 2021). To help employees improve and stay relevant, AI can tailor training modules based on performance data and skills assessments (Vrontis et al., 2021). This approach improves employee performance and shows an organization's commitment to development, increasing retention.

AI and predictive analytics can improve HRM strategic workforce planning. Using historical data and market trends, AI can help HR professionals predict skill gaps and talent shortages. Companies use this data to plan recruitment, training, and succession (Faulds & Raju, 2021). AI has helped PwC develop workforce planning prognostic models to ensure qualified staff are available when needed.

Organizational diversity and inclusion can benefit from AI-powered market research tools. AI can analyze demographic and survey data to help HR departments identify biases and areas for improvement (Kaplan & Haenlein, 2020). This tool provides practical knowledge to improve workplace inclusivity and address unconscious biases in recruitment and promotion. HRM is increasingly using AI-driven chatbots and virtual assistants for employee wellbeing and mental health. AI-powered tools can answer employee questions, provide 24/7 support, and manage stress and mental health. HR can quickly intervene if employee communication indicates emotional or psychological distress. This proactive approach fosters a caring workplace.

By focusing on the unexplored territory of AI-driven market research, Human resource management and customer insights, this study aims to bridge the gap in the existing literature and offer fresh perspectives. The significance of this research lies in uncovering the untapped potential of AI in market research, as it paves the way for innovative methodologies and novel insights. Understanding how AI-driven customer insights can revolutionize market research practices is essential for businesses seeking a competitive edge in today's data-driven landscape. Moreover, this study aims to stimulate further exploration and encourage academia and industry alike to recognize the transformative role of AI in the domain of market research.

Thus this chapter delves into *the role of artificial intelligence (AI) in enhancing customer insights and market research.* It meticulously explores a wide array of studies conducted are leveraged to extract and analyze customer-related data from various sources.

By compiling and assessing existing research across different functional themes, activity levers, and research contexts, this systematic literature review aims to establish a robust body of scientific evidence supporting the pivotal role of AI-powered marketing in driving more competent business outcomes. Through its comprehensive examination of these studies, the review unveils the futuristic potential of AI-powered marketing, which promises to revolutionize customer insights and fuel a new era of more effective market dynamics.

Following a discussion of the study's conceptual foundation in Section 2, we will go into greater depth regarding its review approach and structure in Section 3. The publications we reviewed and our thoughts on the TCCM framework are summarized in Section 4. Section 5 discusses where the field is headed next. Section 6 concludes with a discussion of the implications.

2. CONCEPTUAL FRAMEWORK

2.1. Evolution of AI in Market Research and Enhanced Customer Insight

Qualitative market research has grown in importance in recent decades. Companies now realise consumer perceptions matter (Zolnowski, 2020). Early market research used quantitative methods like surveys and statistical analyses to study consumer habits. Qualitative approaches became more popular as competition increased and consumer tastes diversified (Chen et al 2020). In the 1950s and 1960s, psychologists and sociologists used focus groups to study consumer behaviour, sparking qualitative market research. These preliminary analyses sought to understand consumers' decision-making and how marketing and branding affect sentiment. In the 1970s and 80s, ethnographers observed customers in their daily lives to learn about their habits.

Modern qualitative market research tools include in-depth interviews and social media analysis. Qualitative market research provides a deep, nuanced understanding of consumer behaviour and preferences to help businesses make informed product development, branding, and marketing decisions (Schmidt et al., 2023). Companies need qualitative research in today's fast-changing business environment. AI has revolutionized market research by analyzing data and generating new insights. Market researchers can expect AI to grow in importance as the industry develops (Tran et al 2021). It is essential for businesses to succeed in the data-driven economy (Chen et al., 2020).

Facial coding is an AI-powered technology that reads emotions and expressions. It can reveal what drives people to buy. Sentiment analysis can reveal the emotional impact of campaigns, products, and services by deciphering written or verbal responses. Brands like sentiment analysis' confidence metrics. How confident respondents are in their answers can tell researchers about consumer behaviour. Voice AI can help researchers decipher spoken responses' tone, inflection, and other vocal cues, revealing consumer mindsets and actions. Facial coding, sentiment analysis, and voice AI can improve product development, branding, and marketing (Sanny et al., 2020, Rosca et al., 2018). AI in digitally transformed qualitative research has transformed the study process.

2.2. Motivation and Prospective of AI and Market Research

Artificial intelligence (AI) has transformed data collection, analysis, and application, giving market researchers new opportunities. Davenport et al. (2020) found that AI can automate business processes, learn from historical data, and generate algorithm-based consumer and market insights. Training machines with ML, AI-driven chatbots, predictive analytics, and NLP lets them process big data and generate market intelligence (Smith & Jones, 2021). It understands and interacts with human emotions and feelings, or facilitates them. Current technologies include sentiment analysis, NLP, text-to-speech, RNN, chatbots that mimic human speech, and robots with affective signal sensing hardware.

Marketing uses sentiment analysis to understand customers' opinions and improve products and services (Al Ajrawi et al. 2021; Jang et al. 2013).Social media simplifies stock market interactions for investors. Business has changed with sentiment analysis (Bhardwaj et al. 2015). Different sentiment and emotion recognition methods have pros and cons. Researcher challenges include context, ridicule, multi-emotion statements, Web slang, and lexical and syntactical ambiguity. Without standardized rules for expressing feelings across platforms, people express emotions differently: some strongly, others suppress them, and some structure their messages logically (Birim et al., 2022). Thus, researchers struggle to create a method that works across all domains.

Table 1. Potential applications of AI in market research

Applications of AI in MR
1. Survey automation (Chatbots)
2. Web scrapping (AI-powered bot)
3. Speech analysis
4. Personalised marketing
5. Customer segmentation
6. Predicative Analysis
7. Customer support (virtual assistant)
8. Sentiment analysis
9. Image and Video analysis
10. Customer feedback and reviews (NLP)

Users' interactions with business intelligence and analytics data have also begun to shift due to the rise of conversational interfaces (Bhardwaj et al. 2015). The use of chatbots, which mimic human conversations, has also increased, particularly in the field of customer service. Businesses implementing intelligent chatbots have a heavy burden of monitoring their behaviour (Jang et al. 2013). Chatbots have great revenue-generating potential, which is why messaging services like Facebook Messenger have started investing heavily in them to provide customer service and other functions(Moris., 2023; Sanny et al., 2020, Wang el., 2019). By concentrating on each customer separately in an effort to foresee their actions and motivations, predictive marketing helps restore a human dimension to our otherwise impersonal online and offline experiences. Marketers who are attempting to make sense of such behaviours can gain a great deal of leverage by employing predictive analytics built on machine-learning algorithms. Machine learning and complex algorithms may not be able to completely replace human decision-making, but they may help humans greatly expand their capacity for intelligence and problem-solving(Johnson et al., 2020).

As AI continues to evolve, market research stands on the cusp of unprecedented advancements(Dastane & Haba, 2023). AI-driven methodologies are creating a wealth of opportunities for businesses seeking to leverage data for competitive advantage. By harnessing the potential of NLP, chatbots, sentiment analysis, and predictive analytics, market researchers are poised to unearth richer insights, elevate data collection methods, and devise more precise strategies for a dynamic and ever-changing market landscape.

2.3 Ethical Considerations of AI in Market Research

The use of artificial intelligence has revolutionized market research by providing tools to analyze data and generate insights. It is expected that artificial intelligence will become more integral to marketing research as it evolves and grows. In order to use AI effectively in market research, ethical considerations need to be considered as with any new technology

The ethical considerations businesses must take into account when using AI include transparency, privacy, and bias.((Holmes et al., 2021; Tsamados, 2021). These studies examine AI decision-making bias and the need for strong ethics to prevent unfair treatment. Studies show that AI systems must address fairness concerns to achieve impartial results for all. Trust is another AI autonomy ethical issue. As society and customers adopts AI systems, confidence in them is crucial (Shin, 2022; Gutierrez Lopez et al., 2023).

Privacy and data protection are moral issues. Buttarelli (2018) distinguishes privacy and data protection, but AI ethics prioritizes informational privacy. Data security risks arise from machine learning AI (Kim et al., 2020) More intriguing and specific to AI is the possibility that AI and its ability to detect patterns may pose privacy risks without direct access to personal data. Most jurisdictions have strong data protection laws, but AI may raise ethical and data protection issues. AI may use or generate emotional personal data, which is rare, worsening the situation (Tsamados, 2021; Gutierrez Lopez et al., 2023).

Data protection and security are linked. ICT cybersecurity persists beyond AI. Model poisoning may threaten AI systems (Jagielski et al. 2018). These systems can find and exploit new vulnerabilities (Krafft et al. 2020). Ethical issues with AI autonomy include freedom and dependence. Developers who mishandle AI-based applications can leak sensitive data and lose machine control, according to Kooli (2023a). AI system responsibility and decision-making may increase human dependence on these technologies. AI overuse may reduce autonomy and agency, raising ethical questions about human-AI decision-making.

Businesses must maintain high ethical standards as artificial intelligence changes market research. Transparency, fairness, privacy, and data protection must guide AI implementation. Trusting AI systems is essential for their widespread adoption. AI-driven market research must balance these ethical concerns with the potential benefits of AI to serve businesses and society responsibly and equitably.

3. REVIEW APPROACH AND STRUCTURE

This chapter presents a systematic literature review (SLR) on the utilization of Artificial Intelligence (AI) techniques in customer insights and market research. The review follows a structured methodology involving rigorous search, selection, and analysis of relevant research articles published between 2000 and 2023. The Scopus database was chosen as the primary source for conducting the literature search due to its comprehensive coverage across various disciplines and relevance to the research topic. The Search Query - (TITLE-ABS-KEY (artificial AND intelligence) AND TITLE-ABS-KEY (customer AND insight) AND TITLE-ABS-KEY (market AND research)) AND (LIMIT-TO (DOCTYPE, "ar")) AND (LIMIT-TO (PUBSTAGE, "final")) AND (LIMIT-TO (SRCTYPE, "j")) AND (LIMIT-TO (LANGUAGE, "English")) was employed in the academic database.

The inclusion criteria considered articles focused on the utilization of AI techniques in customer insights and market research, published between 2000 and 2023, and written in the English language. The exclusion criteria ensured that articles not directly related to the research topic, published outside the designated timeframe, or written in languages other than English.

The data extraction process involved extracting key information from each article, including author(s), publication year, research methods employed, AI techniques utilized, industry focus, and findings.

Figure 1. SLR protocol flow diagram

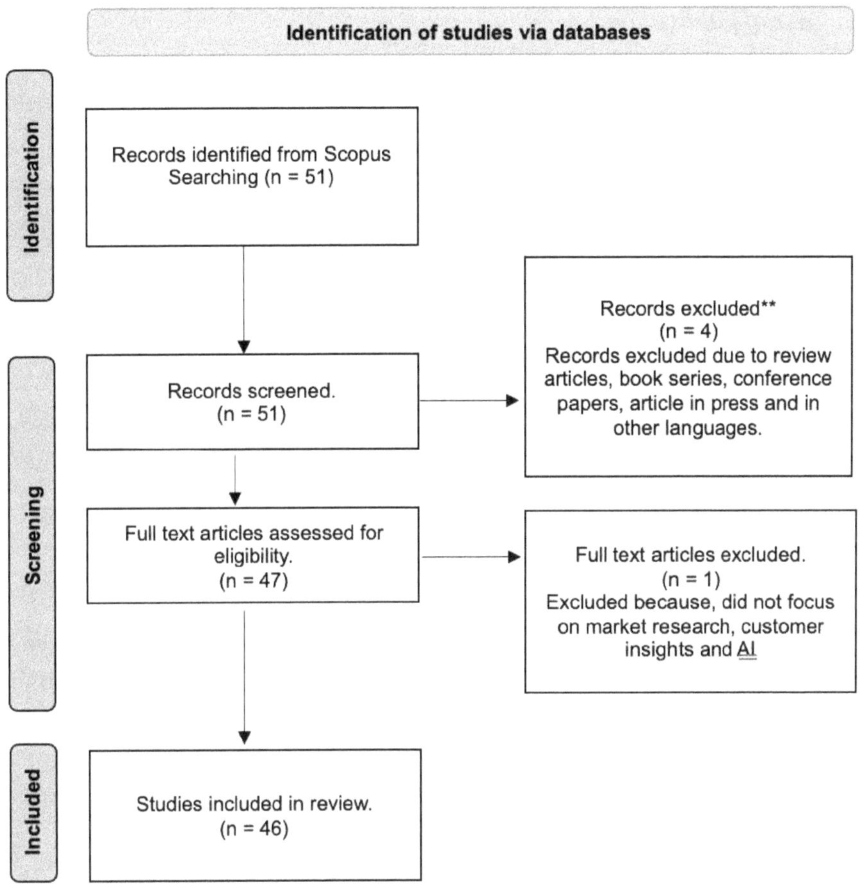

We organized the articles by theory, contexts, characteristics (antecedents, outcomes, themes), and methodology according to the TCCM framework (Paul & Rosado Serrano, 2019). Then, we used content analysis to discuss the TCCM's four pillars: theory development; contextual factors; defining characteristics; and research methodology. Results were more trustworthy when the TCCM framework was used to structure the evaluation and analysis of the content of the literature. The research gaps were identified through a gap analysis, and a plan for future study was developed with a focus on individual pillars of the TCCM framework.

4. ANALYSIS AND DISCUSSION

Table 2. Year of publication

Year	No. of Articles
2023	8
2022	7
2021	13
2020	6
2019	5
2018	1
2017	1
2011	4
2000	1
Total	46
Source: Authors Compilation	

From 2000 to 2016, there were only five published articles on Artificial Intelligence, Customer Insight, and Market Research. However, starting from 2017, the number of published articles began to increase. In 2019, there were 5 articles published, followed by 1 article each in 2017 and 2018. The highest number of articles, 13, was published in 2021. Subsequently, the number remained relatively consistent, with 6 articles in 2020, 7 articles in 2022, and 8 articles in 2023.

Table 3. Contributing journals

Name of Journals	No. of Articles		Name of Journals	No. of Articles
Advances In Intelligent Systems And Computing	2		Electronics Switzerland	1
Journal Of Business Research	2		European Journal Of Marketing	1
ACM International Conference Proceeding Series	2		Fujitsu Scientific And Technical Journal	1
Annals Of Operations Research	2		IEEE Access	1
Artificial Intelligence For Engineering Design Analysis And Manufacturing AIEDAM	2		IFAC Papers online	1
Bulletin Of Electrical Engineering And Informatics	2		Industrial Marketing Management	1
Cogent Business And Management	2		International Journal Of Emerging Markets	1
Communications In Computer And Information Science	2		Journal Of Cleaner Production	1
Computational Intelligence And Neuroscience	2		Journal Of Service Management	1
Developments In Marketing Science Proceedings Of The Academy Of M1arketing Science	2		Journal Of System And Management Sciences	1
Digital Policy Regulation And Governance	2		Lecture Notes On Data Engineering And Communications Technologies	1
Proceedings Of The International Astronautical Congress Iac	2		Management Science Letters	1
Qualitative Research In Financial Markets	1		On The Horizon	1
Religions	1		Operations Research Perspectives	1
SN Computer Science	1		Strategic Direction	1
Source: Authors Compilation				

4.1. Theory, Context, Characteristics, and Methodology (TCCM) Framework Discussion

4.1.1 Theoretical Foundation

The Policy-based Management Theory emphasizes using policies to govern and manage complex systems, such as enterprise and carrier IP networking.This theory facilitates the automation and optimization of network operations, ensuring efficient resource allocation, security enforcement, and quality of service, with a focus on policy-based management for enterprise and carrier IP networking (Hamada et al., 2001).

Framework Foresight Method is a strategic planning approach that anticipates future scenarios and emerging trends. In the context of AI, studies explores the future needs and expectations of students in various aspects of their lives, including living, learning, working, playing, connecting, and participating (Swanson., 2017). This theory aids in identifying opportunities for integrating AI-driven solutions in educational settings to enhance the overall student experience.

The Stimuli-Organism-Response (S-O-R) Theory is a psychological framework explaining the relationship between environmental stimuli, individual organism processing, and behavioral responses.(Buhalis D. et al., 2019). In the context of AI applications in tourism and hospitality, the S-O-R Theory helps understand how technological disruptions driven by AI innovations influence customer behavior and responses, thereby impacting customer satisfaction, loyalty, and decision-making in the tourism and hospitality industry.

Machine Learning and Governance, Business Strategies refer to the application of machine learning algorithms and principles in the development of governance and business strategies. This theory explores the intersection of artificial intelligence and policy-making, investigating how AI technologies, such as machine learning, influence policy formation, business strategies, and decision-making processes across different sectors (Lauterbach., 2019).

The Unified Theory of Acceptance and Use of Technology (UTAUT) Model is a widely used framework to assess the acceptance and adoption of new technologies. In the context of AI's involvement in Christian education in Vietnam, the UTAUT model helps understand the factors influencing people's attitudes towards using AI technology for religious education. It considers variables such as performance expectancy, effort expectancy, social influence, and facilitating conditions to predict individuals' intentions to use AI in religious education. (Tran et al., 2021).

The Technology Adoption Model is a widely used theory to understand how individuals and organizations adopt and accept new technologies. In the context of AI applications, this model helps identify the determinants of technology adoption, assess perceived usefulness and ease of use, and predict the potential success of AI initiatives in different domains. Exploring impact of age and gender on sentiment analysis using machine learning (Kumar et al., 2020). Exploratory research on digitalization transformation practices within supply chain management context in developing countries specifically Egypt in the MENA region (Khalifa and Elghany

., 2021). Competitive strategies of mobile applications in online taxi services: The cases of Snapp and Tap30 in Iran (Arbatani et al., 2021).

The Use and Gratification Theory is a communication theory focusing on how individuals actively seek out and use media to satisfy specific needs and desires. In the context of AI applications in electronic commerce, this theory helps understand the factors influencing customers' acceptance of using chatbots. It examines how customers perceive and use chatbot services to fulfill specific needs during online shopping and customer service interactions (Mahapatra & Singh., 2023).

This model focused on segmenting customers based on their perceived value of personalized AI-driven banking services and conducted technology testing to evaluate the feasibility and customer acceptance of these technological advancements. The researchers utilized the *Lean Startup Method/Pricing Strategy* model to guide their analysis. This approach focused on adopting lean startup principles and implementing appropriate pricing strategies to maximize the success rate of the business model when integrating AI-based analytics and marketing automation. Nordin et al. (2019) proposed " the Behavioral Intention (BN) model, which helped understand consumer behavioral patterns and intentions in the market. By applying this model, the researchers aimed to gain valuable insights into market trends and consumer preferences, enhancing their ability to predict market disruptions and make data-driven decisions for businesses.

4.2 Context

Industry-Specific Context: This chapter encompasses a wide array of industries and sectors where artificial intelligence (AI) has been explored and implemented. The industries studied include consumer and industrial electronics, education, tourism, policy (Lauterbach., 2019)and ethics, customer engagement, customer experience, supply chain management(Khalifa et al., 2021), the automotive industry, social media, religious education, online taxi services (Arbatani et al., 2021) banking and finance (Gambhir et al., 2022), retail (online shopping) (Behera et al., 2023), information and communication technology (ICT) and telecommunications, and supply chain retailers(Alomar et al., 2022).

Countries' Contribution to the Research: The studies presented in this chapter reflects valuable contributions from diverse countries and regions, providing comprehensive insights into AI's implications and adoption on a global scale. Notable countries that have contributed to the studies include the United States, Indonesia, Egypt, Germany, Vietnam, Iran, India, and various countries across Asia and North America.

Each of these countries offers a unique and distinctive context for AI research, considering their specific economic, cultural, and social characteristics. The diversity of countries in the study underscores the global interest in harnessing AI technologies and understanding their impact on various industries and sectors. Furthermore, this wide representation of countries contributes to the depth and richness of the research, providing valuable insights into AI's potential implications and adoption on an international scale.

4.3 Characteristics

The studies included in the framework exhibit a diverse set of characteristics, each focusing on specific variables to comprehensively understand the multifaceted nature of artificial intelligence (AI) and its implications in various domains. Hamada et al. (2000) delve into policy-based management for enterprise and carrier IP networking, studying variables related to the implementation and enforcement of rules to optimize network performance. Swanson (2017) explores emerging student needs across six aspects of student life, including living, learning, working, playing, connecting, and participating. The study examines variables associated with evolving student demands in the education sector, providing insights for educational institutions to adapt effectively.

Lauterbach (2019) investigates the intersection of AI and policy, focusing on machine learning and governance's integration into business strategies. The research considers variables related to the formulation of effective business strategies leveraging AI technologies and the impact of AI in policy decision-making. Sanny et al. (2020) analyze customer satisfaction factors influencing chatbot acceptance in Indonesia. The variables studied encompass brand image and customer satisfaction, shaping customers' attitudes towards AI-powered chatbots and influencing overall customer experience.

Schmidt et al. (2023) propose a strategic framework for incorporating multiple AI benefits in marketing planning. The study examines variables related to pricing strategy and the success rate of business models, seeking to enhance marketing effectiveness and overall business performance. Tran and Nguyen (2021) conduct preliminary research on social attitudes toward AI's involvement in Christian education in Vietnam. The study explores variables associated with the integration of AI technologies in religious education to enhance learning experiences.

Schmidt et al. (2023) develop a strategic framework for incorporating AI benefits in marketing planning, focusing on variables related to big data and machine learning-based analytics, aiming to enhance marketing efficiency and decision-making.

Gigante and Zago (2023) examine applications of DARQ technologies in personalized banking. The study explores variables concerning value segmentation and technology testing, assessing DARQ technologies' effectiveness in the banking sector. Mikalef et al. (2023) explore AI competencies for organizational performance in B2B marketing. The study focuses on variables related to B2B marketing capabilities and their impact on organizational performance, aiming to enhance business-to-business relationships.

Behera et al. (2023) study the creation of sustainable growth with explainable artificial intelligence in consumer packaged goods retailers. The research explores variables concerning the adoption of explainable AI and its contribution to sustainable growth in the retail sector. Collectively, these studies provide valuable insights into AI's diverse applications and implications across different industries, sectors, and countries, highlighting the dynamic nature of AI research on a global scale.

4.4 Methodology

Across the studies analyzed, there is a notable diversity in research methodologies, with both qualitative and quantitative approaches being employed to explore the applications and implications of artificial intelligence. In terms of the distribution between qualitative and quantitative methodologies, the papers show a relatively balanced representation. Several studies opt for qualitative methods, such as conceptual papers, in-depth interviews, and comparative case studies. These qualitative approaches are effective in providing a deeper understanding of complex phenomena, capturing rich insights, and exploring various perspectives in specific contexts. For instance, qualitative stimulation and in-depth interviews allow researchers to simulate scenarios and gather detailed responses from a limited number of participants, facilitating a more comprehensive exploration of emerging trends and needs in the education and customer experience domains. On the other hand, quantitative methodologies are also prevalent in the studies. Researchers frequently utilize surveys, interviews with larger sample sizes, and statistical analyses, such as factor analysis and structural equation modeling (SEM). Surveys and large-scale interviews offer a broader perspective by collecting data from a significant number of respondents, providing valuable insights into customer preferences, market trends, and attitudes towards AI applications in various sectors. The application of statistical techniques like factor analysis and SEM enables researchers to analyze complex relationships between variables and assess the impact of AI on organizational performance and customer satisfaction. The diverse methodologies and sample sizes used in the studies reflect the multidimensional nature of AI research. The combination of qualitative and quantitative methods allows researchers to approach the subject from different angles, considering both breadth and depth in their investigations. This comprehensive approach not only enriches our understanding of the implications of AI across different industries and sectors but also provides evidence-based insights for policymakers, businesses, and practitioners to make informed decisions in the rapidly evolving field of artificial intelligence.

5. DIRECTIONS FOR FUTURE RESEARCH

Ethical AI Governance: Given the increasing prominence of AI applications, it is imperative to investigate ethical AI governance and policy frameworks in-depth. Future research could delve into the ethical considerations surrounding AI decision-making processes, privacy concerns, and transparency in AI algorithms. This research could provide guidelines for policymakers, businesses, and AI developers to ensure responsible and accountable AI deployment.

Longitudinal Studies: As AI technology continues to evolve rapidly, conducting longitudinal studies over extended periods could offer valuable insights into the long-term impacts and trends of AI adoption. Tracking the changing perceptions, attitudes, and experiences of customers and stakeholders towards AI-powered services and products would be essential for staying abreast of AI's evolving dynamics.

Personalization and Customer Experience: Further research could explore the effectiveness of personalized AI-driven customer experiences in different industries. Investigating how AI-powered chatbots, virtual assistants, and recommendation systems impact customer satisfaction, brand loyalty, and overall customer experience would be instrumental in refining customer-centric AI strategies.

AI and Marketing Strategy: The exploration of AI's role in marketing strategy development could provide marketers with a better understanding of how to leverage AI capabilities for market segmentation, targeted advertising, and content optimization. Integrating AI-driven analytics into marketing planning can potentially enhance marketing effectiveness and return on investment. Future research could examine the challenges and opportunities of AI adoption in emerging markets, including India, Malaysia, Vietnam, and Qatar. Understanding the cultural, economic, and regulatory factors that influence AI acceptance and adoption in these regions could facilitate the development of context-specific AI strategies.

Explainable AI: Building on the studies that highlighted the significance of explainable AI in customer insights and retail contexts, further research could delve into methodologies and techniques for enhancing AI explainability. Advancements in explainable AI can facilitate trust-building with consumers, regulators, and stakeholders and pave the way for widespread AI adoption.

AI and Sustainability: Given the growing interest in sustainability, investigating how AI technologies can contribute to sustainable practices in various industries, including supply chain management and consumer packaged goods, could provide valuable insights. This research could uncover opportunities for reducing environmental impacts, optimizing resource utilization, and promoting sustainable business practices.

Table 4. Future research agenda

Future Research Agenda	Areas of Study	Research Questions
Explore the long-term impact of AI adoption on consumer behavior in emerging markets.	Consumer Behavior in Emerging Markets	- How does the adoption of AI technologies influence consumer behavior in emerging markets over an extended period?
Investigate the ethical implications of using AI-driven predictive analytics in the healthcare industry.	Healthcare Ethics	- What are the ethical concerns surrounding AI-powered predictive analytics in healthcare, and how can they be addressed effectively?
Examine the role of AI-based personalization in enhancing customer loyalty and retention in the e-commerce sector.	Customer Loyalty in E-commerce	- How does AI-powered personalization impact customer loyalty and retention in the e-commerce industry?
Analyze the potential of AI in optimizing supply chain management in the automotive industry.	AI in Automotive Supply Chain	- How can AI technologies be leveraged to streamline supply chain management processes and enhance efficiency in the automotive sector?
Investigate the use of AI-driven sentiment analysis in improving marketing strategies for social media influencers.	Marketing Strategies for Social Media Influencers	- How can AI-driven sentiment analysis be employed to enhance marketing strategies and audience engagement for social media influencers?
Explore the intersection of AI and virtual reality in creating immersive customer experiences in the entertainment and gaming industries.	AI and Virtual Reality in Entertainment and Gaming	- How can AI and virtual reality technologies be combined to create immersive and personalized experiences for entertainment and gaming consumers?
Examine the application of AI in predicting demand patterns and optimizing inventory management in the retail sector.	AI in Demand Forecasting and Inventory Management	- How accurate and effective are AI-based demand forecasting models in optimizing inventory management for retailers?
Investigate the potential of AI-driven chatbots in improving customer service and support in the telecommunications industry.	AI Chatbots in Telecommunications	- How do AI-driven chatbots impact customer service and support experiences in the telecommunications sector?
Analyze the use of AI and big data analytics in enhancing decision-making processes in the financial services sector.	AI and Big Data Analytics in Financial Decision-making	- How can AI and big data analytics be employed to facilitate data-driven decision-making in the financial services industry?
Examine the integration of AI and Internet of Things (IoT) technologies in creating smart and sustainable cities.	AI and IoT in Smart Cities	- What are the potential applications and benefits of integrating AI and IoT in the development of smart and sustainable cities?

Source: Authors Compilation

The presented table 3 outlines a promising research agenda in the dynamic domain of "Artificial Intelligence and Market Research and Customer Insights," drawing upon the robust TCCM framework. This agenda envisions exploring the far-reaching influence of AI adoption on consumer behavior, customer experiences, and decision-making processes across diverse industries and contexts. Unveiling intriguing gaps and areas of study, the table directs attention to critical domains that beckon further investigation to unlock profound insights into the ramifications of AI implementation. Noteworthy subjects include the ethical implications of AI in healthcare, the optimization of supply chain management through AI-driven innovations, and the augmentation of customer loyalty and retention in the ever-evolving e-commerce landscape. The thought-provoking research questions presented in the table offer compelling pathways for future exploration. These inquiries delve into the enduring effects of AI adoption in burgeoning markets, the seamless integration of AI and IoT in the genesis of smart cities, and the transformative potential of AI-powered sentiment analysis in fashioning unparalleled marketing strategies with influencers. In essence, this concise yet impactful table paves the way for an exhilarating journey into the realms of AI's transformative prowess, charting an enlightened course to unravel the complexities of industries, consumer behavior, and business paradigms within the ever-evolving landscape of market research and customer insights.

6. CONCLUSION

This chapter has presented a comprehensive overview of the applications and implications of Artificial Intelligence (AI) in the domains of customer insights and market research. The analysis of various studies has demonstrated the diverse and transformative impact of AI across different industries and countries. The findings reveal that AI has significantly enhanced customer experiences, market segmentation, and personalized services in sectors such as banking, education, tourism, and retail. Additionally, AI-driven sentiment analysis, machine learning, and big data analytics have emerged as powerful tools for understanding consumer behavior and preferences.

6.1 Implications of the Study

The implications of the studies on artificial intelligence (AI) are manifold and hold significant value for diverse stakeholders and application domains. The investigation of policy-based management for enterprise and carrier IP networking sheds light on the necessity of formulating robust policies and strategies to govern AI applications in the telecommunications sector effectively (Ledro., 2021). Policymakers can draw upon these insights to create frameworks that promote the responsible and efficient use of AI technologies in networking operations, ensuring compliance with ethical and regulatory considerations. In the realm of education, understanding emerging student needs in various aspects of student life, including living, learning, working, playing, connecting, and participating, provides educational institutions with valuable guidance for tailoring services and support systems accordingly(Mahapatra et al 2021; Micus et al., 2023; Lu et al., 2020). By addressing these diverse needs, educational organizations can enhance student experiences and overall well-being, contributing to improved academic outcomes. Policymakers and businesses must pay attention to the ethical implications of AI technologies to ensure transparency, fairness, and accountability in decision-making processes. Ethical AI governance is crucial for fostering public trust in AI systems and mitigating potential risks associated with their widespread adoption. By understanding customer preferences and leveraging AI for personalized services, companies can elevate customer satisfaction and cultivate strong brand loyalty, contributing to long-term business success.

Furthermore, the development of a strategic framework for incorporating AI benefits in marketing planning encourages businesses to embrace big data and machine learning-based analytics for innovation. Data-driven marketing strategies can better align with customer expectations, resulting in improved marketing outcomes and enhanced customer engagement. In terms of market insights and consumer behavior, the use of Behavioral Intention (BN) as an AI algorithm offers businesses a deeper understanding of consumer preferences and actions. By analyzing behavioral patterns, organizations can make data-driven decisions, leading to more effective marketing strategies and product development, thus driving business growth.

Exploring AI competencies concerning B2B marketing capabilities and organizational performance provides actionable insights for businesses seeking improved marketing effectiveness and operational efficiency. Enhancing AI capabilities within organizations can contribute to superior marketing outcomes and overall business performance.

In essence, this chapter highlights the remarkable potential of AI in revolutionizing customer insights and market research. As AI technologies continue to evolve, businesses and organizations that harness its capabilities wisely and ethically will be better positioned to thrive in an increasingly data-driven and competitive landscape. By leveraging AI's power to gain deeper customer understanding and generate actionable insights, companies can elevate their offerings and forge lasting connections with their target audiences, driving success and sustainability in the dynamic world of business.

REFERENCES

Al Ajrawi, S., Agrawal, A., Mangal, H., Putluri, K., Reid, B., Hanna, G., & Sarkar, M. (2021). Evaluating business yelp's star ratings using sentiment analysis. *Materials Today: Proceedings*. Advance online publication. doi:10.1016/j.matpr.2020.12.137

Alomar, M. A. (2022). Performance Optimization of Industrial Supply Chain Using Artificial Intelligence. *Computational Intelligence and Neuroscience*, *2022*, 1–10. doi:10.1155/2022/9306265 PMID:35942447

Arbatani, T. R., Norouzi, E., Omidi, A., & Valero-Pastor, J. M. (2021). Competitive strategies of mobile applications in online taxi services: The cases of Snapp and Tap30 in Iran. *International Journal of Emerging Markets*, *16*(1), 113–130.

Behera, R. K., Bala, P. K., & Rana, N. P. (2023). Creation of sustainable growth with explainable artificial intelligence: An empirical insight from consumer packaged goods retailers. *Journal of Cleaner Production*, *399*, 136605. doi:10.1016/j.jclepro.2023.136605

Bhardwaj, A., Narayan, Y., & Dutta, M. (2015). Sentiment analysis for Indian stock market prediction using sensex and nifty. *Procedia Computer Science*, *70*, 85–91. doi:10.1016/j.procs.2015.10.043

Birim, S., Kazancoglu, I., Mangla, S. K., Kahraman, A., & Kazancoglu, Y. (2022). The derived demand for advertising expenses and implications on sustainability: A comparative study using deep learning and traditional machine learning methods. *Annals of Operations Research*. Advance online publication. doi:10.100710479-021-04429-x PMID:35017781

Buhalis, D., Harwood, T., Bogicevic, V., Viglia, G., Beldona, S., & Hofacker, C. (2019). Technological disruptions in services: Lessons from tourism and hospitality. *Journal of Service Management*, *30*(4), 484–506. doi:10.1108/JOSM-12-2018-0398

Buttarelli, G. (2018). *Choose humanity: Putting dignity back into digital*. In Speech at 40th international conference of data protection and privacy commissioners, Brussels. https://www.privacyconference2018.org/system/files/2018-10/Choose%20Humanity%20speech_0.pdf

Chen, L., Zhang, C., & Liu, Y. (2020). Application of Predictive Analytics in Market Research: A Case Study on Customer Behavior Prediction. *JMR, Journal of Marketing Research*, *45*(2), 197–210.

Dastane, O., & Haba, H. F. (2023). *The Landscape of Digital Natives Research: A Bibliometric and Science Mapping Analysis*. FIIB Business Review. doi:10.1177/23197145221137960

Davenport, T., Guha, A., Grewal, D., & Bressgott, T. (2020). How artificial intelligence will change the future of marketing. *Journal of the Academy of Marketing Science*, *48*(1), 24–42. doi:10.100711747-019-00696-0

Duan, Y., Edwards, J. S., & Dwivedi, Y. K. (2019). Artificial intelligence for decision making in the era of Big Data–evolution, challenges and research agenda. *International Journal of Information Management*, *48*, 63–71. doi:10.1016/j.ijinfomgt.2019.01.021

Evans, M., & Ghafourifar, A. (2019). *Build A 5-star customer experience with artificial intelligence*. https://www. forbes. com/sites/allbusiness/2019/02/17/ customer-experienceartificial-intelligence

Faulds, D. J., & Raju, P. S. (2021). The work-from-home trend: An interview with Brian Kropp. *Business Horizons*, *64*(1), 29–35. doi:10.1016/j.bushor.2020.10.005 PMID:33106707

Gambhir, V., Asnate-Salazar, E., Prithi, M., Alvarado-Tolentino, J. & Tongkachok, K. (2022). *Using Artificial Intelligence and Deep Learning Methods to Analysis the Marketing Analytics and Its Impact on Human Resource Management Systems*. Academic Press.

Gigante, G., & Zago, A. (2023). DARQ technologies in the financial sector: Artificial intelligence applications in personalized banking. *Qualitative Research in Financial Markets*, *15*(1), 29–57. doi:10.1108/QRFM-02-2021-0025

Haenlein, M., & Kaplan, A. (2019). A Brief History of Artificial Intelligence: On the Past, Present, and Future of Artificial Intelligence. *California Management Review*, *61*(4), 5–14. Advance online publication. doi:10.1177/0008125619864925

Hamada, T., Bystrom, L. J., & Berndt, H. (2001). Networking Technology Convergence in the Photonic Age—TINA Vision on IP Control and Management. *IEICE Transactions on Communications*, *84*(12), 3086–3095.

Holmes, W., Porayska-Pomsta, K., Holstein, K., Sutherland, E., Baker, T., Shum, S. B., Santos, O. C., Rodrigo, M. T., Cukurova, M., Bittencourt, I. I., & Koedinger, K. R. (2021). Ethics of AI in education: Towards a community-wide framework. *International Journal of Artificial Intelligence in Education*. Advance online publication. doi:10.100740593-021-00239-1

Huang, M. H., & Rust, R. T. (2021). A strategic framework for artificial intelligence in marketing. *Journal of the Academy of Marketing Science*, *49*(1), 30–50. doi:10.100711747-020-00749-9

Jagielski, M., Oprea, A., & Biggio, B. (2018). Manipulating machine learning: poisoning attacks and countermeasures for regression learning. 2018 IEEE symposium on security and privacy (SP). doi:10.1109/SP.2018.00057

Jang, H. J., Sim, J., Lee, Y., & Kwon, O. (2013). Deep sentiment analysis: Mining the causality between personality-value-attitude for analyzing business ads in social media. *Expert Systems with Applications*, *40*(18), 7492–7503. doi:10.1016/j.eswa.2013.06.069

Johnson, M., & Smith, J. (2020). Enhancing Data Collection through Chatbots: A Review of Interaction and User Experience. *Journal of Consumer Behaviour*, *15*(4), 432–446.

Kashyap, R., & Dwesar, R. (2021). Artificial Intelligence in Marketing. Artificial Intelligence and Machine Learning in Business Management: Concepts, Challenges, and Case Studies, 1-14.

Khalifa, N., Abd Elghany, M. & Abd Elghany, M. (2021). Exploratory research on digitalization transformation practices within supply chain management context in developing countries specifically Egypt in the MENA region. *Cogent Business and Management, 8*(1).

Kim, S., Lee, H., & Park, J. (2020). Harnessing Sentiment Analysis for Brand Management: A Comprehensive Review of AI-Driven Approaches. *Journal of Market Research and Analysis*, *18*(1), 56–72.

Kooli, C. (2023). Chatbots in education and research: A critical examination of ethical implications and solutions. *Sustainability (Basel)*, *15*(7), 5614. doi:10.3390u15075614

Krafft, T., Hauer, M., & Fetic, L. (2020) *From principles to practice: an interdisciplinary framework to operationalise AI ethics*. VDE and Bertelsmann Stiftung. https://www.ai-ethics-impact.org/resource/blob/1961130/c6db9894ee73aefa489d6249f5ee2b9f/aieig—report—download-hb-data.pdf

Kumar, S., Gahalawat, M., Roy, P. P., Dogra, D. P., & Kim, B. (2020). Exploring impact of age and gender on sentiment analysis using machine learning. Electronics (Switzerland), 9(2). doi:10.3390/electronics9020374

Lauterbach, A. (2019). Artificial intelligence and policy: Quo vadis? *Digital Policy, Regulation and Governance*, *21*(3), 238–263. doi:10.1108/DPRG-09-2018-0054

Ledro, C. (2021). Artificial intelligence applied to customer relationship management: An empirical research. *Proceedings of the European Conference on Innovation and Entrepreneurship, ECIE*, 1153.

Lu, V. N., Wirtz, J., Kunz, W. H., Paluch, S., Gruber, T., Martins, A., & Patterson, P. G. (2020). Service robots, customers and service employees: What can we learn from the academic literature and where are the gaps? *Journal of Service Theory and Practice*, *30*(3), 361–391. doi:10.1108/JSTP-04-2019-0088

Mahapatra, P., & Singh, S. K. (2021). Artificial Intelligence and Machine Learning: Discovering New Ways of Doing Banking Business. Artificial Intelligence and Machine Learning in Business Management: Concepts, Challenges, and Case Studies, 53-80.

Malik, R., Jindal, T., & Sharma, A. (2022). Role of Artificial Intelligence in Reshaping Retail. *2022 2nd International Conference on Advance Computing and Innovative Technologies in Engineering, ICACITE 2022*, 660. 10.1109/ICACITE53722.2022.9823675

Margherita, E. G., & Bua, I. (2021). The role of human resource practices for the development of Operator 4.0 in Industry 4.0 organisations: A literature review and a research agenda. *Businesses*, *1*(1), 18–33. doi:10.3390/businesses1010002

Micus, C., Schramm, S., Boehm, M., & Krcmar, H. (2023). *Methods to analyze customer usage data in a product decision process: A systematic literature review* (Vol. 10). Operations Research Perspectives.

Mikalef, P., Islam, N., Parida, V., Singh, H., & Altwaijry, N. (2023). Artificial intelligence (AI) competencies for organizational performance: A B2B marketing capabilities perspective. *Journal of Business Research*, *164*, 113998. doi:10.1016/j.jbusres.2023.113998

Mustak, M., Salminen, J., Plé, L., & Wirtz, J. (2021). Artificial intelligence in marketing: Topic modeling, scientometric analysis, and research agenda. *Journal of Business Research*, *124*, 389–404. doi:10.1016/j.jbusres.2020.10.044

Nordin, M. A. B. W., Vedenyapin, D., Alghifari, M. F., & Gunawan, T. S. (2019). The disruptometer: An artificial intelligence algorithm for market insights. *Bulletin of Electrical Engineering and Informatics*, *8*(2), 727–734. doi:10.11591/eei.v8i2.1494

Rangaswamy, A., Moch, N., Felten, C., van Bruggen, G., Wieringa, J. E., & Wirtz, J. (2020). The role of marketing in digital business platforms. *Journal of Interactive Marketing*, *51*(August), 72–90. doi:10.1016/j.intmar.2020.04.006

Sanny, L., Susastra, A. C., Roberts, C., & Yusramdaleni, R. (2020). The analysis of customer satisfaction factors which influence chatbot acceptance in Indonesia. *Management Science Letters, 10*(6), 1225–1232. doi:10.5267/j.msl.2019.11.036

Schmidt, S., Karampournioti, E., Wiedmann, K. & Buckler, F. (2023). *Special Session: Marketing Research Automation and Robotization (M-RAR): A Chance for Marketing Practice and a Risk for Marketing Science/Scientists? An Abstract.* Academic Press.

Shakil, M.T.H. & Rajasekaran, R. (2023). *A Data Science Approach in Quantitative Market Research.* Academic Press.

Shakir, M. Z., & Ramzan, N. (2021). AI for emerging verticals: Human-robot computing, sensing and networking. AI for Emerging Verticals: Human-robot computing, sensing and networking, 1-364.

Shin, D. (2022). How do people judge the credibility of algorithmic sources? *AI & Society, 37*(1), 1–16. doi:10.100700146-021-01158-4

Smart Insights. (2018). *How AI is changing the role of the marketer in 2018.* https://www. smartinsights.com/managing-digital-marketing/managing-marketing-technology/h ow-ai-is-changing-the-role-of-the-marketer-in-2018/

Smith, A., & Jones, B. (2021). Unveiling Customer Sentiments: A Comprehensive Analysis of Sentiment Analysis in Market Research. *Market Insights Review, 15*(3), 126–143.

Swanson, J. (2017). The future of student life: Working. *On the Horizon, 25*(3), 165–168. doi:10.1108/OTH-05-2017-0022

Tran, K., & Nguyen, T. (2021). Preliminary research on the social attitudes toward the ai's involved Christian education in Vietnam: Promoting ai technology for religious education. *Religions, 12*(3), 1–20. doi:10.3390/rel12030208

Tsamados, A., Aggarwal, N., Cowls, J., Morley, J., Roberts, H., Taddeo, M., & Floridi, L. (2021). The ethics of algorithms: key problems and solutions. *Ethics, Governance, and Policies in Artificial Intelligence*, 97-123.

Vlačić, B., Corbo, L., Silva, S. C., & Dabić, M. (2021). The evolving role of artificial intelligence in marketing: A review and research agenda. *Journal of Business Research, 128*, 187–203. doi:10.1016/j.jbusres.2021.01.055

Vrontis, D., Makrides, A., Christofi, M., & Thrassou, A. (2021). Social media influencer marketing: A systematic review, integrative framework and future research agenda. *International Journal of Consumer Studies*, *45*(4), 617–644. doi:10.1111/ijcs.12647

Wang, H., Li, J., & Zhang, Y. (2019). Chatbots for Data Collection: Enhancing User Experience in Market Research. *Journal of Consumer Behaviour*, *28*(4), 564–578.

Wilson-Nash, C., Goode, A., & Currie, A. (2020). Introducing the socialbot: A novel touchpoint along the young adult customer journey. *European Journal of Marketing*, *54*(10), 2621–2643. doi:10.1108/EJM-07-2019-0555

Wirtz, J., & Zeithaml, V. (2018). Cost-effective service excellence. *Journal of the Academy of Marketing Science*, *46*(1), 59–80. doi:10.100711747-017-0560-7

Zaki, H. O., Fernandez, D., Dastane, O., Aman, A., & Sanusi, S. (2023). Virtual reality in digital marketing: Research agenda based on bibliometric reflection. *Marketing Intelligence & Planning*, *41*(4), 505–524. doi:10.1108/MIP-12-2022-0568

Zolnowski, A. & Frey, D. (2020). *Analyzing the role of artificial intelligence in the development of human-centered service*. Academic Press.

Compilation of References

Ab Rahman, Z. N., & Ismail, N. (2018). Determinant Factors for Managing Innovation in the Malaysian Public Sector. *MATEC Web of Conferences, 150*, 1–5. 10.1051/matecconf/201815005042

Ababneh, O. M. A. (2021). How do green HRM practices affect employees' green behaviors? The role of employee engagement and personality attributes. *Journal of Environmental Planning and Management, 64*(7), 1204–1226. doi:10.1080/09640568.2020.1814708

Abdelhay, S. (2023) How Artificial Intelligence can affect the process of recruitment and improve the quality of new hired employees. *Resmilitaris, 13*(3), 2517-2533.

Abdul Rahman, N. A., Ahmi, A., Jraisat, L., & Upadhyay, A. (2022). Examining the trend of humanitarian supply chain studies: Pre, during and post COVID-19 pandemic. *Journal of Humanitarian Logistics and Supply Chain Management, 12*(4), 594–617. doi:10.1108/JHLSCM-01-2022-0012

Abouelmehdi, K., Beni-Hessane, A., & Khaloufi, H. (2018). Big healthcare data: Preserving security and privacy. *Journal of Big Data, 5*(1), 1. doi:10.118640537-017-0110-7

Abraham, L. N., & Bariyaa, J. (2020). Status of Principals' ICT Usage in Secondary School Administration in Rivers State. *African Research Review, 14*(1), 61–71. doi:10.4314/afrrev.v14i1.6

Abreu, P. W., Aparicio, M., & Costa, C. J. (2018). Blockchain technology in the auditing environment. *Iberian Conference on Information Systems and Technologies, CISTI,* 1–6. 10.23919/CISTI.2018.8399460

Accounting Today. (2017). Scoping out the audit of the future; A virtual roundtable of experts looks at how technology and other trends are reshaping a core service of the accounting profession. *Accounting Today, 31*(6), 6,52,53. Retrieved from https://search.proquest.com/docview/1910741844/fulltext/3D17D388739842BBPQ/1?accountid=11528

Aggarwal, K. (2021). *The impact of company characteristics on human resource disclosure index: A study on Service sector companies in India.* FIIB Business Review. doi:10.1177/23197145211010871

Ahmad, M. F., Husin, N. A. A., Ahmad, A. N. A., Abdullah, H., Wei, C. S., & Nawi, M. N. M. (2022). Digital Transformation: An Exploring Barriers and Challenges Practice of Artificial Intelligence in Manufacturing Firms in Malaysia. *Journal of Advanced Research in Applied Sciences and Engineering Technology*, *29*(1), 1. Advance online publication. doi:10.37934/araset.29.1.110117

Ahmad, S. (2015). Green Human Resource Management: Policies and practices. *Cogent Business & Management*, *2*(1), 1030817. doi:10.1080/23311975.2015.1030817

Ahmi, A. (2022). *Bibliometric Analysis using R for Non-Coders: A practical handbook in conducting bibliometric analysis studies using Biblioshiny for Bibliometrix R package.* Academic Press.

Al Ajrawi, S., Agrawal, A., Mangal, H., Putluri, K., Reid, B., Hanna, G., & Sarkar, M. (2021). Evaluating business yelp's star ratings using sentiment analysis. *Materials Today: Proceedings*. Advance online publication. doi:10.1016/j.matpr.2020.12.137

Al Badi, F. K., Alhosani, K. A., Jabeen, F., Stachowicz-Stanusch, A., Shehzad, N., & Amann, W. (2022). Challenges of AI Adoption in the UAE Healthcare. *Vision (Basel)*, *26*(2), 193–207. doi:10.1177/0972262920988398

Al Shobaki, M. M., Naser, S. S. A., Amuna, Y. M. A., El Talla, A., Al Shobaki, M. M., Naser, S. S. A., Amuna, Y. M. A., El, S. A., & The, T. (2017). The Efficiency of Information Technology and its Role of e- HRM in the Palestinian Universities To cite this version : HAL Id : hal-01572642 The Efficiency of Information Technology and its Role of e- HRM in the Palestinian Universities. *International Journal of Engineering and Information Systems*, *1*(5), 36–55. http://www.ijeais.org/wp-content/uploads/2017/07/IJEAIS170705.pdfThisVersionisavailableat:http://hdl.handle.net/10419/167316www.ijeais.org36

Albert, E. (2019). AI in talent acquisition: A review of AI-applications used in recruitment and selection. *Strategic HR Review*, *18*(5), 215–221. doi:10.1108/SHR-04-2019-0024

Aldulaimi, S. H., Abdeldayem, M. M., Mowafak, B. M., & Abdulaziz, M. M. (2021). Experimental perspective of artificial intelligence technology in human resources management. *Studies in Computational Intelligence*, *954*, 487–511. doi:10.1007/978-3-030-72080-3_26

Al-Kumaim, N. H., Alhazmi, A. K., Mohammed, F., Gazem, N. A., Shabbir, M. S., & Fazea, Y. (2021). Exploring the impact of the covid-19 pandemic on university students' learning life: An integrated conceptual motivational model for sustainable and healthy online learning. *Sustainability (Basel)*, *13*(5), 1–21. doi:10.3390u13052546

Allal-Chérif, O., Yela Aránega, A., & Castaño Sánchez, R. (2021). Intelligent recruitment: How to identify, select, and retain talents from around the world using artificial intelligence. *Technological Forecasting and Social Change*, *169*(January), 120822. Advance online publication. doi:10.1016/j.techfore.2021.120822

Alomar, M. A. (2022). Performance Optimization of Industrial Supply Chain Using Artificial Intelligence. *Computational Intelligence and Neuroscience*, *2022*, 1–10. doi:10.1155/2022/9306265 PMID:35942447

Alshurideh, M., Al Kurdi, B., & Salloum, S. A. (2019). Examining the main mobile learning system drivers effects: A mix empirical examination of both the Expectation-Confirmation Model (ECM) and the Technology Acceptance Model (TAM). *International Conference on Advanced Intelligent Systems and Informatics*, 406–417.

Aman, A., Rafiq, M., & Dastane, O. (2023). A cross-cultural comparison of work engagement in the relationships between trust climate – Job performance and turnover intention: Focusing China and Pakistan. *Heliyon*, *9*(9), e19534. doi:10.1016/j.heliyon.2023.e19534 PMID:37809562

Aman, A., Rafiq, M., Dastane, O., & Sabir, A. A. (2022). Green corridor: A critical perspective and development of research agenda. *Frontiers in Environmental Science*, *10*, 982473. doi:10.3389/fenvs.2022.982473

Amar, J. R. (2022, November 1). *Smart scheduling: How to solve workforce-planning Challenges with AI.* McKinsey.

Amos, Z. (2022, February 4). *Hive Life, Business and Techbusiness News.* Retrieved from How HR Technology Is Transforming APAC Businesses: https://hivelife.com/hr-technology/

AmpC. (2009). Retrieved from Culture Amp: https://www.cultureamp.com/

Anayat, S. (2023). Human resources management after industry 4.0: Blending AI and HRM. *Strategic Human Resource Management in the Hospitality Industry: A Digitalized Economic Paradigm*, 97–115. doi:10.4018/978-1-6684-7494-5.ch005

Antipova, T. (2018). Using blockchain technology for government auditing. *Iberian Conference on Information Systems and Technologies, CISTI,* 1–6. 10.23919/CISTI.2018.8399439

Antonija Bozickovic, Service Desk Institute. (n.d.). *Five Ethical Issues of AI in the Modern Workplace.* Retrieved from https://www.servicedeskinstitute.com/five-ethical-issues-of-ai-in-the-modern-workplace/

APEC. (2005). *APEC Privacy Framework.* https://www.apec.org/Publications/2005/12/APEC-Privacy-Framework

Appelbaum, D., & Nehmer, R. A. (2017a). Designing and auditing accounting systems based on blockchain and distributed ledger principles. *Feliciano School of Business*, 1–19. Retrieved from https://pdfs.semanticscholar.org/edc2/4c3ae8cb7f4f978c9353d47986168265fe03.pdf

Appelbaum, D., & Nehmer, R. A. (2017b). Using drones in internal and external audits: An exploratory framework. *Journal of Emerging Technologies in Accounting*, *14*(1), 99–113. Advance online publication. doi:10.2308/jeta-51704

Appelbaum, D., & Smith, S. S. (2018). Blockchain basics and hands-on guidance: Taking the next step toward implementation and adoption. *The CPA Journal*, *88*(6), 28–37. http://web-1ebscohost-1com-10000f4h3028c.han.ub.fau.de/ehost/pdfviewer/pdfviewer?vid=16&sid=fc526975-895b-430e-8f7b-c92229f39f1b%40sessionmgr4007

Arbatani, T. R., Norouzi, E., Omidi, A., & Valero-Pastor, J. M. (2021). Competitive strategies of mobile applications in online taxi services: The cases of Snapp and Tap30 in Iran. *International Journal of Emerging Markets*, *16*(1), 113–130.

Aria, M., & Cuccurullo, C. (2017). bibliometrix: An R-tool for comprehensive science mapping analysis. *Journal of Informetrics*, *11*(4), 959–975. doi:10.1016/j.joi.2017.08.007

Ari, E., Karatepe, O. M., Rezapouraghdam, H., & Avci, T. (2020). A Conceptual Model for Green Human Resource Management: Indicators, Differential Pathways, and Multiple Pro-Environmental Outcomes. *Sustainability (Basel)*, *12*(17), 7089. doi:10.3390u12177089

Armstrong, M., & Taylor, S. (2023). *Armstrong's Handbook of Human Resource Management Practice: A Guide to the Theory and Practice of People Management*. Kogan Page Publishers.

Arora, M., Prakash, A., Mittal, A., & Singh, S. (2021). HR Analytics and Artificial Intelligence-Transforming Human Resource Management. *2021 International Conference on Decision Aid Sciences and Application, DASA 2021*, 288–293. 10.1109/DASA53625.2021.9682325

Avila, O. (2023, February). *The Future of AI on Employee Benefits*. Retrieved from KPMG: https://kpmg.com/ae/en/home/insights/2023/02/the-future-of-ai-on-employee-benefits.html

Avrahami, D., Pessach, D., Singer, G., & Chalutz Ben-Gal, H. (2022). A human resources analytics and machine-learning examination of turnover: Implications for theory and practice. *International Journal of Manpower*, *43*(6), 1405–1424. doi:10.1108/IJM-12-2020-0548

Bach, M. P., Čeljo, A., & Zoroja, J. (2016). Technology acceptance model for business intelligence systems: Preliminary research. *Procedia Computer Science*, *100*, 995–1001. doi:10.1016/j.procs.2016.09.270

Bachmann, N., Tripathi, S., Brunner, M., & Jodlbauer, H. (2022). The contribution of data-driven technologies in achieving the sustainable development goals. *Sustainability (Basel)*, *14*(5), 2497. doi:10.3390u14052497

Baer, S. (2023, March 28). Council Post: How To Incorporate Artificial Intelligence Into Learning And Development. *Forbes*. https://www.forbes.com/sites/forbeshumanresourcescouncil/2023/03/28/how-to-incorporate artificial-intelligence-into-learning-and-development/

Baes, H. (2022, August 18). *Applicant Tracking Systems: The Ultimate Guide for Job Seekers in 2022*. Jobscan. https://www.jobscan.co/applicant-tracking-systems/

Baharom, A. (2019). Talent management: Malaysian public universities vs private industries. *Journal of Human Development and Communication*, *8*, 83–96.

Baig, A., Brown, J. S., & Forrest, W. HV, V., Hjartar, K., & Yee, L. (2023, January 6). Where Is Tech Going in 2023? *Harvard Business Review*. https://hbr.org/2023/01/where-is-tech-going-in-2023

Bajunid, I. A., & Wong, W. C. K. (2016). Private higher education institutions in Malaysia. In A Global Perspective on Private Higher Education. doi:10.1016/B978-0-08-100872-0.00008-2

Baker, T. (2013). *The end of the performance review: A new approach to appraising employee performance*. Springer. doi:10.1057/9781137347503

Baldegger, R., Caon, M., & Sadiku, K. (2020). Correlation between entrepreneurial orientation and implementation of AI in human resources management (HRM). *Technology Innovation Management Review*, *10*(4), 72–79. doi:10.22215/timreview/1348

Baliga, A. (2017). *Understanding blockchain consensus models*. Whitepaper.

Bankar, S., & Shukla, K. (2023). Performance Management and Artificial Intelligence: A Futuristic Conceptual Framework. In Contemporary Studies of Risks in Emerging Technology, Part B (pp. 341–360). Emerald Publishing Limited. doi:10.1108/978-1-80455-566-820231019

Bankins, S. (2021). The ethical use of artificial intelligence in human resource management: A decision-making framework. *Ethics and Information Technology*, *23*(4), 841–845. doi:10.100710676-021-09619-6

Barocas, S., Hardt, M., & Narayanan, A. (2019). *Fairness and Machine Learning. fairmlbook*. Academic Press.

Baron, J. (2017). Blockchain What you need to know. *Accounting Today*, *31*(11), 47.

Basu, S., Majumdar, B., Mukherjee, K., Munjal, S., & Palaksha, C. (2023). Artificial Intelligence–HRM Interactions and Outcomes: A Systematic Review and Causal Configurational Explanation. *Human Resource Management Review*, *33*(1), 100893. doi:10.1016/j.hrmr.2022.100893

Bazarbash, M. (2019). *Fintech in financial inclusion: machine learning applications in assessing credit risk*. International Monetary Fund.

Bedard, J. L. (2023, August 24). *Boston Consulting Group*. Retrieved from How Generative AI Will Transform HR: https://www.bcg.com/publications/2023/transforming-human-resources-using-generative-ai

Behera, R. K., Bala, P. K., & Rana, N. P. (2023). Creation of sustainable growth with explainable artificial intelligence: An empirical insight from consumer packaged goods retailers. *Journal of Cleaner Production*, *399*, 136605. doi:10.1016/j.jclepro.2023.136605

Ben Amara, N., & Atia, L. (2016). E-Training-and-Its-Role-in-Human-Resources-Development. *Global Journal of Human Resource Management*, *4*(1), 1–12.

Benevene, P., & Buonomo, I. (2020). Green Human Resource Management: An Evidence-Based Systematic Literature Review. *Sustainability (Basel)*, *12*(15), 15. Advance online publication. doi:10.3390u12155974

Berhil, S., Benlahmar, H., & Labani, N. (2019). A review paper on artificial intelligence at the service of human resources management. *Indonesian Journal of Electrical Engineering and Computer Science*, *18*(1), 32–40. doi:10.11591/ijeecs.v18.i1.pp32-40

Bertot, J. C., Gorham, U., Jaeger, P. T., Sarin, L. C., & Choi, H. (2014). Big data, open government and e-government: Issues, policies and recommendations. *Information Polity*, *19*(1-2), 5–16. doi:10.3233/IP-140328

Bhardwaj, A. (2020, August 18). *Startup Talky*. Retrieved from Big Mistakes Companies Make While Training Their Employees: https://startuptalky.com/7-big-mistakes-while-training-employees/?_gl=1*1160n0z*_ga*WjdpLTMyb00yU2dBdXlfUnJGZDBIbFFYNUE4TVZsb 2ZSNVI3dlBhaWNCT1NOQy1vbTBxbHpIOW4wVExveG92RA

Bhardwaj, A., Narayan, Y., & Dutta, M. (2015). Sentiment analysis for Indian stock market prediction using sensex and nifty. *Procedia Computer Science*, *70*, 85–91. doi:10.1016/j.procs.2015.10.043

Bhutta, U., Martins, J. N., Mata, M. N., Raza, A., Dantas, R. M., Correia, A. B., & Rafiq, M. (2021). Intellectual Structure and Evolution of Accounting Conservatism Research: Past Trends and Future Research Suggestions. *International Journal of Financial Studies*, *9*(3), 35. doi:10.3390/ijfs9030035

Bible, W., Raphael, J., Riviello, M., Taylor, P., & Valiente, I. O. (2017). Blockchain technology and its potential impact on the audit and assurance profession. In *CPA Canada, AICPA & UW CISA*. Retrieved from https://www.aicpa.org/interestareas/frc/assuranceadvisoryservices/blockchain-impact-on-auditing.html%0Ahttps://www.aicpa.org/content/dam/aicpa/interestareas/frc/assuranceadvisoryservices/downloadabledocuments/blockchain-technology-and-its-potential-impact

Bibri, S. E. (2021). Data-driven smart sustainable cities of the future: An evidence synthesis approach to a comprehensive state-of-the-art literature review. *Sustainable Futures : An Applied Journal of Technology, Environment and Society*, *3*, 100047. doi:10.1016/j.sftr.2021.100047

Birim, S., Kazancoglu, I., Mangla, S. K., Kahraman, A., & Kazancoglu, Y. (2022). The derived demand for advertising expenses and implications on sustainability: A comparative study using deep learning and traditional machine learning methods. *Annals of Operations Research*. Advance online publication. doi:10.100710479-021-04429-x PMID:35017781

Black, J. S., & Esch, P. V. (2020). AI-enabled recruiting: What is it and how should a manager use it? *Business Horizons*, *63*(2), 215–226. doi:10.1016/j.bushor.2019.12.001

Blasch, E., Pham, T., Chong, C.-Y., Koch, W., Leung, H., Braines, D., & Abdelzaher, T. (2021). Machine learning/artificial intelligence for sensor data fusion–opportunities and challenges. *IEEE Aerospace and Electronic Systems Magazine*, *36*(7), 80–93. doi:10.1109/MAES.2020.3049030

Bodie, M. T., Cherry, M. A., McCormick, M. L., & Tang, J. (2017). The law and policy of people analytics. *U. Colo. L. Rev.*, *88*, 961. https://heinonline.org/HOL/LandingPage?handle=hein.journals/ucollr88&div=31&id=&page=

Bondarouk, T., Parry, E., & Furtmueller, E. (2017). Electronic HRM: Four decades of research on adoption and consequences. *International Journal of Human Resource Management*, *28*(1), 98–131. doi:10.1080/09585192.2016.1245672

Bone, B. Y. J. (2018). Five trends shaping digital transformation. *Internal Auditor*, (October), 19–21.

Boxall, P., Ang, S. H., & Bartram, T. (2011). Analysing the 'black box'of HRM: Uncovering HR goals, mediators, and outcomes in a standardized service environment. *Journal of Management Studies*, *48*(7), 1504–1532. doi:10.1111/j.1467-6486.2010.00973.x

Bradu, P., Biswas, A., Nair, C., Sreevalsakumar, S., Patil, M., Kannampuzha, S., Mukherjee, A. G., Wanjari, U. R., Renu, K., Vellingiri, B., & Gopalakrishnan, A. V. (2022). Recent advances in green technology and Industrial Revolution 4.0 for a sustainable future. *Environmental Science and Pollution Research International*. Advance online publication. doi:10.100711356-022-20024-4 PMID:35397034

Brandon, D. (2016). The blockchain : The future of business information systems? *International Journal of the Academic Business World*, *10*(2), 33–40.

Brisco, R. (2022). Understanding Industry 4.0 Digital Transformation. *Proceedings of the Design Society*, *2*, 2423–2432. doi:10.1017/pds.2022.245

Broby, D., & Paul, G. (2017). The financial auditing of distributed ledgers, blockchain and cryptocurrencies. *Journal of Financial Transformation*.

Brynjolfsson, B. Y. E., & McAfee, A. (2017). Artificial Intelligence for Real. *Harvard Business Review*, (1), 1–31. https://starlab-alliance.com/wp-content/uploads/2017/09/AI-Article.pdf

Brynjolfsson, E., & Mitchell, T. (2017). What can machine learning do? Workforce implications. *Science*, *358*(6370), 1530–1534. doi:10.1126cience.aap8062 PMID:29269459

Budhwar, P., Chowdhury, S., Wood, G., Aguinis, H., Bamber, G. J., Beltran, J. R., Boselie, P., Lee Cooke, F., Decker, S., DeNisi, A., Dey, P. K., Guest, D., Knoblich, A. J., Malik, A., Paauwe, J., Papagiannidis, S., Patel, C., Pereira, V., Ren, S., ... Varma, A. (2023). Human resource management in the age of generative artificial intelligence: Perspectives and research directions on ChatGPT. *Human Resource Management Journal*, *33*(3), 606–659. doi:10.1111/1748-8583.12524

Budhwar, P., Malik, A., De Silva, M. T., & Thevisuthan, P. (2022). Artificial intelligence–challenges and opportunities for international HRM: A review and research agenda. *International Journal of Human Resource Management*, *33*(6), 1065–1097. doi:10.1080/09585192.2022.2035161

Bughin, J., Seong, J., Manyika, J., Chui, M., & Joshi, R. (2018). *Notes from the AI Frontier | Modeling the Impact of AI on the World Economy*. McKinsey Discussion Paper. https://www.mckinsey.com/featured-insights/artificial-intelligence/notes-from-the-AI-frontier-modeling-the-impact-of-ai-on-the-world-economy

Buhalis, D., Harwood, T., Bogicevic, V., Viglia, G., Beldona, S., & Hofacker, C. (2019). Technological disruptions in services: Lessons from tourism and hospitality. *Journal of Service Management*, *30*(4), 484–506. doi:10.1108/JOSM-12-2018-0398

Bulut, A., & Batur Dinler, Ö. (2023). The Effect of Industry 4.0 and Artificial Intelligence on Human Resource Management. *Uluslararası Doğu Anadolu Fen Mühendislik ve Tasarım Dergisi*, *5*(2), 143–166. doi:10.47898/ijeased.1306881

Burgess, L. (2023, July 31). *Capterra Inc. Retrieved from Are SMEs Leveraging AI in HR To Help With Decision-Making Processes?* https://www.capterra.com.au/blog/4107/study-on-the-future-of-ai-in-hr-australia#:~:text=of%20this%20article.-,One%20in%20five%20Australian%20SMEs%20use%20AI%20in%20HR,and%20personalising%20employee%20training%20programs

BusinessLine. (2018, October 8). *The Hindu Businessline: Economy. HR Consulting Firm Mercer Buys Indian Start-up Mettl for ₹250 crore*. Retrieved from HR Consulting Firm Mercer Buys Indian Start-up Mettl for ₹250 crore: https://www.thehindubusinessline.com/companies/hr-consulting-firm-mercer-buys-indian-start-up-mettl-for-250-crore/article25156969.ece

Buterin, V. (2014). A next-generation smart contract and decentralized application platform. In *Etherum*. Retrieved from http://blockchainlab.com/pdf/Ethereum_white_paper-a_next_generation_smart_contract_and_decentralized_application_platform-vitalik-buterin.pdf

Buttarelli, G. (2018). *Choose humanity: Putting dignity back into digital*. In Speech at 40th international conference of data protection and privacy commissioners, Brussels. https://www.privacyconference2018.org/system/files/2018-10/Choose%20Humanity%20speech_0.pdf

Cachat-Rosset, G., & Klarsfeld, A. (2023). Diversity, Equity, and Inclusion in Artificial Intelligence: An Evaluation of Guidelines. *Applied Artificial Intelligence*, *37*(1), 2176618. doi:10.1080/08839514.2023.2176618

Caldes, R. (2019). Big data and artificial intelligence in public sector human resource management. *Rev. Catalana Dret Pub.*, *58*(9).

Canhoto, A. I., & Clear, F. (2020). Artificial intelligence and machine learning as business tools: A framework for diagnosing value destruction potential. *Business Horizons*, *63*(2), 183–193. doi:10.1016/j.bushor.2019.11.003

Cao, Y., Vasek, J., & Dusik, M. (2018). Design towards AI-powered workplace of the future. Lecture Notes in Computer Science (Including Subseries Lecture Notes in Artificial Intelligence and Lecture Notes in Bioinformatics), 10921 LNCS, 3–20. doi:10.1007/978-3-319-91125-0_1

Cărbune, N. (2022). Human resources management and training of highperforming managers. In Competitiveness and sustainable development (pp. 130-132). doi:10.52326/csd2022.22

Career Coach Institute Website. (2010). *Defining coaching*. Retrieved from http://www.careercoachinstitute.com/about-us.html

Cascio, W. F., & Montealegre, R. (2016). How Technology Is Changing Work and Organizations. *Annual Review of Organizational Psychology and Organizational Behavior*, *3*(1), 349–375. doi:10.1146/annurev-orgpsych-041015-062352

Cath, C. (2018). Governing artificial intelligence: Ethical, legal and technical opportunities and challenges. *Philosophical Transactions. Series A, Mathematical, Physical, and Engineering Sciences*, *376*(2133), 20180080. doi:10.1098/rsta.2018.0080 PMID:30322996

Cellier, F. E. (2001). *Discrete event modeling and simulation technologies: A tapestry of systems and AI-based theories and methodologies*. Springer Science & Business Media.

Chai, K. E., Lines, R. L., Gucciardi, D. F., & Ng, L. (2021). Research Screener: A machine learning tool to semi-automate abstract screening for systematic reviews. *Systematic Reviews, 10*(1), 1–13. doi:10.118613643-021-01635-3 PMID:33795003

Chaparro, F. (2017). *A 'Big Four' accounting firm is accepting bitcoin payments.* Retrieved November 30, 2017, from Business Insider US website: https://www.businessinsider.my/a-big-four-accounting-firm-is-accepting-bitcoin-payments-2017-11/?r=US&IR=T

Charlesworth, A. (2014). *The comprehensibility theorem and the foundations of artificial intelligence.* Minds and Machines. doi:10.100711023-014-9349-3

Chatterjee, S. (2020). AI strategy of India: Policy framework, adoption challenges and actions for government. *Transforming Government: People Transforming Government, 14*(5), 757–775. doi:10.1108/TG-05-2019-0031

Chen, L. (2017). Continuous Delivery: Overcoming adoption challenges. *Journal of Systems and Software, 128*, 72–86. doi:10.1016/j.jss.2017.02.013

Chen, L., Zhang, C., & Liu, Y. (2020). Application of Predictive Analytics in Market Research: A Case Study on Customer Behavior Prediction. *JMR, Journal of Marketing Research, 45*(2), 197–210.

Chenoy, D., Ghosh, S. M., & Shukla, S. K. (2019). Skill development for accelerating the manufacturing sector: the role of 'new-age' skills for 'Make in India'. *International Journal of Training Research, 17*(1), 112-130.

Chin, T., Hu, Q., Rowley, C., & Wang, S. (2021). *Business models in the Asia-Pacific: dynamic balancing of multiple cultures, innovation and value creation.* Taylor & Francis.

Chitrao, P., Bhoyar, P. K., Divekar, R., & Bhatt, P. (2022, February 24-26). Study on Use of Artificial Intelligence in Talent Acquisition. *2022 Interdisciplinary Research in Technology and Management (IRTM).* doi:10.100700146-020-00960-w

Chitturu, S., Lin, D.-Y., Sneader, K., Tonby, O., & Woetzel, J. (2017). Artificial intelligence and Southeast Asia's future. Academic Press.

Chomanski, B. (2019). Massive technological unemployment without redistribution: A case for cautious optimism. *Science and Engineering Ethics, 25*(5), 1389–1407. doi:10.100711948-018-0070-0 PMID:30357558

Chowdhury, S., Dey, P., Joel-Edgar, S., Bhattacharya, S., Rodriguez-Espindola, O., Abadie, A., & Truong, L. (2023). Unlocking the value of artificial intelligence in human resource management through AI capability framework. *Human Resource Management Review, 33*(1), 100899. doi:10.1016/j.hrmr.2022.100899

Circle, V. (2023, August 22). *Vantage Circle: human resource management.* Retrieved from Role of AI in HR: A Complete Guide: https://blog.vantagecircle.com/ai-in-hr/

Clack, L. (2021). Employee engagement: Keys to organizational success. The Palgrave handbook of workplace well-being, 1001-1028.

Colbert, A., Yee, N., & George, G. (2016). The digital workforce and the workplace of the future. *Academy of Management Journal*, *59*(3), 731–739. doi:10.5465/amj.2016.4003

Collins, L., Fineman, D. R., & Tsuchida, A. (2017). *People Analytics: Recalculating the Route.* Deloitte Insights. Available at https://www2.deloitte.com/insights/us/en/focus/human-capital-trends/2017/people-analytics-in-hr.html

Cong, Y., Du, H., & Vasarhelyi, M. A. (2018). Technological disruption in accounting and auditing. *Journal of Emerging Technologies in Accounting*, *15*(2), 1–10. doi:10.2308/jeta-10640

Cooke, F. L., Schuler, R., & Varma, A. (2020). Human resource management research and practice in Asia: Past, present and future. *Human Resource Management Review*, *30*(4), 100778. doi:10.1016/j.hrmr.2020.100778

da Silva, L. B. P., Soltovski, R., Pontes, J., Treinta, F. T., Leitão, P., Mosconi, E., de Resende, L. M. M., & Yoshino, R. T. (2022). Human resources management 4.0: Literature review and trends. *Computers & Industrial Engineering*, *168*(March), 108111. Advance online publication. doi:10.1016/j.cie.2022.108111

Da Silva, M., Flood, C. M., & Herder, M. (2022). Regulation of health-related artificial intelligence in medical devices: The Canadian story. *UBCL Rev.*, *55*, 635.

Dai, J. (2017). *Three essays on audit technology: Audit 4.0, blockchain, and audit app* (Rutgers University). Retrieved from https://rucore.libraries.rutgers.edu/rutgers-lib/55154/PDF/1/

Dai, J., & Vasarhelyi, M. A. (2016). Imagineering audit 4.0. *Journal of Emerging Technologies in Accounting*, *13*(1), 1–15. Advance online publication. doi:10.2308/jeta-10494

Dai, J., & Vasarhelyi, M. A. (2017). Toward blockchain-based accounting and assurance. *Journal of Information Systems*, *31*(3), 5–21. doi:10.2308/isys-51804

Dai, J., Wang, Y., & Vasarhelyi, M. A. (2017). Blockchain: An emerging solution for fraud. *The CPA Journal*, *87*(6), 12–14. http://esc-web.lib.cbs.dk/login?url=http://search.ebscohost.com/login.aspx?direct=true&db=bth&AN=123973389&site=ehost-live&scope=site

Dastane, O., & Haba, H. F. (2023). The landscape of digital natives research: a bibliometric and science mapping analysis. *FIIB Business Review.*

Dastane, D. O. (2020). Impact of leadership styles on employee performance: A moderating role of gender. *Australian Journal of Business and Management Research*, *5*(12), 27–52. doi:10.52283/NSWRCA.AJBMR.20200512A03

Dastane, O., Aman, A., Satar, B. M., & Safie, N. (Eds.). (2023). *Digital Natives as a Disruptive Force in Asian Businesses and Societies.* IGI Global. doi:10.4018/978-1-6684-6782-4

Dastane, O., Fandos-Roig, J. C., & Sánchez-García, J. (2023). It's free! Still, would I learn? Unearthing perceived value of education apps for better entrepreneurial decisions. *Management Decision*. Advance online publication. doi:10.1108/MD-09-2022-1292

Dastane, O., & Haba, H. F. (2023). The Landscape of Digital Natives Research: A Bibliometric and Science Mapping Analysis. *FIIB Business Review*. doi:10.1177/23197145221137960

Dastane, O., & Haba, H. F. (2023). What drives mobile MOOC's continuous intention? A theory of perceived value perspective. *The International Journal of Information and Learning Technology*, *40*(2), 148–163. doi:10.1108/IJILT-04-2022-0087

Daugherty, P. R., & Wilson, H. J. (2018). *Human+ machine: Reimagining work in the age of AI*. Harvard Business Press.

Daugherty, P. R., Wilson, H. J., & Chowdhury, R. (2018). Using artificial intelligence to promote diversity. *MIT Sloan Management Review*.

Davenport, T. H., & Ronanki, R. (2018). Artificial Intelligence for the Real World. *Harvard Business Review*, *96*(1), 108–116.

Davenport, T. H., & Ronanki, R. (2018). Don't start with moon shots. *Harvard Business Review*, 108–116.

Davenport, T., Guha, A., Grewal, D., & Bressgott, T. (2020). How artificial intelligence will change the future of marketing. *Journal of the Academy of Marketing Science*, *48*(1), 24–42. doi:10.100711747-019-00696-0

Davis, F. D. (1989). Perceived usefulness, perceived ease of use, and user acceptance of information technology. *Management Information Systems Quarterly*, *13*(3), 319–339. doi:10.2307/249008

De Loo, I. (2002). The troublesome relationship between action learning and organizational growth. *Journal of Workplace Learning*, *14*(6), 245–255. doi:10.1108/13665620210441207

del Castillo, M. (2018). *Northern trust, PwC launch 'Instant' blockchain audits*. Retrieved March 19, 2018, from Coindesk.com website: https://www.coindesk.com/northern-trust-and-pwc-launch-instant-blockchain-audits

Delacroix, S., & Lawrence, N. D. (2019). Bottom-up data trusts: Disturbing the 'one size fits all' approach to data governance. *International Data Privacy Law, 9*(4), 236-252.

Delecraz, S., Eltarr, L., Becuwe, M., Bouxin, H., Boutin, N., & Oullier, O. (2022). Responsible Artificial Intelligence in Human Resources Technology: An innovative inclusive and fair by design matching algorithm for job recruitment purposes. *Journal of Responsible Technology, 11*(November), 100041. doi:10.1016/j.jrt.2022.100041

Deloitte. (2019a). Deloitte's 2019 global blockchain survey. Deloitte Insights.

Deloitte. (2019b). *Deloitte debuts ' Blockchain In a Box ' (BIAB)*. Retrieved from https://www2.deloitte.com/us/en/pages/about-deloitte/articles/press-releases/blockchain-in-a-box.html

Deloitte. (2019c). *Irish banking industry first in Europe in building new education platform based on blockchain*. Retrieved from https://www2.deloitte.com/ie/en/pages/technology/articles/Irish_banking_industry_first_in_Europe_in_building_new_education_platform_based_on_blockchain.html

Deshpande, A., Stewart, K., Lepetit, L., & Gunashekar, S. (2017). *Distributed Ledger Technologies/Blockchain: Challenges, opportunities and the prospects for standards. British Standards Institution*. BSI. doi:10.7249/RR2223

DesJardins, J. (2016). Is it Time to Jump off the Sustainability Bandwagon? *Business Ethics Quarterly*, *26*(1), 117–135. doi:10.1017/beq.2016.12

Dhanpat, N., Buthelezi, Z. P., Joe, M. R., Maphela, T. V., & Shongwe, N. (2020). Industry 4.0: The role of human resource professionals. *SA Journal of Human Resource Management*, *18*(May), 10. doi:10.4102ajhrm.v18i0.1302

Drage, E., & Mackereth, K. (2022). Does AI Debias Recruitment? Race, Gender, and AI's "Eradication of Difference.". *Philosophy & Technology*, *35*(4), 89. Advance online publication. doi:10.100713347-022-00543-1 PMID:36246553

Duan, Y., Edwards, J. S., & Dwivedi, Y. K. (2019). Artificial intelligence for decision making in the era of Big Data–evolution, challenges and research agenda. *International Journal of Information Management*, *48*, 63–71. doi:10.1016/j.ijinfomgt.2019.01.021

Dumont, J., Shen, J., & Deng, X. (2017). Effects of Green HRM Practices on Employee Workplace Green Behavior: The Role of Psychological Green Climate and Employee Green Values. *Human Resource Management*, *56*(4), 613–627. doi:10.1002/hrm.21792

Dunn, S. (1990). Root metaphor in the old and new industrial relations. *British Journal of Industrial Relations*, *28*(1), 1–31. doi:10.1111/j.1467-8543.1990.tb00350.x

Dutta, B. (2022, September 9). *Artificial Intelligence*. Retrieved from Top 8 AI-powered tools for Human Resources: https://www.analyticssteps.com/blogs/top-8-ai-powered-tools-human-resources

Dwivedi, D. N., Tadoori, G., & Batra, S. (2023). Impact of women leadership and ESG ratings and in organizations: A time series segmentation study. *Academy of Strategic Management Journal*, *22*(S3), 1–6.

Dwivedi, D., Batra, S., & Pathak, Y. K. (2023). A machine learning based approach to identify key drivers for improving corporate's esg ratings. *Journal of Law and Sustainable Development*, *11*(1), e0242. doi:10.37497dgs.v11i1.242

Dwivedi, D., & Ghanashyama, M. (2023). Human Creativity vs. Machine Creativity: Innovations and Challenges. Multidisciplinary Approaches. In Z. Fields (Ed.), *AI, Creativity, Innovation, and Green Collaboration* (pp. 19–28). IGI Global.

Dwivedi, Y. K., Hughes, L., Ismagilova, E., Aarts, G., Coombs, C., Crick, T., Duan, Y., Dwivedi, R., Edwards, J., Eirug, A., Galanos, V., Ilavarasan, P. V., Janssen, M., Jones, P., Kar, A. K., Kizgin, H., Kronemann, B., Lal, B., Lucini, B., ... Williams, M. D. (2021). Artificial Intelligence (AI): Multidisciplinary perspectives on emerging challenges, opportunities, and agenda for research, practice and policy. *International Journal of Information Management*, *57*, 101994. doi:10.1016/j.ijinfomgt.2019.08.002

Earley, P. C., & Ang, S. (2003). *Cultural intelligence: Individual interactions across cultures*. Academic Press.

EDGE. (2012). *EDGE*. Retrieved from https://getedge.ai/

Electo, C. I., Golash, R., & Ma, K. (2008). Ledgerium Whitepaper. In *Ledgerium* [Version 2.2]. Retrieved from https://whitepaper.ledgerium.io/ledgerium-foundation

Enholm, I. M., Papagiannidis, E., Mikalef, P., & Krogstie, J. (2022). Artificial intelligence and business value: A literature review. *Information Systems Frontiers*, *24*(5), 1709–1734. doi:10.100710796-021-10186-w

EU GDPR. (2016). *General data protection regulation (GDPR)* (Regulation (EU) 2016/679 of the European Parliament and of the Council of 27 April 2016 on the protection of natural persons with regard to the processing of personal data and on the free movement of such data, and repealing Directive 95/46/EC, Issue). https://data.europa.eu/eli/reg/2016/679/oj

Eubanks, B. (2022). *Artificial intelligence for HR: Use AI to support and develop a successful workforce*. Kogan Page Publishers.

Evans, M., & Ghafourifar, A. (2019). *Build A 5-star customer experience with artificial intelligence*. https://www. forbes. com/sites/allbusiness/2019/02/17/customer-experienceartificial-intelligence

EY. (2019a). *EY launches smart contract testing service for blockchain clients*. Retrieved April 16, 2019, from https://www.ey.com/en_gl/news/2019/04/ey-launches-smart-contract-testing-service-for-blockchain-clients

EY. (2019b). *EY Ops Chain industrializes the blockchain at scale for enterprises*. Retrieved April 16, 2019, from https://www.ey.com/en_gl/news/2019/04/ey-ops-chain-industrializes-the-blockchain-at-scale-for-enterprises

EY. (2019c). *Multimillion-dollar investment in EY Blockchain Analyzer delivers new upgrades for blockchain and cryptocurrency audit and tax services*. Retrieved April 16, 2019, from https://www.ey.com/en_gl/news/2019/04/multimillion-dollar-investment-in-ey-blockchain-analyzer-delivers-new-upgrades-for-blockchain-and-cryptocurrency-audit-and-tax-services

Fang, L., Shi, S., Gao, J., & Li, X. (2022). The mediating role of green innovation and green culture in the relationship between green human resource management and environmental performance. *PLoS One*, *17*(9), e0274820. doi:10.1371/journal.pone.0274820 PMID:36173966

Farrukh, M., Raza, A., & Rafiq, M. (2023). Environmentally specific authentic leadership and team green creative behavior based on cognitive-affective path systems. *International Journal of Contemporary Hospitality Management*, *35*(10), 3662–3680. doi:10.1108/IJCHM-04-2022-0530

Farrukh, M., Raza, A., Sajid, M., Rafiq, M., Hameed, R., & Ali, T. (2021). Entrepreneurial intentions: The relevance of nature and nurture. *Education + Training*, *63*(7/8), 1195–1212. doi:10.1108/ET-01-2021-0028

Faulds, D. J., & Raju, P. S. (2021). The work-from-home trend: An interview with Brian Kropp. *Business Horizons*, *64*(1), 29–35. doi:10.1016/j.bushor.2020.10.005 PMID:33106707

Fedorova, A., Zarubina, A., Pikulina, Y., Moskovskikh, A., Balandina, T., & Gafurova, T. (2019). Digitalization of the Human Resource Management : Russian Companies Case. *SOCIOINT 2019- 6th International Conference on Education, Social Sciences and Humanities,* 1227–1230. https://www.ocerints.org/socioint19_e-publication/abstracts/papers/713.pdf

Feijóo, C., Kwon, Y., Bauer, J. M., Bohlin, E., Howell, B., Jain, R., Potgieter, P., Vu, K., Whalley, J., & Xia, J. (2020). Harnessing artificial intelligence (AI) to increase wellbeing for all: The case for a new technology diplomacy. *Telecommunications Policy*, *44*(6), 101988. doi:10.1016/j.telpol.2020.101988 PMID:32377031

Fernandez, D., Dastane, O., Omar Zaki, H., & Aman, A. (2023). Robotic process automation: bibliometric reflection and future opportunities. *European Journal of Innovation Management.* doi:10.1108/EJIM-10-2022-0570

Fong, V. (2019). *Luno Is The First Cryptocurrency Exchange to Receive Full Approval in Malaysia.* Retrieved October 22, 2019, from https://fintechnews.my/21843/blockchain/luno-becomes-first-cryptocurrency-exchange-to-receive-full-approval-in-malaysia/

Francisco, K., & Swanson, D. (2018). The supply chain has no clothes: Technology adoption of blockchain for supply chain transparency. *Logistics*. doi:10.3390/logistics2010002

Friend, H. R. M. (2023). *FriendHRM- Best Online CRM, HR management software in Malaysia.* FriendHRM. https://www.friendhrm.com

Gabriel Szydlo, S., Ronit, B., & Yoav, M. (2023). Human-Machine Collaboration in AI-Assisted Surgery: Balancing Autonomy and Expertise. In P. S. Dr. Stanislaw (Ed.), Artificial Intelligence in Medicine and Surgery - An Exploration of Current Trends, Potential Opportunities, and Evolving Threats. IntechOpen. doi:10.5772/intechopen.111556

Gal, D. (2020). Perspectives and Approaches in AI Ethics: East Asia. In M. D. Dubber, F. Pasquale, & S. Das (Eds.), *The Oxford Handbook of Ethics of AI* (pp. 606–624). Oxford University Press. doi:10.1093/oxfordhb/9780190067397.013.39

Gambhir, V., Asnate-Salazar, E., Prithi, M., Alvarado-Tolentino, J. & Tongkachok, K. (2022). *Using Artificial Intelligence and Deep Learning Methods to Analysis the Marketing Analytics and Its Impact on Human Resource Management Systems.* Academic Press.

Garg, V., Srivastav, S., & Gupta, A. (2018). Application of Artificial Intelligence for Sustaining Green Human Resource Management. *2018 International Conference on Automation and Computational Engineering, ICACE 2018,* 113–116. 10.1109/ICACE.2018.8686988

Gartner. (2023). *Gartner.* Retrieved from AI in HR: A Guide to Implementing AI in Your HR Organization: https://www.gartner.com/en/human-resources/topics/artificial-intelligence-in-hr

Gautam, A. (2019, June 28). *SHRM.* Retrieved from Artificial Intelligence and Employee Engagement: Connecting the dots: https://blog.shrm.org/sasia/blog/artificial-intelligence-and-employee-engagement-connecting-the-dots

Gélinas, D., Sadreddin, A., & Vahidov, R. (2022). Artificial Intelligence in Human Resources Management: A Review and Research Agenda. *Pacific Asia Journal of the Association for Information Systems, 14*(6), 1–42. doi:10.17705/1pais.14601

Getchell, K. M., Carradini, S., Cardon, P. W., Fleischmann, C., Ma, H., Aritz, J., & Stapp, J. (2022). Artificial intelligence in business communication: The changing landscape of research and teaching. *Business and Professional Communication Quarterly, 85*(1), 7–33. doi:10.1177/23294906221074311

Ghosh, A. (2019). *How blockchain is streamlining settlements between telecom companies.* Retrieved from KPMG website: https://info.kpmg.us/news-perspectives/technology-innovation/blockchain-streamlining-settlements-between-telecom-companies.html

Ghosh, S. (2023). *PwC.* Retrieved from AI: Possibilities of Transforming the Workplace: https://www.pwc.in/consulting/transformation-consulting/artificial-intelligence.html

Gibbons, P. (2015). *The science of successful organizational change: How leaders set strategy, change behavior, and create an agile culture.* FT Press.

Gigante, G., & Zago, A. (2023). DARQ technologies in the financial sector: Artificial intelligence applications in personalized banking. *Qualitative Research in Financial Markets, 15*(1), 29–57. doi:10.1108/QRFM-02-2021-0025

Giordano, A. (2019). Accountants embrace distributed ledgers. *Global Finance, 33*(3), 72–72.

Giraud, L., Zaher, A., Hernandez, S., & Akram, A. A. (2022). The impacts of artificial intelligence on managerial skills. *Journal of Decision Systems,* 1–34. doi:10.1080/12460125.2022.2069537

Girisha, M. C. (2020). E-Human Resource Management (E-Hrm) Practices in Automotive Industry in Karnataka. *Mukt Shabd Journal, 9*(4), 152–163. https://www.researchgate.net/publication/340524950

Glikson, E., & Woolley, A. W. (2020). Human trust in artificial intelligence: Review of empirical research. *The Academy of Management Annals, 14*(2), 627–660. doi:10.5465/annals.2018.0057

Goel, S. (2021, April 25). *ETHR World.* Retrieved from How AI Can Be A Game Changer in HR Functions: https://hr.economictimes.indiatimes.com/news/trends/ai-in-hr/how-ai-can-be-a-game-changer-in-hr-functions/82245378

Goffin, R. D., & Olson, J. M. (2011). Is it all relative? Comparative judgments and the possible improvement of self-ratings and ratings of others. *Perspectives on Psychological Science*, *6*(1), 48–60. doi:10.1177/1745691610393521 PMID:26162115

Goralski, M. A., & Tan, T. K. (2020). Artificial intelligence and sustainable development. *International Journal of Management Education*, *18*(1), 100330. doi:10.1016/j.ijme.2019.100330

Greller, W., & Drachsler, H. (2012). Translating learning into numbers: A generic framework for learning analytics. *Journal of Educational Technology & Society*, *15*(3), 42–57.

Grewal-Carr, V., & Stephen, M. (2016). *Blockchain enigma. Paradox. Opportunity*. Deloitte.

Grover, P., Kar, A. K., & Dwivedi, Y. K. (2022). Understanding artificial intelligence adoption in operations management: Insights from the review of academic literature and social media discussions. *Annals of Operations Research*, *308*(1–2), 177–213. doi:10.100710479-020-03683-9

Guardtime. (2019). *KPMG forms strategic alliance with Guardtime*. Retrieved from https://guardtime.com/blog/kpmg-forms-strategic-alliance-with-guardtime

Guetterman, T. C., Chang, T., DeJonckheere, M., Basu, T., Scruggs, E., & Vydiswaran, V. V. (2018). Augmenting qualitative text analysis with natural language processing: Methodological study. *Journal of Medical Internet Research*, *20*(6), e231. doi:10.2196/jmir.9702 PMID:29959110

Gupta, M. (2021). The Role of Artificial Intelligence in Adopting Green HRM Practices. In G. Rana, A. Khang, R. Sharma, A. K. Goel, & A. K. Dubey (Eds.), *Reinventing Manufacturing and Business Processes Through Artificial Intelligence* (1st ed.). CRC Press. doi:10.1201/9781003145011-1

Gupta, S. K., & Bhatia, N. (2023). *A Decade of Trend in the Employee Turnover Intention Study in India: A Systematic Review and Recommendation*. FIIB Business Review. doi:10.1177/23197145231158907

Haba, H. F., Bredillet, C., & Dastane, O. (2022). Green consumer research: Trends and way forward based on bibliometric analysis. Cleaner and Responsible Consumption, 100089.

Haber, S., & Stornetta, W. S. (1991). *How to time-stamp a digital document*. Lecture Notes in Computer Science. Including Subseries Lecture Notes in Artificial Intelligence and Lecture Notes in Bioinformatics. doi:10.1007/3-540-38424-3_32

Haenlein, M., & Kaplan, A. (2019). A Brief History of Artificial Intelligence: On the Past, Present, and Future of Artificial Intelligence. *California Management Review*, *61*(4), 5–14. Advance online publication. doi:10.1177/0008125619864925

Halili, S. H., Sulaiman, S., Sulaiman, H., & Razak, R. (2021). Embracing industrial revolution 4.0 in universities. *IOP Conference Series. Materials Science and Engineering*, *1088*(1), 012111. doi:10.1088/1757-899X/1088/1/012111

Hamada, T., Bystrom, L. J., & Berndt, H. (2001). Networking Technology Convergence in the Photonic Age—TINA Vision on IP Control and Management. *IEICE Transactions on Communications*, *84*(12), 3086–3095.

Hameed, I., Haq, M. A., Khan, N., & Zainab, B. (2022). Social media usage and academic performance from a cognitive loading perspective. *On the Horizon*, *30*(1), 12–27. doi:10.1108/OTH-04-2021-0054

Hameed, I., Khan, A. K., Sabharwal, M., Arain, G. A., & Hameed, I. (2019). Managing successful change efforts in the public sector: An employee's readiness for change perspective. *Review of Public Personnel Administration*, *39*(3), 398–421. doi:10.1177/0734371X17729869

Hameed, Z., Khan, I. U., Islam, T., Sheikh, Z., & Naeem, R. M. (2020). Do green HRM practices influence employees' environmental performance? *International Journal of Manpower*, *41*(7), 1061–1079. doi:10.1108/IJM-08-2019-0407

Hancock, B. S. (2023, July 10). *McKinsey*. Retrieved from How Generative AI Could Support—Not Replace—Human Resources: https://www.mckinsey.com/capabilities/people-and-organizational-performance/our-insights/the-organization-blog/how-generative-ai-could-support-not-replace-human-resources

Handoko, B. L., Sabrina, S., Ayuanda, N., & ... (2019). Admission of information technology in external audit profession: Impact of organizational, social and individual factors. *2019 International Conference on Information Management and Technology (ICIMTech)*, *1*, 36–41. 10.1109/ICIMTech.2019.8843720

Harshman, R. (2021, December 16). *Automation. Demand for Automation is Rising: Asia Pacific Needs to Prepare for a Hybrid Human-Digital Workforce*. Retrieved from Demand for Automation is Rising: Asia Pacific Needs to Prepare for a Hybrid Human-Digital Workforce.

Hassoun, A., Prieto, M. A., Carpena, M., Bouzembrak, Y., Marvin, H. J. P., Pallarés, N., Barba, F. J., Punia Bangar, S., Chaudhary, V., Ibrahim, S., & Bono, G. (2022). Exploring the role of green and Industry 4.0 technologies in achieving sustainable development goals in food sectors. *Food Research International*, *162*, 112068. doi:10.1016/j.foodres.2022.112068 PMID:36461323

Hays, S. W. (2019). Changing roles and duties within government's human resources profession: contemporary models and challenges. In *Handbook of Public Management Practice and Reform* (pp. 205–223). Routledge.

He, T., Sun, Z., Shi, Q., Zhu, M., Wang, H., Wang, J., Wen, F., & Lee, C. (2019). Self-Powered Intuitive Control Interface Towards Diversified Gaming, AI, and Online Shopping Applications. *2019 20th International Conference on Solid-State Sensors, Actuators and Microsystems and Eurosensors XXXIII, TRANSDUCERS 2019 and EUROSENSORS XXXIII*, 2452–2455. 10.1109/TRANSDUCERS.2019.8808310

Hecklau, F., Galeitzke, M., Flachs, S., & Kohl, H. (2016). Holistic Approach for Human Resource Management in Industry 4.0. *Procedia CIRP*, *54*, 1–6. doi:10.1016/j.procir.2016.05.102

Hmoud, B., & László, V. (2019). Will Artificial Intelligence Take Over Human resources Recruitment And Selection. *Network Intelligence Studies*, 21-30.

Hoelscher, J. (2018). Taking the lead on blockchain. *Internal Auditor*, (February), 19–21. Retrieved from https://search.proquest.com/docview/1680732671?accountid=12492%0Ahttps://sfx.mit.edu/sfx_local?url_ver=Z39.88-2004&rft_val_fmt=info:ofi/fmt:kev:mtx:journal&genre=unknown&sid=ProQ:ProQ%3Aabicomplete&atitle=Risk+Watch&title=Independent+Banker&issn=00193674&

Holmes, W., Porayska-Pomsta, K., Holstein, K., Sutherland, E., Baker, T., Shum, S. B., Santos, O. C., Rodrigo, M. T., Cukurova, M., Bittencourt, I. I., & Koedinger, K. R. (2021). Ethics of AI in education: Towards a community-wide framework. *International Journal of Artificial Intelligence in Education.* Advance online publication. doi:10.100740593-021-00239-1

Horak, S., & Yang, I. (2019). Whither seniority? Career progression and performance orientation in South Korea. *International Journal of Human Resource Management*, *30*(9), 1419–1447. doi:10.1080/09585192.2017.1362659

Horodyski, P. (2023). Applicants' perception of artificial intelligence in the recruitment process. *Computers in Human Behavior Reports*, *11*(January), 100303. doi:10.1016/j.chbr.2023.100303

Hosseini, Z., Nyholm, S., le Blanc, P. M., Preenen, P. T. Y., & Demerouti, E. (2023). Assessing the artificially intelligent workplace: An ethical framework for evaluating experimental technologies in workplace settings. *AI and Ethics*. Advance online publication. doi:10.100743681-023-00265-w PMID:36846834

Hou, R., Ye, X., Zaki, H. B. O., & Omar, N. A. B. (2023). Marketing Decision Support System Based on Data Mining Technology. *Applied Sciences (Basel, Switzerland)*, *13*(7), 4315. doi:10.3390/app13074315

HROnboard. (2013). Retrieved from HROnboard: https://hronboard.me/about/

HROne. (2022). Retrieved from HROne Co.: https://www.hrone.com/about-us/

HROne. (n.d.). HROne Co. Retrieved from 2005: https://www.hrone.com/blog/ai-and-hr-analytics-in-china/

Huang, M. H., & Rust, R. T. (2021). A strategic framework for artificial intelligence in marketing. *Journal of the Academy of Marketing Science*, *49*(1), 30–50. doi:10.100711747-020-00749-9

Huang, S. M., Hung, W. H., Yen, D. C., Chang, I. C., & Jiang, D. (2011). Building the evaluation model of the IT general control for CPAs under enterprise risk management. *Decision Support Systems*, *50*(4), 692–701. Advance online publication. doi:10.1016/j.dss.2010.08.015

Huang, X., Yang, F., Zheng, J., Feng, C., & Zhang, L. (2023). Personalized human resource management via HR analytics and artificial intelligence: Theory and implications. *Asia Pacific Management Review*, (4), 598–610. Advance online publication. doi:10.1016/j.apmrv.2023.04.004

Hunkenschroer, A. L., & Luetge, C. (2022). Ethics of AI-Enabled Recruiting and Selection: A Review and Research Agenda. In Journal of Business Ethics (Vol. 178, Issue 4, pp. 977–1007). Springer Science and Business Media B.V. doi:10.100710551-022-05049-6

Hupfer, S. (2020, March 3). Deloitte Insights. *Talent and Workforce Effects in the Age of AI*, p. 2.

Hussain, A., Mkpojiogu, E. O. C., Abubakar, H., & Hassan, H. M. (2019). A mobile usability test assessment of an online shopping application. *Journal of Computational and Theoretical Nanoscience*, *16*(5–6), 2511–2516. doi:10.1166/jctn.2019.7923

Hutt, R. (2016). Beyond bitcoin: 4 surprising uses for blockchain. *World Economic Forum.*

Ilija, M. (2019). *The Chinese branch of Walmart and Vechain team up on PwC blockchain safety platform.* Retrieved from https://cryptomaniaks.com/walmart-china-vechain-pwc-blockchain-food-safety

Imperatori, B., Bissola, R., Butera, F., & Bodega, D. (2020). Work and HRM in the 4.0 era: Insights and research directions. *Studi Organizzativi*, *2*(2), 9–26. doi:10.3280/SO2019-002001

Imran, M., Salisu, I., Aslam, H. D., Iqbal, J., & Hameed, I. (2019). Resource and information access for SME sustainability in the era of IR 4.0: The mediating and moderating roles of innovation capability and management commitment. *Processes (Basel, Switzerland)*, *7*(4), 211. doi:10.3390/pr7040211

Instahyre. (2014). *Instahyre*. Retrieved from https://www.instahyre.com/

ISA 500: Audit Evidence. (2009). doi:10.4324/9781315762395-4

Isari, D., Bissola, R., & Imperatori, B. (2019). HR Devolution in the Digital Era: What Should We Expect? *Advanced Series in Management*, *23*, 41–61. doi:10.1108/S1877-636120190000023004

Ivanova, M. (2019). Robots, artificial intelligence, and service automation in travel agencies and tourist information centers. In *Robots, artificial intelligence, and service automation in travel, tourism and hospitality* (pp. 221–237). Emerald Publishing Limited. doi:10.1108/978-1-78756-687-320191011

Iwu, C. G., Eme-ukandu, N., & Allen-ile, C. (n.d.). ADMINISTRATIO Effects of the Use of Electronic Human Resource Management (E- HRM) Within Human Resource Management (HRM) Functions at Universities 1. *Introduction and Purpose.*, *8*(1), 5–20.

Jackson, N. C., & Dunn-Jensen, L. M. (2021). Leadership succession planning for today's digital transformation economy: Key factors to build for competency and innovation. *Business Horizons*, *64*(2), 273–284. doi:10.1016/j.bushor.2020.11.008

Jackson, S. E., Renwick, D. W. S., Jabbour, C. J. C., & Muller-Camen, M. (2011). State-of-the-Art and Future Directions for Green Human Resource Management: Introduction to the Special Issue. *German Journal of Human Resource Management*, *25*(2), 99–116. doi:10.1177/239700221102500203

Jacob Fernandes França, T., São Mamede, H., Pereira Barroso, J. M., & Pereira Duarte dos Santos, V. M. (2023). Artificial intelligence applied to potential assessment and talent identification in an organisational context. *Heliyon*, *9*(4), e14694. Advance online publication. doi:10.1016/j.heliyon.2023.e14694 PMID:37035361

Jagielski, M., Oprea, A., & Biggio, B. (2018). Manipulating machine learning: poisoning attacks and countermeasures for regression learning. 2018 IEEE symposium on security and privacy (SP). doi:10.1109/SP.2018.00057

Jaiswal, A., Arun, C. J., & Varma, A. (2022). Rebooting employees: Upskilling for artificial intelligence in multinational corporations. *International Journal of Human Resource Management*, *33*(6), 1179–1208. doi:10.1080/09585192.2021.1891114

Jang, H. J., Sim, J., Lee, Y., & Kwon, O. (2013). Deep sentiment analysis: Mining the causality between personality-value-attitude for analyzing business ads in social media. *Expert Systems with Applications*, *40*(18), 7492–7503. doi:10.1016/j.eswa.2013.06.069

Järvelä, S., Nguyen, A., & Hadwin, A. (2023). Human and artificial intelligence collaboration for socially shared regulation in learning. *British Journal of Educational Technology*, *54*(5), 1057–1076. doi:10.1111/bjet.13325

Jatobá, M., Santos, J., Gutierriz, I., Moscon, D., Fernandes, P. O., & Teixeira, J. P. (2019). Evolution of Artificial Intelligence Research in Human Resources. *Procedia Computer Science*, *164*, 137–142. doi:10.1016/j.procs.2019.12.165

Javaid, M.0, Haleem, A., Singh, R. P., & Suman, R. (2022). Artificial intelligence applications for industry 4.0: A literature-based study. *Journal of Industrial Integration and Management*, *7*(01), 83–111. doi:10.1142/S2424862221300040

Javaid, M., Haleem, A., Pratap Singh, R., Khan, S., & Suman, R. (2022). Sustainability 4.0 and its applications in the field of manufacturing. *Internet of Things and Cyber-Physical Systems*, *2*, 82–90. doi:10.1016/j.iotcps.2022.06.001

Jiang, X. (2018). The application of blockchain in auditing. *2nd International Conference on Education Science and Economic Management (ICESEM 2018)*, *184*(January), 1018–1023. 10.2991/icpel-18.2018.10

Jia, Q., Guo, Y., Li, R., Li, Y., & Chen, Y. (2018). A conceptual artificial intelligence application framework in human resource management. *Proceedings of the International Conference on Electronic Business (ICEB)*, 106–114.

Jin, J., Rafiq, M., Hayat, N., Yang, Q., & Al Mamun, A. (2023). Discovering the Adoption of Eco-Friendly Furniture Among Chinese Customers. In N. Mansour & L. M. Bujosa Vadell (Eds.), *Finance, Accounting and Law in the Digital Age: The Impact of Technology and Innovation in the Financial Services Sector* (pp. 273–283). Springer International Publishing. doi:10.1007/978-3-031-27296-7_25

Jobscan. (2023). *About Us*. Jobscan. https://www.jobscan.co/about/

Johnson, R.D., Stone, D.L., & Lukaszewski, K.M. (2020). *The benefits of eHRM and AI for talent acquisition*. Academic Press.

Johnson, D. G., & Verdicchio, M. (2017). Reframing AI discourse. *Minds and Machines*, *27*(4), 575–590. doi:10.100711023-017-9417-6

Johnson, M., & Smith, J. (2020). Enhancing Data Collection through Chatbots: A Review of Interaction and User Experience. *Journal of Consumer Behaviour, 15*(4), 432–446.

Kacina, J., Harler, M. C., & Rajnic, M. (2017). *SophiaTX Whitepaper The Blockchain for Business*. Retrieved from https://www.sophiatx.com/storage/web/SophiaTX_Whitepaper_v1.9.pdf

Kafi, A., Zainuddin, N., Saifudin, A. M., Shahron, S. A., Razalli, M. R., Musa, S., & Ahmi, A. (2023). Meta-analysis of food supply chain: Pre, during and post COVID-19 pandemic. *Agriculture & Food Security, 12*(1), 1–22. doi:10.118640066-023-00425-5 PMID:36883120

Kagan, R. A., Gunningham, N., & Thornton, D. (2011). Fear, duty, and regulatory compliance: lessons from three research projects. Explaining compliance: Business responses to regulation, 37-58.

Kamal, K., Alaghbari, M., & Atteia, M. (2016). E-training & employees ' performance a practical study on the ministry of education in the Kingdom of Bahrain E-Training & Employees ' Performance a Practical Study on the Ministry of Education in the Kingdom of Bahrain. *Journal of Resources Development and Management, 18*(March), 1–8.

Kamarul Bahrin, M. A., Fauzi Othman, M., Nor Azli, N. H., & Farihin Talib, M. (2016). Industry 4.0: A Review on Industrial Automation and Robotic. *Jurnal Teknologi, 78*(6–13), 137–143. www.jurnalteknologi.utm.my

Kashyap, R., & Dwesar, R. (2021). Artificial Intelligence in Marketing. Artificial Intelligence and Machine Learning in Business Management: Concepts, Challenges, and Case Studies, 1-14.

Kaur, M., Rekha, A., & Resmi, A. (2021). Research landscape of artificial intelligence in human resource management: A bibliometric overview. In *Artificial Intelligence and Speech Technology* (pp. 255–262). CRC Press. doi:10.1201/9781003150664-29

Kaushal, N., & Ghalawat, S. (2023). Research perspective of artificial intelligence and HRM: A bibliometric study. *International Journal of Business Innovation and Research, 31*(2), 168–196. doi:10.1504/IJBIR.2023.131432

Khalifa, N., Abd Elghany, M. & Abd Elghany, M. (2021). Exploratory research on digitalization transformation practices within supply chain management context in developing countries specifically Egypt in the MENA region. *Cogent Business and Management, 8*(1).

Khalifa, M., Al Baz, M., & Muttar, A. K. (2022). The Impact of Applying Artificial Intelligence on Human Resources Crisis Management: An Analytical Study on COVID19. *Information Sciences Letters, 11*(1), 269–276. doi:10.18576/isl/110127

Kim, J. (2012). Past and future of the labor force in emerging Asian economies. *Japan and the World Economy, 24*(2), 87–100. doi:10.1016/j.japwor.2012.01.004

Kim, P. T. (2018). Big Data and artificial intelligence: New challenges for workplace equality. *U. Louisville L. Rev., 57*, 313.

Kim, S., Lee, H., & Park, J. (2020). Harnessing Sentiment Analysis for Brand Management: A Comprehensive Review of AI-Driven Approaches. *Journal of Market Research and Analysis, 18*(1), 56–72.

Kim, S., Wang, Y., & Boon, C. (2021). Sixty years of research on technology and human resource management: Looking back and looking forward. *Human Resource Management, 60*(1), 229–247. doi:10.1002/hrm.22049

King, K. (2019). *Using Artificial Intelligence in Marketing: How to harness AI and maintain the competitive edge.* Kogan Page Publishers.

Kiran, P. R., Chaubey, A., & Shastri, R. K. (2023). Role of HR analytics and attrition on organisational performance: A literature review leveraging the SCM-TBFO framework. *Benchmarking*. Advance online publication. doi:10.1108/BIJ-06-2023-0412

Kokina, J., Mancha, R., & Pachamanova, D. (2017). Blockchain emergent industry adoption and implications for accounting. *Journal of Emerging Technologies in Accounting, 14*(2), 91–100. doi:10.2308/jeta-51911

Kooli, C. (2023). Chatbots in education and research: A critical examination of ethical implications and solutions. *Sustainability (Basel), 15*(7), 5614. doi:10.3390u15075614

Korpela, K., Hallikas, J., & Dahlberg, T. (2017). Digital supply chain transformation toward blockchain integration. *Proceedings of the 50th Hawaii International Conference on System Sciences.* 10.24251/HICSS.2017.506

KPMG. (2019a). *Accounting for cryptoassets – What's the impact on your financial statements?* Author.

KPMG. (2019b). *Ten key regulatory challenges of 2019.* Retrieved from https://assets.kpmg/content/dam/kpmg/us/pdf/2018/12/ten-key-regulatory-challenges-pov-v5-web.pdf

Krafft, T., Hauer, M., & Fetic, L. (2020) *From principles to practice: an interdisciplinary framework to operationalise AI ethics.* VDE and Bertelsmann Stiftung. https://www.ai-ethics-impact.org/resource/blob/1961130/c6db9894ee73aefa489d6249f5ee2b9f/aieig—report—download-hb-data.pdf

Kramar, R. (2014). Beyond strategic human resource management: Is sustainable human resource management the next approach? *International Journal of Human Resource Management, 25*(8), 1069–1089. doi:10.1080/09585192.2013.816863

Kristoff, B. H., Hoen, B. T., Adrian, L., & Stang, V. (2018). *Digitalization & hr.* Academic Press.

Kshetri, N. (2020). Evolving uses of artificial intelligence in human resource management in emerging economies in the global South: Some preliminary evidence. *Management Research Review, 44*(7), 970–990. doi:10.1108/MRR-03-2020-0168

Kuhn, D. (2019). *Amazon, Deloitte, Fidelity partner with IDEO CoLab on blockchain accelerator.* Retrieved July 11, 2019, from Coindesk website: https://www.coindesk.com/amazon-deloitte-messari-partner-with-ideo-colab-on-blockchain-startup-accelerator

Kumar, S., Gahalawat, M., Roy, P. P., Dogra, D. P., & Kim, B. (2020). Exploring impact of age and gender on sentiment analysis using machine learning. Electronics (Switzerland), 9(2). doi:10.3390/electronics9020374

Kuner, C., Svantesson, D. J. B., Cate, F. H., Lynskey, O., & Millard, C. (2017). Machine learning with personal data: Is data protection law smart enough to meet the challenge? *International Data Privacy Law*, *7*(1), 1–2. doi:10.1093/idpl/ipx003

Lager, D., & Milojkovic, E. (2018). *Digitalization and the renewal of employee engagement surveys.* https://gupea.ub.gu.se/bitstream/handle/2077/57453/gupea_2077_57453_1.pdf?sequence=1

LaGrandeur, K. (2015). Emotion, artificial intelligence, and ethics. *Beyond artificial intelligence: The disappearing human-machine divide*, 97-109.

Lai, P. (2017). The literature review of technology adoption models and theories for the novelty technology. *Journal of Information Systems and Technology Management*, *14*(1), 21–38. doi:10.4301/S1807-17752017000100002

Lauterbach, A. (2019). Artificial intelligence and policy: Quo vadis? *Digital Policy, Regulation and Governance*, *21*(3), 238–263. doi:10.1108/DPRG-09-2018-0054

Lazim, R. M., Nawi, N. M., Masroon, M. H., Abdullah, N., & Iskandar, M. C. M. (2020). Adoption of IR4.0 into Agricultural Sector in Malaysia: Potential and Challenges. *Advances in Agricultural and Food Research Journal*, *1*(2), 2. Advance online publication. doi:10.36877/aafrj.a0000140

Ledro, C. (2021). Artificial intelligence applied to customer relationship management: An empirical research. *Proceedings of the European Conference on Innovation and Entrepreneurship, ECIE*, 1153.

Lee, K.-F. (2018). AI superpowers: China, Silicon Valley, and the new world order. Houghton Mifflin.

Lee, J. D., & See, K. A. (2004). Trust in automation: Designing for appropriate reliance. *Human Factors*, *46*(1), 50–80. doi:10.1518/hfes.46.1.50.30392 PMID:15151155

Lee, J., Cho, H., Kim, Y., & Kim, J. (2020). Fostering AI literacy through educational policies: Current trends and recommendations. *Computers & Education*, *150*, 103841.

Lee, J., Suh, T., Roy, D., & Baucus, M. (2019). Emerging technology and business model innovation: The case of artificial intelligence. *Journal of Open Innovation*, *5*(3), 44. doi:10.3390/joitmc5030044

Lee, N. T., Resnick, P., & Barton, G. (2019). *Algorithmic bias detection and mitigation: Best practices and policies to reduce consumer harms* (Vol. 2). Brookings Institute.

Lepak, D. P., & Shaw, J. D. (2008). Strategic HRM in North America: Looking to the future. *International Journal of Human Resource Management, 19*(8), 1486–1499. doi:10.1080/09585190802200272

Liang, T.-P., Robert, L., Sarker, S., Cheung, C. M., Matt, C., Trenz, M., & Turel, O. (2021). Artificial intelligence and robots in individuals' lives: How to align technological possibilities and ethical issues. *Internet Research, 31*(1), 1–10. doi:10.1108/INTR-11-2020-0668

Liboni, L. B., Cezarino, L. O., Jabbour, C. J. C., Oliveira, B. G., & Stefanelli, N. O. (2019). Smart industry and the pathways to HRM 4.0: Implications for SCM. *Supply Chain Management, 24*(1), 124–146. doi:10.1108/SCM-03-2018-0150

Lin, H.-C. (2017). Nurses' satisfaction with using nursing information systems from technology acceptance model and information systems success model perspectives: a reductionist approach. *CIN: Computers, Informatics. Nursing, 35*(2), 91–99. PMID:27618401

Li, W., Waris, I., Sun, C., Hameed, I., Bhutto, M. Y., & Ali, R. (2022). Understanding the role of corporate social responsibility and sustainable supply chain management in shaping the consumers' intention to use sharing platforms. *Frontiers in Psychology, 13*, 970444. doi:10.3389/fpsyg.2022.970444 PMID:36072017

Li, Z. (2017). Will blockchain change the audit? *China-USA Business Review, 16*(6), 294–298. doi:10.17265/1537-1514/2017.06.006

Loureiro, S. M. C., Guerreiro, J., & Tussyadiah, I. (2021). Artificial intelligence in business: State of the art and future research agenda. *Journal of Business Research, 129*, 911–926. doi:10.1016/j.jbusres.2020.11.001

Lu, V. N., Wirtz, J., Kunz, W. H., Paluch, S., Gruber, T., Martins, A., & Patterson, P. G. (2020). Service robots, customers and service employees: What can we learn from the academic literature and where are the gaps? *Journal of Service Theory and Practice, 30*(3), 361–391. doi:10.1108/JSTP-04-2019-0088

Mackenzie, K. (2023). *How is AI used in human resources? 7 ways it helps HR*. Retrieved from Workable Technology Limited: https://resources.workable.com/tutorial/artificial-intelligence-in-human-resources

Mahapatra, P., & Singh, S. K. (2021). Artificial Intelligence and Machine Learning: Discovering New Ways of Doing Banking Business. Artificial Intelligence and Machine Learning in Business Management: Concepts, Challenges, and Case Studies, 53-80.

Mahbod, R., & Hinton, D. (2019). Blockchain the future of the auditing and assurance profession. *Armed Forces Comptroller, 64*(1), 23–27.

Mahfod, J., Khalifa, N. Y., & Faisal Al, M. (2017). Electronic human resource management (E-HRM) system. *International Journal of Economic Research, 14*(15), 563–576.

Maity, S. (2019). Identifying opportunities for artificial intelligence in the evolution of training and development practices. *Journal of Management Development*, *38*(8), 651–663. doi:10.1108/JMD-03-2019-0069

Malgieri, G., & Comandé, G. (2017). Why a Right to Legibility of Automated Decision-Making Exists in the General Data Protection Regulation. *International Data Privacy Law*, *7*(4), 243–265. doi:10.1093/idpl/ipx019

Malik, A., Budhwar, P., & Srikanth, N. R. (2020). Gig Economy, 4IR and Artificial Intelligence: Rethinking Strategic HRM. In Human & Technological Resource Management (HTRM): New Insights into Revolution 4.0 (pp. 75–88). Emerald Publishing Limited. doi:10.1108/978-1-83867-223-220201005

Malik, A., Srikanth, N., & Budhwar, P. (2020). Chapter 4: Digitisation, Artificial Intelligence (AI) and HRM. In J. Crawshaw, P. Budhwar, & A. Davis (Eds.), *Human Resource Management: Strategic and International Perspectives* (3rd ed., pp. 88–111). SAGE.

Malik, R., Jindal, T., & Sharma, A. (2022). Role of Artificial Intelligence in Reshaping Retail. *2022 2nd International Conference on Advance Computing and Innovative Technologies in Engineering, ICACITE 2022*, 660. 10.1109/ICACITE53722.2022.9823675

Malik, A., Budhwar, P., & Kazmi, B. A. (2023). Artificial intelligence (AI)-assisted HRM: Towards an extended strategic framework. *Human Resource Management Review*, *33*(1), 100940. Advance online publication. doi:10.1016/j.hrmr.2022.100940

Malik, S. Y., Cao, Y., Mughal, Y. H., Kundi, G. M., Mughal, M. H., & Ramayah, T. (2020). Pathways towards sustainability in organizations: Empirical evidence on the role of green human resource management practices and green intellectual capital. *Sustainability (Basel)*, *12*(8), 1–24. doi:10.3390u12083228

Mansor, D. (2021, August 30). How Malaysia Can Navigate Its Future Economy With AI – Microsoft Malaysia News Center. *Microsoft Malaysia News Center*. https://news.microsoft.com/en-my/2021/08/30/how-malaysia-can-navigate-its-future-economy-with-ai/

Mansour, E. M. (2016). Factors affecting the adoption of Computer Assisted Audit Techniques in audit process: Findings from Jordan. *Business and Economic Review*, *6*(1), 248–271. doi:10.5296/ber.v6i1.8996

Mantello, P., & Ho, M. T. (2023). Emotional AI and the future of wellbeing in the post-pandemic workplace. *AI & Society*. Advance online publication. doi:10.100700146-023-01639-8 PMID:36776535

Manuti, A., & Monachino, D. (2020). Managing knowledge at the time of artificial intelligence: An explorative study with knowledge workers. *East European Journal of Psycholinguistics*, *7*(2). Advance online publication. doi:10.29038/eejpl.2020.7.2.man

Marda, V. (2018). Artificial intelligence policy in India: A framework for engaging the limits of data-driven decision-making. *Philosophical Transactions. Series A, Mathematical, Physical, and Engineering Sciences*, *376*(2133), 1–19. doi:10.1098/rsta.2018.0087 PMID:30323001

Margherita, E. G., & Bua, I. (2021). The role of human resource practices for the development of Operator 4.0 in Industry 4.0 organisations: A literature review and a research agenda. *Businesses*, *1*(1), 18–33. doi:10.3390/businesses1010002

MarketingH. (2018). Retrieved from HROnboard: https://hronboard.me/blog/hronboard-acquired-by-elmo-software/

Marler, J. H., & Boudreau, J. W. (2017). An evidence-based review of HR Analytics. *International Journal of Human Resource Management*, *28*(1), 3–26. doi:10.1080/09585192.2016.1244699

Maskey, S. (2022, March 23). *Forbes Technology Council*. Retrieved from How AI Is Primed To Disrupt HR And Recruiting: https://www.forbes.com/sites/forbestechcouncil/2022/03/23/how-ai-is-primed-to-disrupt-hr-and-recruiting/?sh=11c1b5b41078

McKinsey. (2018). *AI, Automation, and the Future of Work: Ten Things to Solve for*. McKinsey Global Institute. http://dln.jaipuria.ac.in:8080/jspui/bitstream/123456789/1335/1/MGI-Briefing-Note-AI-automation-and-the-future-of-work_June2018.pdf

Mehrotra, S. a. (2022). Recruitment Through AI in Selected Indian Companies. Metamorphosis. *Journal of Management Research*, *21*(1), 31–39.

Mer, A., & Srivastava, A. (2023). Employee Engagement in the New Normal: Artificial Intelligence as a Buzzword or a Game Changer? In The Adoption and Effect of Artificial Intelligence on Human Resources Management, Part A (pp. 15–46). Emerald Publishing Limited. doi:10.1108/978-1-80382-027-920231002

Mer, A., & Virdi, A. S. (2023). Navigating the paradigm shift in HRM practices through the lens of artificial intelligence: A post-pandemic perspective. *The Adoption and Effect of Artificial Intelligence on Human Resources Management, Part A*, 123-154.

Mer, A., & Virdi, A. S. (2023). Navigating the Paradigm Shift in HRM Practices Through the Lens of Artificial Intelligence: A Post-pandemic Perspective. In P. Tyagi, N. Chilamkurti, S. Grima, K. Sood, & B. Balusamy (Eds.), *The Adoption and Effect of Artificial Intelligence on Human Resources Management, Part A* (pp. 123–154). Emerald Publishing Limited. doi:10.1108/978-1-80382-027-920231007

Mercer, L. L. C. (2009). *Mercer LLC*. Retrieved from https://mettl.com/en/about/

Mercer. (2019). *Mercer's 2019 Global Performance Management Survey*. Marsh & McLennan Companies. https://www.imercer.com/uploads/common/HTML/LandingPages/AnalyticalHub/june2019-mercer-2019-global-performance-management-survey-executive-summary.pdf

Miao, F., Holmes, W., Huang, R., & Zhang, H. (2021). *AI and education: A guidance for policymakers*. UNESCO Publishing.

Micus, C., Schramm, S., Boehm, M., & Krcmar, H. (2023). *Methods to analyze customer usage data in a product decision process: A systematic literature review* (Vol. 10). Operations Research Perspectives.

Mikalef, P., Islam, N., Parida, V., Singh, H., & Altwaijry, N. (2023). Artificial intelligence (AI) competencies for organizational performance: A B2B marketing capabilities perspective. *Journal of Business Research*, *164*, 113998. doi:10.1016/j.jbusres.2023.113998

Mishra, V., & Singh, J. (2022). *Health Technology Assessment of Telemedicine Interventions in Diabetes Management: Evidence from UAE.* FIIB Business Review. doi:10.1177/23197145221130651

Mittelstadt, B. (2019). Principles alone cannot guarantee ethical AI. *Nature Machine Intelligence*, *1*(11), 501–507. doi:10.103842256-019-0114-4

Modgil, S., Singh, R. K., & Hannibal, C. (2022). Artificial intelligence for supply chain resilience: Learning from Covid-19. *International Journal of Logistics Management*, *33*(4), 1246–1268. doi:10.1108/IJLM-02-2021-0094

Morshidi, A., b, K. Y. S., Yussof, K. M., Idris, R. Z., Idris, R., & Abas, A. (2022). Online work adjustment in the sustainable development context during COVID-19 pandemic: A systematic literature review. *International Journal of Work Innovation*, *3*(3), 269–288. doi:10.1504/IJWI.2022.127668

Mullainathan, S., & Spiess, J. (2017). Machine Learning: An Applied Econometric Approach. *The Journal of Economic Perspectives*, *31*(2), 87–106. doi:10.1257/jep.31.2.87

Muralidhar, S., Bharadwaj, A., & Bhat, K. P. (2022). Artificial intelligence and human resource management: A conceptual study. *BOHR International Journal of Advances in Management Research*, *2*(1), 72–80. doi:10.54646/bijamr.2023.20

Murday, J., Bell, L., Heath, J., Kong, C. H., Chang, R., Fonash, S., & Baba, M. (2013). Implications: People and physical infrastructure. Convergence of knowledge, technology and society: Beyond convergence of nano-bio-info-cognitive technologies, 287-370.

Murphy, J. W., & Largacha-Martínez, C. (2021). Is it possible to create a responsible AI technology to be used and understood within workplaces and unblocked CEOs' mindsets? *AI & Society*. Advance online publication. doi:10.100700146-021-01316-8

Murray, J. (2018). The Coming World of Blockchain: A Primer for Accountants and Auditors. *The CPA Journal.*

Mushfiqur, R., Mordi, C., Oruh, E. S., Nwagbara, U., Mordi, T., & Turner, I. M. (2018). The impacts of work-life-balance (WLB) challenges on social sustainability: The experience of Nigerian female medical doctors. *Employee Relations*, *40*(5), 868–888. doi:10.1108/ER-06-2017-0131

Mushtaq, R., Dastane, O., Rafiq, M., & Başar, B. D. (2023). Women financial inclusion research: A bibliometric and network analysis. *International Journal of Social Economics*, *50*(8), 1169–1185. doi:10.1108/IJSE-06-2022-0438

Mustak, M., Salminen, J., Plé, L., & Wirtz, J. (2021). Artificial intelligence in marketing: Topic modeling, scientometric analysis, and research agenda. *Journal of Business Research, 124*, 389–404. doi:10.1016/j.jbusres.2020.10.044

Muster, V., & Schrader, U. (2011). Green Work-Life Balance: A New Perspective for Green HRM. *German Journal of Human Resource Management: Zeitschrift Für Personalforschung, 25*(2), 140–156. doi:10.1177/239700221102500205

Nakamoto, S. (2008). *Bitcoin: A peer-to-peer electronic cash system.* Retrieved from http://www.academia.edu/download/54517945/Bitcoin_paper_Original_2.pdf

Nam, K., Dutt, C. S., Chathoth, P., Daghfous, A., & Khan, M. S. (2021). The adoption of artificial intelligence and robotics in the hotel industry: Prospects and challenges. *Electronic Markets, 31*(3), 553–574. doi:10.100712525-020-00442-3

Naqvi, S. R., Sareen, P., Sharma, T., & Naqvi, A. (2023). Enhancing Employee Experience with HR Bots: A Study in Mega Company. *2023 10th International Conference on Computing for Sustainable Global Development (INDIACom),* 227-230.

Naseri, M. B., & Elliott, G. (2011). Role of demographics, social connectedness and prior internet experience in adoption of online shopping: Applications for direct marketing. *Journal of Targeting. Measurement and Analysis for Marketing, 19*(2), 69–84. doi:10.1057/jt.2011.9

Nash, K. S. (2016). IBM pushes blockchain into the supply chain. *The Wall Street Journal.*

Nathalie, B., Gauthier, M., Morin, J.-H., & Arber, S. (2019). The Potential Impact of Blockchain Technology on Audit Practice. *Journal of Strategic Innovation and Sustainability, 14*(2), 35–59. doi:10.33423/jsis.v14i2.1370

Ng, C. (2019). Blockchain in the Accounting Curriculum. *Pennsylvania CPA Journal, 90*(1), 14–15. Retrieved from http://eds.a.ebscohost.com/eds/Citations/FullTextLinkClick?sid=e1bbad5a-8886-4460-aecb-cce09bbdbc59@sessionmgr4007&vid=6&id=pdfFullText

Nguyễn, T. (2023). *The Influence of ChatGPT and AI Tools on Vietnamese Education.* Academic Press.

Nishant, R., Kennedy, M., & Corbett, J. (2020). Artificial intelligence for sustainability: Challenges, opportunities, and a research agenda. *International Journal of Information Management, 53*, 102104. doi:10.1016/j.ijinfomgt.2020.102104

Noor, Z. (2015, April). Impact of Job Promotion and Job Advancement on Job Satisfaction in Universities of Kpk Province of Pakistan. *Science International (Lahore), 27*(2), 1499–1505.

Nordin, M. A. B. W., Vedenyapin, D., Alghifari, M. F., & Gunawan, T. S. (2019). The disruptometer: An artificial intelligence algorithm for market insights. *Bulletin of Electrical Engineering and Informatics, 8*(2), 727–734. doi:10.11591/eei.v8i2.1494

Norman, C. S., Payne, M. D., & Vendrzyk, V. P. (2009). Assessing information technology general control risk: An instructional case. *Issues in Accounting Education*, *24*(1), 63–76. Advance online publication. doi:10.2308/iace.2009.24.1.63

Norvig, P., & Russell, S. (2016). *Artificial intelligence: a modern approach* (Global Edition). Pearson Education Limited.

Ntoutsi, E., Fafalios, P., Gadiraju, U., Iosifidis, V., Nejdl, W., Vidal, M. E., Ruggieri, S., Turini, F., Papadopoulos, S., Krasanakis, E., Kompatsiaris, I., Kinder-Kurlanda, K., Wagner, C., Karimi, F., Fernandez, M., Alani, H., Berendt, B., Kruegel, T., Heinze, C., ... Staab, S. (2020). Bias in data-driven artificial intelligence systems—An introductory survey. *Wiley Interdisciplinary Reviews. Data Mining and Knowledge Discovery*, *10*(3), e1356. doi:10.1002/widm.1356

Nuttall, K. S. (2023). *Deloitte*. Retrieved from Generation AI: Ready or Not, Here We Come!: https://www.deloitte.com/au/en/services/consulting/analysis/generation-ai-ready-or-not.html?id=au:2ps:3gl:4con-daegenerationaireport2023-2023:6con:20230905:paid_search_2&utm_source=google&utm_medium=cpc&utm_campaign=con-daegenerationaireport2023-2023&ut

Occean, P. S. (2017, February 27). *Digital HR: Platforms, people, and work*. Retrieved from 2017 Global Human Capital Trends: https://www.deloitte.com/global/en/our-thinking/insights/topics/talent/human-capital-trends/digital-transformation-in-hr.html

Ogbeibu, S., Emelifeonwu, J., Pereira, V., Oseghale, R., Gaskin, J., Sivarajah, U., & Gunasekaran, A. (2023). Demystifying the roles of organisational smart technology, artificial intelligence, robotics and algorithms capability: A strategy for green human resource management and environmental sustainability. *Business Strategy and the Environment*, 1–20. doi:10.1002/bse.3495

Olsen, T. L., & Tomlin, B. (2020). Industry 4.0: Opportunities and challenges for operations management. *Manufacturing & Service Operations Management*, *22*(1), 113–122. doi:10.1287/msom.2019.0796

Omar, S. A., Hasbolah, F., & Zainudin, U. M. (2017). The Diffusion of Artificial Intelligence in Governance of Public Listed Companies in Malaysia. *International Journal of Business Economics and Law*, *14*(2), 1–9.

Oracle. (2019). *Oracle | From Fear to Enthusiasm* (Global Study 2019 Oracle and Future Workplace AI@Work). Oracle. https://www.oracle.com/webfolder/s/assets/ebook/ai-work/index.html?source=:ow:ms:pt:RC_PDMK191009P00032:LPD400002437&intcmp=:ow:ms:pt:RC_PDMK191009P00032:LPD400002437

Oswal, N., Khaleeli, M., & Alarmoti, A. (2020). Recruitment in the Era of Industry 4.0: use of Artificial Intelligence in Recruitment and its impact. *PalArch's Journal of Archaeology of Egypt/Egyptology*, *17*(8), 39-47.

Paesano, A. (2021). Artificial intelligence and creative activities inside organizational behavior. *The International Journal of Organizational Analysis*.

Palos-Sánchez, P. R., Baena-Luna, P., Badicu, A., & Infante-Moro, J. C. (2022). Artificial Intelligence and Human Resources Management: A Bibliometric Analysis. *Applied Artificial Intelligence, 36*(1), 2145631. Advance online publication. doi:10.1080/08839514.2022.2145631

Panda, G., Dash, M. K., Samadhiya, A., Kumar, A., & Mulat-weldemeskel, E. (2023). Artificial intelligence as an enabler resiliency : past literature, present debate and future research directions. *International Journal of Industrial Engineering and Operations Management.* doi:10.1108/IJIEOM-05-2023-0047

Panos, S., & Bellou, V. (2016). Maximizing e-HRM outcomes: A moderated mediation path. *Management Decision, 54*(5), 1088–1109. doi:10.1108/MD-07-2015-0269

Pan, Y., & Froese, F. J. (2023). An interdisciplinary review of AI and HRM: Challenges and future directions. *Human Resource Management Review, 33*(1), 100924. Advance online publication. doi:10.1016/j.hrmr.2022.100924

Pavlou, C. (2022, May). *efront.* Retrieved from AI in HR: The Good, The Bad, And The Ugly: https://www.efrontlearning.com/blog/2022/05/ai-in-hr.html

Pawczuk, L., Massey, R., & Schatsky, D. (2018). Breaking blockchain open Deloitte's 2018 global blockchain survey. Deloitte. doi:10.1002/ejoc.201200111

Perkinson, J., & Miller, R. (2016). Unimpeachable blockchains: Could blockchain revolutionise the accounting profession? In Acuity (Vol. 3). Academic Press.

Pessach, D., Singer, G., Avrahami, D., Chalutz Ben-Gal, H., Shmueli, E., & Ben-Gal, I. (2020). Employees recruitment: A prescriptive analytics approach via machine learning and mathematical programming. *Decision Support Systems, 134*, 113290. doi:10.1016/j.dss.2020.113290 PMID:32501316

Peterson, J., Tahssain-Gay, L., Salvetat, D., Perez, F., & Hennekam, S. (2023). How managers approach data analytics: A typology through a Resource Orchestration perspective. *Management Decision, 61*(5), 1225–1243. doi:10.1108/MD-03-2022-0316

Pham, N. T., Hoang, H. T., & Phan, Q. P. T. (2020). Green human resource management: A comprehensive review and future research agenda. *International Journal of Manpower, 41*(7), 845–878. doi:10.1108/IJM-07-2019-0350

Pillai, R., Ghanghorkar, Y., Sivathanu, B., Algharabat, R. S., & Rana, N. P. (2023). Adoption of artificial intelligence (AI) based employee experience (EEX) chatbots. *Information Technology & People.* Advance online publication. doi:10.1108/ITP-04-2022-0287

Pillai, R., & Sivathanu, B. (2020). Adoption of artificial intelligence (AI) for talent acquisition in IT/ITeS organizations. *Benchmarking, 27*(9), 2599–2629. doi:10.1108/BIJ-04-2020-0186

Pillai, R., & Srivastava, K. B. L. (2022). Smart HRM 4.0 for achieving organizational performance: A dynamic capability view perspective. *International Journal of Productivity and Performance Management.* Advance online publication. doi:10.1108/IJPPM-04-2022-0174

Pizzoferrato, A. (2023). European Legislation and AI information systems applicable to HRM. In Law, Technology and Labour (pp. 179-185). Università di Bologna.

Polas, M. R. H., Afshar Jahanshahi, A., Kabir, A. I., Sohel-Uz-Zaman, A. S., Osman, A. R., & Karim, R. (2022). Artificial Intelligence, Blockchain Technology, and Risk-Taking Behavior in the 4.0IR Metaverse Era: Evidence from Bangladesh-Based SMEs. *Journal of Open Innovation*, *8*(3), 168. doi:10.3390/joitmc8030168

Pozzi, F. A., & Dwivedi, D. (2023). ESG and IoT: Ensuring Sustainability and Social Responsibility in the Digital Age. In S. Tiwari, F. Ortiz-Rodríguez, S. Mishra, E. Vakaj, & K. Kotecha (Eds.), *Artificial Intelligence: Towards Sustainable Intelligence. AI4S 2023. Communications in Computer and Information Science* (Vol. 1907). Springer., doi:10.1007/978-3-031-47997-7_2

PricewaterhouseCoopers. (2020). *PwC's Global Artificial Intelligence Study: Sizing the prize*. PwC. https://www.pwc.com/gx/en/issues/data-and-analytics/publications/artificial-intelligence-study.html

Prikshat, V., Islam, M., Patel, P., Malik, A., Budhwar, P., & Gupta, S. (2023). AI-Augmented HRM: Literature review and a proposed multilevel framework for future research. *Technological Forecasting and Social Change*, *193*(April), 122645. doi:10.1016/j.techfore.2023.122645

Prikshat, V., Malik, A., & Budhwar, P. (2023). AI-augmented HRM: Antecedents, assimilation and multilevel consequences. *Human Resource Management Review*, *33*(1), 100860. doi:10.1016/j.hrmr.2021.100860

Przegalinska, A., & Jemielniak, D. (2023). *Strategizing AI in Business and Education*. Cambridge University Press., doi:10.1017/9781009243520

Pte, I. (2017). *Ideatory Pte*. Retrieved from https://impress.ai/about-us/

Puhovichova, D., & Jankelova, N. (2020). Changes of human resource management in the context of impact of the fourth industrial revolution. *International Scientific Journal, 141*(3), 138–141. https://stumejournals.com/journals/i4/2020/3/138

PWC. (2018). Blockchain is here. What's your next move? In PwC's Global Blockchain Survey 2018.

PwC. (2018). Blockchain is here. What's your next move? In *PwC's Global Blockchain Survey 2018*. Retrieved from https://www.pwc.com/gx/en/issues/blockchain/blockchain-in-business.html?WT.mc_id=CT11-PL1000-DM2-TR1-LS4-ND30-TTA5-CN_US-GX-xLoSBlockchain-StratITForecast&_cldee=a3BvbWFsbGV5QGdtYWlsLmNvbQ%3D%3D&eq=CT11-PL1000-DM2-CN_US-GX-xLoSBlockchain-StratITForecast&e

PwC. (2019a). *Financial Service Technology 2020*. Retrieved from https://www.pwc.com/gx/en/financial-services/assets/pdf/technology2020-and-beyond.pdf

PwC. (2019b). *PwC and VeChain help Walmart China build its Blockchain Traceability System*. Retrieved June 25, 2019, from PwC website: https://www.pwccn.com/en/press-room/press-releases/pr-250619.html

PWC. (2020). *Sizing the prize | What's the real value of AI for your business and how can you capitalise?* [PWC's Global AI Study]. PWC. https://www.pwc.com/gx/en/issues/analytics/assets/pwc-ai-analysis-sizing-the-prize-report.pdf?source=:ow:ms:pt:RC_PDMK191009P00032:LPD400002437

Qamar, Y., Agrawal, R. K., Samad, T. A., & Jabbour, C. J. C. (2021). When technology meets people: The interplay of artificial intelligence and human resource management. *Journal of Enterprise Information Management*, *34*(4), 1339–1370. doi:10.1108/JEIM-11-2020-0436

Radonjić, A., Duarte, H., & Pereira, N. (2021, June). (2022). Artificial intelligence and HRM: HR managers' perspective on decisiveness and challenges. *European Management Journal*. Advance online publication. doi:10.1016/j.emj.2022.07.001

Rafiq, M., & Chin, T. (2019). Three-Way Interaction Effect of Job Insecurity, Job Embeddedness and Career Stage on Life Satisfaction in A Digital Era. *International Journal of Environmental Research and Public Health*, *16*(9), 1580. doi:10.3390/ijerph16091580 PMID:31064119

Rafiq, M., Dastane, O., & Mushtaq, R. (2023a). Waste reduction as ethical behaviour: A bibliometric analysis and development of future agenda. *Journal of Global Responsibility*, *14*(3), 360–379. doi:10.1108/JGR-09-2022-0098

Rafiq, M., Farrukh, M., Attiq, S., Shahzad, F., & Khan, I. (2023b). Linking job crafting, innovation performance, and career satisfaction: The mediating role of work engagement. *Work (Reading, Mass.)*, *75*(3), 877–886. doi:10.3233/WOR-211363 PMID:36683474

Rafiq, M., Jafar, R. M. S., Ahmad, W., Dastane, O., & Sial, M. A. (2022). Job Embeddedness: Cross-cultural Comparison Between China and Pakistan During COVID-19 Pandemic. *Vision (Basel)*.

Rafiq, M., Jafar, R. M. S., Ahmad, W., Dastane, O., & Sial, M. A. (2022). Job Embeddedness: Cross-cultural Comparison Between China and Pakistan During COVID-19 Pandemic. *Vision (Basel)*. doi:10.1177/09722629221129980

Rafiq, M., & Weiwei, W. (2017). Managerial trust outlook in China and Pakistan. *Human Systems Management*, *36*(4), 363–368. doi:10.3233/HSM-17157

Rahman, M., Ming, T. H., Baigh, T. A., & Sarker, M. (2021). Adoption of artificial intelligence in banking services: An empirical analysis. *International Journal of Emerging Markets*. doi:10.1108/IJOEM-06-2020-0724

Raisch, S., & Krakowski, S. (2021). Artificial intelligence and management: The automation–augmentation paradox. *Academy of Management Review*, *46*(1), 192–210. doi:10.5465/amr.2018.0072

Ramachandran, K. K., Apsara Saleth Mary, A., Hawladar, S., Asokk, D., Bhaskar, B., & Pitroda, J. R. (2022). Machine learning and role of artificial intelligence in optimizing work performance and employee behavior. *Materials Today: Proceedings*, *51*, 2327–2331. doi:10.1016/j.matpr.2021.11.544

Rana, G., & Sharma, R. (2019). Emerging human resource management practices in Industry 4.0. *Strategic HR Review*, *18*(4), 176–181. doi:10.1108/SHR-01-2019-0003

Rangaswamy, A., Moch, N., Felten, C., van Bruggen, G., Wieringa, J. E., & Wirtz, J. (2020). The role of marketing in digital business platforms. *Journal of Interactive Marketing*, *51*(August), 72–90. doi:10.1016/j.intmar.2020.04.006

Ras, E., Wild, F., Stahl, C., & Baudet, A. (2017). Bridging the skills gap of workers in industry 4.0 by human performance augmentation tools - Challenges and roadmap. *ACM International Conference Proceeding Series, Part F1285*, 428–432. 10.1145/3056540.3076192

Regona, M., Yigitcanlar, T., Xia, B., & Li, R. Y. M. (2022). Opportunities and Adoption Challenges of AI in the Construction Industry: A PRISMA Review. *Journal of Open Innovation*, *8*(1), 45. doi:10.3390/joitmc8010045

Ren, T., Jin, X., Rafiq, M., & Chin, T. (2019). Moderation of Housing-related Factors on Psychological Capital–Job Embeddedness Association. *Frontiers in Psychology*, *10*, 1618. doi:10.3389/fpsyg.2019.01618 PMID:31649569

Renwick, D., Redman, T., & Maguire, S. (2008). *Green HRM: A review, process model, and research agenda*. University of Sheffield Management School. https://onlinelibrary.wiley.com/doi/abs/10.1111/j.1468-2370.2011.00328.x

Renwick, D. W. S., Redman, T., & Maguire, S. (2013). Green Human Resource Management: A Review and Research Agenda*. *International Journal of Management Reviews*, *15*(1), 1–14. doi:10.1111/j.1468-2370.2011.00328.x

Rezzani, A., Caputo, A., & Cortese, C. G. (2020). An analysis of the literature about the application of Artificial Intelligence to the Recruitment and Personnel Selection. *Bollettino di Psicologia Applicata*, 25–33.

Richardson, C., & Wong, H. W. (2018). Expatriate academics in Malaysia: Motivation, adjustment, and retention. *Journal of Management Development*, *37*(3), 299–308. doi:10.1108/JMD-12-2017-0421

Rodgers, W., Murray, J. M., Stefanidis, A., Degbey, W. Y., & Tarba, S. Y. (2023). An artificial intelligence algorithmic approach to ethical decision-making in human resource management processes. *Human Resource Management Review*, *33*(1), 100925. doi:10.1016/j.hrmr.2022.100925

Ronquillo, C. E., Peltonen, L. M., Pruinelli, L., Chu, C. H., Bakken, S., Beduschi, A., ... Michalowski, M. (2021). Artificial intelligence in nursing: Priorities and opportunities from an international invitational think-tank of the Nursing and Artificial Intelligence Leadership Collaborative. *Journal of Advanced Nursing*, *77*(9), 3707–3717. doi:10.1111/jan.14855 PMID:34003504

Rozario, A. M., & Vasarhelyi, M. A. (2018). Auditing with Smart Contracts. *The International Journal of Digital Accounting Research, 18*(December), 1–27. doi:10.4192/1577-8517-v18_1

Rupp, D. E., Shapiro, D. L., Folger, R., Skarlicki, D. P., & Shao, R. (2017). A critical analysis of the conceptualization and measurement of organizational justice: Is it time for reassessment? *The Academy of Management Annals*, *11*(2), 919–959. doi:10.5465/annals.2014.0051

Sadu, I. (2018). Auditing blockchain. *Internal Auditor*, *75*(6), 17–19.

Sae-Lim, P., & Jermsittiparsert, K. (2019). Is the fourth industrial revolution a panacea? Risks toward the fourth industrial revolution: Evidence in the Thai economy. *International Journal of Innovation. Creativity and Change*, *5*(2), 732–752.

Safara, F. (2022). A Computational Model to Predict Consumer Behaviour During COVID-19 Pandemic. *Computational Economics*, *59*(4), 1525–1538. doi:10.100710614-020-10069-3 PMID:33169049

Saleh, A., Al-Shameri, A. S., Sarah, S., & Omar, B. (2022). *HR Digitalization as a Critical HR practice to Navigate through Covid-19 for the Improvement of the Employee Job Performance: Review Paper*. Academic Press.

Samsurijan, M. S., Ebekozien, A., Nor, A. N. A., Shaed, M. M., & Radin, B. R. F. (2022). Artificial intelligence in urban services in Malaysia: A review. *PSU Research Review*. doi:10.1108/PRR-07-2021-0034

Sanny, L., Susastra, A. C., Roberts, C., & Yusramdaleni, R. (2020). The analysis of customer satisfaction factors which influence chatbot acceptance in Indonesia. *Management Science Letters*, *10*(6), 1225–1232. doi:10.5267/j.msl.2019.11.036

Sanyaolu, E. a. (2022). *Role of Artificial Intelligence in Human Resource Management: Overview of its Benefits and Challenges*. Academic Press.

Schmidt, S., Karampournioti, E., Wiedmann, K. & Buckler, F. (2023). *Special Session: Marketing Research Automation and Robotization (M-RAR): A Chance for Marketing Practice and a Risk for Marketing Science/Scientists? An Abstract*. Academic Press.

Schwartz, J. (2020). *The social enterprise at work: Paradox as a path forward*. Deloitte Insights.

Shah, N., Michael, F., & Chalu, H. (2020). E-HRM and Motivation: A Case of Manufacturing Companies in Tanzania. *East African Journal of Business and Economics*, *2*(1), 53–71. doi:10.37284/eajbe.2.1.241

Shakil, M.T.H. & Rajasekaran, R. (2023). *A Data Science Approach in Quantitative Market Research*. Academic Press.

Shakir, M. Z., & Ramzan, N. (2021). AI for emerging verticals: Human-robot computing, sensing and networking. AI for Emerging Verticals: Human-robot computing, sensing and networking, 1-364.

Sharma, C., Sakhuja, S., & Nijjer, S. (2022). Recent trends of green human resource management: Text mining and network analysis. *Environmental Science and Pollution Research International*, *29*(56), 84916–84935. doi:10.100711356-022-21471-9 PMID:35790632

Sharma, R., Mithas, S., & Kankanhalli, A. (2014). Transforming decision-making processes: A research agenda for understanding the impact of business analytics on organisations. *European Journal of Information Systems*, *23*(4), 433–441. doi:10.1057/ejis.2014.17

Sharma, S., & Tiwari, V. (2023). Modelling the Impact of Emotional Intelligence, Career Success and Happiness on Turnover Intention Among Managerial-level Employees in the Information Technology Industry. *FIIB Business Review*, *12*(3), 279–293. doi:10.1177/23197145221121082

Shin, D. (2022). How do people judge the credibility of algorithmic sources? *AI & Society*, *37*(1), 1–16. doi:10.100700146-021-01158-4

Shu, C. (2021, July 29). *TechCrunch*. Retrieved from Employee Engagement Platform Culture Amp Raises $100M at a $1.5B Valuation: https://techcrunch.com/2021/07/29/employee-engagement-platform-culture-amp-raises-100m-at-a-1-5b-valuation/

Shukla, S. K. (2009). *Decision models and artificial intelligence in supporting workforce forecasting and planning*. The University of Texas at San Antonio.

Singapore, P. D. P. C. (2012). *Personal Data Protection Act 2012*. https://sso.agc.gov.sg/Act/PDPA2012

Singh, A., Kanaujia, A., Singh, V. K., & Vinuesa, R. (2023). Artificial intelligence for Sustainable Development Goals: Bibliometric patterns and concept evolution trajectories. *Sustainable Development (Bradford)*, (May), 1–31. doi:10.1002d.2706

Sinniah, S., Mohamed, R. K. M. H., Mior, W. R., Harith, A., Izni, W. N., & Rawshdeh, Z. A. (2019). Talent retention in private universities of Malaysia. *International Journal of Engineering and Advanced Technology, 8*(6), 233–239. doi:10.35940/ijeat.F1038.0986S319

Sithambaram, R. A., & Tajudeen, F. P. (2023). Impact of Artificial Intelligence in Human Resource Management: A Qualitative Study in the Malaysian Context. *Asia Pacific Journal of Human Resources*, *61*(4), 821–844. doi:10.1111/1744-7941.12356

Sivathanu, B., & Pillai, R. (2018). Smart HR 4.0 – how industry 4.0 is disrupting HR. *Human Resource Management International Digest*, *26*(4), 7–11. doi:10.1108/HRMID-04-2018-0059

Smart Insights. (2018). *How AI is changing the role of the marketer in 2018*. https://www.smartinsights.com/managing-digital-marketing/managing-marketing-technology/h ow-ai-is-changing-the-role-of-the-marketer-in-2018/

Smith, A., & Jones, B. (2021). Unveiling Customer Sentiments: A Comprehensive Analysis of Sentiment Analysis in Market Research. *Market Insights Review*, *15*(3), 126–143.

Smith, S. S. (2018). Blockchain augmented audit – benefits and challenges for accounting professionals. *Journal of Theoretical Accounting Research*, *14*(1), 117–138. http://search.ebscohost.com/login.aspx?direct=true&AuthType=cookie,ip,shib,uid&db=bsu&AN=131747318&lang=pt-br&site=eds-live&authtype=sso

Sofiah, A. (2023, August 24). *More than half of HR leaders surveyed in Singapore and Malaysia share concerns about the ethical use of AI*. Human Resources Online. https://www.humanresourcesonline.net/more-than-half-of-hr-leaders-surveyed-in-singapore-and-malaysia-share-concerns-about-the-ethical-use-of-ai

Song, Y., & Wu, R. (2021). Analysing human-computer interaction behaviour in human resource management system based on artificial intelligence technology. *Knowledge Management Research and Practice*, *00*(00), 1–10. doi:10.1080/14778238.2021.1955630

Soni, H. (2023, February 1). *10 Areas AI Impacts Performance Management Practices*. About Leaders. https://aboutleaders.com/performance-management-practices/

Sonik, D., & Colarossi, A. (2020). *Becoming Artificial: A Philosophical Exploration Into Artificial Intelligence and What it Means to be Human* (Vol. 73). Andrews UK Limited.

Spoke, M. (2015). *How blockchain tech will change auditing for good*. Retrieved from Coindesk.com website: https://www.coindesk.com/blockchains-and-the-future-of-audit

Staff, C. P. A. J. (2019). Auditing implications of blockchain and cybersecurity: Certified Public Accountant. *The CPA Journal*, *89*, 38–39. http://eds.a.ebscohost.com/eds/Citations/FullTextLinkClick?sid=e1bbad5a-8886-4460-aecb-cce09bbdbc59@sessionmgr4007&vid=8&id=pdfFullText

Stahl, A. (2021, October 3). How AI Will Impact The Future Of Work And Life. *Forbes*. https://www.forbes.com/sites/ashleystahl/2021/03/10/how-ai-will-impact-the-future-of-work-and-life/

Stahl, G., Björkman, I., Farndale, E., Morris, S. S., Paauwe, J., Stiles, P., Trevor, J., & Wright, P. (2012). Six principles of effective global talent management. *Sloan Management Review*, *53*(2), 25–42.

Statista. (2020). *Global business and HR leaders use of AI to assist workers 2020*. Statista. https://www.statista.com/statistics/1120120/global-business-and-hr-leaders-use-of-ai-to-assist-workers/

Stone, D. L., Deadrick, D. L., Lukaszewski, K. M., & Johnson, R. (2015). The influence of technology on the future of human resource management. *Human Resource Management Review*, *25*(2), 216–231. doi:10.1016/j.hrmr.2015.01.002

Sultan, K., Ruhi, U., & Lakhani, R. (2018). Conceptualizing Blockchains: Characteristics & Applications. *11th IADIS International Conference. Information Systems*, *2018*, 49–57. https://arxiv.org/abs/1806.03693

Sun, T. Q., & Medaglia, R. (2019). Mapping the challenges of Artificial Intelligence in the public sector: Evidence from public healthcare. *Government Information Quarterly*, *36*(2), 368–383. doi:10.1016/j.giq.2018.09.008

Sun, X. (2021). 5G joint artificial intelligence technology in the innovation and reform of university English education. *Wireless Communications and Mobile Computing*, *2021*, 1–10. doi:10.1155/2021/2460916

Swan, M. (2015). Blockchain: Blueprint for a new economy. In Climate Change 2013 - The Physical Science Basis. doi:10.1017/CBO9781107415324.004

Swanson, J. (2017). The future of student life: Working. *On the Horizon*, *25*(3), 165–168. doi:10.1108/OTH-05-2017-0022

Tambe, P., Yakubovich, V., & Cappelli, P. (2019, February). Artificial Intelligence in Human Resources Management: Challenges and a Path Forward. *California Management Review*, *61*(4), 15–42. doi:10.1177/0008125619867910

Tamminga, J., & Parham, S. (2018). The Adaptation of the Logistic Industry to the Fourth Industrial Revolution: The Role of Human Resource Management. *Journal of Business Management & Social Sciences Research*, *7*(9), 179–191. https://www.researchgate.net/publication/327531057

Tan, J. (2023, August 18). *HRM Asia*. Retrieved from AI's Dual Impact on Singapore's HR Landscape: https://hrmasia.com/ais-dual-impact-on-singapores-hr-landscape/

Tapscott, D., & Tapscott, A. (2017). How blockchain will change organizations. *MIT Sloan Management Review*, *58*(2), 10. doi:10.7551/mitpress/11645.003.0010

Tariq, M. U., Poulin, M., & Abonamah, A. A. (2021). Achieving operational excellence through artificial intelligence: Driving forces and barriers. *Frontiers in Psychology*, *12*, 686624. doi:10.3389/fpsyg.2021.686624 PMID:34305744

Telukdarie, A., & Munsamy, M. (2019). Digitization of Higher Education Institutions. *IEEE International Conference on Industrial Engineering and Engineering Management, December*, 716–721. 10.1109/IEEM44572.2019.8978701

Teune, L. (2023). *Is AI a Diamond in the Rough for HR? Identifying the Attributions Towards AI-enabled HR practices. A Grounded Theory Approach*. University of Twente.

Tewari, I., & Pant, M. (2020). Artificial Intelligence Reshaping Human Resource Management: A Review. *2020 IEEE International Conference on Advent Trends in Multidisciplinary Research and Innovation (ICATMRI)*, 1–4. 10.1109/ICATMRI51801.2020.9398420

Tilo, D. (2023, June 28). HR minister: Malaysia needs to retrain 50% of workforce amid AI rise. *Human Resources Director (HRD)*. https://www.hcamag.com/asia/specialisation/learning-development/hr-minister-malaysia-needs-to-retrain-50-of-workforce-amid-ai-rise/450731

Tiwari, P. C., Pal, R., Chaudhary, M. J., & Nath, R. (2023). Artificial intelligence revolutionizing drug development: Exploring opportunities and challenges. *Drug Development Research*, ddr.22115. doi:10.1002/ddr.22115 PMID:37712494

Topol, E. (2019). *Deep medicine: how artificial intelligence can make healthcare human again.*

Tran, K., & Nguyen, T. (2021). Preliminary research on the social attitudes toward the ai's involved Christian education in Vietnam: Promoting ai technology for religious education. *Religions*, *12*(3), 1–20. doi:10.3390/rel12030208

Trong Tuan, L. (2013). Competitive intelligence and other levers of brand performance. *Journal of Strategic Marketing*, *21*(3), 217–239. doi:10.1080/0965254X.2013.765501

Tsamados, A., Aggarwal, N., Cowls, J., Morley, J., Roberts, H., Taddeo, M., & Floridi, L. (2021). The ethics of algorithms: key problems and solutions. *Ethics, Governance, and Policies in Artificial Intelligence*, 97-123.

Tschang, F. T., & Mezquita, E. A. (2020). Artificial Intelligence as Augmenting Automation: Implications for Employment. *The Academy of Management Perspectives*.

Tuncer, S., & Ramirez, A. (2022). Exploring the Role of Trust During Human-AI Collaboration in Managerial Decision-Making Processes. In HCI International 2022 – Late Breaking Papers: Interacting with eXtended Reality and Artificial Intelligence. doi:10.22215/etd/2022-15336

Tysiac, K., & Drew, J. (2018). Accounting firms: The next generation. *Journal of Accountancy*, *225*(6), 26–32. http://web.b.ebscohost.com.ezproxy.ub.gu.se/ehost/pdfviewer/pdfviewer?vid=1&sid=d1eed4fe-a91b-49a5-85ab-238e241ec257%40pdc-v-sessmgr05

Ulrich, D., Kryscynski, D., Ulrich, M., & Brockbank, W. (2017). *Competencies for HR professionals who deliver outcomes*. Academic Press.

UN. (2023). *12.6 Sustainability Reporting (Businesses)* [SDG 12 Data and Progress]. SDG 12 Hub. https://sdg12hub.org/sdg-12-hub/see-progress-on-sdg-12-by-target/126-sustainability-reporting-businesses

Valuer. (2022). *Innovative Companies & SDG 12: Responsible Consumption and Production*. https://www.valuer.ai/blog/aligning-business-with-sdg-12-by-collaborating-with-startups

Varadaraj, D. A., & Al Wadi, D. B. M. (2021). A Study on Contribution of Digital Human Resource Management towards Organizational Performance. *The International Journal of Management Science and Business Administration*, *7*(5), 43–51. doi:10.18775/ijmsba.1849-5664-5419.2014.75.1004

Varma, A., Budhwar, P. S., & DeNisi, A. (2023). *Performance management systems: A global perspective*. Taylor & Francis. doi:10.4324/9781003306849

Varma, A., Dawkins, C., & Chaudhuri, K. (2023). Artificial intelligence and people management: A critical assessment through the ethical lens. *Human Resource Management Review*, *33*(1), 100923. doi:10.1016/j.hrmr.2022.100923

Varma, J. R. (2019). Blockchain in Finance. *Vikalpa*, *44*(1), 1–11. doi:10.1177/0256090919839897

Vishwakarma, L. P., & Singh, R. K. (2023). An Analysis of the Challenges to Human Resource in Implementing Artificial Intelligence. In The Adoption and Effect of Artificial Intelligence on Human Resources Management, Part B (pp. 81–109). Emerald Publishing Limited. doi:10.1108/978-1-80455-662-720230006

Vlačić, B., Corbo, L., Silva, S. C., & Dabić, M. (2021). The evolving role of artificial intelligence in marketing: A review and research agenda. *Journal of Business Research*, *128*, 187–203. doi:10.1016/j.jbusres.2021.01.055

Vos, J. F. J., & Boonstra, A. (2022). The influence of cultural values on Enterprise System adoption, towards a culture – Enterprise System alignment theory. *International Journal of Information Management*, *63*, 102453. doi:10.1016/j.ijinfomgt.2021.102453

Votto, A. M., Valecha, R., Najafirad, P., & Rao, H. R. (2021). Artificial Intelligence in Tactical Human Resource Management: A Systematic Literature Review. *International Journal of Information Management Data Insights*, *1*(2), 100047. doi:10.1016/j.jjimei.2021.100047

Vrontis, D., Christofi, M., Pereira, V., Tarba, S., Makrides, A., & Trichina, E. (2022). Artificial intelligence, robotics, advanced technologies and human resource management: A systematic review. *International Journal of Human Resource Management*, *33*(6), 1237–1266. doi:10.1080/09585192.2020.1871398

Vrontis, D., Makrides, A., Christofi, M., & Thrassou, A. (2021). Social media influencer marketing: A systematic review, integrative framework and future research agenda. *International Journal of Consumer Studies*, *45*(4), 617–644. doi:10.1111/ijcs.12647

WaghmareIS. (2018). A Study of E-Recruitment: From the Perspective of Job Applicants. doi:10.13140/RG.2.2.17695.61605

Walters, J. (2023, September 6). *HR technology*. Retrieved from Singapore's HR Leaders Embracing AI: Survey: https://www.hcamag.com/asia/specialisation/hr-technology/singapores-hr-leaders-embracing-ai-survey/458641

Waltl, B., & Vogl, R. (2018). Increasing Transparency in Algorithmic- Decision-Making with Explainable AI. *Datenschutz und Datensicherheit - DuD, 42*(10), 613-617. doi:10.1007/s11623-018-1011-4

Wang, H., Li, J., & Zhang, Y. (2019). Chatbots for Data Collection: Enhancing User Experience in Market Research. *Journal of Consumer Behaviour*, *28*(4), 564–578.

Wang, X., Waris, I., Bhutto, M. Y., Sun, H., & Hameed, I. (2022). Green initiatives and environmental concern foster environmental sustainability: A study based on the use of reusable drink cups. *International Journal of Environmental Research and Public Health*, *19*(15), 9259. doi:10.3390/ijerph19159259 PMID:35954613

Wang, Y., & Kogan, A. (2018). Designing confidentiality-preserving Blockchain-based transaction processing systems. *International Journal of Accounting Information Systems*, *30*, 1–18. Advance online publication. doi:10.1016/j.accinf.2018.06.001

Waris, I., Barkat, W., Ahmed, A., & Hameed, I. (2022). Fostering sustainable businesses: Understanding sustainability-driven entrepreneurial intention among university students in Pakistan. *Social Responsibility Journal*, *18*(8), 1409–1426. doi:10.1108/SRJ-10-2020-0399

Waris, I., Farooq, M., Hameed, I., & Shahab, A. (2021). Promoting sustainable ventures among university students in Pakistan: An empirical study based on the theory of planned behavior. *On the Horizon*, *29*(1), 1–16. doi:10.1108/OTH-10-2020-0035

Watthanabut, B. (2019). From HR 4.0 to better supply chain flexibility: Role of talent on boarding and a development in Thailand. *International Journal of Supply Chain Management*, *8*(5), 804–815.

Wilkinson, J. E., & Kao, C. P. (2019). Aspects of socio-emotional learning in Taiwan's pre-schools: An exploratory study of teachers' perspectives. *International Journal of Child Care and Education Policy*, *13*(1), 1–17. doi:10.118640723-019-0057-6

Wilson, H. J., Daugherty, P. R., & Morini-Bianzino, N. (2017). The jobs that artificial intelligence will create. *MIT Sloan Management Review*, *58*(4), 14–16.

Wilson-Nash, C., Goode, A., & Currie, A. (2020). Introducing the socialbot: A novel touchpoint along the young adult customer journey. *European Journal of Marketing*, *54*(10), 2621–2643. doi:10.1108/EJM-07-2019-0555

Winarno, B. H., Prayitno, E., & Samudra, S. T. (2019). Continuance intention to use MOOCs: Integrating the Technology Acceptance Model (TAM) and Task Technology Fit (TTF) model. *Journal of International Conference Proceedings*, *2*(2), 46–49. doi:10.32535/jicp.v2i2.601

Wirtz, J., & Zeithaml, V. (2018). Cost-effective service excellence. *Journal of the Academy of Marketing Science*, *46*(1), 59–80. doi:10.100711747-017-0560-7

Worcman, V. (2023, February 9). *How Bites AI is Unleashing Employee Training and Development*. Bites. https://mybites.io/blog/employee-training-powered-by-ai/

World Economic Forum. (2020). *The Future of Jobs Report 2020*. Geneva: World Economic Forum.

WSBA. (2017). *Wall Street blockchain alliance adds KPMG as corporate member*. Retrieved from https://www.wsba.co/uploads/3/7/9/4/3794101/wsbafinal11-15.pdf

Wu, B., & Chen, X. (2017). Continuance intention to use MOOCs: Integrating the technology acceptance model (TAM) and task technology fit (TTF) model. *Computers in Human Behavior*, *67*, 221–232. doi:10.1016/j.chb.2016.10.028

Wu, F., Lu, C., Zhu, M., Chen, H., Zhu, J., Yu, K., Li, L., Li, M., Chen, Q., Li, X., Cao, X., Wang, Z., Zha, Z., Zhuang, Y., & Pan, Y. (2020). Towards a new generation of artificial intelligence in China. *Nature Machine Intelligence*, *2*(6), 6. Advance online publication. doi:10.103842256-020-0183-4

Wu, W., Huang, T., & Gong, K. (2020). Ethical Principles and Governance Technology Development of AI in China. *Engineering (Beijing)*, *6*(3), 302–309. doi:10.1016/j.eng.2019.12.015

Xref. (2013). Retrieved from Xref: https://www.xref.com/company/about-us

Xue, X., Rafiq, M., Meng, F., & Peerzadah, S. A. (2023). 21st anniversary of job embeddedness: A retrospection and future research agenda. *Work*, (Preprint), 1-15.

Yalenios, J., & d'Armagnac, S. (2023). Work transformation and the HR ecosystem dynamics: A longitudinal case study of HRM disruption in the era of the fourth industrial revolution. *Human Resource Management*, *62*(1), 55–77. doi:10.1002/hrm.22114

Yang, X. (2019). Accelerated Move for AI Education in China. *ECNU Review of Education*, *2*(3), 347–352. doi:10.1177/2096531119878590

Yermack, D. (2017). Corporate governance and blockchains. *Review of Finance*, rfw074. Advance online publication. doi:10.1093/rof/rfw074

Yong, J. Y., Yusliza, M. Y., Ramayah, T., Farooq, K., & Tanveer, M. I. (2022). Accentuating the interconnection between green intellectual capital, green human resource management and sustainability. *Benchmarking: An International Journal,* 1463–5771. doi:10.1108/BIJ-11-2021-0641

Yusof, H., Farhana Mior Badrul Munir, M., Zolkaply, Z., Jing, L. C., Yu Hao, C., Swee Ying, D., … Kok Leong, T. (2018). Behavioral intention to adopt blockchain technology: Viewpoint of the banking institutions in Malaysia. *International Journal of Advanced Scientific Research and Management, 3*(10), 1–6. Retrieved from www.ijasrm.com

Zain, M., Rose, R. C., Abdullah, I., & Masrom, M. (2005). The relationship between information technology acceptance and organizational agility in Malaysia. *Information & Management*, *42*(6), 829–839. doi:10.1016/j.im.2004.09.001

Zaki, H. O., Fernandez, D., Dastane, O., Aman, A., & Sanusi, S. (2023). Virtual reality in digital marketing: Research agenda based on bibliometric reflection. *Marketing Intelligence & Planning*, *41*(4), 505–524.

Zavvy. (2023, June 9). *AI in HR Examples: 9 Companies Successfully Using AI Innovation in Key People Processes.* Retrieved from Zavvy: https://www.zavvy.io/blog/ai-in-hr-examples

Zhang, Y., Zhang, M., Li, J., Liu, G., Yang, M. M., & Liu, S. (2021). A bibliometric review of a decade of research: Big data in business research – Setting a research agenda. *Journal of Business Research, 131*(December), 374–390. doi:10.1016/j.jbusres.2020.11.004

Zhang, C., Dai, J., & Vasarhelyi, M. A. (2018). The impact of disruptive technologies on accounting and audiiting education. *The CPA Journal*, *88*(9), 20–26.

Zhang, L., Pei, D., & Vasarhelyi, M. A. (2017). Toward a new business reporting model. *Journal of Emerging Technologies in Accounting*, *14*(2), 1–15. doi:10.2308/jeta-10570

Zhang, Y., Xu, S., Zhang, L., & Yang, M. (2021). Big data and human resource management research: An integrative review and new directions for future research. *Journal of Business Research*, *133*(April), 34–50. doi:10.1016/j.jbusres.2021.04.019

Zielinski, D. (2023, January 10). *SHRM.* Retrieved from 2023 HR Technology Trends: Talent Marketplaces, Expanding AI and Optimizing Existing Systems: https://www.shrm.org/resourcesandtools/hr-topics/technology/pages/2023-hr-technology-trends.aspx

Zirar, A., Ali, S. I., & Islam, N. (2023). Worker and workplace Artificial Intelligence (AI) coexistence: Emerging themes and research agenda. *Technovation, 124*(June), 102747. doi:10.1016/j.technovation.2023.102747

Zolnowski, A. & Frey, D. (2020). *Analyzing the role of artificial intelligence in the development of human-centered service*. Academic Press.

Zoogah, D. B. (2011). The Dynamics of Green HRM Behaviors: A Cognitive Social Information Processing Approach. *German Journal of Human Resource Management*, *25*(2), 117–139. doi:10.1177/239700221102500204

About the Contributors

Muhammad Rafiq is working as an Assistant Professor at Graduate Business School, UCSI University, Kuala Lumpur, Malaysia. He received his Ph.D. in Business Administration specialization in Human Resource Management from the Harbin Institute of Technology, China, in 2018. His teaching and research interests lie in Human Resource Management and Organizational Behaviour. He has vast experience in publications and reviewing in top publishers like Elsevier, Taylor & Francis, Wiley, Springer, Sage, Inderscience, etc. Moreover, he has published more than 35 research articles in International Journals. He is serving as an Associate Editor of Vision Journal of Business Perspective, International Journal Of Productivity and Performance Management, Academic Editor of PlosOne Journal and reviewer of numerous journals.

Muhammad Farrukh is currently involved in teaching and research activities in the Department of Economics, Shenzhen MSU-BIT China. He had been an active member of the founding teams of two education institutes, a health care setup, and an Advertising venture. He holds a Ph.D. in Intrapreneurship. His area of research revolves around entrepreneurship, Intrapreneurship, and Industrial-organizational psychology.

Mushtaq Rizwan, currently heading the MSc Data Science & Business Analytics program at the Department of Finance, Economics & Law, is distinguished by his profound expertise in Financial Economics. Holding an MS in Banking & Finance and a PhD from EDC Paris Business School, his research is centered around CSR disclosure, firm innovation, access to finance, and the application of AI and ML in finance. An esteemed educator, he imparts knowledge in Financial Risk Management, Portfolio Management, Financial Markets, Corporate Finance, and Data Analytics Tools.

Omkar Dastane obtained his Ph.D. in Business from Curtin University and is working as an Assistant Professor and Head of Program (MBAs) at the UCSI Graduate Business School, UCSI University, Kuala Lumpur, Malaysia. Dr Omkar is also Certified Management and Business Educator approved by CABS, UK. Dr. Omkar's research mainly emphasizes digital consumer behavior, consumer perception and values, technological impact on businesses, and scale development studies in the marketing domain. His research has been published in several international journals and books including the Journal of Retailing and Consumer Services, Marketing Intelligence & Planning among others. Dr Omkar is appointed as as an Editor of Arab Gulf Journal of Scientific Research (Emerald, Scopus, WoS). He is also an active reviewer for Web of Science and Scopus Indexed Journals.

* * *

Kamaal Allil, a highly respected academic and expert in digital marketing, holds a PhD in Digital Marketing and a Master's in Marketing Analytics. Currently, he holds a distinguished position as a senior lecturer at Hertfordshire Business School. Dr. Allil is widely admired for his innovative teaching methods and the ability to inspire enthusiasm in his students. His research interests lie at the intersection of data analytics, marketing and business psychology, with a particular focus on understanding consumer behavior in the digital landscape. This allows him to provide up-to-the-minute insights in the classroom, enabling his students to stay at the forefront of industry trends. Beyond academia, his expertise in digital marketing strategies and business analytics plays a crucial role in reshaping the way organizations understand and reach their target markets.

Azueryn Annatassia Dania Aqeela Azizan is a student of business analytic at UNSW Business School, UNSW Sydney, Australia.

Pradnya Bhatkulkar is a seasoned HR professional with over a decade of expertise in human resources management, specializing in talent management, employee relations, and organizational development. She excels in implementing strategic HR initiatives aligned with business objectives, fostering a positive workplace culture, and enhancing employee engagement. Pradnya's adept navigation of complex personnel issues showcases her comprehensive knowledge of HR policies and regulations, coupled with effective communication skills. Renowned for her commitment to diversity and inclusion, she has played a pivotal role in implementing programs that promote equality within organizations. Pradnya's adaptability to industry trends and forward-thinking approach make her a valuable asset in the ever-evolving field of human resources. With a proven track record of driving HR excellence and a passion for cultivating collaborative teams, Pradnya Bhatkulkar continues to significantly contribute to the success and growth of the organizations she serves.

Dwijendra Nath Dwivedi is a professional with 19+ years of subject matter expertise creating right value propositions for analytics and AI. A post-Graduate in Economics from Indira Gandhi Institute of Development and Research and perusing PHD from crackow university of economics Poland. He has published more than 25 papers in many reputed journals. He has presented in more than 17 international conference and published paper on AI adoption in many areas. Academic interest includes econometrics, climate risk and Text Mining.

Aziatul Waznah Ghazali holds a Diploma in Accounting and Bachelor in Accounting from Universiti Teknologi MARA and a Master's degree in the same field from University of Strathclyde, Scotland. She obtained another Master's degree in 2014 and pursue her PhD, which is also in the area of accounting from Kingston University London in 2018. Her academic career began with her appointment as a lecturer at Universiti Teknologi MARA (UiTM) in 2010. She was then appointed as a senior lecturer in 2019 at Universiti Sains Malaysia (USM) and continues her career in Universiti Kebangsaan Malaysia (UKM). As for her research interest, she specialises in quantitative studies involving financial reporting, corporate governance, auditing and financial criminology. She also has a keen interest in social enterprises, as well as in environmental and sustainable reporting. Her works based on those researches have been published in established refereed journals, international, regional, and national proceedings, as well as technical reports and training modules.

Irfan Hameed holds a Ph.D. degree in marketing. He is an assistant professor at the Faculty of Business Management, UCSI University, Kuala Lumpur, Malaysia, and also associated with Rabat Business School, International University of Rabat, Rabat, Morocco. He has over 15 years of academic and research experience. His area of research is consumer behavior and management issues in implementing sustainable policies. He has been writing on sustainable issues for a long in journals including Environment, Development and Sustainability, International Journal of Consumer Studies, British Food Journal, Social Responsibility Journal, Journal of Hospitality and Tourism Insights, Management of Environmental Quality, Journal of Marketing for Higher Education, Human Behavior and Emerging Technologies, Energy Efficiency, Environmental Science and Pollution Research, etc.

Rafiq Idris is a senior lecturer at Universiti Malaysia Sabah and he is also a Rector of University College of Sabah Foundation, Kota Kinabalu, Malaysia.

Rizal Idris is a senior lecturer and a head of international program at his faculty.

Muhammad Imran is working as an International Senior Lecturer in School of Business Management, Universiti Utara Malaysia, Sintok, Kedah, Malaysia 06010.

Zulaikha Amirah Johari is a full-time PhD in Accountancy candidate at the Faculty of Economics & Management at Universiti Kebangsaan Malaysia. She received her Master's degree in Forensic Accounting & Financial Criminology from the Faculty of Accountancy, Universiti Teknologi MARA. She is currently working on a contract basis as a Research Assistant for a project funded by the Malaysian Ministry of Higher Education at the Accounting Research Institute (ARI), Universiti Teknologi MARA. Her areas of expertise include forensic accounting and financial criminology.

Naveed R. Khan is Assistant Professor at UCSI, Kuala Lumpur, Malaysia. Dr. Khan has earned his Ph.D. in HRM from University Pendidikan Sultan Idris, Malaysia. He has published widely in SSCI, ESCI, Scopus, and HEC indexed journals of international repute. One of his research papers has been included as a book chapter, published by McGraw Hill.

Ghana Mahanty leads MENA Data science, UAE and Global Data Science Center of Excellent, India for Visa Inc. He is a data enthusiast with expertise in mobilizing the organization to deliver value out of data and specializing in business management, data transformation strategy, and machine learning and artificial intelligence solutions for Retail Banking and Payment industry. He has worked extensively across North America, Asia, Europe and Middle East regions. Currently pursuing PhD. in Economics from Department of Analytical and Applied Economics, Utkal University, Bhubaneswar, India. His research area of interests are machine learning, artificial intelligence, macro econometric and structural data modelling, panel modelling, money, banking and payments.

Fazeelat Masood is Assistant Professor at Bahria Business School. Dr. Masood has earned her Ph.D. in Management Sciences from Bahria University, Karachi. Her research interests are quality of life, well-being, social entrepreneurship, and tourism. She has published in a few research journals. One of her research papers was accepted for presentation at the British Academy of Management Conference 2019 and another at the Asian Academy of Management Conference 2021.

Yusarina Mat Isa holds a PhD in Accounting specializing in financial criminology from Universiti Teknologi MARA, Malaysia. She graduated with MSc in

Accounting and Financial Management from Lancaster University, United Kingdom and Bachelor of Accountancy from Universiti Tenaga Nasional, Malaysia. She is an associate member of Institute of Internal Auditors Malaysia. She formerly worked as a senior executive in banking supervision with Bank Negara Malaysia from 2002 to 2007. She later joined the Faculty of Accountancy, Universiti Teknologi MARA in 2007 and is currently a senior lecturer at the faculty. Her teaching portfolio at the faculty includes subjects from various fields including external auditing, internal auditing, corporate governance and financial reporting. Her research interests cover financial crimes, auditing, risk management, banking operations and regulatory enforcement.

Mohammad Shaukhi Md Radzi is a senior lecturer at history program at Faculty of Social Sciences & Humanities, Universiti Malaysia Sabah.

Sitinurbayu Mohd Yusoff is a lecturer in Communication program at her faculty in Universiti Malaysia Sabah.

Azizan Morshidi is a lecturer at Industrial Relations Program, Faculty of Social Sciences & Humanities, Universiti Malaysia Sabah, Malaysia.

Hafizah Omar Zaki is a Senior Lecturer in Marketing at the Faculty of Economics and Management (FEP), Universiti Kebangsaan Malaysia (UKM). She is currently the Head of Emerging Technology & Big Data (ETBD) cluster at the Centre of Global Business and Digital Economy (GloBDE), FEP-UKM. She holds a Ph.D in Marketing - specializing in advertising and branding from University of Malaya (UM); an MBA - specialising in Human Resource Management from UKM; and a Degree in Multimedia Management from Multimedia University (MMU). Her research and publications involves advertising, branding, digital marketing and digital business amidst the advancement of technology use. Some of her astonishing awards include receiving the Harvard Business School Alumni Club of Malaysia Scholarship in 2012, and an Apple Teacher Award in 2021. She has been engaging in coordinating research and academic forums with the governmental bodies such as MOSTI, EPU, and organizations such as Cradle Fund Sdn. Bhd. To balance her career in the academia, she has also engaged in societal programs such as voluntary teaching programmes for schools (i.e., schools at ukm etc.), and engaging in car boot sale to fund the high schoolers and orphanage. She practices work-life-balance by filling her out of work time with gardening, baking and carpentry.

Saeed Mohammed Qurtas Barzani is the author of the benefits and challenges of adopting Human Resource Management 4.0 in public universities in Malaysia.

Nurhizam Safie M. Satar is as professor of information system and Dean of Faculty of Information Science and Technology, UKM Bangi.

Zuraidah Mohd Sanusi is a Professor at the Faculty of Accountancy, Universiti Teknologi MARA. She is currently holding the post of Director of Centre for Profiling and Assessment, Institute Leadership & Development, Universiti Teknologi MARA. She is also a senior research fellow at the Accounting Research Institute, Universiti Teknologi MARA. She holds a Doctorate in Business Administration (Accounting) from Universiti Kebangsaan Malaysia and has a Master of Science Degree and a Bachelor of Science Degree in Accounting from Syracuse University, New York, USA. She has been working with UiTM for more than 30 years. Her research interests span auditing, forensic accounting, corporate reporting, corporate governance, management accounting and management. Much of her work has been on improving the competencies, judgement, and performance of auditors, managers, employees of companies, enforcement agencies and social enterprises.

Fauzie Sarjono is a senior lecturer in Industrial Relations Program and a Deputy Dean of Academic & Internationalisation in his faculty at Universiti Malaysia Sabah.

Nur Aima Shafie is a fellow at Accounting Research Institute, Universiti Teknologi MARA, Shah Alam. She also is a senior lecturer at Faculty of Accountancy of the same university. She holds PhD in Accounting specializing in financial criminology from Universiti Teknologi MARA, Malaysia. She is an associate editor for Asia-Pacific Management Accounting Journal (APMAJ). Her research interest span corporate governance, financial reporting, risk management and social enterprise.

Anusha Thakur is an independent researcher with 25 solo research papers in the World's reputed books and journals. Anusha's exemplary contributions without the conventional Ph.D. degree, and in a span of nearly three years, have earned her the title of the Best Woman Researcher of the Year - (Category - Below 35 years) during the 4th International Inspirational Women Awards (IIWA), 2023 in New Delhi, on 17th June 2023. Anusha has also been conferred the prestigious "Shiksha Bharati Award", in October 2023 by the "Indian Achievers Forum" in recognition of her extraordinary professional achievements and contribution towards nation-building. One of her published chapters, *Impact of Mood of the Millennial Customers on Purchase of Apparels Online*, published by IGI Global, USA, was chosen to be included as a reprinted chapter in 2021 for the book *Research Anthology on E-Commerce Adoption, Models, and Applications for Modern Business* by the Information Resources Management Association (USA). Anusha serves as an Editorial Review Board member for the *International Journal of Enterprise Information Systems*

(IJEIS). She is also a peer reviewer for several publications with renowned publishers such as IGI Global, USA, and Common Ground Research Networks journals and books. Anusha has pursued B. Tech in Electronics and Instrumentation Technology from Tumkur, Karnataka, and a Master's in Business Administration (MBA) in the Department of Economics and International Business from the University of Petroleum & Energy Studies, (UPES) Dehradun. Anusha has also completed a post-graduation certification course in Market Research and Data Analytics from MICA, Ahmedabad. She has work experience of approximately 4+ years in the Market Research Industry as a Senior Research Analyst with extensive knowledge of market research in diversified industries.

Index

A

Administration 50, 132, 134-135, 138
AI 1-15, 18-21, 23-28, 30-37, 39-63, 66-76, 78, 80-81, 83, 85-93, 96, 108-113, 115, 117, 119, 123, 137, 140-147, 149-169, 172-198, 200-201, 231-238, 242-246, 248-249, 251-254
AI Adoption 9, 47, 52, 55, 59-60, 140, 142-143, 152-156, 158-159, 192, 246, 248
AI Competencies 182, 184, 192-193, 196-197, 244, 249
Algorithmic Hiring 166
Artificial Intelligence 1, 3, 12-14, 26-28, 30-34, 36-37, 39-40, 42-44, 46-47, 54, 59-66, 68, 73, 81-83, 85-92, 104, 107-117, 119-120, 124, 137, 140-141, 143, 158-166, 168, 172-175, 179-183, 185, 198-201, 221, 225, 231-232, 234-235, 237-238, 240, 242-245, 247-248, 250-255
Asia 2-9, 12-13, 15-17, 19-25, 32, 36, 45-46, 114, 160, 163-164, 182-184, 186, 188-191, 195-196, 198-199, 243
Auditing 22, 157, 195, 202-211, 213, 215-223, 226-228

B

Bibliometric Study 63, 97, 105
Bibliometrix 85-86, 94, 96, 111
Biblioshiny 86, 94, 96, 103, 111
Blockchain Technology 162, 202-205, 207-223, 227, 229

C

Career Coaching 78, 84
Collaboration 21, 35, 39, 47, 51, 56, 89, 109, 172-174, 179, 186, 190-194, 196-197, 199, 201, 213, 217
Compensation Planning 76, 84
Cultural and Legal Implications 184, 189-190, 196-197
Customer Insights 231, 233-234, 238, 246-249

D

Data-Driven Decision Making 167, 182, 187
Disruptive Technology 202

E

Efficiency 2-4, 6-7, 21, 30, 37, 48, 56-57, 68, 72, 80, 109, 122-124, 126, 130, 132, 134, 141, 149, 151-153, 185, 188, 196, 203, 207-208, 210, 217, 233, 244, 249
Employee Engagement 1, 4-5, 26, 32, 34-35, 38, 40, 44, 46, 49-50, 68, 70-73, 84, 108, 115, 136, 148, 152, 157-158, 171-174, 177-178, 182-183, 187-188, 192, 196
Employee Experience 3, 11, 38, 66-69, 72-73, 75, 79-81, 84, 166, 168, 175-176, 180
Employee Growth 187
Ethics 41, 48, 55, 58, 60-61, 63, 112, 160,

177, 180, 237, 243, 251-252, 254

F

Future of Work 2, 11, 48, 54, 67, 81, 161, 164, 186

G

Green HRM 140, 142-143, 147-154, 156-158, 160, 162-163, 165

H

HR Department 118, 123-124, 126, 129
HRM 2-5, 7-13, 15, 18, 31, 42-43, 46-49, 51-61, 63, 65, 67-68, 83, 85-86, 88-90, 92-93, 108-112, 115-116, 118, 120-126, 128, 130-137, 140, 142-143, 147-163, 165, 182-198, 200, 233-234
HRM 4.0 118, 120-122, 136-137
Human Resource Functions 30
Human Resource Management 1, 3, 12-14, 17, 26-27, 30-31, 43-44, 46-47, 62-63, 65-66, 85-92, 96, 104, 106, 108-117, 119, 123, 125, 134-138, 140, 142, 147, 158-165, 173, 182-183, 185, 190-191, 193-196, 198-201, 234, 251
Human Resources 3, 10, 30-33, 36, 40-45, 57, 61-63, 82, 86, 89, 91, 111-117, 127, 130-132, 135, 140, 142, 149, 163-164, 169, 180, 183, 195, 199
Human-AI Collaboration 190-191, 196, 201

I

Industrial Revolution (IR4.0) 118
Innovation 1, 7, 9, 11, 13-14, 22, 26, 28-29, 32, 46-49, 54-55, 57, 59-64, 67, 82-83, 109-110, 113, 115, 121, 124, 126, 134, 136, 138, 142, 146, 148-149, 160, 162-164, 179, 186, 192-193, 198, 207, 224, 227, 249, 253
Integrating Artificial Intelligence 47, 66, 68
IR 4.0 136, 140-142, 146

L

Learning and Adaptation 47, 55

M

Malaysia 1, 15, 85, 102, 118, 120-122, 127-128, 130, 132-134, 137-140, 145-146, 152, 154, 158, 160-164, 202, 215, 225, 229, 246
Management 2-7, 9-10, 12-18, 20-22, 24-31, 34, 36, 38, 41, 43-48, 50, 59, 61-65, 67-68, 75, 77, 82-83, 85-93, 96, 104, 107-117, 119-121, 123, 125-128, 130-142, 147-149, 151-155, 158-170, 173-175, 179-183, 185-186, 188-196, 198-202, 208-209, 217-218, 221, 224-227, 229, 234, 241-244, 246, 248, 250-254
Market Research 231-238, 240, 247-250, 252, 254-255

O

Organization 8, 17-18, 30-31, 35-36, 38-39, 41-42, 44, 47, 49-50, 53-59, 67-68, 70, 72-73, 76, 78-80, 84, 120-126, 130, 133, 140, 142, 148-149, 151, 153-155, 157, 167, 169, 171, 173-175, 177-178, 185, 189, 194, 213-214, 217, 221, 233
Organizational Strategy 48, 57-58

P

Performance Management 7, 9, 15, 29, 34, 38, 41, 50, 111, 137, 151, 153, 162, 164, 166-167, 173-175, 183, 186, 188, 192

Personnel Management 67-68, 85, 131, 185
Public Universities of Malaysia 118

R

Retention 5, 8, 15, 21, 54, 67-68, 72, 74, 79-80, 137-138, 147, 171-172, 174-175, 178, 182, 187-188, 196, 233, 248

S

Systematic Literature Review 80, 115, 117, 159, 201, 234, 238, 253

T

Talent Management 2-3, 6, 14, 19, 21, 25, 36, 48, 67, 128, 134, 152, 188
TCCM 231, 234, 239, 241, 248
Technologies 2-3, 9-11, 15-16, 19-20, 22, 24-25, 28, 30-33, 36, 41-42, 48, 53-54, 59, 61, 69, 71-72, 79-80, 88, 110, 117, 119-120, 124, 126, 133, 141-146, 149-151, 154-155, 157, 160, 167-169, 174-178, 180, 183, 185-186, 188, 190, 204, 216, 219-224, 226, 229, 232, 235, 237, 242, 244, 246, 248-249, 251, 253
Technology Adoption 155, 216, 219, 225, 227, 242
Transformative Role 11, 47, 234

W

Workplace Dynamics 19, 48

www.ingramcontent.com/pod-product-compliance
Lightning Source LLC
LaVergne TN
LVHW081337300926
849161LV00008B/1992